*The Soviet
High Command,
1967–1989*

The SOVIET HIGH COMMAND, 1967–1989

Personalities and Politics

DALE R. HERSPRING

PRINCETON UNIVERSITY PRESS

PRINCETON, NEW JERSEY

Copyright © 1990 by Princeton University Press
Published by Princeton University Press, 41 William Street,
Princeton, New Jersey 08540
In the United Kingdom: Princeton University Press, Oxford

All Rights Reserved

Library of Congress Cataloging-in-Publication Data
Herspring, Dale R. (Dale Roy)
The Soviet high command, 1967–1989 : personalities and politics /
Dale R. Herspring.
p.   cm.
Includes index.
ISBN 0-691-07844-0—ISBN 0-691-02318-2 (pbk.)
1. Soviet Union—Armed Forces—History—20th century.   2. Soviet Union—
Politics and government—1945–   3. Generals—Soviet Union.
I. Title.
UA770.H48   1990
355'.0092'247—dc20   89-35220

This book has been composed in Linotron Garamond

Princeton University Press books are printed on acid-free paper,
and meet the guidelines for permanence and durability of the
Committee on Production Guidelines for Book Longevity of the
Council on Library Resources

Printed in the United States of America by Princeton University Press,
Princeton, New Jersey
        10 9 8 7 6 5 4 3 2 1
(Pbk.) 10 9 8 7 6 5 4 3 2 1

TO GARY FORD

. . . in and of itself, a leader's personality does not count for much, but in combination with a whole set of other, broader elements, it can take on significant historical meaning.

—*Robert C. Tucker,*
"A Choice of Lenins?"

Contents

Preface

From all appearances the USSR is in a state of flux; *perestroika, glasnost'*, and *demokratizatsiia* have become household words not only in the Soviet Union but in the West as well. Nowhere is this state of flux more evident, however, than in the Soviet military. Top-level military officers have been relieved of their positions, Gorbachev has warned of lean times for the military, the symbolic role of the marshals has been downgraded, new arms control agreements have been concluded, and there is increasing talk of a new concept of "military sufficiency" that could lead to major modifications in Soviet force structure.

Contrary to some who see Gorbachev as a modern-day Sir Galahad out to slay the evil military-industrial complex, this study concludes that despite some differences of opinion, up to this point the relationship between Gorbachev and the marshals has been more symbiotic than conflictual, and that Gorbachev's changes are part of an evolutionary process that began with the appointment of Nikolai Ogarkov as chief of the General Staff. Ogarkov was the first senior military officer who understood both the interrelationship between political and military factors and how their careful management could work to benefit the country's national security, and who was prepared to work closely with the country's political leadership in the national security area.

The result is that despite some occasional disagreements, the West is confronted with a relatively united national security apparatus in the Soviet Union. This suggests that there is a need to rethink the popular view that anything Gorbachev favors must be opposed by the marshals and generals. Likewise, it suggests that unilateral concessions to the Soviet Union aimed at strengthening Gorbachev against hard-line marshals would be self-defeating.

This book is divided into five parts. The first section, chapters one and two, sets the stage for the main part of the book. In addition to a methodological introduction, it contains a chapter dealing with the impact of the Khrushchev period on issues of direct interest to the high command, thereby setting the stage for the Grechko period. The second section, chapters three and four, deals with the period from 1967 to 1976, when Grechko served as defense minister and Zakharov and Kulikov as chiefs of the General Staff. Primary focus is placed on the military's increasing emphasis on conventional weapons and its intensified efforts to adapt to the demands of modern technology. On the political side, attention is paid to Grechko's attempts to block efforts by civilian leaders to cut back military spending and his attempts to undermine Brezhnev's efforts to improve East-West relations through the SALT I treaty.

Section three, which includes chapters five and six, deals with the period when the top two positions were occupied by Ustinov and Ogarkov. From a military-technical standpoint, this period was marked by an effort by Ogarkov to focus the military's attention on the high-technology conventional weapons he believed to be the wave of the future; on the political side it was characterized by increasing acrimony as Ogarkov became disenchanted with Brezhnev's policies and eventually came into open opposition with both his defense minister and general secretary on these issues.

The fourth section covers the period from 1984 to 1989 and focuses on Sokolov, Akhromeyev, and Yazov. Special attention is devoted to the good working relationship between Akhromeyev, Yazov, and Gorbachev and the implications of this close relationship for the Soviet national security apparatus. Finally, the conclusion looks at the future of the Soviet high command and its relations with the country's top political leadership.

Acknowledgments

This book has been in the making for several years. Articles on Marshals Ogarkov and Akhromeyev, on General Yazov and the role of the Soviet military under Gorbachev convinced me of both the need for such a book as well as the importance of integrating the large amount of Soviet military writings available to me while they were still fresh in my mind. Despite my best intentions, however, I doubt this book would ever have been written had it not been for the encouragement—and prodding—of my friends and colleagues. First and foremost I am indebted to William E. Griffith who repeatedly reminded me of the need to finish a "second book." In addition, a number of other specialists in the field, such as William E. Odom and Timothy J. Colton, encouraged me to put my thoughts down on paper. Most important, however, was my family, who not only provided me with the necessary support but also made numerous sacrifices in their own lives to permit me the time to work on this book.

This book deals with a very difficult and complex subject. And I make no pretense of being an expert on all of the topics covered in it. Indeed, the primary reason why I was able to write this book and emerge feeling that it is a more or less accurate portrayal of the evolution of the Soviet high command over the past twenty-odd years is because a number of my colleagues spent long hours reading, checking, and commenting on various aspects of it. Those whose comments were of particular help include Peter Almquist, Karen Dawisha, Robert Einhorn, Raymond Garthoff, Rose Gottemoeller, Thane Gustafson, John Hines, Erik Hoffmann, Stuart Kaufman, Ken Kennedy, Michael MccGwire, John McDonnell, John Parker, Bruce Parrott, Fred Starr, and Notra Trulock. Special thanks go to

Robbin Laird who not only provided useful comments on the manuscript, but also organized a seminar at the Institute for Defense Analysis to discuss its implications for the military balance in Europe. I should also like to express my appreciation to Adrienne Anne Shirley for her expert editorial assistance in the preparation of the book. Obviously, any errors of fact or interpretation in the book are my own responsibility, and the book does not represent official U.S. government policy. Unless otherwise noted, all translations from the Russian are by the author.

Finally, some of the most important encouragement I received while writing this book came from an unexpected source. Shortly after I began the first draft I learned that my step-brother was seriously ill. His strength, personal courage, and optimistic approach to life in dealing with this most serious, painful, and ultimately terminal illness served as an inspiration to me—and to all who came in contact with him. When confronted on a daily basis with the less desirable side of life, some law enforcement officials develop a sense of cynicism, bitterness, and hatred; others, like Gary, who had worked in law enforcement for more than twenty years, rise above such constraints and in doing so become a source of inspiration for those around them. In recognition of the difference he made in the lives of so many people, this book is dedicated, with affection, to Gary Ford.

List of Acronyms

ABM	Anti-Ballistic Missile
ASW	Anti-Submarine Warfare
AWACS	Airborne Warning and Control System
BMP	*Boevaia mashina pekhoty* (Armored Personnel Carrier)
CDE	Conference on Disarmament in Europe
FBIS	Foreign Broadcast Information Service
FBS	Forward-Based Systems
ICBM	Intercontinental Ballistic Missile
INF	Intermediate-range Nuclear Forces
MBFR	Mutual Balanced Force Reductions
MIRV	Multiple Independently Targeted Reentry Vehicle
NCO	Noncommissioned Officer
OMG	Operational Maneuver Group
PVO	*Protovovozdushnaia oborona strany* (Air Defense Forces)
SALT	Strategic Arms Limitation Talks
SLBM	Submarine-Launched Ballistic Missile
SNF	Strategic Nuclear Force
SRF	Strategic Rocket Forces
START	Strategic Arms Reduction Talks
TASS	*Telegrafnoe agentstvo Sovetskogo Soiuza* (Telegraphic Agency of the Soviet Union)
TMO, TSMA, TVD	Theater of Military Operations

PART I

The Setting

CHAPTER 1

The Methodological Framework

*I*n the short time he has been in office, Mikhail Gorbachev has made clear that he intends to effect major changes in the Soviet political system. Perestroika, glasnost', and demokratizatsiia, his codewords for the reform of the country's morbid economic and political system, are said to be the order of the day. While the jury is still out deliberating on how effective he will be in implementing his policies in the long run, he has already had a major impact. This is particularly evident in his relations with the Soviet high command.

Since he took over as general secretary, Gorbachev has sacked the country's defense minister and commander of air defense forces; warned the marshals they will have to do more with less; downgraded the symbolic importance of the armed forces; provided a major impetus to arms control agreements; announced unilateral reductions in the country's armed forces; and is now presiding over the introduction of what the Kremlin calls a policy of "military sufficiency."

At first glance, all these actions would appear to run counter to the interests of the Soviet military. Indeed, even before Gorbachev had become a major figure, Jeremy Azrael was arguing that because of a number of factors—the cutbacks in the rate of military expenditures, the appointment of Ustinov as defense minister, Brezhnev's comments on the unwinnability of nuclear war, the ousting of Marshal Ogarkov, and the failure of the political leadership to get the country's economic house in order—the military had become deeply concerned over the direction in which politicians were taking the country.[1] More recently, several Western writers have suggested

---

[1] Jeremy Azrael, *The Soviet Civilian Leadership and the Military High Command, 1976–1986*, Rand Report, R-3521, June 1987, p. 2.

that the military leadership does not fully support the changes in security policy that Gorbachev has introduced. Tsuyoshi Hasegawa, for example, argues that the new approach advocated by Gorbachev marks such a major break with past Soviet military thinking, that "the rejection of Clausewitz's axiom"—i.e., that war is the continuation of politics by other means—"is far from being accepted by the military." Similarly, Seweryn Bialer has suggested that the Soviet military does not fully accept some of the premises upon which Gorbachev's "national security" is based, and Robert Legvold sees potential disagreement between civilian and military officials over how to interpret and implement these new concepts.[2]

It has now been more than ten years since a major study has been done in the West of the role played by senior military officers in the Soviet Union. As a result, Western analysts have generally been forced to rely either on secondary sources or, at best, on a cursory review of the relevant literature.

This study attempts to fill the gap by providing the first in-depth analysis of the evolution of the Soviet high command over the past twenty years. In the process, I argue that while some of the things Gorbachev is doing are a source of resentment and even hostility on the part of the officer corps, at the highest level there is more support than opposition to most of what he is proposing. Indeed, it is the thesis of this book that beginning with the appointment of Marshal Nikolai Ogarkov as chief of the General Staff in 1977, the high command has shown an increasingly sophisticated understanding of the various components of Soviet national security; it has been prepared to work closely with the political leadership to enhance the country's security, whether this means new weapons or the negotiation of an arms control agreement. In fact, Ogarkov emerges as one of the most important figures in the Soviet military of the past twenty years primarily because he was the first senior

---

[2] Tsuyoshi Hasegawa, "Gorbachev, the New Thinking of Soviet Foreign-Security Policy and the Military: Recent Trends and Implications," in Peter Juviler and Hiroshi Kimura, eds., *Gorbachev's Reforms* (New York: Albine de Gruyter, 1988), p. 138; Seweryn Bialer, "New Thinking and Soviet Foreign Policy," *Survival* 30, no. 4 (July–August 1988): 298, 303; Robert Legvold, "Gorbachev's New Approach to Conventional Arms Control," *The Harriman Institute Forum* 1, no. 1 (January 1988): 5–6; and Matthew Evangelista, "Economic Reform and Military Technology in Soviet Security Policy," *The Harriman Institute Forum* 2, no. 1 (January 1989): 1–8.

military officer to recognize both the value of arms control to the Soviet military and the importance, when dealing with politicians, of making short-term sacrifices in favor of longer-term gains.

However, Ogarkov's attempt to work closely with the Brezhnev leadership was unsuccessful. The continuing decay of the country's economy, the absence of strong and decisive political leadership, the deterioration of East-West relations, and the weapons buildup by the Reagan administration—especially in strategic nuclear programs—all combined to convince Ogarkov that there was little to be gained from a cooperative relationship with the Brezhnev leadership. As a consequence, Ogarkov went into opposition, working—quite openly, by Soviet standards—to undercut many of the general secretary's main security-related policies.

The situation facing Sergei Akhromeyev when he took over as chief of the General Staff in 1984 was in many ways very similar to that which had confronted Ogarkov. He, too, recognized the value of arms control agreements to Soviet military security, was deeply concerned over the country's failing economy, and, like Ogarkov, believed that the future of military competition lay in the area of high-technology conventional weapons. He, too, had to make a decision on whether or not to work closely with the country's general secretary.

Based on the available evidence, Akhromeyev's initial approach to Gorbachev's appointment as general secretary was to wait and see. It was not that he opposed what the new general secretary was proposing. However, he first wanted to be sure that the new political leader was both serious about reforming the country's economy and in a position to implement his policies. While the latter issue still remains in doubt, it was becoming clear by the middle of 1986 that Gorbachev was "for real," that he meant what he said about tackling the country's underlying economic problems. As a consequence, Akhromeyev decided to support Gorbachev's national security policies. In return, he was given considerable latitude in designing arms control policies, in determining the military's response to a tighter budget, and in defining the content of any policy of military sufficiency. Thus, there was a greater symbiosis between the interests of the high command, under Akhromeyev and Yazov, and Gorbachev than has often been assumed. Barring a major change in Gorbachev's approach to dealing with the military, this state of affairs is likely to continue in the future, despite Akhromeyev's retirement in December 1988 and Gorbachev's announcement of unilateral cuts in Soviet forces.

THE CONCEPTUAL FRAMEWORK

This study will suggest a new variation on an old approach to analyzing Soviet politics. In essence, it maintains that a focus on individual decision makers (in this case high-ranking military officers), their personalities, backgrounds, and relationships, when combined with the traditional focus on specific issues, can provide an added dimension to our understanding of Soviet military politics. Issues are important; indeed, they provide the bases for almost any type of analysis—this study included. However, this study attempts to go beyond issue-oriented analyses by providing a two-dimensional approach: in addition to looking at the key issues, it provides an in-depth analysis of the main decision makers and the role they played in framing and implementing policies in these areas. The result, it is hoped, will be a more comprehensive understanding of both the issues and the individuals who shape them.

There has been a tendency by many in the West to believe that with the exception of top officials such as Gorbachev, Khrushchev, or Stalin, individuals play a peripheral role in Communist political systems. Part of the reason for this belief is the assumption that the actions of such individuals are to a large degree determined by either their institutional affiliation or their party membership—that military officers act in accordance with either the interests of the armed forces or those of the party. While no one would deny the importance of these affiliations, I argue that individuals can have a very important—and in some cases lasting—impact on politics in the Soviet Union.[3] This does not mean that bureaucratic structures do

---

[3] The idea of looking at an individual's personality as a means for understanding Soviet politics is not new; in fact, it has been the focal point for a number of important studies. Up to this point, however, it has not been applied to the Soviet military. Examples of such individualistic/psychological studies include Jerry Hough, "Soviet Succession: Issues and Personalities," *Problems of Communism* 31, no. 5 (September–October 1982): 20–40; Robert C. Tucker, *Stalin as a Revolutionary* (New York: Norton, 1973); and Victor Wolfenstein, *The Revolutionary Personality: Lenin, Trotsky, Gandhi* (Princeton, N.J.: Princeton University Press, 1967).

not also have an important impact on decision making. Indeed, decisions are heavily influenced—and sometimes dominated—by the institutional framework within which they are formulated and implemented. Even when the institutional framework plays an important role, however, individuals can make, and have made, a difference. This is true not only in crisis periods, but in the day-to-day life of a bureaucracy. Marshals Grechko, Ogarkov, and Akhromeyev are examples of such individuals. After all, it is these men who were most influential in deciding the military's interests and in overseeing the implementation of policies approved by the political leadership.

It is therefore the thesis of this book that focusing on individual decision makers—in this case in the military—can serve as an important window onto the evolution of Soviet politics. This is particularly true of the armed forces, where important and fundamental changes have been under way for the past twenty years. Indeed, the Soviet military is now undergoing changes that will have major implications for the USSR and the West for years to come.

Focusing on individual decision makers is a way of tracing the evolution of changes not only within the institution itself, but between the institution and the party leadership as well. The historical record is replete with examples of Soviet military officers who have had a major impact both within the armed forces and in the broader political spectrum. For example, in the 1920s and 1930s such Soviet military leaders as Mikhail Frunze, Mikhail Tukhachevskii, and Boris Shaposhnikov all had a major impact on the evolution of the Soviet military and Soviet warfighting doctrine. Indeed, many of the concepts that the Soviet high command uses today are derived from the writings of individuals such as Tukhachevskii. Similarly, Marshal Georgii Zhukov had considerable influence both within the military and on the evolution of Soviet military politics. Rodion Malinovskii, Vasilii Sokolovskii, Matvei Zakharov, Sergei Shtemenko, Pavel Rotmistrov, and other military officers have also left their mark on the evolution of postwar military thinking. More recently, senior officers such as Andrei Grechko, Nikolaii Ogarkov, and Sergei Akhromeyev have played a key role in the development of the Soviet military and its relationship to the political leadership.

Because of the nature of its data—the lack of access to key decision makers until quite recently—this study proceeds from the assumption that it will not be possible to differentiate among an individual's ideas, perceptions, and policy choices. It also assumes that it is possible to detect major debates between individual political and military leaders by using the Soviet press. Even in the worst of times, the press is the key arena in which differences of opinion have been expressed.

Top-level military decision makers operate within the confines of an institutional framework—in particular, the General Staff. The Soviet General Staff was established by Frunze in 1924 when it was called the Staff of the Workers' and Peasants' Red Army. In 1935 it was renamed the General Staff, and in 1936 the General Staff Academy was opened. During the Second World War the General Staff functioned as an executive agency for the Supreme High Command. In this context, the General Staff was responsible for coordinating actions in areas such as operations, intelligence, transportation, logistics, and communications. In effect, it was the "brain of the army," to use Shaposhnikov's phrase.

While a detailed description of the postwar General Staff is not available, it appears to be charged with strategic planning for all of the military services. Officers from the various branches are assigned to the General Staff—a much sought-after assignment that is considered to enhance one's career. According to a Soviet source, the primary function of the General Staff is "the coordination of actions of the main staffs of the services of the Armed Forces, the staff of the Rear Services, the staff of Civil Defense, the main and central administrations of the Ministry of Defense, the staffs of military districts, groups abroad, air defense districts, and fleets."[4] In short, the General Staff is the most important military structure in the Soviet Union. It is far more powerful than its American equivalent—the Joint Chiefs of Staff—which in comparison with the Soviet General Staff has very limited powers. Most observers agree that during a war the General Staff would play a central role in the command of Soviet forces. As a consequence of its independence from the various services, the General Staff has been spared some of the service parochialism that pervades many Western political systems. However, it

---

[4] V. Kulikov, "General'nyi shtab" ("The General Staff"), in A. Grechko, ed, *Sovetskaia Voennaia Entsiklopediia*, vol. 2 (Moscow: Voennoe izdatel'stvo, 1976), p. 513.

too has experienced its share of problems. It has its own biases and has often found it difficult to impose its will on independent-minded services—for example, during most of the 1970s, when Admiral Gorshkov was arguing for an independent naval strategy.

To a large degree, the influence the General Staff is able to exert over the other services derives from the personal standing of each particular chief of staff. If he is a weak individual and faces strong service chiefs with solid political support, his influence will be limited. But if he is not supported by an equally strong defense minister and general secretary, even a strong chief of the General Staff will have only limited influence. This is particularly true if the chief of the General Staff intends to bring about major changes in the operations of the military: the chief of the General Staff can obviously order those below him to modify their behavior, for example, by paying greater attention to technical qualifications in personnel appointments. But if he is not supported by his defense minister or the political-military leadership in general, he is likely to have only moderate success.

The ability of the chief of the General Staff to bring about change is even more restricted when the changes he seeks go against the grain of prevailing attitudes or policies in society at large. During his time on the General Staff, Ogarkov, for example, was a strong proponent of what is now called perestroika in the personnel area (i.e., greater emphasis on personal responsibility, technical expertise, initiative, and creativity). His ability to bring about change, however, was severely limited as this policy was not being pushed by the political leadership throughout Soviet society in general. Gorbachev's strong support makes Yazov's task of restructuring the military much easier.

The defense minister's ability to influence events within the armed forces is more circumscribed than is often assumed. Although he is clearly the country's top military officer, not only must he go through the General Staff for information, but the General Staff retains primary responsibility for the implementation of defense policies. This puts a premium on the personal relationship between the chief of staff and the defense minister. If there is discord, the defense minister can expect problems in having his way within the armed forces. This can be particularly difficult when the defense minister is a civilian: he is then often perceived as an "outsider" and generally lacks either the technical or the bureaucratic expertise necessary to keep the General Staff in line.

Under most circumstances, the defense minister is the primary interface between civilians and the military. He represents the interests of the high command to the political leadership and in turn ensures that decisions by the political leadership are effectively implemented. While this is the way the relationship is supposed to work, in practice this has not always been the case. If the chief of the General Staff disagrees strongly with the views and policies of the political leadership, and the latter is not strong enough to enforce them, a situation might develop similar to that of the early 1980s, when Ogarkov openly disputed with the political leadership over the nature of East-West relations.

A senior military officer has the greatest opportunity to have an impact on the military during a period of change—particularly if such change is initiated by a vigorous general secretary. In such a situation bureaucratic structures are at their weakest and most open to modification. A dynamic military officer—whether he be chief of the General Staff or defense minister—has a very good opportunity to see his ideas implemented, especially if they are supported by other senior military officers and if he has a good working relationship with the general secretary. This, in essence, is what has been happening under Gorbachev.

A military officer can also have a negative impact on the political process if he opposes change and is strong and assertive enough to stand up to the political leadership. The historical record suggests, in fact, that it is much easier to prevent changes than it is to introduce them. This is what happened during Grechko's tenure as defense minister. He opposed Brezhnev's policies vis-à-vis the budget and arms control and, despite Brezhnev's efforts to get him to change his views, remained defiant until his death in 1976.

Past Approaches

The emphasis on individual decision makers advocated in this book differs from the other major approaches suggested by Western analysts, although it is not necessarily in conflict with them. The focus of other studies can be divided into two categories. First, there is the high command itself. Perhaps because of the difficulty of obtaining sufficient data, or the tendency of political scientists to shy away from analyses of military issues, the nature of bureaucratic politics within the upper ranks of the Soviet armed forces is not well understood. In fact, with three notable exceptions, almost all book-length studies dealing directly with the high command tend to focus on civil-military interactions, not on differences within the top military leadership. The three exceptions are D. Fedotoff-White's history of the early years of the Soviet army, John Erickson's study of the evolution of the Soviet army, and Edward L. Warner's study of the Soviet military.[5] Other book-length studies provide insights into various aspects of the high command, but their information is fragmentary at best. The situation is somewhat better when it comes to articles. Here there are a number of works that discuss politics within the high command, although these, too, are primarily interested in how these differences influence civil-military relations.

Given the paucity of studies devoted to intrabureaucratic politics within the Soviet military, it is not surprising that no attempt has been made thus far to conceptualize relationships within this institution. In view of the important—indeed, key—role that many writers believe this organization plays in Soviet defense policy, such an analysis is long overdue.

The situation is different when it comes to the second area of focus, that of civil-military relations in the Soviet Union. Here a number of general approaches have been suggested as conceptual frameworks for understanding military politics in the Soviet Union. Erickson's analysis of the Soviet high command utilizes what might be labeled a historical-analytical approach. In good historical fashion, Erickson's work is exhaustive in its coverage of key events and personalities and provides the reader with an in-depth understanding of the historical development of the Soviet high command. What it lacks, however, is the systematic approach to the analysis of data common to contemporary social science. Events or persons are discussed and analyzed only insofar as Erickson believes them to

[5] D. Fedotoff-White, *The Growth of the Red Army* (Princeton, N.J.: Princeton University Press, 1944); John Erickson, *The Soviet High Command* (London: Macmillan, 1962); idem, *The Road to Stalingrad* (New York: Harper and Row, 1975); idem, *The Road to Berlin* (Boulder, Colo.: Westview, 1983); idem, *The Russian Imperial/Soviet General Staff*, College Station Papers, no. 3 (College Station, Tex.: Texas A and M University Press, 1981); Edward L. Warner III, *The Military in Contemporary Soviet Politics* (New York: Praeger, 1977).

be significant. At one point, for example, a political officer or political apparatus will figure prominently, while at another it will be ignored. Similarly, while the importance of the military as an institution will be stressed in one instance, it will be the personality of the individual that figures prominently in another. Such an approach makes for good history and even better reading but has limited utility for an analyst interested in understanding those common factors or variables that drive Soviet politics.

In an effort to come to grips with this problem, Roman Kolkowicz has suggested an approach that relies heavily on Samuel Huntington's methodology, developed in his *The Soldier and the State.* Huntington argues that the military is characterized by a high degree of expertise, responsibility, and corporateness. This means that a military officer tends to perceive himself as a specialist "peculiarly expert at directing the application of violence under certain conditions." His feeling of responsibility is manifested in his "sense of obligation to utilize his craft for the benefit of society." Finally, corporateness is evidenced in the "bureaucratic" nature of the profession.[6] Kolkowicz applies this paradigm to the Soviet Union and argues that the Soviet military's expertise leads to greater demands for professional autonomy; that its sense of professional responsibility has resulted in a strict code of honor and discipline; and that the bureaucratic nature of the military's organizational structure appears in its "easily discernable and stable" levels of authority. These attributes clash with the "Party's ideal image of an open institution, one easy to penetrate and manipulate."[7] The result, in Kolkowicz's analysis, is conflict, as the party constantly attempts to deny the military the institutional autonomy it seeks: "The incompatibility

---

[6] Samuel P. Huntington, *The Soldier and the State* (New York: Vintage, 1964), pp. 12, 15, 16.

[7] Roman Kolkowicz, *The Soviet Military and The Communist Party* (Princeton, N.J.: Princeton University Press, 1967), p. 21. Kolkowicz has also published several articles making similar points, for example, "Military Intervention in the Soviet Union: Scenario for Post-Hegemonial Synthesis," in Roman Kolkowicz and Andrzej Korbonski, eds., *Soldiers, Peasants, and Bureaucrats* (London: Allen and Unwin, 1982); "The Military," in H. Gordon Skilling and Franklyn Griffiths, eds., *Interest Groups in Soviet Politics* (Princeton, N.J.: Princeton University Press, 1971); "The Impact of Modern Technology on the Soviet Officer Corps," *Orbis* 11, no. 2 (Summer, 1977); and "Interest Groups in Soviet Politics: The Case of the Military," in Dale R. Herspring and Ivan Volgyes, eds., *Civil-Military Relations in Communist Systems* (Boulder, Colo.: Westview, 1978).

between the Party's ideal model of a thoroughly politicized instrument of the socialist state (which also must be militarily effective and disciplined) on the one hand, and the military's 'natural' tendencies toward orthodoxy on the other, creates friction and tension between the two institutions." This situation creates the basis for interest group politics. Furthermore, the advent of modern technology has exacerbated tensions, as the party finds itself increasingly dependent on the expertise of the military. As Kolkowicz argued: "In short, the growing complexity and proliferation of military equipment and weapons, and the greater need for military professionals able to attend to them, have set new boundaries to the Party's rule over the military, for they have heightened its dependence on the experts, forcing it to treat them with circumspection."[8] Looked at from the perspective of this study, Kolkowicz's model suggests a relatively high degree of institutional cohesion and corporateness combined with an effort by the military to expand its institutional autonomy whenever possible. For the party this means that civil-military relations are a never-ending struggle to assert primacy over an often rebellious military.

William Odom has criticized Kolkowicz by arguing that civil-military relations are not the zero-sum game they believe them to be.[9] He admits the existence of a sense of corporateness within "most military establishments," but argues that military expertise is not unique because an increased intertransferability of skills and knowledge between civilian and military arenas is taking place. Senior military officers are moving closer to what Morris Janowitz has called "military managers."[10]

Odom's preferred approach relies heavily on totalitarian theory. He asserts that the key factor uniting military and political leaders is their shared values or ethos. Both owe allegiance to a set ideology, and both have a stake in the perpetuation of the system. Political

[8] Kolkowicz, *The Soviet Military and the Communist Party*, pp. 10, 35.

[9] William E. Odom, "The Party-Military Connection, a Critique," in Herspring and Volgyes, *Civil-Military Relations*, p. 28. Among Odom's other writings having direct relevance for this study are his "A Dissenting View on the Group Approach to Soviet Politics," *World Politics* 27, no. 4 (July 1976): 542–67; and *The Soviet Volunteers* (Princeton: N.J.: Princeton University Press, 1973).

[10] See Morris Janowitz, *The Professional Soldier* (New York: The Free Press, 1960), p. 6.

conflicts may occur, but they do so within one large bureaucracy. All are subordinated to the political leadership: "In short, . . . behavior in the Soviet military is viewed as fundamentally a bureaucratic political matter; and politics within bureaucracies is essentially a struggle by the top leadership to impose its value preferences on the lower bureaucratic levels." In Odom's view, the idea of conflict between two identifiably different interest groups is a Western concept having little relevance for politics in the Soviet Union. The civil-military boundary exists as an administrative and bureaucratic reality, but Odom maintains that Western scholars have often made too much of that boundary in explaining Soviet political behavior. The result is that as members of the party and representatives of a relatively permeable institution, the marshals are "executants," not policy-makers. They do not "frame the issues, they can only respond to the way the issues are framed above them."[11] Alliances and battles over policy occur, but they cut across institutional lines.

Another approach, one that falls somewhere between the positions taken by Odom and Kolkowicz, was articulated by Timothy Colton. Colton takes issue with both Kolkowicz and Odom. He argues that Kolkowicz overstates the magnitude of the control/conflict problem, and he raises questions about Odom's schema, suggesting in his own work that "clusters of military and party officials are bound together on particular issues and pursue their interests on such issues cooperatively."[12]

Colton's alternative approach focuses on military participation in the political process. He accepts Kolkowicz's starting point, i.e., that the military and the party are two distinct institutions, and maintains that conflict does not pervade the relationship as Kolkowicz argues mainly because up to this point the military's core interests (e.g., pay and status) have been satisfied. Conflict becomes more probable the closer one gets to these core interests. Conversely, the boundary between the civilian and military arenas tends to become more permeable the further one moves from these basic interests

---

[11] Odom, "The Party-Military Connection," pp. 37, 44.

[12] For the purposes of this study Colton's two most important works are *Commissars, Commanders and Civilian Authority: The Structure of Soviet Military Politics* (Cambridge, Mass.: Harvard University Press, 1979), and "The Party-Military Connection: A Participatory Model," in Herspring and Volgyes, *Civil-Military Relations*, pp. 53–75, 62.

(e.g., national industrial policy and foreign policy). Furthermore, the nature of the relationship between civilian and military authorities depends on the situation. In one instance an issue may lead to conflict, while in another cooperation may be the norm. Future analyses, Colton advises, should concentrate on areas of military participation. Toward this end, he develops a matrix which shows patterns of military participation arranged according to the scope of the issues and the means employed.

Based on his analysis of events over the past sixty years, Colton argues that military participation has been greatest in matters dealing with what are generally considered the military's prerogative (e.g., discipline, promotion, and tactics) and less so as broader issues such as education and nationality questions have become the focus of attention. But although Colton's paradigm provides a framework for analysis, the many boxes in its matrix remain empty. With a few notable exceptions (the Zhukov affair, for example) it is not clear how past events in Soviet civil-military relations are to fit this matrix. Thus, at this stage at least, it remains more a guide to action than a model.

In order to fill in the blanks of Colton's model, it will be necessary not only to examine a wide variety of issues over time, but also to analyze roles played and perceptions held by various participants. In this writer's opinion, generals are important not only as representatives of a highly cohesive organization that tends to constrain their behavior on issues, but also as those individuals who implement either group interests or party policy.[13]

Because they are based on the existence of conflict or cooperation, Kolkowicz's and Odom's models tend to be more relevant in one period than another. Grechko's relationship with Brezhnev was

---

[13] While these three models represent the most clearly articulated approaches to civil-military relations in the USSR, there are a number of other studies that deal to varying degrees with this topic. The more useful recently published book-length studies include Jonathan R. Adelman, *The Revolutionary Armies* (Westport, Conn.: Greenwood, 1980); Jonathan R. Adelman, ed., *Communist Armies in Politics* (Boulder, Colo.: Westview, 1982); Yosef Avidar, *The Party and the Army in the Soviet Union* (Jerusalem: The Magnes Press, 1983); Herspring and Volgyes, *Civil-Military Relations*; David Holloway, *The Soviet Union and the Arms Race*, 2d ed. (New Haven: Yale University Press, 1984); Ellen Jones, *Red Army and Society* (Boston: Allen and Unwin, 1985); Kolkowicz and Korbonski, *Soldiers, Peasants, and Bureaucrats*; Roman Kolkowicz and Ellen Propper Mickiewicz, eds., *The Soviet Calculus of Nuclear War* (Lexington, Mass.: Lexington Books, 1984).

conflictual in many instances (although not as conflictual as the conflictual model suggests); the situation under Gorbachev is much different. Similarly, although the relationship between Ogarkov and Brezhnev during the late 1970s more closely approximated the unitary model, by the beginning of the 1980s, it had become conflictual.

Compared to the other two models, Colton's approach is the most useful because it does not assume conflict or unity in most instances. In fact, its purpose is to track the extent of military participation in politics. As noted above, however, it tends to focus primarily on the issues involved, not on the decision makers.

Focus on the Individual

In his study of leadership in the Soviet Union, Robert C. Tucker divided the leadership process into three "interlocking phases."[14] The first is the *diagnostic* phase during which the community or group's concerns are determined by its leadership. In essence, the leadership analyzes the group's strengths and weakness, weighs them against its long- and short-term goals, and decides when it is important to act. Second, it must determine the best *strategy* for achieving its goals. Finally, the leadership must *mobilize* whatever assets it has available in an attempt to maximize its chances of achieving the group's ends.

For the military leadership in the Soviet Union, these three phases represent the various stages through which the country's top generals must move in attempting to affect national security policy. First, within the military, the generals must decide what kind of a military is desirable for the coming months and years. For example, should the armed forces rely more on conventional or nuclear weapons? Assuming the decision is made in favor of conventional weapons, what strategy will enable Soviet forces to become fully effective? Finally, what resources—defined in the broadest sense—are available for implementing any changes in warfighting strategy?

Looking at the civil-military interface, the generals must go through a similar process. What is the military's view on a sensitive topic such as arms control? How likely is it to have an adverse im-

[14] Robert C. Tucker, *Political Culture and Leadership in Soviet Russia* (New York: Norton, 1987), p. 13.

pact on the country's force structure? How will the political leadership react if the generals oppose it? Assuming a decision is made in favor of arms control, what is the best mix of weapons?

Following Tucker, this book will use a three-phased approach in studying the role of the USSR's top military leadership in the national security decision making process. Special attention will be focused on how these individuals affected policy both within the military establishment and vis-à-vis political authorities. In essence, then, this study attempts to do two things at once. On the one hand, it offers an alternative approach for looking at Soviet military politics. On the other hand, it takes an in-depth look at the evolution of the high command's role in military politics. In an effort to combine these two sometimes only partially related factors, I am employing the framework suggested by Tucker. This framework will not be applied mechanically, i.e., it will not be allowed to dominate the interpretation of the data. However, to ensure that the study retains its conceptual relevance, a section at the end of the main three parts of the book will analyze the conceptual relevance of the study in terms of the framework suggested by Tucker. It is hoped that the study will thus be of interest both to those whose primary concern is methodology as well as to those more interested in policy debates.

METHODOLOGICAL ISSUES

The Players

For the purpose of this study, "the top military leadership in the Soviet Union" will refer to the two most influential military officers in the Soviet armed forces: the defense minister and the chief of the General Staff (who also serves as first deputy defense minister). Focusing on these two individuals serves two purposes. First, while it is obvious that other officers play important roles, these are the two most important decision makers in the Soviet armed forces. As Condoleezza Rice has noted, "The Chief of the General Staff (who participates in the deliberations of the Defense Council) and the Minister of Defense are both decision makers in their roles on the Council. They also provide the link between political authority and military direction and management. It is not surprising that political authorities have the final say in the selection of these key actors."[15] Focusing on these officers will provide a better understanding of the ideas and actions of the individuals at the top. In addition, this focus should help broaden our knowledge of how they relate to both their subordinates and the civilian leadership. As numerous studies of the Soviet Union have shown, patronage is often the key to power. A close consideration of these individuals may provide a better understanding of how this process works in a relatively closed bureaucracy like the Soviet armed forces.

Based on the recent historical record, when the defense minister is a professional soldier, he is often the most influential voice in the military. However, when the top position is occupied by a civilian, he tends to avoid detailed discussions of technical military issues. This task is then passed on to the chief of staff. Even when the defense minister is a professional soldier, however, the chief of staff tends to be the most authoritative voice within the military on technical issues such as strategy or command and control. Much of the defense minister's time appears to be occupied with broader issues; overseeing the actual operation of the armed forces is left to the chief of staff, especially to the General Staff, which has primary responsibility within the military for planning and wartime activities. In terms of specific individuals, the 1967–1988 period includes eight officers: the defense ministers include Andrei Grechko (1967–1976), Dmitrii Ustinov (1976–1984), Sergei Sokolov (1984–1987), and Dmitrii Yazov (1987–present). The chiefs of staff include Matvei Zakharov (1960–1963 and 1964–1971), Viktor Kulikov (1971–1977), Nikolai Ogarkov (1977–1984), and Sergei Akhromeyev (1984–1988).[16]

This study uses 1967 as the starting point for three reasons. First, that year marks the advent of a new and energetic defense

---

[15] Condoleezza Rice, "The Party, the Military, and Decision Authority in the Soviet Union," *World Politics* 40, no. 1 (October 1987): 67.

[16] While coverage of Zakharov's actions as chief of the General Staff should technically have covered 1960–1963 and 1964–1967, both time periods fall outside the framework of this study. Consequently, while some mention will be made of Zakharov's role during the Khrushchev and post-Khrushchev periods, primary attention will be given to his activities under Grechko's tenure as defense minister. Furthermore, on December 15, 1988, it was announced that Marshal Akhromeyev had retired and been replaced by General Mikhail Moiseyev as chief of the General Staff. Given the short amount of time he has occupied this high-level post, Moiseyev will not be dealt with in a separate section, although his appointment and its significance is discussed in the conclusion to this study.

minister, Andrei Grechko. Second, it came during a period of considerable turmoil and change in Soviet military warfighting strategy and one of renewed concern over the impact of modern technology on the armed forces. Finally, it predates major changes in Soviet attitudes toward arms control and difficulties with the military budget. Both of these latter issues were to play an important part in the marshals' relationships with their political superiors over the next twenty-odd years. Finally, 1967 takes in most of the Brezhnev period (1964–1982), thereby ensuring a high degree of continuity in evaluating developments since that time.

The Issues

In an effort to look at both the nature of politics within the Soviet military establishment as well as the dynamics of civil-military relations, a distinction will be made between primarily military factors and political ones. It is useful in considering the Soviet context to note the distinction normally made in Soviet military writings between military-technical and sociopolitical issues. In defining the military-technical component of military doctrine, the *Soviet Encyclopedic Dictionary* states:

> The military-technical content of Soviet military doctrine embraces a wide circle of questions relating to the construction and training of the armed forces, their maintenance at a high level of combat readiness, the improvement of their technical equipment and control systems, and the further development of Soviet military art, i.e., defining the paths, means, and methods of tracing and executing missions by the armed forces so that they may reliably protect the socialist homeland in a future war in the event one is unleashed by an aggressor.

In looking at the political side of military doctrine, the *Soviet Encyclopedic Dictionary* notes that "the sociopolitical side embraces questions touching on the methodological, economic, social, and legal principles of achieving the goals of a possible future war. It is definitive and possesses the greatest stability, as it expresses the class essence and political goals of the state, which are relatively constant over a prolonged period."[17] The dividing line between the two is

---

[17] "Doktrina voennaia" ("Military Doctrine"), in N. V. Ogarkov, ed., *Voennyi Entsik-*

often blurred in practice; this study, following Colton, will consider purely military affairs as falling within the domain of the marshals. In practice, the political leadership would appear to be only remotely involved in the technical sphere, although it reserves the right to intervene in this area as well, as did Stalin and, to a lesser degree, Khrushchev. The test of a senior military officer's influence will be the degree to which he is able to modify or change policies in either sector. For its part, the party leadership clearly preserves for itself the right to have the last word, believing, as it does, that the sociopolitical aspect of every situation is "definitive."

A number of issues could have been selected as indicators of leadership influence either within the military or in the high command's relations with senior party officials. For the purposes of this study, however, two were chosen in each category: Soviet warfighting strategy and the management of the armed forces for the strictly military issues, and arms control and the budgetary process for the political-military issues. There are two reasons for this decision. First, these are four of the most important topics the Soviet military and political leadership have faced over the past twenty years. Second, given the enormity of the internal and external variables that have had an impact on the Soviet national security process since 1967, it was felt that this approach would permit a more systematic analysis by ensuring both that each factor would be analyzed throughout the entire period under study and that each issue would be investigated in an in-depth manner.

Furthermore, following Colton, I am not assuming on any of these variables that conflict will necessarily exist between civilian and military officials. Technical issues will generally be considered as the professional prerogative of the military, and political issues will generally be viewed as the responsibility of political officials. Indeed, while there is a greater probability of conflict between military and civilian leaders when political issues are involved, this may not always be the case.

The discussion of warfighting strategy will focus on an issue that has been one of the major concerns of senior military officers: the

---

lopedicheskii Slovar' (*Military Encyclopedic Dictionary*) (Moscow: Voennoe izdatel'stvo, 1983), p. 240.

relative importance of nuclear and conventional weapons in the Kremlin's strategic and force structure. For example, how does the country's national security leadership see the relationship between the two types of weapons? Assuming that conventional weapons are assigned an important role, is escalation to the use of nuclear systems nevertheless considered to be inevitable? Is there a different attitude toward the relationship between such systems when viewed in various contexts—the Third World, the theater level, or in the event of a world war? How important is parity at the nuclear level? To what degree does the existence of nuclear and conventional weapons complicate Soviet battlefield tactics or strategy? Assuming—as this writer does—that there is a close correlation between warfighting strategy and force structure, to what degree is the nature of the Soviet military arsenal changing over time?

Military technology is defined by the *Military Encyclopedic Dictionary* as "the weapons, military and non-military devices, apparatuses, mechanisms, and other technical means with which the armed forces are equipped for carrying out their combat and daily tasks." Not only is such equipment critical for military operations, but as the *Military Encyclopedic Dictionary* notes, the speed of new technological developments is "one of the basic factors of a high level of combat capability."[18] On a practical level, the primary task for the high command is twofold. First, it must obtain the necessary equipment, and second, it must ensure that the military organization is managed in the most efficient manner possible. This includes not only modifying Soviet warfighting strategy to accommodate new technologies, but also—perhaps even more important—making certain that Soviet military personnel specifically and the armed forces as an institution are putting the available equipment to the best possible use. What is the high command's conception of the ideal Soviet soldier or officer? To what degree does reality agree with this ideal? Assuming there is any discrepancy, is the high command able to change the situation? Any attempt by political authorities to dictate policy in either of these areas would signify an expansion of political authority and a diminishment of the power of the country's top military leadership.

---

[18] Ibid., p. 737.

Turning to the sociopolitical side of Soviet national security affairs, arms control impinges directly on the military since it raises fundamental questions about the nature of Soviet foreign policy and has serious implications for the Kremlin's military posture—the marshals may be forced to give up some valuable pieces of equipment. Generals and admirals have tended to believe that military strength is the key to maintaining a country's security. And while an argument can be made for arms control negotiations as a way of regulating the military growth of the other side, actual cuts in one's military arsenal are another matter. In essence, diplomacy is sometimes useful, but only as an appendage to military force. Consequently, the country's top military officers may be suspicious of any attempt to reduce military forces while relying on political arrangements as compensation. Furthermore, arms control agreements are bound to affect the country's military force structure. A country's military posture is dictated by a number of factors, and the removal of a category or class of weapons from the inventory has serious consequences for the military's ability to prosecute a war at various levels. In short, arms control means giving up something to get something; even if it can be argued that the gains outweigh the losses, it is not surprising that many military officers—both East and West—are often uncomfortable with the political arrangements that cause adjustments, even minor ones, in strategy and force structure. On the other hand, arms control can be particularly important to a political leadership attempting to save money that is normally allocated to military systems for use in the civilian economy. If an arrangement can be made that permits a reallocation of economic resources to help satisfy consumer pressures or facilitate economic rejuvenation without seriously undermining the country's security, then the political leadership will often consider it a good arrangement. Given the overlapping nature of military and political interests here, arms control is a potential area of conflict between the USSR's political and military leaders. Indeed, this was the main reason why it was selected for inclusion in this study. In its most simplistic version, most generals will probably oppose arms control, while the political leadership will be its most likely proponents.

The budgetary process is another potential source of discord between politicians and generals. Military officers of every nation never believe they have sufficient funds to meet all of the threats facing their country, while politicians constantly feel called upon to curb what appears to be the military's insatiable appetite for more guns and missiles. Which is more important, a new missile or tackling the country's never ending crises in agriculture?

Given the very political nature of both arms control and the budgetary process, Soviet political leaders are bound to be sensitive to attempts by senior Soviet military officers to interfere in decision making in these areas. The military as an institution and the country's top generals as representatives of that institution consider themselves to have a legitimate right to express their views in both areas; indeed, when it comes to arms control, it can be argued that the military is a key player in the formulation of policy if only because it traditionally has had a monopoly over military data and can influence the process by changing the ways in which that data is presented. However, in accordance with the principle of democratic centralism—one of the primary features of any Leninist party—once the political leadership makes a decision on an issue like arms control, the military is expected to give its full support. Similarly, while generals are expected to push their favorite programs within the budgetary process, they will also be expected to support a decision on the allocation of resources once the Politburo makes it— even if they are not happy about all its aspects. Thus, a decision by senior military officers to oppose the political leadership on either of these issues will not be taken lightly. Here we have two key questions: how effective are the top military leaders in convincing the political leadership to adopt positions on arms control congenial to the military? How effective are they in lobbying for a share of the country's budget?

Finally, how much influence was in fact exercised by the country's top military officers? This major concern may be addressed through various questions. How effective were they in enforcing their will, both on issues related to warfighting strategy and technology within the military establishment and in the broader military-political arena on topics such as arms control and the budget? On the technical side, were these individuals reactive? Did they simply respond to major changes in Soviet warfighting strategy over the years, or did they originate some of the new ideas? Likewise, were they out in front on the need to make the military more responsive to the demands of high technology, or did they delegate this to their subordinates? One assumes that a strong military leader would tend to adopt an aggressive stance on both issues, particularly that of management, since management is primarily a matter of making organizational and personnel modifications where the intensity of bureaucratic interests could be assumed to be low. During a time of change, however, when resistance to new ideas and approaches may be rampant, a strong leader will sometimes need to exercise a heavy hand over the armed forces in order to ensure that the necessary changes and adaptations are carried out. He will in any case tend to be an active participant in the discussion of these issues within the military. Furthermore, given the different nature of the responsibilities of the defense minister (who focuses on broad military-political matters) and the chief of staff (who deals with more technical day-to-day issues) one would expect to find that it is the chief of staff who takes the lead in this area.

Turning to the sociopolitical area, a strong chief of staff or defense minister will tend to be outspoken in advocating what he considers to be the military's primary interests as to arms control or the budget. He will tend to be less confrontational on these issues than in dealing with warfighting strategy or technology, however, since issues of arms control and the budget are normally considered the responsibility of political authorities. In practical terms this means that where a senior military officer might openly advocate a change in the way the military deals with officer education (e.g., an increase in the time all officers must devote to the study of technical subjects), when it comes to politically sensitive issues such as arms control, he will adopt a more indirect approach. Rather than openly disagreeing with the line followed by the political leadership on arms control, he could withhold his support (perhaps by ignoring the political leadership's call for an arms control agreement) or oppose the leadership's line by emphasizing the aggressive nature of imperialism while the general secretary is emphasizing the value of a SALT I agreement. As to the budget, the senior officer could argue for the importance of a strong military deterrent just when the political leadership is hinting at the need for greater emphasis on consumer goods. Given his broader responsibilities as well as his presence on the country's top national-security decision-making bodies (i.e., the Defense Council and the Politburo), the defense minister would be most likely to take the lead in this area. An exception might be when the defense minister is a political appointee who tends to identify closely with the general secretary. The chief of the General Staff might then become a strong spokesman for the armed forces. In fact, if the chief of staff is a strong leader and believes the general secretary is following a policy that threatens the country's security interests, it is possible that there will be differences of opinion between the two top military officers, with the defense minister supporting the party line while the chief of staff dissents. Indeed, this is exactly what happened in the early eighties as Ogarkov and Ustinov quarreled over the Kremlin's policy toward the West.

Key Questions

This study will not only provide an in-depth analysis of the evolution of Soviet attitudes and policies toward four of the most important issues facing the Soviet high command over the past twenty years, it will also attempt to answer a number of other questions.

Political Influence. To what degree were the seven senior military officers able to translate their authority within the military establishment into influence in the political sphere? One assumes that the ability to exercise a high degree of control within the military is a prerequisite for influence at the political level. But to what degree does power in the former lead to influence in the latter area?

Determining the degree of influence exerted by an individual is difficult in any system. The closed nature of the Soviet system complicates the situation even further. For example, during the early years of his tenure as minister of defense, Grechko had a sympathetic general secretary, one who supported his efforts to build up the armed forces. During the latter part of his time as minister of defense, however, there was clear conflict between the two men. And positions favored by Grechko—for example, on the budget—prevailed. This was not solely a result of Grechko's efforts. In fact, he could almost certainly not have accomplished his goal of avoiding a cutback in military spending on his own. He needed allies and found them in the political leadership. Nevertheless, it appears clear that he helped influence events, just as Ogarkov influenced the way Soviet warfighting strategy and force structure developed in the early eighties.

Political Style. All eight of the military officers covered by this study differed in style. Some were aggressive, outspoken, even abrasive, while others were quiet and passive. To what degree is style a reflection of power? Is it only an aggressive leader who is influential, or does being outspoken, especially in a system like the USSR, suggest that the individual is politically weak? In short, is it possible to identify a style closely associated with a successful military officer?

Personal Qualifications.   Much has been said and written in recent years about the changing nature of the Soviet elite. For example, it has been argued that it is becoming better educated and more cosmopolitan. While the eight generals and marshals covered here are not statistically representative of the Soviet officer corps, they do provide us with an interesting overview of the personal characteristics of senior military officers. Do these men share qualifications that make for a successful career?

Personal Ties.   If the Soviet military does, in fact, reflect civilian politics in the Soviet Union, then the majority of these top military individuals were selected for their high positions because of their personal ties to top civilian and military leaders. If this is true, it confirms the commonly held belief that personal ties are crucial in the selection of top military officers.

Institutional and Organizational Constraints.   While one assumes that the top two military officers have primary authority over implementing developments within the armed forces, how successful do they end up being when it comes to introducing radical changes? For example, if the chief of staff decides to introduce major changes in the personnel area—changes aimed at producing a Soviet soldier with attitudes toward efficiency and productivity that vary from those in the population as a whole—will he be able to successfully implement such modifications on his own? It is often argued that organizational constraints limit a senior military officer's ability to have a serious effect on the course of events within the Soviet Union. Senior military officers are thought to be most effective as to peripheral issues; core issues, such as personnel, force structure, and strategy, appear to be set by organizational constraints. Assuming the defense minister or chief of staff is determined to effect major changes, will he need the strong backing of political authorities? If so, will this have an impact on his autonomy in dealing with sociopolitical issues in relation to the military as an institution or to political officials? Does he pay a price for relying for assistance on political authorities? If so, where in the leadership process is this most visible?

Interpreting Soviet Writings

For those unfamiliar with writings on military issues and policy debates in the West, this book's general approach may appear strange. While the situation may be changing, instead of private conversations with key participants and official (or more often unofficial) copies of key decision memoranda, the analyst of Soviet affairs must rely primarily on the public writings and speeches of the individuals concerned. He or she then must attempt to relate these to changes in the force structure and to the overall evolution of Soviet political-military affairs.

Furthermore, the format traditionally used by Soviet officials to communicate their positions and ideas has often been confusing to Westerners. For example, where Western policy-makers are often very blunt in their expressions of policy choices, up until very recently Soviet officials generally adopted a more indirect approach. There are a number of reasons for this, from an awareness of Lenin's warning against factionalism to a desire to avoid taking an unambiguous stand on a disputed issue. Not long ago such an action could have cost an individual his or her life. In practice, this means that an individual may use historical examples to make a point rather than openly arguing that a policy of détente is unwise. In the early 1980s, for example, one of the key areas of disagreement between Marshal Ogarkov and Defense Minister Ustinov centered on the relevance of the period from 1937 to 1941 for the present. Ogarkov argued that the early 1980s resembled the late 1930s, thereby signaling his disagreement with Brezhnev's policy of improving relations with the West. Ogarkov was arguing that Stalin had attempted to improve relations with Nazi Germany, and that had led to the disastrous and almost successful German invasion of the USSR. By implication, any attempt to improve relations with Washington threatened to have the same effect. Ustinov, on the other hand, was optimistic about the possibility of improved East-West relations and denied that the 1930s and Nazi Germany were relevant to the present.

The situation is similar when it comes to military-technical matters. Soviet writers do not generally signal their differences on existing strategy or tactics by openly criticizing current policy. They tend rather to argue that a new approach to the problems facing the Soviet military is in order. For example, during the mid-1960s, when Khrushchev's primary reliance on nuclear weapons came under fire, Soviet military writers focused on the insufficiency of the "single-variant" approach and called instead for a balanced force structure. To Soviet military officers, the message was clear: despite the importance of nuclear weapons, a modern military needed to have a balanced military force—conventional as well as nuclear weapons.

In both cases noted above, the contrast—between Ogarkov and Ustinov or between "single-variant" and "balanced" force structures—was clear by Soviet standards. Few analysts would argue that there was no difference of opinion between the Kremlin's top two military officers or that Khrushchev's single-variant strategy was not under fire from the Soviet military. Unfortunately, the situation is not always so clear-cut. This is what makes Kremlinology as much an art as a science. Often a difference of opinion is signaled by the change of a single word. For example, the program adopted by the Twenty-seventh Party Congress in 1986 noted that the party was "making every effort to ensure" that the military had everything it needed. This language contrasted sharply with the phraseology that had been used up to that point, namely, that the party was "taking steps to ensure" that the military had what it needed. This change was not accidental: it signaled a major effort by Gorbachev to cut back the Soviet military budget. But in other instances what may at first appear to be a signal may turn out to be nothing more than a variation in language. For example, during the early 1980s both Ogarkov and Ustinov used language that suggested that the international world had become more threatening. They would note that the danger of war had increased, or that the world was balanced on the abyss of a nuclear holocaust. While there is no doubt that Soviet military leaders viewed the outside world as more threatening, one cannot draw a direct correlation between gradations of perceived threat and the language they employed. In some instances, the same writer shifts between more and less threatening phrases over time. The point is not that such language is not important—the overall trend was clear—but that such changes must be viewed within the context of the overall evolution of Soviet thinking on a given topic.

And more often than not, a creative interpretation is required in attempting to understand the significance of any statement.

This brings us to the question of disinformation. In the past some have questioned reliance on written Soviet material on military issues as a guide to understanding the Soviet policy-making process. There is no question that more is hidden from the researcher than is revealed in print. For example, the analyst is unlikely to have access to leaks from the highest party circles, much less come across a transcript of a Politburo or Defense Council meeting. Nevertheless, an extensive review of relevant Soviet materials over a specific period can provide the analyst with a general sense of trends, relationships, and leadership views on questions of key importance to the future of the Soviet state—even if some bits and pieces of disinformation occasionally creep in. And regarding the suggestion that most of what is written is meant primarily to mislead foreign readers, I would agree with James McConnell's observation that

> it is a peculiar form of inflated Western self-esteem that turns a literature read for profit in the Soviet Union into a performance for its own benefit. Moscow is, of course, aware of alien eavesdropping; hence, much of the rigid propaganda conventions, the misleading statements, guarded language that borders on the opaque. The substance of the message is not affected, however; the Kremlin cannot afford to deceive its own cadres. If disinformation be defined as communication that the Soviet elite, skilled in reading the literature of its specialty, would declare to be an untruth, then there is very little disinformation in the Soviet press. [19]

In fact, a close reading of the Soviet military press—the vast majority of which goes unread since it is not translated into English—shows that it has long been more open and has long indicated more debate among elites than is generally believed in the West.

There is also the question of the reliability of Western data on the Soviet military. Western estimates of Soviet military capabilities are just that—estimates. They are subject to error, not to mention problems that occur as a result of the interjection of political considerations. Given the lack of reliable Soviet data on questions such as

[19] James M. McConnell, "Shifts in Soviet Views on the Proper Focus of Military Development," *World Politics* 37, no. 3 (April 1985): 319.

size of military budget, however, the analyst has no alternative but to rely on figures produced by U.S. government agencies. To be credible, these data should be at least indirectly supported by the speeches and writings of top-level officials.

Finally, it should be noted that in spite of attempts to sift through an entire mountain of data, it is always possible that, given the closed nature of the Soviet Union, new information will become available which will call into question the findings of this or any other study. While such a recognition is humbling, it is a fact of life with which the analyst must be prepared to live.

Sources

In carrying out research for this study, primary emphasis was placed on Soviet sources. First, a search was conducted of articles by Moscow's senior military officers in the country's three most important political-military newspapers: *Pravda*, *Izvestiia* and *Krasnaia zvezda*. Generally, articles by the defense minister appeared in *Pravda*, although other officers were also represented from time to time and the defense minister would also publish articles in the other two newspapers. *Izvestiia* was utilized by a wide variety of senior military officers, and, as might be expected, the greatest number of articles by senior military officers appeared in the military newspaper *Krasnaia zvezda*. In a few instances, more obscure regional newspapers such as *Pravda vostoka* and *Sovetskaia Litva* were also consulted.

All issues of the major political-military journals were combed for articles of value. This included the journals *Kommunist*, *Kommunist vooruzhennykh sil*, *Voennyi vestnik*, *Voenno-istoricheskii zhurnal*, and *Morskoi sbornik*. When available, English-language translations of the classified General Staff journal, *Voennaia mysl'* were also utilized. Other journals such as *Voprosy istorii KPSS*, *Novyi mir*, and *Partiinaia zhizn'* were also checked; in a number of cases these carried important articles. Just as *Pravda* tended to contain the most important and authoritative newspaper articles, *Kommunist* was the most significant journal. In general, one *Kommunist* article per year, usually in February or March, was devoted to military affairs. It was usually written by the defense minister or chief of staff and often contained new ideas or authoritative statements on key questions of importance to the Soviet armed forces. If one were to consult only one source over the past ten years as a guide to the most important thinking at the highest levels of the Soviet military, this source would be *Kommunist*.

A number of Russian-language books were also consulted. The collected speeches of political leaders such as Brezhnev, Andropov, Chernenko, Gorbachev, and Ustinov were reviewed, as were books and pamphlets written by Grechko, Kulikov, Ogarkov, Ustinov, and Yazov. In addition, other key Soviet works by writers such as Sokolovskii, Gareyev, and Kir'ian were also used.

Among the English-language works available in the West on the Soviet military, journals such as the *International Defense Review*, *Orbis*, *International Security*, and *World Politics* were indispensable. The same is true of works by authors such as Christopher Donnelly, John Hines, Charles Peterson, Notra Trulock, Michael MccGwire, and James McConnell. The most important book-length Western source on the Soviet military is the journal *Soviet Armed Forces Review Annual* edited by David Jones. Without this latter publication Western analysts would be hard pressed to keep up with current developments in the Soviet armed forces.

CHAPTER 2

The Legacy of Khrushchev

*T*he *Khrushchev era* exerted a profound influence on the attitudes of the high command. On the military-technical side the major preoccupation of the high command after Khrushchev would be to reverse his deification of nuclear weapons at the expense of conventional systems toward the creation of a more balanced force structure. Politically, the primary legacy of Khrushchev's tenure in office was a deep sense of suspicion—a feeling on the part of the high command that political leaders would willingly sacrifice the country's security to improve their own domestic position. The high command saw arms control, for example, not as a means for improving the country's security, but as part of an effort to take money away from the armed forces to satisfy domestic needs.

One of the most important and disturbing elements of this period from the standpoint of the high command was that Khrushchev not only interfered in such traditionally military areas such as warfighting strategy and force structure, but also forced the generals to move in a direction that the vast majority of them believed to be militarily unsound. While most of the USSR's top military officers recognized the critical importance of nuclear weapons in a future war, almost all of them believed that the key to military success lay in a balanced military force. In practice this included not only modern nuclear weapons, but a robust conventional force as well. Without the latter, they believed, it would be impossible to seize territory or to follow up on gains made as the result of nuclear strikes. Khrushchev, however, had a different view on this matter.

In a speech before the Supreme Soviet on January 14, 1960, Khrushchev asserted that large standing armies, surface navies, and fleets of bomber aircraft were becoming obsolete. Nuclear weapons,

32

he maintained, were the basis of Soviet military strength; a future war would begin with "rocket strikes deep in the interior." Furthermore, he asserted that "in modern times a nation's defense capability depends on firepower, not on the number of men under arms." Given the centrality of nuclear weapons in a future war, it would be possible for the USSR to reduce conventional forces.[1]

The implication of Khrushchev's line was that a world war could best be prevented not by balanced military forces but by the threat of nuclear retaliation. As one Western expert put it, "Khrushchev's conception was limited to one sole option: preparation for atomic war by means of a minimal deterrent strategic force."[2] One of the most immediate consequences of Khrushchev's 1960 speech was that the Strategic Rocket Forces (SRF), which had been formed in 1959, began to be viewed as the most important of the five Soviet services, while the relative significance of the other services diminished. As he stated in his speech on the navy and air force:

> Given the present development of military technology, military aviation and the navy have lost their former importance. This type of armament is not being reduced but replaced. Military aircraft are being almost entirely replaced by rockets. We have now sharply reduced and probably will further reduce and even halt production of bombers and other obsolete equipment. In the navy the submarine fleet is assuming great importance and surface ships can no longer play the role they played in the past.[3]

A significant segment of the country's conventional forces was thus quickly becoming a thing of the past.

In arguing that any attack would lead to massive retaliation, Khrushchev's approach bore a resemblance to the "mutual assured destruction" concept popular in the West:

> Let us assume . . . that some state or group of states succeeded in preparing and carrying out a surprise attack on a power possessing nuclear and rocket weapons. But could the attacking side . . . be able to put out of commission at once all stocks of nuclear weapons

---

[1] N. S. Khrushchev, *Disarmament for Durable Peace and Friendship* (Moscow: Foreign Languages Publishing House, 1960), pp. 38–39.

[2] Yosef Avidar, *The Party and the Army in the Soviet Union* (Jerusalem: The Magnes Press, 1983), p. 249.

[3] Khrushchev, *Disarmament for Durable Peace and Friendship*, p. 38.

and all the rocket installations on the territory of the power being attacked? Of course not. The state that has been suddenly attacked . . . will always be able to give the aggressor a proper rebuff.[4]

Khrushchev's attempt to push nuclear weapons (his "single-variant" strategy, as it has sometimes been labeled) was primarily motivated by a belief that he could save money needed for domestic purposes by pushing the less expensive nuclear deterrent. Thus, in 1963, in the midst of his drive for an expansion of the chemicals industry, Khrushchev criticized the military-industrial complex, arguing that "there are large reserves for increased production even in the defense industry, but they are little used because these factories are absolutely closed off—and they're also closed to criticisms of shortcomings and negligence."[5] Throughout the remainder of 1963 Khrushchev continued to criticize the military budget while at the same time arguing for the primacy of the chemical industry. A key, unstated premise of his argument was that it was more important to put money into the chemical sector than into expensive and unnecessary conventional weapons. By the end of 1964 the Supreme Soviet had ratified a state budget that called for a reduction in military expenditures by roughly 600 million rubles.[6]

To make matters worse, Khrushchev made it very clear throughout his tenure that he did not trust his generals. In 1959, for example, he stated, "I do not trust the appraisal of generals on questions of strategic importance."[7] Clearly, this was a man who felt he understood military matters better than his generals. Given such an attitude, it is not surprising that senior military officers were less than enthusiastic about him and his approach.

Indeed, from the very beginning top military officers showed misgivings about Khrushchev's "single-variant" strategy. This was

---

[4] Ibid., pp. 40–41.

[5] N. S. Khrushchev, "Vse rezervy promyshlennosti i stroitel'stva—na sluzhbu kommunizma!" ("All Industrial and Structural Reserves—for the Service of Communism"), *Pravda*, April 26, 1963.

[6] "O gosudarstvennom plane razvitiia narodnogo khoziaistva SSSR na 1964–1965 gody" ("Concerning the State Plan for the Development of the People's Economy of the USSR for the Years 1964–1965"), *Pravda*, December 17, 1963.

[7] Khrushchev to a Kremlin Press Conference, November 8, 1959, as cited in Raymond D. Senter, "Khrushchev, the Generals and Goldwater," *The New Republic*, November 21, 1964, p. 8. I am indebted to Ted Warner for bringing this citation to my attention.

particularly evident in defense minister Malinovskii's carefully structured comments to the Twenty-second Party Congress in 1961. Malinovskii stated that

> —if a world war takes place, it "will inevitably take the form of a nuclear rocket war";
> —the main weapon would "be the nuclear weapon and the basic means of delivering it to the target will be the rocket";
> —the use of atomic and thermonuclear weapons meant that it would be possible to achieve "decisive military results in the shortest period of time and over enormous territory";
> —a future war "will take on an unprecedentedly destructive character. It will lead to the death of hundreds of millions of people, and whole countries will be turned into lifeless deserts covered with ashes";
> —since any war between the superpowers would inevitably escalate to the use of nuclear weapons, the USSR must prepare its forces to fight a nuclear war.[8]

With the importance of conventional forces very much in mind, however, he added that all components of the Soviet force structure would play an important role in a war: "Despite the fact that in the next war the decisive weapon will be nuclear rockets, we have nevertheless reached the conclusion that final victory over the aggressor can only be secured as a result of combined action by all the arms of the Armed Forces. . . . We are likewise of the opinion that under present conditions, the next war will be conducted, despite heavy losses, by armed forces numbering many millions."[9] This placed him clearly in opposition to Khrushchev's emphasis on the primacy of nuclear weapons.

Malinovskii was not the only senior military officer prepared to speak out against Khrushchev's one-variant strategy. For example, Admiral Gorshkov, while conceding the importance of nuclear missiles, argued for a balanced force structure: "it does not follow from this [i.e., the importance of nuclear armed missiles] that the need for other forces has diminished. Victory in contemporary war can be accomplished only through the use of all means of armed conflict.

---

[8] Rodion Ya. Malinovskii, "Bessmertnyi podvig sovetskogo naroda" ("The Immortal Feat of the Soviet People"), *Pravda*, June 22, 1961.

[9] Ibid.

The geographic conditions of our nation, washed by many seas and oceans, dictate particularly that the navy henceforth will occupy an important place in the system of the Soviet Armed Forces."[10] In November, Marshal Moskalenko made a statement similar to Malinovskii's comments in June.[11] Likewise, Marshal Rotmistrov, chief of soviet tank forces wrote in 1962 that "nuclear weapons, powerful though they are, do not conquer territory. The soldier has to get there in order to do this, he has to advance in depth and wage battle boldly—this is what armored troops are suitable for."[12] Marshal Chuikov entered the fray in 1963, arguing that "to ignore the objective laws of balanced development of all types of weapons and of the different branches in the forces and their coordinated use in warfare necessarily has catastrophic consequences."[13] The bottom line for these officers was that there were no short cuts to a secure military deterrent. It was not long before Khrushchev was ousted from the political leadership. The dissatisfaction among Soviet generals over strategy and budget almost certainly played a role in the decision to remove him.

Khrushchev's elevation of nuclear weapons in general and the Strategic Rocket Forces (SRF) in particular had practical consequences for other services. As a leading Soviet theorist stated:

> All this naturally led to a change in the organizational structure of the Armed Forces, and to a reevaluation of the role and importance of Services and branches of the Armed Forces. The Strategic Missile Forces were organized and remain in continuous readiness for delivering a crushing nuclear retaliatory strike against an aggressor. They became the primary Service of the Armed Forces and a reliable means for containing the aggressive aspirations of imperialism.[14]

---

[10] Admiral S. G. Gorshkov, "Nadezhnyi strazh bezopasnosti rodiny" ("Reliably Guarding the Security of the Motherland"), *Sovetskii flot*, February 23, 1960, as quoted in George E. Hudson, "Soviet Naval Doctrine and Soviet Politics, 1953–1975," *World Politics* 29, no. 1 (October 1976): 101.

[11] K. Moskalenko, "V sovershenstve vladet' vsemi sredstvami zashchity rodiny" ("Commanding with Perfection All Means of Defending the Motherland"), *Kommunist vooruzhennykh sil*, no. 22 (November 1961): 37.

[12] A. Rotmistrov, "Sovremennye tanki i iadernoe oruzhie" ("Modern Tanks and Nuclear Weapons"), *Izvestiia*, October 20, 1962.

[13] V. Chuikov, "Sovremennye sukhoputnye voiska" ("Modern Infantry Forces"), *Izvestiia*, December 22, 1963.

[14] M. I. Cherednichenko, "On Features in the Development of Military Art in the

The most immediate impact of this enhanced role for the SRF was felt by the ground forces. In September 1964 they lost their status as an independent command as the post of commander in chief of ground forces was suspended, and they were placed under the direct administration of the ministry of defense. Nuclear weapons became the key to Soviet military prowess.

The clearly subordinate role assigned to ground forces was noted by a well-known Soviet theorist who, in describing the ground forces of the time, observed that "the Ground Forces were charged with the tasks of destroying enemy troop formations and aircraft using operational-tactical nuclear weapons. A special role was assigned to the organization of coordinated nuclear strikes between operational-tactical missile forces and tactical aviation, and also to the mobile operations and helicopters."[15] Conventional forces such as the ground forces were relegated to the role of securing areas once they had been neutralized by nuclear weapons. This in effect led to the "nuclearization" of the Soviet armed forces. Hines, Peterson, and Trulock put it best when they observed: "In effect, nuclear weapons became the first echelon of Soviet military operations, with all the other forces relegated to an exploitation role. This represents probably the only period in which Soviet military theory and planning relied on an absolute weapon."[16] The logical conclusion of this development was that the USSR could live with a smaller number of conventional forces. And by 1960 Khrushchev had in fact succeeded in reducing the size of the Soviet military by 2,140,000 troops to a low of 3,623,000. To add insult to injury, Khrushchev proposed in 1960 the elimination of another 1,200,000, down to a total of 2,423,000—although during the fall of 1961, ostensibly in response to the Berlin crisis, he announced the cancellation of further cuts.[17] Khrushchev returned to the subject again in 1964, hinting at the possibility of further troop cuts, although no further reductions in force were to occur.

Postwar Period," *Voenno-istoricheskii zhurnal*, no. 6 (Moscow: June 1970), translated by the U.S. Air Force, in *Selected Military Writings, 1970–1975* (Washington, D.C.: Government Printing Office, 1976), p. 120.

[15] Cherednichenko, "On Features in the Development of Military Art," p. 122.

[16] John G. Hines, Phillip A. Peterson, and Notra Trulock II, "Soviet Military Theory from 1945–2000: Implications for NATO," *The Washington Quarterly*, Fall 1986, p. 120.

[17] N. S. Khrushchev, *Disarmament for Durable Peace and Friendship*, p. 35.

In 1961, with the publication of the first edition of *Military Strategy*, the preeminence of nuclear weapons took on canonical status. Written by a number of military officers under the direction of Marshal Sokolovskii, chief of the General Staff from 1952 to 1960, the book declared that "military strategy in the conditions of modern warfare becomes the strategy of deep rocket-nuclear strikes in combination with actions by all services of the armed forces with the aim of simultaneously striking and destroying the economic potential and the armed forces on the whole depth of the enemy's territory for attaining the objectives of the war in a short time."[18]

Military Strategy did not entirely ignore the role of ground forces. Indeed, it could be argued, as Warner has maintained, that this book was a compromise document, one that "combined a greatly increased emphasis upon strategic missiles and nuclear weapons with a determined defense of the continuing need to prepare for massive ground-based theater operations."[19] While the book clearly recognized the importance of ground operations (and thus deviated at least in theory from Khrushchev's one-variant strategy), there is no question that nuclear weapons were now the basis of Soviet military strategy. Indeed, for the next twenty-odd years this book and its subsequent editions would be cited especially in the West as evidence of the supreme importance of nuclear weapons in Soviet warfighting strategy. Meanwhile, despite hints of dissatisfaction, Khrushchev was forcing a revision of many segments of Soviet warfighting doctrine. In discussing the problem of encirclement and the annihilation of enemy forces, for example, a Soviet theorist argued that nuclear weapons would play a crucial role: "The basis for actions for the encirclement and annihilation of defending groups is the use of nuclear weapons and a swift attack from several directions."[20] Thus a "zone of radioactive contamination" could be set up to prevent the withdrawal of enemy forces. Similarly, nuclear weapons

[18] V. D. Sokolovskii, ed., *Voennaia Strategiia* (*Military Strategy*) (Moscow: Voenizdat, 1962), p. 16.

[19] Edward L. Warner III, *The Military in Contemporary Soviet Politics* (New York: Praeger, 1977), p. 145.

[20] Maj. Gen. B. Golovchiner, "Encirclement and Annihilation of Groupings of Defending Troops," *Voennaia mysl'*, no. 8 (August 1964), in Joseph D. Douglass Jr. and Amoretta M. Hoeber, *Selected Readings from Military Thought, 1963–1973* (Washington, D.C.: Government Printing Office, 1982) vol. 5, pt. 1, p. 42.

would help to ensure that reserves would not be brought up to relieve those encircled and would be an effective vehicle for destroying the other side's nuclear systems. This does not mean that non-nuclear forces would not play a useful role. It seems, however, that the idea of employing conventional forces independent of the use of nuclear systems did not occur to Soviet writers at this time. Another Soviet writer put it best when, in discussing problems involved in the destruction of the other side's reserves, he observed that "nuclear rocket weapons . . . are among the most reliable and important means . . . against reserves."[21] Still another stated that the "forward detachments" that had played such an important role during World War II would be restructured and assigned the task of "ensuring a more rapid and complete exploitation of nuclear strikes delivered by . . . advancing forces."[22]

From a structural standpoint, the nuclearization of Soviet forces had two major drawbacks. First, the incorporation of tactical nuclear weapons into the force structure created a need to disperse troops so as to avoid the destruction of many troops with a single nuclear weapon. This in turn resulted in the creation of small, highly mobile units and thus increased the problems of coordinating forces in a nuclear environment. Second, the restructuring of these forces into smaller units meant that Soviet forces would give up a certain degree of "staying power." This could become a serious problem if Soviet forces had to fight a protracted conventional war.

The American decision to develop a strategy of flexible response, with its emphasis on nonstrategic as well as strategic weapons, served as an impetus for renewed concern among senior Soviet generals and marshals. They worried that while the U.S. built up both its nuclear and conventional forces, the Kremlin would be outflanked. Not only would the U.S. have a larger nuclear force as a result of its efforts to expand and modernize its Intercontinental Ballistic Missile (ICBM) and Sea-Launched Ballistic Missile (SLBM)

---

[21] Maj. Gen. Kh. Dzhelaukov, "Combating Strategic Reserves in a Theater of Military Operations," *Voennaia mysl'*, no. 11 (November 1984), in Douglass and Hoeber, *Selected Readings*, vol. 5, pt. 1, p. 91.

[22] Col. I. Vorob'iev, "Forward Detachments in Offensive Operations and Battles," *Voennaia mysl'*, no. 4 (April 1965), in Douglass and Hoeber, *Selected Readings*, vol. 5, pt. 1, p. 98.

forces, it would also be in an advantageous position in areas in which it would be too dangerous to use nuclear weapons. After all, the Cuban missile crisis in 1962 had shown that in some cases the possession of nuclear weapons by both sides made the use of force too risky. In fact, the chief of the General Staff, Marshal Matvei Zakharov, was forced into early retirement in March 1963 apparently for criticizing Khrushchev's interference in military affairs. His replacement by Marshal Biriuzov, head of the SRF, was another defeat for those who favored a balanced force development in the Soviet military. After Khrushchev had been ousted from office, Zakharov—who had been restored to his post in 1964 after Marshal Biriuzov was killed in an airplane crash—published an article in which he attacked certain unnamed "subjectivist" and "harebrained" leaders—he clearly had Khrushchev in mind. He also attacked outside interference in military affairs by individuals who knew nothing about such things.[23] Meanwhile, Marshal Chuikov continued the high command's criticism of Khrushchev's policy, arguing that Washington's abandonment of total reliance on nuclear weapons was an example the Soviet Union should follow.[24]

REEVALUATING THE ROLE OF CONVENTIONAL WEAPONS

According to a Soviet source, a major reappraisal of Soviet military policy in fact took place immediately after Khrushchev's ouster: "After the October 1964 Plenum of the Central Committee of the CPSU, certain incorrect views within the military-scientific circles connected with the overvaluation of the potential of the atomic weapon, its influence on the character of war, and on the future development of the Armed Forces were overcome."[25] This reassessment was to have a major impact on the issues studied by Soviet military science over the next five to ten years. To begin with,

[23] M. V. Zakharov, "Vlastnoe trebovanie vremeni" ("The Imperative Demand of Our Time"), *Krasnaia zvezda*, February 4, 1965.

[24] Marshal V. Chuikov, "Modern Ground Forces," *Izvestiia*, December 22, 1963, cited in Thomas W. Wolfe, *Soviet Strategy at the Crossroads* (Cambridge, Mass.: Harvard University Press, 1964), p. 244.

[25] S. A. Tiushkevich, *Sovetskie Vooruzhennye Sily: istoriia stroitel'stva* (*The Soviet Armed Forces: A History of Their Development*) (Moscow: Voenizdat, 1978), p. 476.

Soviet writers started to consider the possibility that conventional weapons might be used, at least initially, in a future war. This renewed interest in the role of conventional weapons was evident in an order issued by Marshal Malinovskii and published in *Voennaia mysl'*. It noted, inter alia, the importance of studying military problems "chiefly under conditions of the employment of nuclear weapons, but also under conditions of the conduct of military operations with conventional weapons."[26]

By 1965 various approaches to the role of nuclear weapons had begun to appear in public comments on military strategy. In reality, however, their differences reflected the different functions the writers played within the Soviet armed forces. Some, such as Colonel Rybkin, who is often considered one of the most hawkish among Soviet military writers on the topic, parroted the official line, i.e., argued for the primacy of nuclear weapons. Rybkin took on those who had expressed concern over the consequences of placing primary reliance on nuclear weapons by stating that while a nuclear war would result in numerous casualties, to argue "that victory in a nuclear war would be completely impossible would be not only incorrect theoretically, but dangerous from a political point of view." In focusing on the latter point, Rybkin observed that "an a priori rejection of the possibility of victory is harmful because it could lead to moral disarmament, to a lack of belief in victory, to fatalism and passivism."[27] In evaluating Rybkin's comments, it is important to note that he was a political officer, a long-time professor at the Lenin Political-Military Academy. Accordingly, it was his task not to consider alternative strategies, but to gain support among the troops for the existing doctrine. However much some military officers at this time may have doubted the wisdom of primary reliance on nuclear weapons, this was the official party/governmental policy. Similar attitudes were evident in other "official" publications during the mid-1960s, especially those published under the auspices of the

---

[26] See "Under the Banner of the Great Lenin," *Voennaia mysl'*, no. 2 (February 1966): 13–14, cited in Raymond L. Garthoff, "Continuity and Change in Soviet Military Doctrine since the 1960s," paper delivered at the Conference on the Dynamics of Soviet Defense Policy, Kennan Institute for Advanced Russian Studies, September 21–23, 1987.

[27] E. Rybkin, "O sushchnosti mirovoi raketno-iadernoi voiny" ("On the Essence of a World Nuclear-Missile War"), *Kommunist vooruzhennykh sil*, no. 17 (September 1965): 55, 56.

Main Political Directorate. A book entitled *The History of Military Art*, published in 1966 as part of the authoritative Officers' Library series, for example, reiterated the Khrushchev line, noting that

> a future war, if the imperialists unleash it against the socialist countries, will be a world war; the main forces of the world will be drawn into it, and it will be a war of the two coalitions with opposing socio-political systems. . . . A world war will inevitably assume the nature of a nuclear rocket war with the main means of destruction in the war being the nuclear rocket weapon and the basic manner of delivering it to the target being rockets of various types.[28]

Likewise, in 1967 a book entitled *L. I. Lenin and the Soviet Armed Forces*, authored by professors at the Lenin Political Military Academy, argued that "war will inevitably become a world nuclear rocket war and will draw into the armed struggle the main countries of the world."[29] Similar statements appeared in books published in 1968 as well.

Meanwhile, Soviet military (as opposed to political) officers had began to explore the possibility of alternative strategies. They did not play down the importance of nuclear weapons; indeed, according to Khrushchev, Grechko himself, while in charge of the ground forces, had pushed hard for the introduction of small-yield tactical nuclear weapons into the Soviet ground forces. But Soviet writers began to argue that the Soviet military must be prepared to fight all kinds of war, both nuclear and conventional.[30] Thus Colonel General Lomov, a professor at the General Staff Academy, wrote in 1965 that "the armed forces must master the methods of waging operations in existing organizations with the limited use of nuclear weapons and without them, that is, with the use of conventional means."[31] In 1966 Soviet specialists were writing that "it is neces-

---

[28] A. A. Strokov, *Istoriia voennogo iskusstva* (*The History of Military Art*) (Moscow: Voenizdat, 1966), p. 590.

[29] A. S. Zheltov, ed., *V. I. Lenin i Sovetskie Vooruzhennye Sily* (*V. I. Lenin and the Soviet Armed Forces*) (Moscow: Voenizdat, 1967), p. 226.

[30] Nikita Khrushchev, *Khrushchev Remembers: The Last Testament*, vol. 2 (New York: Penguin Books, 1974), pp. 84–85.

[31] N. A. Lomov, "Vliianie sovetskoi voennoi doktriny na razvitie voennogo iskusstva" ("The Influence of Soviet Military Doctrine on the Development of Military Art"), *Kommunist vooruzhennykh sil*, no. 21 (November 1965): 22.

sary to be ready to wage various kinds of wars: world and local, swift and protracted, with the use of the nuclear weapon and without it."[32] While exploring the possibility of greater reliance on conventional weapons, the Soviet military continued to believe that a conflict would inevitably involve nuclear weapons.

The reasons for these two strains of thought in Soviet military writings have become clearer with the appearance of classified Soviet military writings from the period. For example, a textbook on general tactics in use at the Frunze Military Academy in 1966 stated: "The present textbook brings to light the essence of contemporary combined-arms battle, its nature and basic principles, gives recommendations on the organization and conduct of combat operations of a division (brigade) with the use of conventional means of attack, but under threat of the use of nuclear weapons on the enemy."[33] While there were significant differences between the statements of Soviet writers concerned with agitation and propaganda and those of officers who worried about tactics and strategy, they were fulfilling different functions. This difference in emphasis between military-political and military-technical officers has given rise to considerable confusion in the West. Those like Richard Pipes,[34] who has argued that the Soviets continued to assign primary importance to nuclear weapons throughout the 1960s, have tended to cite statements by political-military officers such as Rybkin to bolster their case. Those, on the other hand, who argue for a gradual change, a shift to greater reliance on a combined-arms approach, have assigned primary importance to the writings of regular military officers. Major changes were in fact under way. Despite the public position adopted by political officers, greater attention was being given to conventional systems and the limited use of nuclear weapons. In fairness to Soviet political-military officers, however, they had no alternative but to argue for the Khrushchev line. After all, it re-

---

[32] N. Ya. Sushko and T. R. Kondratkov, eds., *Metodologicheskie problemy voennoi teorii i praktiki* (*Methodological Problems of Military Theory and Practice*) (Moscow: Voenizdat, 1966), p. 127, cited in Hines et al., "Soviet Military Theory," p. 121.

[33] V. G. Reznichenko, ed., *Taktika (Tactics)* (Moscow: 1966) p. ii, cited in Hines et al., "Soviet Military Theory," p. 122.

[34] See, for example, Richard Pipes, *U.S.-Soviet Relations in an Age of Détente* (Boulder, Colo.: Westview, 1981), pp. 135–70, and Richard Pipes, "Soviet Strategic Doctrine: Another View," *Strategic Review*, Fall 1982, pp. 53–57.

mained the official dogma. Furthermore, if one accepted the argument that it was unlikely or impossible to win a nuclear war, how could one expect Soviet soldiers to fight under nuclear conditions, if it came to that? Discussion among experts over the proper approach to warfighting was fine, but until an authoritative decision was made on the subject, those responsible for the maintenance of morale would continue to follow the old line.

Despite the increased attention paid to conventional weapons, Soviet military writers clearly believed at this point that escalation to the use of nuclear weapons was probably inevitable. As Colonel General Lomov put it, "it is obvious that the probability of escalation of a limited war into a world nuclear war is quite high, if the nuclear powers are drawn into a local conflict, and under certain circumstances it can become inevitable."[35] Thus, if escalation is considered highly probable even if the conflict occurs far from the Soviet homeland, a conflict on the USSR's borders must be considered as even more likely to involve the use of nuclear weapons.

Grechko avoided taking a public stance on the relationship between conventional and nuclear weapons. Indeed, he seemed at this time to be hedging his bets in the nuclear-conventional controversy. In discussing the initial period of a war, for example, he seemed to side with those who emphasized the importance of nuclear weapons; he remarked that the next war would be qualitatively different from the last one and noted that "new forms of combat give rise to a number of completely different problems. It is sufficient to mention the delivery of a nuclear first strike, its impact on the vitality of the rear, industrial objects, and so forth."[36] On the other hand, Grechko was criticizing Khrushchev's single-variant strategy as early as 1960, when he remarked that "military science justly considers that it is impossible to achieve victory in a war without routing the enemy's armed forces and depriving him of the possibility of restoring them."[37] And in 1966 he argued against those in the Soviet military

---

[35] Lomov, "The Influence of Soviet Military Doctrine," p. 15.

[36] A. Grechko, "25 let tomu nazad" ("25 Years Ago"), *Voenno-istoricheskii zhurnal*, no. 6 (1966): 15.

[37] A. Grechko, "Great Victory," *Pravda*, May 9, 1960, cited in John McDonnell, "Khrushchev and the Soviet Military-Industrial Complex: Soviet Defense Policy, 1959–1961" (unpublished manuscript), p. 39.

"who are inclined to give a simplified view or who keep silent or smooth over insufficiencies in the construction and preparation of the armed forces."[38] Within the context of the time, such a comment could be easily interpreted as a criticism of those insisting on a simplified (i.e., single-variant) view of warfighting.

The emergence of nuclear weapons led to what Soviet theoreticians have called a "revolution in military affairs." The demands on Soviet technology increased significantly and, in turn, complicated military operations. To begin with, the firepower of nuclear systems meant that the amount of usable force available to a commander increased geometrically. As one Soviet writer noted:

> As a result of the abrupt qualitative leap in the development of sources of firepower and means of delivering it, and also with the appearance of other latest technical equipment, there has been created the possibility of decreasing the number of personnel of the armed forces directly engaged in combat operations for the direct destruction of the enemy without decreasing, and in fact increasing, their firepower. In the period from 1955 to 1960 the numerical strength of the Soviet Armed Forces was decreased by one-third, but their firepower, as N. S. Khrushchev has noted, increased many times during the same period, thanks to the introduction of the latest forms of modern military equipment.[39]

This increase in firepower complicated the conduct of military operations in a number of ways. First, the Soviet military relies heavily on calculations of the military balance for planning purposes, and the increase in firepower made such calculations more difficult. Not only did the tremendous destructive power of nuclear weapons make more traditional means for figuring the balance irrelevant, these weapons made constant revisions of such calculations necessary throughout the conflict. Computers help in factoring in variables such as mobility and maneuverability, as well as quantitative and qualitative elements, but even computers had their limits—especially in the early 1960s.

The constantly changing nature of the battlefield in a nuclear age also increased the demands for effective means of command and

---

[38] Grechko, "25 Years Ago," p. 6.

[39] Capt. 1st Rank V. Kulakov, "Problems of Military-Technical Superiority," *Voennaia mysl'*, no. 1, (January 1964), cited in Douglass and Hoeber, *Selected Readings*, p. 17.

control. Writing in 1963, a Soviet theorist observed: "Only a constant and comprehensive knowledge of the true situation on the fronts, the prompt supply of information to the appropriate control organs, and the knowledge and consideration of the versatility of enemy actions and his intentions will permit the rapid execution of sound measures, well-founded decisions, and the most purposeful and realistic control of subordinate troops, forces, and means."[40]

Now, however, with the advent of nuclear weapons and the increasing need to integrate them with conventional forces, the situation became more complex. To begin with, coordinating the actions of all forces involved in nuclear operations is more difficult than coordinating conventional operations. Different systems require varying amounts of time to reach a state of readiness, each has a different flight time, and the explosive charge and accuracy of each warhead varies. To be effective, each warhead must strike in a closely coordinated fashion. In addition, the interfacing of conventional and nuclear forces—even with the latter in a clearly subordinate role—means that careful attention must be paid to factors such as nuclear contamination. How long must aircraft or tanks wait until they can operate in a radioactive environment? Furthermore, with the increasing importance of deep operations, one must closely coordinate the actions of troops engaged in such operations with hundreds of other conventional and nuclear related forces. Finally, the equipment itself is much more complex than that used in the past. The result is an increased need for both planning and a better-trained cadre to carry out such operations. As one writer stated, "without a thorough understanding of its character there can be no correct understanding of the essence of modern coordination of forces and equipment or of the procedure and methods of its organization and implementation."[41] What is interesting about this comment, in light of later developments, is that the writer leaves the clear impression that only well-trained military experts are capable of mak-

---

[40] Maj. Gen. V. Kruchinin, "Contemporary Strategic Theory on the Goals and Missions of Armed Conflict," in Douglass and Hoeber, *Selected Readings*, p. 10.

[41] Col. M. Skovorodkin, "Some Questions on Coordination of Branches of Armed Forces in Major Operations," *Voennaia mysl'*, no. 2 (February 1967), cited in Douglass and Hoeber, *Selected Readings*, p. 142.

ing the necessary decisions. War has become so complex that it is increasingly a matter for specialists.

High-technology nuclear weapons are useless without trained personnel. War is no longer a matter of peasants mounting horses, receiving a few hours of training on how to fire a weapon, and then riding off to battle. By the early 1960s, the time required to train an officer to deal with complex weapons systems had increased significantly. And even at that time it was recognized that the problem was likely to get worse. To quote one writer, "The more complex and improved the weapons and technical equipment of the troops, the higher and more varied the demands on the personnel."[42]

CONCLUDING OBSERVATIONS

Seen from the vantage point of Tucker's three interlocking phases of the leadership process, the tasks facing the high command in the mid-1960s were formidable. Its *diagnosis* of the problems facing the Soviet military was far from complete. Indeed, diagnosis appeared limited to a recognition of the need for a modern military force evenly balanced between conventional and nuclear weapons. The task of developing such a force would be a complex one. How, for example, would conventional and nuclear weapons be integrated? What should be their proper mix? Should primary emphasis be placed on building up neglected conventional systems, or should the two types of weapons receive equal emphasis? Likewise, reliance on both nuclear and conventional weapons called for a rethinking of Soviet warfighting strategy. How would the two systems be related as to operational strategy and tactics? Given the complexity of modern warfare, this, too, would be a formidable undertaking.

How to determine the Soviet military's response to modern technology was another area of concern to the high command. The advent of nuclear weapons had placed greater demands on the military, particularly the officer corps. The increasing importance of conventional weapons only served to make these problems more difficult; a way had to be found to interrelate the two. Not only would a premium be placed on technical education and the use of science,

---

[42] Kulakov, "Problems of Military Technical Superiority," p. 22.

but command and control would also be an area of prime concern. Controlling thousands of troops—some in a nuclear and others in a conventional environment—was a formidable task. How serious were these problems? How many resources should be devoted to dealing with them?

Although in the mid-1960s arms control did not confront the high command as a serious problem, the budget did. If Moscow was going to return to a more balanced military force posture, a considerable amount of money would have to be put into conventional weapons, which are by nature more expensive than nuclear systems. This raised the need for a *strategy* for convincing the political leadership to pay for these expensive systems. Domestic priorities were an obvious matter of concern to the Brezhnev leadership, and the high command was faced with the need to argue for a rather large slice of the budgetary pie for the major buildup it was contemplating.

Finally, a decision had to be made on the best means for *mobilizing* the high command's assets to sustain over the long run the buildup it felt to be imperative. Political developments within the upper ranks of the party leadership suggested that it would not be difficult to get high-level support for the budget over the short run. But given the fickleness of politicians and their concern for satisfying consumer demands, the high command was faced with the necessity of ensuring sustained support from within the national security apparatus to offset the inevitable efforts to cut back on the military budget. Furthermore, the legacy of the Khrushchev era, with the general secretary's attempt to dictate even warfighting strategy, had convinced many officers of the need to insulate the military from such challenges. Military-technical issues had to become once again a preserve of the high command.

The Soviet military was obviously in a state of flux. And there was an equally obvious need for a strong leader to diagnose the military's basic interests, plan a strategy for achieving them, and mobilize resources over the long term, thereby guaranteeing the construction of a balanced and highly capable military. Malinovskii had made important contributions to the Soviet armed forces, but he was nearing the end of his life. The situation demanded a younger officer, one who enjoyed good political connections and was fully conversant with the issues at hand.

PART II

The Grechko Era, 1967–1976

CHAPTER 3

Grechko: The Early Years, 1967–1970

*D*uring the first three years of his reign as general secretary, Brezhnev was primarily concerned with consolidating his power. When he took over in 1964 it was as one of several influential—and independent—political leaders. Nikolai Podgornyi, a member of the Politburo and the Secretariat, openly sought to replace him. Petr Shelest, who would become a constant thorn in Brezhnev's side, supported Podgornyi, while others such as Mikhail Suslov, the party's ideologist, Andrei Kosygin, the country's top economist and planner, and Aleksandr Shelepin, head of the party control commission, were independent forces in their own right.

Brezhnev's approach to power was twofold. He sought to maintain a balance of support from a variety of sources while at the same time attempting to have his supporters appointed to key positions in the party apparatus—the most notable examples being the naming of Konstantin Chernenko to head the General Department of the Central Committee in July 1965 and Andrei Kirilenko to the Secretariat in April 1966. At the same time, Brezhnev moved against Shelepin by stripping the party control commission of its authority over the party; by the Twenty-third Party Congress in April 1966 he had succeeded in having Podgornyi dropped from the Secretariat to be replaced by a Brezhnev supporter, Kirilenko. Despite these gains, Brezhnev's power remained limited.

From the high command's standpoint, this period was decidedly better than its predecessor. The more congenial Brezhnev had replaced the combative and antimilitary Khrushchev, the younger Andrei Grechko had replaced the ailing Malinovskii, and the highly regarded Matvei Zakharov had been reappointed chief of the General Staff. Meanwhile, having achieved greater control of their own in-

ternal affairs, the generals faced the task of working out a more effective strategy and force structure, one that would take equal cognizance of nuclear and conventional weapons while at the same time
helping them better to meet the demands of modern technology.

For the present, the new leadership appeared committed to a
massive buildup in military forces. But the commitment was ten-
tative at best, as others in the Soviet leadership appeared to oppose
such a policy. For example, while Brezhnev favored an expanded
military budget, his opponents (most prominently, Podgornyi) insisted on giving priority to consumer interests. Brezhnev's victory
over Podgornyi was thus good news for the high command, and it
was followed by a decision in favor of a broad-based buildup in Soviet military forces. As one writer stated, "What was different and
striking about the decisions reached in 1965 was that, in addition
to their commitment to the expansion of their strategic programs,
the Soviets decided to begin a long-term expansion of other forces
on a multi-service front."[1] Thus, even before Grechko was appointed
defense minister, the high command had succeeded in obtaining
political support for the large-scale conventional and nuclear
buildup it considered imperative. And Brezhnev, while still in the
process of consolidating his power, was unlikely to oppose the marshals over the budgetary issue—at least in the short run. Furthermore, Brezhnev's style of leadership appeared to rely on support
from a number of institutional groups, and this style would place
the military in an advantageous position in dealing with political
authorities.

Despite the more positive relationship to the new Brezhnev
leadership, the legacy of the Khrushchev period remained. What
would Brezhnev do once he had consolidated his position? Would
he attempt to force his will—perhaps in an arbitrary and capricious
fashion, as Khrushchev had done—on the armed forces? At a minimum, the Kremlin's senior military officers would maintain a careful watch on the political leadership. After all, that which had been
given today could be withdrawn tomorrow.

---

[1] Harry Gelman, *The Brezhnev Politburo and the Decline of Detente* (Ithaca, N.Y.: Cornell
University Press, 1984), p. 80.

Enter Grechko

In April 1967 Andrei Grechko was appointed defense minister. The reasons behind his appointment to this lofty position remain unclear. One thesis, based on the testimony of former Czechoslovak General Jan Sejna, is that the Soviet military leadership vehemently opposed the appointment of Ustinov as defense minister after Malinovskii died. According to this thesis, they favored a military candidate, i.e., Grechko, who was also favored by Brezhnev.[2] Another interpretation is that Brezhnev favored Ustinov but was forced by the marshals to accept Grechko.[3] A third explanation is that the Politburo attempted to block Grechko's appointment in favor of Ustinov.[4] There is no evidence to substantiate any of these arguments. There is no evidence, during the period that Brezhnev was building his authority, that the generals possessed sufficient power to force him to do anything. A debate may have occurred, but as Dornberg notes, it probably took place within the military: "If there was a debate over Grechko's appointment, then most likely it was in the defense establishment itself. And if there was an alternative to Grechko, then the only conceivable one could have been Marshal Nikolai Krylov, the commander of strategic missile forces."[5]

In my opinion, the most logical explanation for Grechko's appointment is that Brezhnev wanted an individual with whom he was familiar, one more likely to support him within the Soviet national security leadership. Grechko seemed to fit the bill. To begin with, Grechko and Brezhnev had been wartime comrades in arms; Brezhnev knew him and was presumably comfortable with him. Second, Grechko does not appear to have been a political force in Moscow. In his two-volume memoirs Khrushchev mentioned Grechko only four times, in passing, yet he devoted a whole chapter to Admiral Gorshkov. This may help explain why Brezhnev reportedly insisted on Grechko rather than the civilian Dmitrii Ustinov. He presuma-

---

[2] Christian Duevel, "The Appointment of Ustinov as USSR Minister of Defense," *Radio Liberty Research*, RL 242/76, May 4, 1976, p. 2.

[3] Dusko Doder, *Shadows and Whispers* (New York: Random House, 1986), p. 221.

[4] John Dornberg, *Brezhnev: The Masks of Power* (New York: Basic Books, 1974), p. 213.

[5] Ibid.

bly believed that Grechko's appointment would help shore up his own position within the Soviet political-military leadership. Third, the appointment of Grechko coincided with the Soviet military establishment's increased interest in conventional weapons, which suggests that Grechko may have been proposed by segments of the military to counter any possibility that Krylov might get the job. Finally, from Brezhnev's standpoint, the appointment of Grechko was certainly a plus in 1967—Brezhnev could argue that at a minimum he had avoided having the post go to one of his competitors. Over time Grechko would turn out to be anything but a passive supporter of the general secretary. In fact, Grechko would show that while he might support Brezhnev in many areas, when it came to issues he believed would have a great impact on the military's vital interests, he was perfectly prepared to stand up to and even oppose the country's top political leader. By the early 1970s Grechko would become a force to be reckoned with in Soviet political-military circles. This, however, was a problem for the future, and probably one that Brezhnev did not anticipate in 1967.

The Key Players

The three military officers who were key actors in the high command during the Grechko era shared a number of things. All had the proper class background: Grechko's and Kulikov's parents were peasants, while Zakharov was from a working-class family. All three had served the greater part of their careers in the ground forces (Grechko in the cavalry and infantry, Zakharov in the artillery, and Kulikov in tanks); all three had fought in World War II; all were considered bright, but not brilliant; all appear to have favored a combined-arms approach, one with an increasingly important role for conventional forces. While Zakharov's attitude toward arms control was unclear, both Kulikov and Grechko were strongly opposed to it. Each had a reputation for being outspoken in expressing his views. Indeed, it is hard to detect any major differences between the writings of Zakharov and Kulikov. There are, however, some areas where the three men differed slightly.

During this period neither Kulikov nor Zakharov was as outspoken as Grechko on political issues such as the budget or arms control. This may be due to the position each occupied. The defense minister, at least as long as he is a professional soldier, tends to be the military's primary spokesman on issues like budget and arms control. The same is not true, however, for military-technical issues, where chiefs of the General Staff seem to feel free to express their opinions. Zakharov, for example, had been outspoken in his criticism of Khrushchev's single-variant strategy. Kulikov also tended to focus primarily, but not exclusively, on military-technical issues. Finally, while Grechko was known as a man who could be unyielding in his views, he, like Zakharov, had a reputation for being relatively easy to deal with. Kulikov, on the other hand, is reported to be a difficult person with whom to work. Westerners who have met and talked with him have found him quite abrasive.

MILITARY-TECHNICAL ISSUES

In contrast to his successors, Grechko made no effort to interrelate warfighting strategy, military management arms control, and the budgetary process in diagnosing the military's vital interests. When it came to technology, Grechko recognized its importance: he argued quite vigorously that more should be done to make better use of science and technology and to upgrade the qualifications of officers and noncommissioned officers (NCOs). But he did not attempt to tie the improved use of technology to a new warfighting strategy. Similarly, when it came to strategy, Grechko's prime concern was with building up a balanced military force, not with the creation of a new conceptual approach. If Grechko showed little interest in conceptualizing developments in the military-technical area, his interest in interrelating arms control and budget, the two political variables included in this study, was even lower. Cuts in the military budget were a direct threat to his efforts to build the balanced force structure he believed was so important, and he was strongly opposed to arms control. He saw the latter as the political leadership's instrument for achieving the former, arms control as a way of cutting back on the military budget. In short, Grechko was neither a conceptualizer nor a visionary. Rather, this crusty old-line cavalry and infantry officer was more operationally oriented. It was his task to oversee the rebuilding of the armed forces after the damage Khrushchev's single-variant approach had inflicted on it. And until that process was complete, all other factors would take the back seat.

Warfighting Strategy

Based on his published writings and speeches, Grechko's concept of Soviet warfighting strategy seems to have combined a commitment to a more balanced force structure (i.e., a better balance between conventional and nuclear forces) with a belief that despite the best efforts of both sides, a major conflict, once begun, would inevitably escalate to the use of central systems. As a consequence, Grechko argued for as long as he was defense minister that despite the increasing importance of conventional systems, nuclear weapons would remain the basis of Soviet military power.

While Grechko seemed to recognize the gathering significance of conventional weapons—even mentioning toward the end of his tenure the future importance of high-technology systems—he does not appear to have had a clear idea of where the many changes in military technology and the increasing importance of conventional systems were leading the Soviet military.

While he presided over important discussions about the future of Soviet warfighting strategy in the course of the 1960s, Grechko's approach to this problem differed significantly from the way he dealt with the other three areas covered by this book. Whereas he spoke authoritatively on questions of technology, arms control, and the budget, he adopted what was in essence a less assertive stance with regard to warfighting strategy. Here he spoke in generalities and, while repeatedly endorsing the general trend toward increased reliance on conventional systems, carefully avoided saying or writing anything that might cut off debate. He appears to have believed that open discussion of these issues would be useful.

The Nature of War.   Soviet writing on the nature of war in the latter half of the 1960s can be divided by focus into three categories: local conflicts, theater wars, and a general world war. In all three areas the importance of conventional systems increased over time.

Grechko had little to say on the topic of local wars during the 1960s; his attention was primarily focused on Europe and the need to build up Soviet forces to face the Western threat. Nevertheless, Soviet attitudes toward local wars began to change. In essence, Soviet military writers argued that in addition to world wars, the Red Army must also be prepared to fight local wars, i.e., conflicts not involving the superpowers, ones that would not necessarily escalate to the use of nuclear weapons. It had been previously assumed that if a conflict involved the superpowers, it would inevitably go nuclear, regardless of where it occurred. Now, however, conventional weapons began to seem more important. As one source argued, "The armed forces of the USSR and the socialist countries are confronted with an important task—to be in readiness to repel the aggression of imperialist states not only in a nuclear-missile war, but also in local wars using conventional means of combat."[6] Soviet writers carefully qualified this statement, however, noting that "the danger of local wars to peace lies in their possible escalation to a world war if the nuclear powers are drawn into the conflict."[7] Yet in writing about local wars one influential Soviet theoretician argued that "the decisive role belongs to the ground troops and to air and naval forces utilizing conventional weapons."[8] Meanwhile, the third edition of Sokolovskii's *Military Strategy* openly acknowledged the possibility of a non-nuclear conflict on the local level. In contrast to the first two editions, the third rejected the idea that local wars would inevitably lead to an intercontinental nuclear exchange. From a theoretical standpoint, the possibility of a non-nuclear conflict was no longer doubted. Or, as General Zheltov put it, "it is now entirely possible that a war may be waged with only conventional weapons."[9]

While Grechko did not comment in the latter half of the 1960s specifically on the nature of a conventional war at the theater level, Soviets' attitudes toward the role of conventional weapons in this area also began to change, especially with regard to their role in

[6] V. A. Sikistov and V. A. Matsulenko, "The Armed Forces and Military Art of the Main Capitalist States After World War II," in I. Kh. Bagramian, ed., *Voennaia istoriia*, p. 325, cited in James McConnell, *The Interacting Evolution of Soviet and American Military Doctrines*, Center for Naval Analysis (CNA) 80-1313.00, September 17, 1980, p. 40.

[7] Mark N. Katz, *The Third World in Soviet Military Thought* (Baltimore, Md.: John Hopkins, 1982), p. 39.

[8] V. Zemskov, "Characteristic Features of Modern Wars and Possible Methods of Conducting Them," *Voennaia mysl'*, no. 7 (July 1969), in U.S. Air Force, *Selected Readings from Military Thought, 1963–1973* (Washington, D.C.: Government Printing Office, 1977), p. 54.

[9] A. S. Zheltov et al., *Metodologicheskie problemy voennoi teorii i praktiki* (*Methodological Problems of Military Theory and Practice*) (Moscow: Voenizdat, 1969), p. 359, as cited in Raymond L. Garthoff, "Continuity and Change in Soviet Military Doctrine Since the 1960s," paper delivered at the Conference on the Dynamics of Soviet Defense Policy, Kennan Institute for Advanced Russian Studies, September 21–23, 1987.

Europe. Up to this point Soviet writers had argued that given the stakes involved, a war in Europe would almost immediately escalate to the use of nuclear weapons and would probably result in an intercontinental exchange between the superpowers. Now, however, it was being argued that it would be possible that *even* Europe might be spared the use of nuclear weapons. Brezhnev, for example, hinted at this possibility in April 1967 when he stated that a war in Europe *might* involve nuclear weapons, implying thereby that it might not. Thus, a nuclear war, even in Europe, was not inevitable.[10] Likewise, Army General S. P. Ivanov, the commandant of the Voroshilov General Staff Academy, provided a military rationale for this point of view by arguing that given the destructive power of nuclear weapons, both sides would attempt to utilize all other available methods first: "There is too great a risk of the destruction of one's own government, and the responsibility to humanity for the fatal consequences of the nuclear war is too heavy, for an aggressor to make an easy decision on the immediate employment of nuclear weapons from the very beginning of a war without having used all other means for the attainment of its objectives."[11]

In practical terms this meant that "a situation may arise in which combat operations begin and are carried out for some time . . . without nuclear weapons."[12] Similarly, as one Western analyst has pointed out, a comparison of the fourth and fifth editions of the authoritative *Marxism-Leninism on War and the Army* revealed some significant changes:

> The term "contemporary war" replaced "nuclear war" in the relevant section headings, references to the inevitability of nuclear war were changed to possibility, and a reference to the initial period of the war

---

[10] L. I. Brezhnev, "Rech' na konferentsii evropeiskikh kommunisticheskikh i rabochikh partii, 24 aprel'ia 1967 goda" ("A Speech to the Conference of European Communist and Workers' Parties, April 24, 1967"), in L. I. Brezhnev, *Leninskim kursom (On a Leninist Course)*, vol. 2 (Moscow: Izdatel'stvo politicheskoi literatury, 1973), p. 9.

[11] S. Ivanov, "Soviet Military Doctrine and Strategy," *Voennaia mysl'*, no. 5 (May 1969), in Joseph D. Douglass and Amoretta M. Hoeber, *Selected Readings from Military Thought, 1963–1973*, vol. 5, pt. 2 (Washington, D.C.: Government Printing Office, 1982), p. 28.

[12] S. Shtrik, "The Encirclement and Destruction of the Enemy During Combat Operations Not Involving the Use of Nuclear Weapons," *Voennaia mysl'*, no. 1 (January 1968), in Douglass and Hoeber, *Selected Readings*, vol. 5, pt. 1, p. 187.

as being "the time in which nuclear strikes will be carried out" was deleted. A comment that "water and medications, food products and electricity could prove more necessary than certain types of weapons and military equipment" was omitted from the 1968 edition, and the role of the economy was upgraded.[13]

Taken together, these textual modifications signaled a clear break with the ideas of the early 1960s.

Grechko took the lead in discussing the overall role of conventional weapons, observing in 1967, for example, that "as is known, conventional weapons have not lost their importance today." He went on to assign the following characteristics to a future world war, asserting that such a war would

—have clearly defined goals on the part of the warring sides;
—lead to the death of millions of people;
—result in tremendous physical damage; and
—be characterized by highly destructive, quick, and dynamic combat operations.[14]

Grechko returned to this issue in 1970 when he noted that such a war would be a "decisive conflict between two social systems" and added that the other side would follow a "coalition strategy."[15]

Escalation. According to Grechko, how long would the conventional phase last in a major war? During the late 1960s most Soviet writers, including Grechko, argued that the conventional segment of a conflict, especially that of a theater or world war, would be limited. Ivanov, for example, admitted that a world war would probably involve nuclear weapons sooner or later and would spread to all or the majority of continents and oceans.[16]

The actual decision on whether or not to escalate was considered to be affected by a number of factors. First, as one Soviet theorist

[13] Michael MccGwire, *Military Objectives in Soviet Foreign Policy* (Washington, D.C.: Brookings Institution, 1987), pp. 390–91.

[14] A. Grechko, "Torzhestvo leninskikh idei o zashchite sotsialisticheskogo otechestva" ("A Celebration of the Leninist Idea of the Defense of the Socialist Fatherland"), *Kommunist vooruzhennykh sil*, no. 20 (1967): 35, 37.

[15] A. Grechko, "Vernost' leninskim zavetam o zashchite rodiny" ("Fidelity to the Leninist Precept on the Defense of the Motherland"), *Kommunist vooruzhennykh sil*, no. 7 (1970): 21.

[16] Ivanov, "Soviet Military Doctrine and Strategy," p. 27.

maintained, it would depend "particularly on the capability of both sides to continue the struggle without the use of nuclear weapons."[17] The obvious implication was that once either side found itself losing, it would initiate the use of nuclear weapons. Most Soviet writers considered the chances of controlling such an escalation very dim. To quote one writer, "A world war will be a decisive armed class confrontation between capitalism and socialism and will inevitably escalate into an all-out nuclear war."[18] For his part, in 1969 Grechko publicly came out on the side of those who believed that a war would escalate to involve all of the weapons available to either side. He stated that even if "in some circumstances it is possible that some regiments and battalions will carry out operations with conventional weapons . . . the main and decisive means of combat would be nuclear missiles."[19] Clearly, as far as Grechko was concerned, escalation was inevitable.

Thus, the most that could at this time be said about escalation was that "the spatial scope of non-nuclear military operations will be limited. They will develop in certain conventional and ocean theaters and will take in at first an area of relatively small scope."[20] Inevitably, however, nuclear weapons would be employed despite the best efforts of both sides to prevent their use. From the standpoint of those who may have favored a conventional-weapons-only option, this was not a particularly optimistic prognosis.

Nuclear Parity.   While Grechko refused publicly to embrace the concept of parity, he did give it backhanded support in observing that "we possess military force of such colossal firepower that it is completely sufficient to annihilate any aggressor."[21] The implication of such a statement was that since the USSR would not start a war and Moscow possessed everything necessary to deliver a devastating retaliatory blow against any possible aggressor, the chances of a strategic nuclear conflict had decreased. The idea of "an annihilat-

---

[17] Zemskov, "Characteristic Features of Modern Wars," p. 52.

[18] M. I. Cherednichenko, "Modern War and Economics," *Kommunist vooruzhennykh sil*, no. 18 (September 1971), in U.S. Air Force, *Selected Soviet Military Writings, 1970–1975* (Washington, D.C.: Government Printing Office, 1977), p. 47.

[19] A. Grechko, "V. I. Lenin i stroitel'stvo Sovetskikh Vooruzhennykh Sil" ("V. I. Lenin and the Development of the Soviet Armed Forces"), *Kommunist*, no. 3 (February 1969): 23.

[20] Zemskov, "Characteristic Features of Modern Wars," p. 52.

[21] Grechko, "V. I. Lenin and the Development of the Soviet Armed Forces," p. 22.

ing retaliatory attack" would in time become a key phrase in the Soviet military lexicon—i.e., the lack of such a capability on both sides would begin to be equated with deterrence at the strategic level.

Meanwhile, Soviet writers were arguing that nuclear parity was critical to the conduct of war at the conventional level. And even if they were behind in practice, they maintained that nuclear parity existed. Writing in mid-1966, a Soviet writer stated that "under contemporary circumstances, with the existence of a system for detecting missile launches, an attempt by an aggressor to inflict a surprise preemptive strike cannot give him a decisive advantage for the achievement of victory in war, and moreover will not save him from great destruction and human losses."[22] Ivanov took a similar stance when he observed: "With the existing level of development of nuclear missile weapons and their reliable cover below ground and under water it is practically impossible to prevent an annihilating retaliatory attack."[23] The same line was taken at this time by Soviet negotiators at the SALT I (Strategic Arms Limitation Talks) discussions. Raymond Garthoff, for example, cites a Soviet statement to the effect that even in the event that one side were the first to be subjected to attack, it would undoubtedly retain the ability to inflict a strike of annihilating power. He stated that both sides were in agreement that war between the two countries would be disastrous for both, and that to decide to start such a war would be tantamount to suicide.[24]

In fact, by 1970 even the hard-line Colonel Rybkin was arguing that "a world nuclear war, despite all of the just nature of our aims, we cannot consider as sensible, rational means of resolution of international problems."[25] Nuclear war was still a possibility for Soviet writers, but they clearly did not believe that it was in their interest.

The Role of Nuclear Weapons. Despite hints at the existence of

---

[22] N. I. Krylov, "The Nuclear Missile Shield of the Soviet State," *Voennaia mysl'*, no. 11 (November 1967): 20, cited in Garthoff, "Continuity and Change in Soviet Military Doctrine," p. 19.

[23] Ivanov, "Soviet Military Doctrine and Strategy," p. 28.

[24] Garthoff, "Continuity and Change in Soviet Military Doctrine," p. 18.

[25] E. Rybkin, "The Marxist-Leninist Conception of the Essence of War and Its Sources," *Voennaia mysl'*, no. 8 (August 1970): 14, cited in Garthoff, "Continuity and Change in Soviet Military Doctrine," p. 36.

nuclear parity, both Grechko and his first deputy Zakharov continued to maintain that nuclear weapons were the military's most important weapons system. In a 1970 article in *Izvestiia* Grechko ranked various military services in order of their importance. SRF forces with their long-range nuclear missiles occupied first place, while the ground forces were placed in second. (The air force occupied third, the navy fourth, and the air defense forces fifth.)[26] In an article in *Kommunist* later that year he referred to the SRF as "the basis of the defensive power of the Soviet state."[27] Grechko's reasoning was simple. Given the probability that conventional war would escalate to the use of nuclear weapons, nuclear parity was crucial; otherwise, the West would immediately escalate to the use of nuclear weapons, and the possibility of a conventional phase would disappear. As late as 1971 Admiral Stalbo took a similar stance, describing the navy's primary role in this way: "the principle objective of warfare at sea today is to secure an advantageous position for launching nuclear attacks from the sea against vitally important targets on enemy territory."[28]

Although they recognized the key role played by nuclear weapons, senior Soviet writers went to considerable pains to argue that nuclear missiles were not the absolute weapon. As Zakharov stated, "Soviet military science and Soviet art does not absolutize nuclear-missile weapons; the decisive role in ensuring victory over an opponent will be played by the individual."[29]

Modifying Soviet Force Structure.   Devising conceptual modifications to Soviet military strategy was one thing, coming up with an actual weapons mix that would permit a force of this size and magnitude to be built was something else. Taking the ground forces as an example, Ben Lambeth said it best when he remarked that in the early 1960s, when "these doctrinal themes were being given expres-

[26] A. Grechko, "V boiakh rozhdennaia" ("Born in Battle"), *Izvestiia*, February 22, 1970, and M. Zakharov, "Udarnaia moshch' naroda" ("The Shock Power of the People"), *Izvestiia*, February 23, 1966.

[27] A. Grechko, "Na strazhe mira i sotsializma" ("On Guard Over Peace and Socialism"), *Kommunist*, no. 3 (February 1970): 64.

[28] K. Stalbo, "The Significance of the Seas and Oceans in Combat Actions," *Voennaia mysl'*, no. 3 (March 1971), in Douglass and Hoeber, *Selected Readings*, vol. 2, pt. 2, p. 77.

[29] M. Zakharov, "Rodiny shchit i mech" ("The Motherland's Shield and Sword"), *Izvestiia*, February 22, 1970.

sion, Soviet conventional forces had been reduced to near austerity levels in the wake of Khrushchev's single-minded emphasis on building up the recently created Strategic Rocket Forces."[30] Grechko himself gave strong support to the idea of building up conventional variants when he observed that "these play an important role in strengthening our armed forces and as a result should be preserved, built up in accordance with the new demands of the laws of war."[31] In a conventional conflict or even the conventional phase of a war that might eventually escalate, such forces would play a major role. As one noted Soviet writer stated:

> The most important distinguishing features of the stage of non-nuclear operations are concentration of the main forces for destruction above all of means of nuclear attack at their bases and regions of deployment; retaining in constant readiness the strategic and operational-tactical nuclear means for operations and the regular elaboration of plans for their combat use in accordance with the changing situation; constant and fast reinforcement of groupings of troops in the main zones by moving the reserves forward from the depths of the countries of the coalitions; completing the deployment of naval forces and posts for mobile basing; and the special feature of echeloning and utilizing the forces and means in connection with the necessity of allocating in a number of forms of armed forces, mainly in aircraft, of the so-called "nuclear echelons."[32]

From an operational standpoint, this would be a major undertaking, in terms of both troops and equipment.

In September 1964 the post of ground forces chief had been abolished, and these forces had been subordinated to the Ministry of Defense. This had both emphasized the importance of the nuclear factor and left the ground forces in an awkward situation: they were now symbolically and bureaucratically inferior to the other four services—with obvious implications for the struggle over funds as well as for their role in Soviet military strategy, not to mention problems that would now arise in recruiting new officers and NCOs.

---

[30] Benjamin S. Lambeth, "Selective Nuclear Operations and Soviet Strategy," in Johan J. Holst and Uwe Nerlich, eds., *Beyond Nuclear Deterrence* (New York: Crane, Russak, 1977), pp. 84–85.

[31] Grechko, "A Celebration of the Leninist Idea," p. 35.

[32] Zemskov, "Characteristic Features of Modern Wars," p. 52.

Who would want to be part of what appeared to be at best an appendage of the SRF? One of the first structural changes introduced by Grechko to enhance the Soviet military's ability to operate at the conventional level was to grant the Soviet ground forces once again the status of a separate command. This occurred in September 1967, and Army General Ivan Pavlovskii was appointed ground forces chief. The ground forces were now restored to their previous status.

Shortly thereafter Grechko published an article emphasizing that the Soviet military must develop a capacity for operating on both nuclear and conventional levels: "The Soviet Armed Forces are able to carry out combat operations under any conditions—on the ground, in the air, and at sea, at day or night as well as with and without the use of nuclear weapons."[33] In actuality the Soviets were far behind in both areas. As David Holloway states: "By 1965 the Soviet Union, far from maintaining a lead in missile development and production, now faced the task of catching up with the United States."[34] As a result, between 1966 and 1969 Soviet strategic forces grew by about three hundred silos a year. By 1969 the Kremlin had succeeded in catching up with the Americans in the area of Intercontinental Ballistic Missiles (ICBMs).

Simultaneously with strategic expansion, the Soviets sought to modernize their general purpose forces. For example, shortly after Grechko took over, an exercise called "Dnepr" was held in the Western regions of the Soviet Union. This exercise contrasted with similar undertakings in the past (e.g., "October Storm" in 1965 and "Vlatva" in 1966). Whereas both previous exercises had included a conventional phase, each had quickly escalated to the use of nuclear weapons. This time, however, the exercise was entirely conventional. Given the Soviet penchant for making military exercises as realistic as possible, this suggests that the idea of conventional operations without any necessary involvement of nuclear weapons was taking on increasing operational importance, in marked contrast to the Khrushchev era with its overwhelming emphasis on nuclear weapons. At the same time, increased attention was also paid to the

---

[33] A. Grechko, "Piat'desiat let na strazhe zavoevanii velikogo oktiabria" ("Fifty Years on Guard over the Gains of the Great October"), *Pravda*, February 24, 1968.

[34] David Holloway, *The Soviet Union and the Arms Race* (New Haven: Yale University Press, 1983), p. 43.

weapons systems themselves. The T-62 main battle tank was introduced as were the Armored Personnel Carriers (BMP), an infantry combat vehicle, mobile antiaircraft weapons and modified tactical missile launchers. A motorized rifle division was added to each tank army, air defense systems were strengthened, and the number of conventional artillery pieces was increased. In addition, improvements were made in logistics; air power, particularly airlift, was expanded; and older systems were replaced with the MIG-21 and SU-7. The navy was also given attention. Air and submarine arms were modernized and expanded, helicopter carriers and other surface ships were constructed, and an amphibious capability, including some twelve thousand naval infantry, were added.

Management, Technology, and Leadership

Brezhnev and Grechko were in agreement during the mid-1960s about both the importance of a modern military and the need to allocate more resources to develop and produce new military technology. As Grechko stated:

> In recent years successes developing the economy, in science and technology have made possible the creation of a powerful and qualitatively new material-technical basis for equipping our army and fleet with new weapons and have led to an all-round reorganization of our armed forces. As a result of this fundamental reorganization in military affairs, the military power of our country has significantly increased.[35]

In the short run, at least, Grechko appears to have had some success—the percentage of the defense budget allocated to producing new technology "increased by 4.7 percent in 1966 and 8.2 percent in 1967."[36]

In the meantime Grechko stressed the importance of technology for the future of the Red Army at every opportunity. He spoke in 1969 of the "revolution" and "the fundamental changes in military affairs" occurring as a result of "technological progress."[37] In 1970

---

[35] Grechko, "A Celebration of the Leninist Idea," p. 34.

[36] As cited by Thomas B. Larson in Bruce Parrott, *Politics and Technology in the Soviet Union* (Cambridge, Mass.: MIT Press, 1983), p. 182.

[37] Grechko, "Lenin and the Development of the Soviet Armed Forces," pp. 22, 25.

he emphasized the impact which new weapons were having on military theory, exercises, training, and structure and drew particular attention to the SRF as an area where military structures had been modified to accommodate changing technology.[38]

In fact, Soviet concern over the impact of technology during this period centered in four areas: technology's effect on all aspects of warfare; the way new technology demanded a closer interaction between natural science and military affairs; technology's increased demands on personnel; and the pressure it caused for major changes in command and control.

More complex weapons systems, not to mention the increasing importance of conventional weapons in Soviet planning, were making even simple operations, like calculating the military balance on the battlefield, more complicated. Looking at the military correlation of forces at this time, one Soviet theorist maintained that such calculations had to take into account

—quantitative factors, such as the number of tanks on both sides;
—the firepower of the weapons systems involved;
—the vulnerability of combat systems prior to their launching;
—the vulnerability of weapons systems after launching;
—the quality and availability of support systems; and
—the plans of operation.[39]

These factors were then assigned weights and a figure attained for the overall correlation of military forces. Nuclear weapons vastly complicated this process, as noted above. Not only are these weapons incredibly destructive, they are capable of radically changing the battlefield situation in a very short period of time. The growing importance of conventional weapons further complicated this process. As one Soviet analyst observed: "Formerly in armies of developed states military equipment for the most part was identical. Now they have two different types of weapons—conventional and nuclear missiles—and besides, an enemy can start a war with the mass or

[38] Grechko, "On Guard over Peace and Socialism," pp. 63–64.
[39] Maj. Gen. I. Anureyev, "Determining the Correlation of Forces in Terms of Nuclear Weapons," *Voennaia mysl'*, no. 6 (1967), in Douglass and Hoeber, *Selected Readings*, vol. 5, pt. 1, p. 163.

limited employment of nuclear weapons or with a non-nuclear variant. As a consequence of this the qualitative determination of the combat capabilities of the sides has become more complex."[40]

Calculating the military balance, however, was only the tip of the iceberg. Technology was creating problems for the Soviet army at every turn. As Grechko argued, the Soviet military would have to engage in some major rethinking; more effort, for example, would have to be devoted to solving such critical problems as "improving the quantitative and qualitative relations between people and technology in forces and in creating more goal-oriented relations among branches of forces and within them."[41]

One key to dealing with modern technology was science. The more complex the issues, the more the armed forces needed to rely on it. Without exploiting science it would be impossible to build a modern military. Grechko emphasized this when he observed that "in the course of resolving the task of strengthening the combat capabilities of our army, perfecting military art on the basis of the newest military technology, *Lenin's statement that it is not possible to construct a modern army without science is particularly appropriate.*" Grechko continued to say that in practice this meant that scientific work must have a practical bent—i.e., it must be made directly relevant to problems facing the Soviet military:

> These problems, like modernizing the quantitative and qualitative relationships between people and technology in the forces, creating the most expedient relations between branches of the armed forces and within them—between some types of forces and others—should be at the center of attention in our scientific-theoretical thought. The further modernization of the army's organizational structure, combat capability and combat readiness, as well as the efficient expenditure of means and spending on the strengthening of the defensive capability of the country, depends on their scientific resolution.[42]

---

[40] S. Tiushkevich, "The Methodology for the Correlation of Forces in War," *Voennaia mysl'*, no. 6 (June 1969), cited in Douglass and Hoeber, *Selected Readings*, vol. 5, pt. 2, p. 63.

[41] Grechko, "Lenin and the Development of the Soviet Armed Forces," p. 24.

[42] Grechko, "Lenin and the Development of the Soviet Armed Forces," pp. 23, 24. Emphasis in the original.

In short, for Grechko, without a thorough understanding and full use of modern science it would be impossible to sustain a modern military.

The key question insofar as civil-military relations was concerned was the degree of interrelation between science in the civilian world and science in military affairs. It would later become evident that Grechko believed that the civilian scientific community should be closely tied, if not subordinated to, the demands of the Soviet armed forces. At that time, this position was acceptable to the political leadership as it coincided with Brezhnev's overall goal of building up the country's military capabilities. In latter years as the Soviet economy worsened, however, it would serve as a source of conflict between the two men.

Personnel policy as well was an area of critical importance to Zakharov, and he made no secret of this fact. As he stated in 1967, "The combat readiness of units, ships, and formations depends to a large degree on how quickly and fundamentally personnel can master new technology."[43] From the standpoint of the high command, the situation was complicated by the 1967 Law on Universal Military Obligation, which reduced the time of obligated service from three to two years. In the meantime Grechko was arguing that the reduction in military service, combined with certain linguistic problems in the army, increased the need to modernize military training and education. Indeed, Grechko made this one of the military's top priorities. Writing in 1967, he called the technological preparation of soldiers "one of the most difficult tasks," arguing that "today not only is a minimum of military-technical knowledge necessary, but it must be constantly improved as well." Furthermore, he continued, "it is no secret that not all soldiers possessing a secondary education (and sometimes even those with a higher education) are able to carry out the tasks assigned to them."[44]

Zakharov published an article in 1967 which argued strongly for increased attention to science and technology in the training of Soviet officers. Emphasizing the importance of subjects such as

---

[43] M. Zakharov, "Razvitie voennoi organizatsii sotsialisticheskogo gosudarstva" ("The Development of the Military Organization of the Socialist State"), *Kommunist vooruzhennykh sil*, no. 21 (November 1967): 37.

[44] Grechko, "A Celebration of the Leninist Idea," pp. 35–36.

physics and mathematics, "without which it will not be possible to understand broad developments in science and technology," Zakharov argued for a new approach to officer education. Unless major changes are introduced, he warned, "the Soviet military will not be in a position to deal with the demands of new weapons and weapons systems."[45]

Like Grechko, Zakharov was also concerned about the implications of the 1967 law for military personnel in general. In a 1968 article published on the new law Zakharov maintained that together with "the major quantitative and qualitative changes in the technical capabilities of the Soviet armed forces," this law was placing increased demands on the armed forces.[46] He noted that to a degree an intensified program of premilitary training was compensating for this problem. This program helped acclimate new recruits to military service but did little to train them in areas involving the use of high technology. Consequently, Zakharov, like Grechko, argued that the military would have to improve its training techniques by providing better technical training and, in light of the problem with Russian-language literacy, assistance in this area as well.

Grechko's and Zakharov's expressions of concern over training and education in the latter part of the 1960s must have hit home: by 1970 a Soviet source was playing up cadre qualifications and boasting that the number of officers with an engineering-technical background had increased three-and-a-half times since 1945. The same source claimed that one-fourth of all officers had "higher military or specialist training."[47] To be effective, Soviet writers maintained, an officer had to be knowledgeable in a number of fields, including computer technology.

Grechko also took the lead in calling for greater efforts in modernizing command and control. He argued in 1967 that "a further modernization of the command and control of troops in strategic, operational, and tactical measures has become the most important

---

[45] M. Zakharov, "Iskat' novoe, povyshat' kachestvo obucheniia" ("Finding the New, Raising the Quality of Training"), *Krasnaia zvezda*, April 14, 1967.

[46] M. Zakharov, "Vazhnyi etap voennogo stroitel'stva" ("An Important Stage of Military Construction"), *Krasnaia zvezda*, January 4, 1968.

[47] "Vooruzhennye Sily SSSR v poslevoennyi period" ("The Armed Forces of the USSR in the Postwar Period"), *Kommunist vooruzhennykhsil*, no. 15 (October 1970): 72.

task of our military cadre."[48] Two years later he reiterated his concern, calling for significantly greater attention to the problems of military theory, "in particular to the problems of developing and utilizing new means of automated command and control of personnel."[49] In 1970 he reiterated his concern over command and control, arguing that "fundamental changes in military affairs" had significantly complicated "the character of controlling troops," and that the successful outcome of any battle would depend on the commander's ability to exert complete control over all aspects of the operation.[50] Grechko's consistent emphasis on the problems associated with command and control indicated the intensifying Soviet concern that the Soviet military do more in this critical area.

SOCIOPOLITICAL ISSUES

Grechko's goal during the late 1960s was simple: to minimize the ability of political leaders to interfere in his plans of building a dual-capable, balanced military. Always suspicious of their motives, Grechko worked consistently to maintain a high degree of budgetary support while at the same time attempting to head off any efforts by the Brezhnev leadership to enter into arms control agreements; not only did he not understand and hence was uncomfortable with arms control arrangements, but he also feared they would later be used to justify cutbacks in the military budget.

Economic Costs

To support the massive military buildup occurring in the late 1960s, military writers marshaled a number of arguments. First, they asserted that the relationship between the armed forces and the country's economy had grown closer in recent years:

> Strategy in the past appeared to stand apart from economics and was not seriously considered; it only placed orders for the required material and during wartime used the country's economic resources for conducting the war, often without considering the expenditures.

---

[48] Grechko, "A Celebration of the Leninist Idea," p. 38.
[49] Grechko, "V. I. Lenin and the Development of the Soviet Armed Forces," p. 24.
[50] Grechko, "Fidelity to the Leninist Precept," pp. 20–21.

Now, when the means of armed struggle have sharply risen in price, strategy is compelled to take into account even more completely the capabilities of the country's economy.

The development of nuclear weapons had been a prime factor complicating this relationship. In case of a nuclear war, the leadership must plan to fight with the resources on hand. Other writers go on to state: "The possibilities of production functioning in a period when nuclear strikes are exchanged and during a lengthy period after are quite problematical."[51] The situation is similar in a conventional war: one cannot wait until the war has begun to begin producing and developing the necessary weapons systems.

Military writers tried to support defense expenditures in other ways as well. In addition to emphasizing the need for funds for the country's defense, they argued that the defense sector provided important benefits to the civilian economy. In one instance, Brezhnev was cited to the effect that "today 42 percent of the entire output of the defense industry is destined for civil use. Thus the defense industry is making a great contribution toward improving the material well-being of the Soviet people." Similarly, it was argued that "the defense industry is paving the way to scientific-technical progress."[52]

There was a certain logic to the military's position. Under present conditions a surprise attack, whether conventional or nuclear, could have the most serious implications. At a minimum, the country would suffer very serious losses, and the operation of the economy would almost certainly be interrupted. It was imperative that the country be able to make a smooth transition from peace to war—not only in arenas such as the mobilization of personnel and weapons, but in gearing the country's economy to a war as well. Second, it was vital that the necessary weapons be on hand. Given the major disruptions and damage the country would suffer, immediate replacement of destroyed weapons and equipment would be almost impossible:

[51] V. Sokolovskii and M. Cherednichenko, "Military Strategy and Its Problems," *Voennaia mysl'*, no. 10 (October 1968), in Douglass and Hoeber, *Selected Readings*, vol. 5, pt. 2, pp. 11, 12.
[52] Cherednichenko, "Modern War and Economics," p. 53.

Under present conditions, the economies of capitalist countries are being readied for war in the following manner. Supplies of war material to be used in the war are prepared in advance, during peacetime, in keeping with plans for deploying the armed forces and conducting combat operations for a given period of time subsequent to the initiation of hostilities. At the same time, attention is focused on ensuring that the defense industry and the entire economy are in a state of readiness, that is they are prepared to quickly shift to the large-scale production of military goods under wartime conditions.

If one assumes that in this case the Soviets mean their own system—as is often the case when they discuss the West—then the reader is left with the impression that the dictates of Soviet security require that the country's economy be subordinated to the demands of the military; as the same writer put it, "The readiness of our Soviet economy for a possible imperialist war represents an important factor for restraining the expansionist aspirations of imperialist aggressors."[53]

Military considerations aside, the buildup effected in the late 1960s was a costly undertaking, as Grechko himself admitted in 1967, observing that "it [this buildup] is a matter of a whole complex of measures for strengthening the country."[54] According to one analyst, military spending increased 15.2 percent in 1968 alone.[55] Indeed, throughout the five years covered by this chapter the Soviet military budget steadily grew.[56] No matter what angle one took, the new doctrine with its increasing reliance on conventional weapons would be very expensive. As one Western analyst observed, "The doctrine had major implications for the volume of ordnance needed to support a conventional blitzkrieg, the need to completely reshape the navy and the ground and air forces, and the need to restructure the nation's military-industrial base to be able to compete with an undamaged United States in a protracted conventional war."[57] In practical terms this meant not only support for Soviet

[53] Ibid., pp. 48, 46.

[54] A. Grechko, "A Celebration of the Leninist Idea," p. 32.

[55] Parrott, *Politics and Technology in the Soviet Union*, p. 197.

[56] Thomas W. Wolfe, *Soviet Power and Europe, 1945–1970* (Baltimore, Md.: Johns Hopkins, 1970), p. 429.

[57] MccGwire, *Military Objectives in Soviet Foreign Policy*, p. 398.

strategic deployments but also a major expansion of general service forces (especially in the Far East), the construction of a more robust navy, and a buildup in airborne forces.

As to the economic decision-making process, Harry Gelman has argued that the formal decision to expand the military budget was taken in 1965, while Michael MccGwire ties it to the decision to effect a formal modification of doctrine, which he dates to the December 1966 Plenum.[58] Regardless of which date one accepts, it is clear that by the mid-1960s the Soviets were attempting a long-term expansion of all of their military services. And over the next five years the military budget grew both in absolute terms and as a proportion of the national budget.[59] While necessary from a military standpoint, these rising military expenditures were placing an increasing strain on the Soviet economy.

As might be expected, military spending was a point of contention within the upper ranks of the Soviet political leadership—according to Gelman, as early as 1965.[60] Brezhnev's hope was that despite the expansion of the military budget, the Eighth Five-Year Plan (1966–1970) would lead to a broad-based expansion of the economy especially in the areas of agriculture, heavy industry, and, to a lesser degree, consumer goods. Despite some short-term gains—especially those in the agricultural sector, which were due in large part to good weather—Brezhnev's hopes were not realized, and the struggle over resources intensified. By the end of the 1960s it was clear that the economy was suffering. For example, 1969 turned out to be a very disappointing year for the economic health of the country.[61] Industrial output declined from 10 percent in 1967 to 8.1 percent in 1968 and to 7 percent in 1969. Similarly, labor productivity fell from 5.2 percent in 1968 to 4.4 percent in 1973.[62] To further complicate matters, there were constraints on investment and labor resources, agriculture as usual was a serious problem, technologically the country was increasingly falling behind the West,

[58] Harry Gelman, *The Brezhnev Politburo and the Decline of Detente* (Ithaca, N.Y.: Cornell, 1984), p. 80; MccGwire, *Military Objectives in Soviet Foreign Policy*, p. 398.

[59] Thomas W. Wolfe, "Policymaking in the Soviet Union: A Statement with Supplementary Comments," *Rand Paper*, P-4131, June 1969, p. 23.

[60] Gelman, *The Brezhnev Politburo*, p. 82.

[61] Ibid., p. 125.

[62] Wolfe, *Soviet Power and Europe, 1945–1970*, p. 246.

the defense burden was rising, and the inflexible and inefficient bureaucratic structure made any attempt to rejuvenate the system very difficult.

Grechko was adamant in arguing for the unrestrained growth of the military budget. He maintained that in view of the continuing threat presented by imperialism, "it has been necessary for the party constantly to strengthen the country's defense and to take corresponding measures to raise the combat capabilities and combat readiness of the Soviet armed forces." As if to remind the political leadership of their commitment to strengthening the country's military, he went on to quote Brezhnev's November 1967 speech to the Supreme Soviet with its argument that the leadership would "do everything so as not to be caught unawares."[63] In 1970, Grechko equated the defense budget with the construction of Communism itself, observing that "the Leninist party sees the question of strengthening the combat power of the armed services to be an important prerequisite for the successful construction of communism in our country"[64]; in another article he maintained that current tasks facing the military "demand uninterrupted modernization and development of our military strength."[65] Grechko clearly intended to keep the political leadership's feet to the fire as to funding for the military. Not only did he use an external threat to justify Soviet defense expenditures, he also attempted to make willingness to fund the military a test of Marxist-Leninist manhood. The implication was that those who argued against sustained military buildup were undermining the country's defenses and probably soft on capitalism as well.

The country's mounting economic and technological problems—combined with concern over China and the West's apparent acceptance of strategic parity or equality, its readiness to enter into a less confrontational relationship with the USSR—helped convince Brezhnev of the need for a more relaxed relationship with the West. Not everyone in the Soviet leadership agreed, however. This was particularly true of Grechko and Kulikov.

---

[63] Grechko, "V. I. Lenin and the Development of the Soviet Armed Forces," p. 22.
[64] Grechko, "Fidelity to the Leninist Precept," p. 22.
[65] Grechko, "On Guard over Peace and Socialism," p. 63.

The Military and Arms Control

Throughout the late 1960s Grechko allied himself with individuals such as Suslov, Shelepin, and Shelest, all of whom opposed the arms control process. Indeed, it is reported that Grechko not only refused to endorse the SALT process, but—if Shevchenko is to be-lieved—he was its most outspoken opponent in the upper ranks of the Soviet political-military leadership:

> Defense Minister Grechko remained permanently apoplectic during SALT. His incurable distrust of and violent opposition to all of us involved in the negotiations, affected even the more realistic and so-phisticated generals in a negative way. Grechko would repeatedly and irrelevantly launch into admonitory lectures on the aggressive nature of imperialism, which, he assured us, had not changed. There was no guarantee against a new world war except a continued buildup of Soviet armed might.

While less openly critical of the SALT process in his public writings, Grechko's dislike and distrust of the process is also evident in his published works. In fact, his writings and speeches from the mid-1960s through to the end of his tenure in 1976 suggest a man who, as Shevchenko suggests, "reluctantly accepted the opening of SALT, but almost immediately began a guerrilla campaign that helped to stall the process."[66] In 1966, a year before he took over as defense minister, Grechko belittled international agreements, not-ing that the nonaggression pact with Germany had led to the illu-sion that the country could avoid a conflict and save on defense. This, he argued, contributed to the disastrous defeats suffered by the Soviets at the beginning of the Second World War.[67] In 1968, when it looked like the SALT I discussions would soon be underway, he delivered a major speech, later published in *Pravda*, which claimed that "American imperialism" was the major source of "war and aggression" and warned as if with the Soviet political leadership in mind, that it behooved the country to be "exceptionally vigilant" in dealing with the Americans.[68] In 1969 Grechko attacked the

---

[66] Arkady Shevchenko, *Breaking with Moscow* (New York: Alfred A. Knopf, 1985), p. 202.

[67] Andrei Grechko, "25 let tomu nazad" ("25 Years Ago"), *Voenno-istoricheskii zhurnal*, no. 6 (1966): 6.

[68] Grechko, "Fifty Years on Guard over the Achievements of the Great October."

West for its "military provocations and adventures," its "aggressive war against Vietnam," and its interference in the internal affairs of other countries.[69] Later in that year he argued that events in Czechoslovakia showed the need for Moscow to be on guard in its dealings with the West.[70] In 1970 Grechko warned that imperialists had no respect for international law when it came to matters of war and peace and again compared the situation facing the Kremlin to that which existed prior to the Second World War.[71] He also called the international situation "difficult."[72] Grechko's hostile views appear to have been shared by others in the Soviet military. A colonel writing in *Voennaia mysl'* warned that "underestimation of the threat of war is impermissible; a policy constructed on denials of the danger of war is criminal."[73] Despite Grechko's Aesopian language he was clearly warning the political leadership, now increasingly involved in sensitive negotiations with the Americans, of the dangers involved in any kind of agreement with Washington.

From Grechko's point of view there were good reasons for hesitating to enter into arms negotiations. Like many if not most Soviet military officers, Grechko was deeply suspicious of the West. How could he be sure the West would live up to the agreements? Besides, the idea of restricting weapons systems for the sake of improved East-West relations made no sense to his military mind. Peace, Grechko believed, would be assured not by diplomatic agreements but by the strength of the Soviet military. As he and other Soviet military leaders would repeat ad nauseam over the years, the key to Soviet security was a strong military. Diplomatic maneuvering was fine, but it clearly took second place to Moscow's efforts to build up its armed forces. Furthermore, there was the question of ideology. If the West was as evil as Soviet officers and soldiers had been led to believe, and if the military was expected to be prepared to defend the country in the event of a conflict, how could one justify deals

[69] Grechko, "Lenin and the Development of the Soviet Armed Forces," p. 21.

[70] A. Grechko, "Vsegda nacheku" ("Always on Guard"), *Pravda*, February 23, 1969.

[71] Grechko, "Fidelity to the Leninist Precept on the Defense of the Fatherland," p. 22. See also Grechko, "On Guard over Peace and Socialism," p. 63.

[72] Grechko, "Born in Battle."

[73] M. V. Petrov, "Problems of War and Peace and the World Revolutionary Process," *Voennaia mysl'*, no. 8 (August 1971), in Douglass and Hoeber, *Selected Readings*, vol. 5, pt. 2, p. 111.

with the capitalist devil? If nothing else, such a course of action could lead to moral disarmament.

During the latter half of the 1960s Moscow achieved strategic parity. But despite the impressive gains the Soviet military had made by 1970 in modernizing and expanding its military, from the standpoint of the General Staff much remained to be done. Conventional forces were still being rebuilt, a blue-water navy was still under construction, dual-capable systems were still being developed, and the technological gap vis-à-vis the West remained wide. Grechko was concerned that Brezhnev's effort to reach an accommodation with the West was primarily an excuse for cutting back on the military buildup. Brezhnev was beginning to talk about the importance of consumer goods, about the need to satisfy the people's desire for a better life. One primary means of achieving that end would be a relaxation of East-West tensions which, in turn, would permit a slow-down in military spending.

Grechko also objected to the involvement of civilians in what had hitherto been a military preserve. Soviet security affairs have traditionally been a matter for professional military officers. With the exception of Stalin, civilians have tended to become involved only at the highest levels, and then they have seldom dealt with the more technical issues of strategy, tactics, or operations. With the rise of the SALT process, however, civilians were becoming directly involved in negotiations with the West, negotiations that would determine the structure and composition of a major segment of the Soviet armed forces for years to come. True, the General Staff was a direct participant in these deliberations; furthermore, it had a monopoly over the information necessary to conduct negotiations, which strengthened its hand considerably in intrabureaucratic discussions, and probably had the major say in designing the Soviet position. Still, the presence of civilians was discomfiting. And the military did its best to maintain control of the process. Henry Kissinger, for example, recounts how he had to collude with Soviet Ambassador Dobrynin to exclude overly influential Soviet generals from the Vladivostok summit.[74]

---

[74] Raymond L. Garthoff, *Détente and Confrontation* (Washington, D.C.: Brookings Institution, 1985), p. 430.

From a bureaucratic point of view, the inclusion of civilians in the arms control process meant that the dam had been broken. Civilians would be a part of this process from this time forward. And who could ensure that their role would not grow over the years? As Garthoff reports, by the late 1960s a joint working group had been established between the Ministry of Foreign Affairs and the Ministry of Defense "to study positions and draft positions for higher-level review."[75] And to the Soviet military mind, civilians, especially those from the Foreign Ministry, often appeared to be driven primarily by a desire to reach agreement, even if this would mean compromising (i.e., trading away Soviet advantage) with the other side.

Finally, there was the question of the secrecy that the Soviet military traditionally used to cover up Soviet weakness. If the West does not know the exact figures or the nature of Soviet weapons systems, the military thinks, it will assume the worst, and this strengthens deterrence. This may be why "the Soviet military delegates are reported to have entered the initial rounds of SALT I under the personal instructions of Defense Minister Marshal Grechko to avoid any disclosure of information on Soviet weapons capabilities."[76] In time, the Soviet military adapted to the SALT discussions, and an argument can be made that the agreements that were reached served the interests of Soviet military security. Throughout his period as defense minister, however, Grechko's actions made it clear that he would have preferred not to be involved in the process.

[75] Raymond L. Garthoff, "The Soviet Military and SALT," in Jiri Valenta and William Potter, eds., *Soviet Decisionmaking for National Security* (New York: Allen and Unwin, 1984), p. 155.

[76] Edward L. Warner III, *The Military in Contemporary Soviet Politics* (New York: Praeger, 1977), p. 242.

CHAPTER 4

Defending against the Politicians, 1971–1976

B_{y the early} 1970s it was becoming increasingly clear to Grechko that his efforts to build a dual-capable military force were being threatened by the country's politicians. Brezhnev was "cozying up" to the Americans while at the same time talking more and more about the need to satisfy consumer desires. For Grechko the message was only too clear: relax military tensions, and use the money saved to meet consumer demands. Meanwhile, Grechko's diagnosis of the problems facing the Red Army was relatively simple: more weapons, both conventional and nuclear. He was not comfortable with the idea of making short-term sacrifices now for longer-term advantages later (i.e., accepting a cut in the budget to permit the modernization of the country's economy). He not only found such ideas strange, but he did not trust the politicians to deliver. To his mind, once the funds were given away they would be lost forever.

For Grechko, the task ahead would not be easy. He had to continue mobilizing the funds necessary to build a dual-capable military in the face of efforts by the political leadership to cut the budget. And the strategy he chose was simple: he consistently opposed any improvement in East-West relations, while at the same time refusing to agree to any cuts in the military budget. He would eventually lose on the latter issue, but he succeeded to a greater degree than many would have thought possible.

MILITARY-TECHNICAL ISSUES

Warfighting Strategy

While the quantity of Grechko's comments on doctrinal matters increased significantly during the last five years of his life, primarily with the publication of his 1971 pamphlet, *On Guard For Peace and the Building of Communism*, and his 1975 book, *The Armed Forces of the Soviet State*, he continued to articulate the same general approach he had followed in the 1960s.[1]

The Nature of War.   Grechko continued to argue that conventional weapons were becoming increasingly important, but that the dangers of escalation remained high. Thus, Grechko acknowledged that "a war can begin with the use of either nuclear weapons or conventional means of attack" and observed that "in certain circumstances operations by units and subunits may be carried out only by conventional means."[2] Indeed, Grechko asserted that qualitative improvements in conventional systems had advanced to a point where they could carry out some of the tasks previously assigned to nuclear weapons: "Due to a qualitative improvement in conventional means of destruction and the increase of these weapons in units and formations, there has been a great improvement in the fire, shock and maneuver capabilities of troops, which permits assigning them very decisive missions on the battlefield which they are capable of accomplishing without resorting to nuclear weapons."[3] He added that Soviet military science does not "absolutize" nuclear weapons; indeed one senior Soviet military officer went even further in discussing the relative merits of nuclear and conventional weapons: "A flagrank officer on the Soviet General Staff wrote in 1970 that fulfillment of these objectives would create 'a situation in which the enemy will be defeated even if he attempts to use nuclear weapons.' It was this assessment that probably enabled the same flag-rank officer to conclude that 'there is a real possibility of conducting a conventional war in Europe.' "[4] Furthermore, Grechko

---

[1] A. A. Grechko, *On Guard for Peace and the Building of Communism*, trans. *Joint Publications Research Service*, 54602, December 2, 1971, of the original Russian *Na strazhe mira i stroitel'stva kommunizma* (Moscow: Military Publishing House, 1971), and A. Grechko, *The Armed Forces of the Soviet State* (Washington, D.C.: Government Printing Office, 1975).

[2] Grechko, *On Guard for Peace and the Building of Communism*, p. 43.

[3] Grechko, *The Armed Forces of the Soviet State*, pp. 147–48, 150.

[4] As cited in John G. Hines, Philip A. Peterson, and Notra Trulock II, "Soviet Military Theory from 1945–2000: Implications for NATO," *The Washington Quarterly*, Fall 1986, p. 120. Throughout this chapter reference will be made to Soviet materials such as the lecture materials from the General Staff Academy. These materials have not yet been formally declassified, and the only place they are available to the general public is in the

maintained, nuclear weapons cannot do everything; that was why the USSR was making intensified efforts to develop new conventional weapons: "Nevertheless, no matter how significant might be the role of nuclear weapons, they cannot solve all of the problems of war. Therefore, great efforts are being directed, as before, toward the creation of new—as well as the improvement of existing—conventional types of weapons." Grechko went so far as to associate himself with the need to develop high-technology conventional weapons, something that is generally credited to Ogarkov. Such weapons, Grechko argued, would make use of new types of materials and explosives, new sighting and guidance systems, laser electronics and computer technology. These weapons would be more maneuverable, "with higher mobility and greater speed, greater range and more economical engines." In a discussion of tanks Grechko provided an example of what he had in mind: "The problem of the survivability of tanks is made even more complex because the development of anti-tank guided missiles has essentially only begun and the possibilities of improving these powerful new weapons of anti-tank warfare appear to be quite significant."[5]

Finally, lectures at the General Staff Academy during the mid-1970s indicate that in contrast to the massive nuclear strike approach of the early 1960s, the Soviet high command was telling senior military officers that a war could begin in a number of ways:

—"surprise invasion with unlimited use of nuclear weapons;
—"invasion with initially limited employment of nuclear weapons and subsequently passing over to full use of the complete nuclear arsenal;
—"invasion by groups of armed forces deployed in the theaters of strategic military action without the employment of nuclear weapons;
—"[and] initiation of war through gradual expansion of local wars."[6]

Escalation. Despite the increased importance of conventional weapons and the promise of high-technology variants, Grechko was still less than sanguine about the chances that a major conflict would

---

writings of Hines, Peterson and Trulock. Consequently, all references to these materials are taken from articles by these three individuals.

[5] Grechko, *The Armed Forces of the Soviet State*, pp. 153, 154, 155.
[6] Cited in Hines et al., "Soviet Military Theory," p. 125.

remain conventional. For example, he reiterated his earlier statement that in a major conflict "nuclear missiles will be the decisive means of conflict." Such a conflict, he argued, one that would "decide the fate of all mankind," would inevitably escalate to the use of nuclear weapons.[7] For his part, Kulikov did not address the issue directly and noted only that "the operational art has made a significant new step in its development, with the introduction of nuclear weapons into our inventory and with the further improvement of conventional weapons."[8] This was sensitive territory, and Kulikov clearly decided not to venture into it.

Publication of the hitherto classified Voroshilov Academy lectures of the mid-1970s may provide us with an insight into Grechko's way of thinking and help us to understand why he was not optimistic about the chances of keeping a major conflict conventional. The problem with escalation, students at the Academy were told, was not so much that it would be inevitable, but that the West, when faced with a successful conventional onslaught in Europe, would probably resort to the use of nuclear weapons: "In modern conditions, such [limited] nuclear attacks would primarily be the consequences of the expansion and development of a conventional war in a crucial situation, when the dangers of complete destruction of the enemy group of armed forces and the loss of important and vital strategic enemy territories may become apparent." The use of such weapons, according to these lectures, would lead to Soviet retaliation by "operational and tactical means."[9] This in turn would greatly increase the chances that escalation would involve central systems.

Grechko and his colleagues were in essence arguing that despite the increasingly important role being played by conventional weapons in Soviet and Western force structures, there was still a high probability that a major conflict would escalate—no matter how

[7] A. A. Grechko, "Rukovodiashchaya rol' KPSS v stroitel'stve armii razvitogo sotsialisticheskogo obshchestva" ("The Leading Role of the CPSU in the Construction of an Army of a Developed Socialist Society"), *Voprosy istorii KPSS*, no. 5 (1974): 37.

[8] V. G. Kulikov, "Sovetskie vooruzhennye sily i voennaia nauka" ("The Soviet Armed Forces and Military Science"), *Kommunist*, no. 3 (February 1973): 84–85.

[9] Cited in Notra Trulock, "Soviet Perspectives on Limited Nuclear Warfare," in Fred Hoffman, Albert Wholstetter, and David Yost, eds., *Swords and Shields* (Lexington, Mass: Lexington Books, 1986), p. 61.

hard both sides tried to avoid it. Nevertheless, Soviet military thinkers continued to believe that it was in their interest to avoid escalation. They reasoned as follows: employing nuclear weapons would let the genie out of the bottle—one might be able to get him back in, but there is no assurance that this will be possible. The practical effect is that in addition to the danger of escalation to the use of central systems, which would result in an all-out nuclear war, there would be also a possibility that NATO would employ nuclear weapons against targets in the USSR; e.g., Minsk or Lvov might be targeted in an effort to disrupt Soviet resupply or command-and-control capabilities.

In addition, nuclear weapons would also inhibit the operations of other military forces. Thus, materials from the Voroshilov Academy indicate that the Soviets—and presumably with Grechko in their number—believed that the use of nuclear weapons would have a negative impact, for example, on their rate of advance during a frontal offensive. This was one of the General Staff's key concerns. A nuclear exchange would also inevitably produce tremendous military dislocation, especially to command-and-control facilities. The Soviet military attaches a great deal of importance to strict lines of control in an effort to micro-manage almost all movements on a battlefield, and the use of nuclear weapons could produce a kind of chaos that might make centralized control impossible. Having lost communications, many Soviet units would have to operate independently, something that is an anathema to the Soviet military mind. Such problems would occur, of course, during conventional operations, but not on so large a scale. To quote the lecture materials:

> Actually, assumptions about determining the likely impact of the enemy's nuclear strikes would be very difficult to make at the phase of preparing an operation. The experience of field exercises and scientific calculations indicate the collection of information about the impact on the unit's combat capabilities might take much time. . . . Mutual initial nuclear strikes . . . might change completely the planning of the unit's combat actions.[10]

To make matters worse, the Soviet military normally operates under tight time constraints, i.e., as an integrated whole in which each

---

[10] Cited in Hines et al., "Soviet Military Theory," p. 124.

unit is assigned a task and is expected to perform it in a specific amount of time. Obviously, the use of nuclear weapons with their indeterminate impact on the battlefield could be expected to upset such a timetable even more than would be the case in a conventional war.

Furthermore, while Moscow's armed forces are equipped and trained to fight in a nuclear environment, this involves very cumbersome procedures. Equipment must be decontaminated, and areas affected by nuclear fallout avoided. Thus, in addition to the confusion they create, nuclear weapons would make it necessary for Soviet forces to avoid whole areas: "large territories will become useless for immediate continuation of the operation."[11] The problem, however, is that from a military standpoint, such areas might be critical if the Red Army were to continue a sustained advance westward. The task for Soviet military planners would be to devise a strategy and force structure that would maximize the chances of keeping a conflict conventional.

Nuclear Parity.   A key element in the Kremlin's effort to keep a conflict conventional remained nuclear parity. Until very recently, the USSR had lagged behind the West in this key area, and, in the view of the high command, the West had attempted to use this fact against the Soviet Union by offering arms control negotiations on terms that appeared to be designed to freeze the USSR into an inferior position.

Even with the attainment of parity, strategic weapons remained very important. Grechko, for example, never tired of pointing out that the SRF formed the basis of Soviet military power. In 1971 he again ranked various services in order of preference. The SRF, which he called the basic "striking force" for the Soviet armed forces, once again occupied first place, while the ground forces were placed in second. (The air force occupied third, the navy fourth, and the air defense forces fifth).[12] Kulikov adopted a similar stance in 1973, arguing that "the combat power of the Soviet armed forces is based on the Strategic Rocket Forces, which are equipped with modern automated missile complexes with intercontinental and medium-

---

[11] Cited in Trulock, "Soviet Perspectives on Limited Nuclear Warfare," p. 61.
[12] Grechko, *On Guard for Peace and the Building of Communism*, p. 147.

range missiles."[13] Indeed, throughout his tenure as defense minister, Grechko never deviated from this position. The reason is simple. On the strategic level, for example, the SRF was critical. Strategic nuclear forces provided—and provide—the basis for parity between the superpowers. If the Soviet Union falls behind in the strategic realm, it becomes open to nuclear blackmail, not to mention the problems inherent in fighting a world war from such a position. Nuclear weapons thus serve a crucial role; if a nuclear war were to occur they would be key to Moscow's efforts to fight and survive it.

In the meantime, nuclear weapons were also critical if the Kremlin were to have any hope of keeping a conflict conventional. Seen from the Soviet military's viewpoint, nuclear parity would be the key to deterrence. As long as it were maintained, it would be suicide for either side to begin such a conflict. As one of Moscow's most influential theorists put it in 1973, "an aggressor who would initiate a nuclear war would irrevocably be subjected to a devastating retaliatory nuclear strike by the other side. It would be unrealistic for an aggressor to count on victory in such a war, in view of the enormous risk for the aggressor's own continued existence."[14] In fact, by 1973 Kulikov was arguing that the primary function of the SRF was that of nuclear deterrence, i.e., that of convincing the U.S. that any attack on the USSR would be met by a devastating response.[15] Soviet theorists also believed that it was important for the Soviets to develop nuclear forces at the theater and tactical levels. Failure to do so would encourage the West to use such systems at those levels in the event of a war. Grechko emphasized the importance of tactical nuclear systems in his writings, commenting in 1971 with regard to the ground forces that "the operational and tactical missile units comprise the basis for the firepower of the Ground Troops. This is a qualitatively new branch of arms which is the basic means for employing nuclear weapons in combat and operations."[16]

---

[13] Kulikov, "The Soviet Armed Forces and Military Science," p. 78.

[14] M. I. Cherednichenko, "Military Strategy and Military Technology," *Voennaia mysl'*, no. 4 (April 1973): 42, as cited in Raymond Garthoff, "Continuity and Change in Soviet Military Doctrine Since the 1960s," paper delivered at the Conference on the Dynamics of Soviet Defense Policy, Kennan Institute for Advanced Russian Studies, September 21–22, 1987.

[15] Kulikov, "The Soviet Armed Forces and Military Science," p. 78.

[16] Grechko, *On Guard for Peace and the Building of Communism*, p. 33.

By 1970 Soviet writers were asserting that the West was also beginning to accept the premises of deterrence. As one stated, "American political leaders and strategists have begun to understand that, in connection with the creation of a powerful nuclear potential in the Soviet Union, general nuclear war becomes hopeless and extremely dangerous for the United States as a means for achievement of its aggressive policy."[17] Furthermore, in addition to the deterrent value of such systems, their warfighting capability was also important to the Soviets. For example, if conventional forces were unsuccessful, or if the Soviet Union faced the prospect of a major defeat, it might be forced to escalate to the use of tactical or theater nuclear weapons even if on a limited scale.[18]

Modifying Soviet Force Structure.   The combination of nuclear and conventional systems, and in particular the latter, was causing major changes in Soviet operational procedures and force structure. New concepts had to be developed to achieve a better integration of the two types of forces. As Hines and Peterson stated:

> Serious pursuit of the capability for conventional victory and escalation dominance was extremely ambitious, even given the promise of improved conventional and nuclear technologies. Several actions were required. First, the Soviets had to continue to develop, refine, and acquire the most advanced military technologies and apply this new capability to the military force structure. The second—and perhaps most difficult—task was to adapt and refine operational concepts for force employment that would better exploit the potential of new technological capabilities. Third, they needed to restructure and develop the armed forces in a way that would best enable them to carry out improved operational concepts. Finally, the Soviets would have to exercise, test, and refine new operational ideas and a new force structure to execute the operations successfully.[19]

[17] M. Povaly, "Policy and Military Strategy," *Voennaia mysl'*, no. 7 (July 1970): 18, cited in Garthoff, "Continuity and Change in Soviet Military Doctrine Since the 1960s," p. 49.

[18] Just because Soviet military writers do not believe it is in their interest to engage in limited nuclear warfare, it does not follow that they have not planned for such a contingency. Indeed, the high command prepares for every eventuality, including the limited use of nuclear weapons. See, for example, Notra Trulock's discussion of this issue in his "Soviet Perspectives on Limited Nuclear Warfare."

[19] Phillip A. Peterson and John C. Hines, "The Conventional Offensive in Soviet Theater Strategy," *Orbis* 27, no. 3 (Fall 1983): 703.

Soviet writers argued that to a certain degree a symbiotic relationship exists between nuclear and conventional weapons, that "they are not in opposition to one another. On the contrary, they are closely interrelated, and are developed as an integrated whole."[20]

In order to operate successfully in either environment, the Soviet military leadership gave increasing recognition to the need to work out new operational concepts. Grechko, for example, argued that changes in doctrine as well as the introduction of modern technology was leading to a demand for closer integration between the services. As he observed: "Soviet military science believes that if imperialist reaction should unleash a modern war, it will include active and decisive operations by all services of the armed forces, coordinated as to goal, time and place. Each service of the armed forces and each branch, in fulfilling the missions peculiar to it, will bend its efforts to achieve the overall goals of the war."[21] Kulikov also emphasized the need for greater integration:

> These problems, such as modernizing the quantitative and qualitative relationships between people and technology in forces, the establishment of more expedient relations between branches of the armed forces and within them—between types of troops and others— should be at the center of attention of our military-theoretical thought. The further modernization of organization structure, combat capability and combat readiness of the army . . . depends on it.[22]

In contrast to the past, Grechko argued, when it might have been possible for Soviet forces to operate independently, war under contemporary conditions would be inconceivable without closer cooperation between all those involved: "Like scientific theory, strategy is one, because war is not carried out somehow by one branch of service, but by their united efforts."[23]

Turning to actual battlefield operations, Soviet writers began to discuss several ideas for improving operations so as better to integrate Soviet conventional and nuclear systems, and, if possible, in-

---

[20] I. G. Zav'ialov, "The New Weapon and Military Art," *Krasnaia zvezda*, October 30, 1970, in U.S. Air Force, *Selected Soviet Military Writings, 1970–1975* (Washington, D.C.: Government Printing Office, 1977), p. 211.

[21] Grechko, *The Armed Forces of the Soviet State*, p. 150.

[22] Kulikov, "The Soviet Armed Forces and Military Science," p. 83.

[23] Grechko, *The Armed Forces of the Soviet State*, p. 209.

crease the chances that a conflict would remain conventional. First, there was the concept of deep operations. This idea had grown out of the writings of Mikhail Tukhachevskii, the famed Soviet marshal and military theorist who fell victim to Stalin's purges, and had as its basic idea "the delivery of a simultaneous blow against the entire depth of the enemy's defenses and destruction of his main groupings through the decisive offensive actions of infantry and the mass employment of aviation, artillery, tanks and airborne troops."[24] This concept played a key role in Soviet strategy during the Second World War. In the late 1960s and early 1970s, Soviet writers resurrected it, arguing that "to a certain extent, the provisions of the theory of in-depth operations and battles have retained their significance even for present conditions."[25] Grechko himself singled it out for special attention, maintaining that

> the Soviet theory of in-depth operations and battles was a fundamentally new theory on the conduct of war by massive highly mobile and technically well equipped armies. Its basic idea was the delivery of a simultaneous blow against the entire depth of the enemy's defenses and destruction of his main grouping through the decisive offensive actions of infantry and the mass employment of aviation, artillery, tanks and airborne troops.[26]

In essence, Soviet writers were arguing that the new types of equipment and more destructive weapons that had been developed made this concept even more useful. Ground force troops had been fully mechanized and their firepower had increased significantly. This would make it possible for Soviet forces to attack along the opponent's entire front and fully exploit any breakthroughs that might occur. Thus, while the content of the conception of in-depth operations had changed as compared to World War II, as a result of new levels of military mobility, the general idea remained the same. Instead of one single massive thrust against one single position, it

[24] Ibid. For a discussion of this concept and its origins under Tukhachevskii, see Richard Simpkin, *Deep Battle: The Brainchild of Marshal Tukhachevskii* (London: Brassey's, 1987).

[25] See N. V. Ogarkov, "Glubokaia operatsiia" ("Deep Operation"), in A. Grechko, ed., *Sovetskaia Voennaia Entsiklopediia*, vol. 2 (Moscow: Voennoe izdatel'stvo, 1976), pp. 574–78.

[26] Grechko, *The Armed Forces of the Soviet State*, p. 261.

would now be possible to undertake several, closely coordinated attacks at various points. This idea had particular relevance for a conventional war. Rather than losing time and major resources in trying to overwhelm the defensive positions prepared by the enemy, Soviet forces would attack in a variety of areas; upon determining where the weak point was located, second-echelon forces would seek to exploit it with highly mobile mechanized forces. To quote a Soviet writer, "In modern operations . . . the second echelons are to be used for developing success on the main axes."[27] However, despite the attention paid to this concept during this period, little was written concerning its specific characteristics. For example, what specific types of forces would be employed?

A second concept resurrected in the early 1970s, which was to be of considerable importance during later years, was Theaters of Military Operations (TVDs). In a nutshell, this idea—at least during the first half of the 1970s—referred to a command structure in which several large units would be subordinated to one single commander. Grechko noted its importance in 1973, and Kulikov endorsed it when he recommended the creation of a command level that would strengthen the centralized leadership of front-line commands.[28] Kulikov emphasized the importance of front-line commands in preparing and carrying out strategic operations as well as in independent actions by units and sub-units, "which in the course of a war will be spread out over great distances."[29] Western analysts did not at the time attach any particular significance to references

[27] A. Poltavets, "Use of Support Echelons and Reserves in Offensive Operations, *Voennaia mysl'*, no. 8 (August 1973) in Joseph Douglass and Amoretta Hoeber, *Selected Readings from Military Thought, 1963–1973*, vol. 5, pt. 2 (Washington, D.C.: Government Printing Office, 1982), p. 200.

[28] A. Grechko, "Na strazhe mira i sotsializma" ("On Guard over Peace and Socialism"), *Kommunist*, no. 7 (May 1973): 24. V. Kulikov, "Strategicheskoe rukovodstvo Vooruzhennymi Silami" ("Strategic Leadership of the Armed Forces"), *Voenno-istoricheskii zhurnal*, no. 6 (1975): 86; Kulikov, "The Soviet Armed Forces and Military Science," p. 85. The term Theater of Military Action has been variously translated in the West as TVD (*Teatr voinnykh deistvii*), TMO (Theater of Military Operations), and TSMA (Theater of Strategic Military Action). All three abbreviations will be utilized in this study depending on the author being cited. For a discussion of this topic see John G. Hines and Phillip A. Peterson, "Changing the Soviet System of Control," *International Defense Review* 19, no. 3 (March 1986): 281–89.

[29] Kulikov, "The Soviet Armed Forces and Military Science," pp. 84–86.

like that made by Kulikov to TVDs. Subsequently, however, it would be discovered that what the Soviets were talking about was a new intermediate structure to be located between "the national command authority and the Soviet/Warsaw Pact Fronts."[30] In later years this structure would serve as the focal point for the Kremlin's attempt to ensure control over a number of fronts, thereby maximizing Soviet ability to carry out the kind of complex operations needed to seize Western territory while degrading NATO's nuclear assets and protecting its own.

Faced with the need to counter the NATO nuclear threat, Soviet writers argued that the key to avoiding escalation would be "to beat the enemy to the attack."[31] This meant that Soviets would continue to place a premium on factors such as surprise and speed. The former was crucial because it was the key to neutralizing Western nuclear assets. As Grechko observed, "the problem of surprise today has acquired a particular keenness."[32] Speed, meanwhile, would be critical if the Pact were to seize large parts of NATO territory before the West would be able to use nuclear weapons. The primary goal would be to put NATO into a situation where it would have to use nuclear weapons on its own territory in order to stop a Pact offensive or, equally important, to create a situation in which the Alliance would decide that in view of the degradation it had suffered in its nuclear assets, the use of its remaining weapons would not significantly alter the course of events on the battlefield. Meanwhile, Soviet conventional forces would attempt to destroy NATO's remaining conventional forces as quickly as possible. In the words of one Soviet expert: "Every nuclear strike, depending on its force and accuracy, has an immediate effect on troop combat capability. Therefore every gun capable of firing a nuclear warhead round and every hostile missile launcher should be destroyed as soon as it is spotted. Nuclear ammunition should also be immediately destroyed as soon as it is discovered, at fire positions, bases, or in transport."[33]

---

[30] John G. Hines and Phillip A. Peterson, "Changing the Soviet System of Control," *International Defense Review* 19, no. 4 (March 1986): 281.

[31] N. Zubkov, "General Principles of the Approach to Appraising the Effectiveness of Combined Arms Control Systems," *Voennaia mysl'*, no. 11 (November 1971), in Douglass and Hoeber, *Selected Readings*, vol. 5, pt. 2, p. 147.

[32] Grechko, *The Armed Forces of the Soviet State*, p. 72.

[33] V. P. Chervonobab, "Principles of Military Art and Their Development," *Voennaia*

In the past Grechko had argued that the introduction of nuclear weapons had "required a fundamental revision in all areas of military affairs." But new conventional weapons—"tanks with improved armor protection, increased firepower and higher speed and maneuverability, new medium and heavy artillery pieces, mortars, multiple rocket launchers, recoilless rifles, new antitank weapons and troop air defense weapons"—were also having a major impact on the contemporary battlefield.[34] In short, the Soviet military now had to be prepared for a wide range of contingencies. And during the first half of the 1970s the Soviet military was moving ahead on all fronts to modernize and expand its capabilities to fight a war.

It was under these circumstances that Admiral Gorshkov launched his push for a greater role for the Soviet navy: he published in 1972 a series of articles in the navy's monthly journal, *Morskoi sbornik*, entitled "Navies in War and Peace." Gorshkov, who appears to have been unsatisfied with the allocation of resources to the navy in the Ninth Five-Year Plan, used these articles to argue for a greater role for the navy as an instrument of policy during both war and peacetime. Not only did the navy fulfill an important strategic role as a second-strike deterrent (the so-called "withholding strategy") with its nuclear-missile-carrying submarine fleet, it was also a key vehicle for the projection of Soviet conventional power whether it be anti-submarine warfare (ASW) work, amphibious and antifleet operations, or as a way to project force in the Third World. In essence, Gorshkov was pushing for an even larger Soviet navy by seizing on the greater interest, within the upper ranks of the Soviet military, in a more balanced Soviet force structure. The navy plays a key role in winning wars, Gorshkov argued, and, while the submarine force is critical, to be effective the Soviet navy needs other kinds of ships as well. It must be able to fight either kind of war—nuclear or conventional. To quote MccGwire, "Taken together, these added up to a powerful argument for a larger and better balanced fleet."[35]

Based on the available data, Grechko appears initially to have

---

mysl', no. 11 (November 1971), in Douglass and Hoeber, *Selected Readings*, vol. 5, pt. 2, p. 142.

[34] Grechko, *The Armed Forces of the Soviet State*, p. 147.

[35] Michael MccGwire, *Military Objectives in Soviet Foreign Policy* (Washington, D.C.: Brookings Institution, 1987), p. 465.

opposed Gorshkov on this issue, which is not surprising, given his own interest in closer integration between the various services. Not only did Gorshkov experience difficulties in getting his articles published, but Grechko had an article in the July 1971 issue of *Morskoi sbornik* (the first and only time a defense minister had written an article in the navy's journal in the past twenty years) that differed significantly both in terms and tone from the articles written by Gorshkov.[36] Furthermore, in his 1971 book Grechko called atomic submarines "the main force of the navy" and limited his comments on the Soviet military's international commitments to include only the other socialist states. This does not mean that Grechko did not appreciate the changes that had occurred within the Soviet navy in recent years. Indeed, in his 1971 book he remarked that "the Soviet Navy has emerged from the coastal waters and inland seas. It honorably represents our nation on the expanses of the world oceans."[37] By 1974 Gorshkov and Grechko appeared to have worked out a compromise. Grechko wrote an article in which he acknowledged that "at the present stage the historic function of the Soviet armed forces is not restricted to their function in defending our Motherland and other socialist countries."[38] Gorshkov, in the meantime, published an article in which he moved somewhat closer to Grechko's position, arguing that "the main military mission in war would be an operation against targets on land rather than combat against the enemy fleet."[39] Despite Gorshkov's acknowledgement of the importance of land operations, the publication of his 1976 book, *Seapower and the State*, made it clear that he still saw a more independent role for the navy than the high command thought advisable.[40]

From a practical standpoint, the primary result of Gorshkov's push for a greater role for the Soviet navy was an acceleration in and greater emphasis on the construction of larger, better-armored ships

[36] A. A. Grechko, "The Fleet of our Homeland," *Morskoi sbornik*, no. 7 (1971): 3–9, in *Foreign Broadcast Information Service (FBIS)*, *Daily Report, The Soviet Union*, August 11, 1971, pp. m1–6.

[37] Grechko, *On Guard for Peace and the Building of Socialism*, p. 37.

[38] Grechko, "The Leading Role of the CPSU in the Construction of an Army of a Developed Socialist Society," p. 39.

[39] S. G. Gorshkov, "Morskaia moshch' strany sovetov" ("The Naval Power of the Land of the Soviets"), *Pravda*, July 28, 1974.

[40] S. G. Gorshkov, *Morskaia moshch' gosudarstva* (*The Naval Power of the Government*) (Moscow: Voenizdat, 1976).

that would have the greater endurance necessary to fight a prolonged conflict. For example, the follow-on to the Kresta and Kara class cruisers would "be some 25–30 percent bigger." The same process occurred with regard to amphibious ships, and plans were drawn up for a new type of ship, a heavily armed battlecruiser "that would have the command facilities which had been found so necessary to forward deployment and which would be essential in a protracted war."[41] Soviet strategic programs appeared to have slowed down by the early 1970s. In fact, most analysts agree that by 1970 the Soviet Union had achieved approximate parity with the U.S. on the strategic level. Thereafter, most of the emphasis was placed on qualitative improvements. As one observer noted, "The SRF mission appears to remain one of deterrence, and warfighting if deterrence fails. The recent qualitative improvements do, however, suggest additional redundancy (increased kill-probability) to accommodate the increased numbers of MIRVs [Multiple Independently Targeted Reentry Vehicles], and an overall improvement in reentry (RV [Reentry Vehicle]) accuracy."[42]

Turning to the ground forces, a new main-battle tank, the T-64, had been introduced, marking a qualitative improvement over its predecessor, the T-62. It "is thought to be less vulnerable than the T-62. It mounts a larger gun which is equipped with an automatic loader and improved sighting mechanism to increase accuracy and the rate of fire."[43] In addition, "no less than five battlefield air defense systems, five artillery systems, and two infantry fighting vehicles" were being introduced.[44] Helicopters (especially the Mi-24 or Hind) appeared to be playing a greater role in Soviet ground operations, and efforts were underway to improve logistics. As Donnelly noted:

> To ensure supplies on the high-speed battlefield, logistics, long considered the weak point of the Soviet army, recently has received a lot of attention. In 1976 it was announced that there had been a 500

[41] Michael MccGwire, "A New Trend in Soviet Naval Developments," *International Defense Review* 13, no. 5 (1980): 677.

[42] Richard T. Ackley, "Strategic Rocket Forces," in David R. Jones, ed., *Soviet Armed Forces Review Annual* (Gulf Breeze, Fla.: Academic International Press, 1978), vol. 2, p. 46.

[43] Christopher Donnelly, "Ground Forces," in Jones, *Soviet Armed Forces Review Annual*, p. 59.

[44] John Erickson, "Soviet Military Capabilities," *Current History*, 71 (October 1976): 101.

percent increase in mechanisation of rear services during the preceding seven years. By the beginning of 1977 the Soviets claimed that 90 percent of all ammunition, spares and food delivered to the battlefield would be paletized or packaged for mechanized handling.[45]

Finally, the Soviets also introduced medium-range tactical missiles capable of firing both nuclear and conventional warheads. This led Erickson to comment that "the Soviet command has embraced the 'conventional option' in its own right."[46]

By the time Grechko left the scene in 1976, the Soviet military was well on its way toward developing a meaningful conventional variant. The danger of escalation was still great in Grechko's eyes, but the groundwork for a more robust—and effective—conventional force structure had been laid.

Management, Technology, and Leadership

By the late 1960s Brezhnev had become convinced that the USSR was falling increasingly behind the West in the area of advanced technology. Speaking to the Twenty-fourth Party Congress, he emphasized the importance of the scientific-technical revolution, arguing that it required a "modernization of many aspects of our economy."[47] Despite its seemingly innocuous nature, this issue soon became a point of contention within the upper ranks of the Soviet political leadership. Suslov and several others feared that Brezhnev would use this issue to argue for improved East-West relations and arms control agreements. From Brezhnev's perspective, such an approach would not only provide the USSR with a breathing space in which it could make the necessary adjustments to its economy, it would also lead to a major infusion of Western technology.[48]

Despite his deep-seated opposition to arms control and improved East-West relations, Grechko was caught in a dilemma. He

[45] Donnelly, "Ground Forces," 60.

[46] Erickson, "Soviet Military Capabilities," p. 101.

[47] L. Brezhnev, "Otchetnyi doklad Tsentral'nogo Komiteta KPSS XXIV s"ezdu Kommunisticheskoi partii Sovetskogo Soiuza" ("Accounting Report of the Central Committee of the CPSU to the Twenty-fourth Congress of the Communist party of the Soviet Union"), in L. I. Brezhnev, *Leninskim kursom* (*On a Leninist Course*), vol. 3 (Moscow: Izdatel'stvo politicheskoi literatury, 1973), p. 236.

[48] See Bruce Parrott, *Politics and Technology in the Soviet Union* (Cambridge, Mass.: MIT Press, 1983), pp. 239–65.

could not help providing limited support for Brezhnev's overall foreign policy approach if he backed him on the technology issue. In
Grechko's perception, however, the Red Army was falling increasingly behind in this key area, and the situation would deteriorate
even further unless radical action was taken. Consequently, Grechko
adopted the seemingly contradictory policy of supporting Brezhnev's overall push for an increased emphasis on technology while
continuing to oppose his policies toward arms control and improved
East-West relations. In pressing their technological concerns,
Grechko and Kulikov singled out four areas for particular attention:
the increasing importance of science, personnel qualifications, command and control, and the importance of the General Staff.

As Brezhnev had done in his report to the Twenty-fourth Party
Congress, Grechko continually stressed the importance of increased
reliance on science in dealing with the military's problems. In particular, he argued that the tie between technology and military affairs had become "ever closer and more diversified." He went on to
say that science and technology had in fact become "the determining
factor in the revolutionary changes in military affairs" and commented that "there is no area of military affairs which has not been
influenced by the scientific and technical revolution."[49] In 1972 he
observed that "scientific-technical progress has forced a fundamental
transformation in the technical equipping of the armed forces and
their organization, and in all systems of political and military education.[50]

Kulikov took a similar line in 1973. He stated that technology
played an important role in "modernizing" the Soviet military and
in raising its "combat capabilities and combat readiness." The situation has become more and more complex, he maintained, as the
"high tempo of scientific-technical progress opens broad possibilities for the creation of new weapons systems."[51]

By 1975 Grechko had begun to sound like a technological determinist. Technology, he argued, was "the catalyst of all transfor-

---

[49] Grechko, *On Guard for Peace and the Building of Socialism*, pp. 28, 32.

[50] A. Grechko, "Vooruzhennye sily Soiuza Sovetskikh Sotsialisticheskikh Respublik"
("The Armed Forces of the Union of Soviet Socialist Republics"), *Kommunist*, no. 3 (February 1972), 55.

[51] Kulikov, "The Soviet Armed Forces and Military Science," pp. 81, 82–83.

mations in the means and methods of conducting wars." It was being driven by developments in "the physical-mathematical sciences, nuclear physics, solid-state physics, electronics, radiophysics, cybernetics and metallurgy."[52]

As he had in the past, Grechko now emphasized the need for the military to make better use of science. "The contents, methods, organization, and structure of command and control are in need of further modernization. Today the basis of such changes consists in keeping up with the fast changes in scientific-technical thought and in introducing its achievements into military practice in a timely fashion."[53]

Kulikov made the same point in a *Kommunist* article in *1973:*

> The maintenance of the Armed Forces' combat capability at the appropriate level and the observance of cost-effectiveness depend on the correct, scientifically based choice of direction for the development of weapons and equipment. Scientific leadership methods in the military-technical sphere make it possible correctly to determine the trends and paths of weapons development as well as to take into account the consequences of this process.

Kulikov listed a number of areas where progress was needed in order to deal with the increasing importance of science and technology. These included

—research into operations by coalition forces;
—an analysis of issues related to organization, including questions of manning, mobilization, and training;
—better troop control;
—the use of automated systems, including radioelectronic warfare and computers; and
—research into the psychological training of troops.[54]

Grechko adopted a similar line, noting that "military science has an important role in successfully carrying out the tasks of military development."[55] Or as he put it in 1974:

[52] Grechko, *Armed Forces of the Soviet State*, pp. 138, 148.
[53] A. Grechko, "Na strazhe rodiny" ("On Guard over the Motherland"), *Pravda*, February 23, 1973.
[54] Kulikov, "Soviet Armed Forces and Military Science," p. 81.
[55] Grechko, *On Guard for Peace and the Building of Communism*, p. 42.

In the contemporary stage of development of our society, under complex international conditions and sharply growing scientific-technical progress, the party places before Soviet military science new tasks [and] demands from military-scientific cadre intensified work in the area of military theory, bold thoughts and daring, concentrated effort in the most forward-looking directions, [and] a modernization of the methods of resolving military-scientific problems.[56]

By the next year Grechko was arguing that military theory was playing an even more vital role in resolving "fundamental problems of military construction." What is needed, Grechko reiterated, is an in-depth analysis of "the influence of new means of combat on the methods of military action" and the structure of units.[57] Or as Kulikov argued, "scientific research work should be subordinated above all to the interests of further strengthening the army and the navy."[58] In practice this would mean strengthening the ties between higher educational institutions and the military so that the latest developments in science and technology could be incorporated into the military with a minimum of delay.

From an unscientific sampling of books published during the 1970s it can be seen that science had begun to figure more prominently in Soviet military thinking. As Condoleezza Rice put it: "The drive to uncover the laws of warfare and to make decisions in a scientific fashion led to new methods of planning. Operations research, systems analysis, decision theory, and other methods taken from the hard sciences were instituted in all planning and operations agencies. As a result, major changes were made in both the curriculum of military academies and in the creation of new military specialties."[59] By the end of this period, it was becoming obvious that Moscow's top two soldiers believed that science was becoming even more important. As Kulikov observed in 1976: "The closer the contacts between military theory and practice, and the more fully new types of weapons and military technology are taken into account,

---

[56] Grechko, "The Leading Role of the CPSU and the Development of an Army of a Developed Socialist Society," p. 45.

[57] A. Grechko, "Nauka i iskusstvo" ("Science and Art"), *Pravda*, February 19, 1985.

[58] V. Kulikov, "Sovetskaia voennaia nauka segodnia" ("Soviet Military Science Today"), *Kommunist*, no. 7 (May 1976): 43.

[59] Condoleezza Rice, "The Party, the Military, and Decision Authority in the Soviet Union," *World Politics* 40, no. 1 (October 1987): 61.

the more deeply military thought will penetrate into the nucleus of war phenomena, the more reliable will be the forecasts of future conflicts, the greater the possibilities of success in an armed struggle."[60]

Of all the areas of most concern to Grechko during the first half of the 1970s, none was more important than improving the technical qualifications of military personnel. As Grechko put it, "A high level of technical training is a most important factor of combat readiness." Given the increasing importance of both types of weapons, it was becoming crucial that Soviet forces be trained to fight any type of war. To quote a leading Soviet theorist:

> This gives rise to a most important task, namely to teach the troops how to operate both with and without the use of nuclear weapons and how to make a swift transition from one mode of operation to another—from combat with conventional weapons to combat with nuclear weapons. A problem arises in this connection: how to provide a single plan for conducting one and the same operation—the separate and simultaneous employment of nuclear and conventional weapons. The complexity lies in the fact that it is difficult to foresee at what stage of the operation nuclear weapons can be employed. All this makes it necessary to train troops to successfully conduct combat operations under any circumstances.[61]

To a certain degree, Grechko's efforts during the latter half of the 1960s had begun to pay off. In a 1971 speech published in *Pravda*, for example, he noted that up to forty-five percent of officer positions were "occupied by engineers and technicians."[62] Not satisfied with this situation, Grechko continually emphasized the need to avoid stagnation. One must always look to the future, he felt. As he put it in 1971, "Weapons and combat equipment are continually being improved. In accord with this the demands on all the personnel and particularly the officers are increasing."[63] By 1975 Grechko was reporting that "nearly 100 percent of the positions from brigade commanders and higher and more than 90 percent of the positions

[60] Kulikov, "Soviet Military Science Today," p. 32.

[61] Zav'ialov, "The New Weapon and Military Art," p. 211.

[62] "Rech' tovarishcha A. A. Grechko" ("The Speech of Comrade A. A. Grechko"), *Pravda*, April 3, 1971.

[63] Grechko, *On Guard for Peace and the Building of Communism*, p. 58.

of regimental commanders and 100 percent of the positions of ship commanders of the 1st and 2nd ranks are filled with officers having a higher military education. On the whole, around half of the officers have a higher military or a specialized military education."[64]

Given the high priority assigned to science in general, it comes as no surprise that Grechko also expressed continued concern over the status of command and control. In 1971 he wrote, "The problem of mastering scientific methods of troop command on the basis of new technical means is assuming exceptional urgency"—a point he repeated in 1975.[65] Command and control was defined by Kulikov as "the ability of a commander-in-chief or commander to confidently orient himself in a situation, make an expedient decision for an operation or battle, assign to units and subunits, organize interaction, render total support to troop operations and put the decision which has been made into effect firmly and resolutely."[66] According to Grechko, an effective command-and-control system was becoming particularly important as the problems facing the battlefield commander were becoming increasingly complicated: "command and control of forces have become much more complex than in the past, and because of this the requirements on them have grown considerably."[67]

For his part, Kulikov also called for intensified work on command and control and placed considerable emphasis on automated forms, on radioelectronics in particular. According to Kulikov, these advanced forms of command and control served as the "central nervous system of the Soviet armed forces."[68] Staffs assigned to a commanding officer had the responsibility of assembling all the data necessary for their superior to make the necessary decision. But the contemporary commander is besieged with thousands of pieces of data, any of which could determine the outcome of the battle. Kulikov believed that the use of automated systems (i.e., computers) would provide the commander with necessary information and thus

---

[64] Grechko, *The Armed Forces of the Soviet State*, p. 187.

[65] Grechko, *On Guard for Peace and the Building of Communism*, p. 45; Grechko, *The Armed Forces of the Soviet State*, pp. 209–210.

[66] Kulikov, "Soviet Military Science Today," p. 44.

[67] Grechko, *The Armed Forces of the Soviet State*," p. 210.

[68] Kulikov, "The Soviet Armed Forces and Military Science," p. 87.

help the decision-making process. Having once reached a decision, however, the commander would have to ensure that it would be carried out. Here again, the thought was that computers would facilitate this process. Hundreds of commands could be issued to a wide variety of units at the same time. As Colonel Bondarenko put it:

> It has been calculated that during combat action where nuclear missiles are used, the headquarters of a division will receive more than three times as much information as the headquarters of an equally large formation received during World War II. . . . At the same time, in order to make a decision, the commander needs only those fresh data that reflect the actual situation exactly. All this leads to an increase in the time necessary for processing information and evaluating enemy and friendly forces. However, in modern warfare decisions must be made within a very limited time frame.

The solution to the problem, according to Bondarenko, was "full automation of control," which in turn "encompasses the entire system of troop control."[69] For his part, Grechko called in 1971 for a "further modernization" of the process, and later that year he reiterated his concern over "automated systems of command and control."[70] Command and control continued to figure prominently in Grechko's writings up to his death in 1976.[71] And it seems that some success had been achieved. In 1971 Grechko commented that "automated control systems have been developed for weapons and combat material, in addition to modern means of communication, radar equipment, and various automatic and remote control devices."[72]

Kulikov shared his superior's concern with command and control, but took the matter one step further and argued for a strengthened General Staff. As Kulikov explained it, the increasing importance of timely decisions and the need to coordinate large numbers

---

[69] V. Bondarenko, "Nauchno-tekhnicheskii progress i upravlenie voiskami" ("Scientific-Technical Progress and the Control of Troops), *Kommunist vooruzhennykh sil*, no. 10 (May 1973): 28, 30.

[70] A. Grechko, "Velikaia pobeda" ("The Great Victory"), *Pravda*, May 9, 1971.

[71] See, for example, his discussion of military science in the *Soviet Military Encyclopedia*, especially p. 188, "Voennaia nauka" ("Military Science"), *Sovetskaia Voennaia Entsiklopediia*, vol. 2, pp. 183–88.

[72] Grechko, *On Guard for Peace and the Building of Communism*, p. 31.

of troops in the face of increasingly sophisticated conventional or even nuclear weapons had enhanced the role of the General Staff:

> The rapid [*burnyi*] development of science and technology, basic changes in the means, character, and methods of conducting contemporary wars, the presence of strategic nuclear weapons, and the increasing danger that they will be employed by imperialist states, the exceptional dynamism in the growth of international events, raises, in a significant manner, the role of the General Staff in guaranteeing the security of the Soviet Fatherland, and broadens the scope of its tasks, and complicates their contents.[73]

In Kulikov's mind, the role of the General Staff was all-encompassing. It dealt with political questions ("analyzes and evaluates military-political conditions"), had a role in long-term planning ("determines the development of the means for conducting war and the manner of their application"), ran the military ("organizes the preparation of the armed forces and ensures their high level of combat readiness"), and, finally, played a major role in the development of military theory. Furthermore, in another context Kulikov argued that the General Staff "is the main organ for managing/controlling the armed forces of the state in peace and war."[74]

For Kulikov, the bottom line was that the General Staff had to be the key organ for ensuring a smooth transition from peace to war and, once the latter stage is reached, for conducting operations. Only it would be capable of coordinating and mobilizing all the forces at Soviet disposal in the event of war. In the past, the Soviets had had the luxury of large amounts of time to carry out this transition. In fact, as Kulikov noted, during the early months of the Second World War they had experimented with a number of variants for conducting combat operations until finally coming up with a workable solution. Given current weapons systems, he argued, a similar response to a war would be a recipe for disaster. Kulikov's comments on the General Staff and its increasing importance in an age of high technology provided a basis for Ogarkov's later efforts to argue for an expanded role for the high command in national secu-

---

[73] V. Kulikov, "Mozg armii" ("The Brain of the Army"), *Pravda*, November 13, 1974.

[74] V. Kulikov, "General'nyi shtab" ("The General Staff"), in *Sovetskaia voennaia entsiklopediia*, vol. 2, pp. 510–13.

rity decision making (i.e., to ensure that the Soviet Union would be prepared for a surprise attack and that the transition from peace to war would be smooth). The argument that the high command was in a unique position—and by implication that its powers should be further enhanced—had important implications for civil-military relations.

SOCIOPOLITICAL ISSUES

By the beginning of the 1970s, it was becoming clear that the military budget was out of hand and that in spite of Grechko's opposition, Brezhnev was determined to do something about it. It was also evident that despite Grechko's defeat on the arms control front and his threatened defeat on the budget, he was not about to submit meekly to the principles of democratic centralism; rather, he continued to fight against concessions on either issue up to his death in 1976.

Economic Deterioration

Throughout the early 1970s the economy continued to be beset by problems. To begin with, the weather deteriorated, having an adverse impact on agricultural output. Meanwhile, expenditures needed to subsidize consumer food prices also increased. A falling demographic curve, combined with the added costs involved in extracting increasingly inaccessible raw materials (especially oil) led to a slow-down in the rate of growth of the country's gross national product. As a result, the Soviet GNP fell from 5 percent in the 1960s to 3.8 percent in the first half of the 1970s.[75] Meanwhile, the military budget was continuing to grow at a rate of 4 to 5 percent per annum.[76] In relative terms, this meant that the military budget was growing at an accelerated rate at a time when the money available for domestic programs was decreasing. In addition, given the closed nature of the Soviet military-industrial complex, the fact that

[75] Daniel Bond and Herbert Levine, "The 11th Five-Year Plan, 1981–1985," in Seweryn Bialer and Thane Gustafson, eds., *Russia at the Crossroads* (London: George Allen and Unwin, 1982), p. 88.

[76] Richard F. Kaufman, "Causes of the Slowdown in Soviet Defense," *Soviet Economy* 1, no. 1 (January–March 1985).

during these years the military sector's share of machinery was also increasing significantly meant that the amount of new machinery available for the civilian economy—which in turn would have acted as a spur to technological progress—was also lowered. To quote Gelman, "the rate of growth of most key branches of both heavy and light industry dropped steadily. The slowdown of the expansion of heavy industry—particularly in sectors such as machine tools— threatened to make it increasingly difficult in future years for the civilian economy to supply the industrial inputs required by military industry."[77] The result was increasing technological and economic stagnation.

Both Grechko and Brezhnev wanted a strong military, if for no other reason than because it was the key to Soviet superpower status. The two men differed, however, on how to achieve it. Grechko opposed cuts in research and development because they would assign the Soviet armed forces to permanent technological inferiority vis-à-vis the West. Brezhnev, on the other hand, saw the problem in a somewhat broader context. He believed that unless the scientists involved in military projects devoted more of their time and effort to the nonmilitary sector, the overall strength of the economy would suffer, and, as a result, the country's national security would be weakened. In essence, the USSR ran the risk of having its national security weakened by an endless buildup in its armed forces. Meanwhile, Grechko believed that cuts in procurement or operating expenses would undermine his efforts to build up his balanced force structure. One suspects that Brezhnev did not care where the cuts came from, as long as they occurred.

Undaunted by Grechko's opposition, Brezhnev called for a "full abundance" of consumer goods by the summer of 1974.[78] At the same time, he intensified his efforts to improve relations with the West. If he could get the Americans to agree, the USSR might receive an infusion of technology from the West. This, he hoped, would help raise the technological level of the Soviet Union—in-

---

[77] Harry Gelman, *The Brezhnev Politburo and the Decline of Detente* (Ithaca, N.Y.: Cornell, 1984), 86.

[78] *Pravda*, June 15, 1974, as cited in John Parker, *The Kremlin in Transition*, forthcoming from Unwin Hyman, Inc.

cluding in its military sphere—to that which prevailed in the rest of the world. As Gelman put it:

> It seems likely that the turn to the West, and to the United States in particular, served for Brezhnev as a tacit response to the charge that his strident complaints about the trends in the Soviet economy had not been accompanied by proposals that could remedy these difficulties. He had now furnished one such proposal. . . . The Politburo was apparently "sold" on the thesis that this change over time, would go a long way toward solving the economic problems to which Brezhnev had pointed at the December 1969 Plenum, helping to raise productivity and preventing a continued decline in the growth rate of the Soviet economy. At the same time, the Politburo was undoubtedly convinced that the change would produce ancillary benefits for Soviet military technology.[79]

For his part, Grechko did not appear especially impressed with the new policy. In fact, he made clear throughout the early part of the 1970s that he opposed any cuts in the rate of increase of military spending. To begin with, in 1971 he emphasized again the increasingly close ties between the military and the economy. He argued as well that international conditions made it necessary to strengthen Soviet military forces even more. He also made very clear his preference for heavy industry:

> it is clear that the achievements of our economy during the past five years as well as the new goals outlined by the Twenty-fourth Congress for the economic development of the Soviet state have the most immediate significance for strengthening its defense might and for raising the combat power of the Soviet army and navy.
>
> The development of heavy industry has played and does play a particularly important role in solving this problem. . . . The high development rates of heavy industry . . . will also be maintained during the coming five years.[80]

Despite progress in relations with the West, Grechko made it clear that there was no reason to let up in defense spending, citing the

[79] Gelman, *The Brezhnev Politburo and the Decline of Detente*, p. 130.

[80] "Rech' tovarishcha A. A. Grechko" ("The Speech of Comrade A. A. Grechko"), *Pravda*, April 3, 1971. See also, A. Grechko, "Nesokrushimyi shchit rodiny" ("The Indestructible Shield of the Motherland"), *Pravda*, February 23, 1971; Grechko, *On Guard for Peace and the Building of Communism*, pp. 15, 28, 29, 39.

1971 Party Program demonstrating the party's belief that it was vital for the state to keep defense spending at a high level. Grechko continued his hard-nosed approach to military spending throughout the first half of the 1970s, arguing in 1974 that

> the party . . . teaches us to evaluate the international situation realistically, to take into account not only the positive changes but also the factors that oppose peace. The forces of imperialism and reaction have not laid down their arms. They are striving to poison the international atmosphere, to return to the times of the cold war, endeavoring to increase the allocations for war purposes and to promote the arms race. The party constantly draws the attention of all of us to this—of all Soviet people. *We must preserve a high degree of vigilance, maintain the defense capacity of our state at a proper level and intensify its defenses.*[81]

Likewise, in his 1974 *Kommunist* article he maintained that it was the "economic and military might" of the USSR that kept imperialism in check. He continued in 1975 to express such views.[82] Kulikov supported his defense minister, emphasizing in 1976 the enormous sums the U.S. was spending on its military "more than $100 million."[83] The obvious implication was that at a time when U.S. defense spending was up, the USSR could not cut back on its own military preparations. Whatever others might think about it, Grechko believed that the only *realistic* option for the Soviet political-military elite was to continue to increase its military budget. Indeed, by the time of the publication of his 1975 book, he was warning that the increasingly complex weapons systems required by the Soviet military would necessitate more, not less, from the beleaguered Soviet economy. As he observed:

> The production of new weapons models and combat equipment is placing greater demands upon the country's economy. In order to manufacture these weapons and equipment it is not enough to make use of only the old branches of industry. It is necessary to develop

---

[81] "Grechko Addresses Kerch Meeting," Kiev domestic service in Russian, September 14, 1974, *FBIS, The Soviet Union*, September 17, 1974, p. R1. Emphasis added. See also Kulikov, "Brain of the Army."

[82] Grechko, "V. I. Lenin and the Armed Forces of the Soviet State"; see also Grechko, "Science and Art."

[83] Kulikov, "Soviet Military Science Today," p. 39.

new, long-range branches, capable of producing qualitatively different materials, which would also include such unique materials as
those possessing a high degree of mechanical strength, heat resistance, purity of composition, and other properties.[84]

Such a prognosis was certainly not welcome to Brezhnev, who was
already hard pressed to find ways to pump more money into the
civilian economy.

In the short term, Grechko's opposition to decreases in the defense budget won out. The Twenty-fifth Party Congress in effect
decided that the country would continue to maintain defense expenditures at a high rate of growth and that consumer goods would be
slighted in favor of heavy industry. Brezhnev was successful, however, in getting defense industries to play a greater role in the production of consumer goods.[85] Brezhnev would continue to search for
arms control agreements to limit spending and would continue his
attempt to use foreign economic ties to shore up the technologically
backward Soviet economic system. The opposition of the high command to any cut in the rate of increase of defense spending was,
nevertheless, a problem—one that would only be overcome with the
adoption of the Tenth Five-Year Plan which was unveiled at the
Twenty-fifth Party Congress in March 1976, a month before Grechko's death.

Grechko's concern about the budget was shared by others in the
Soviet political leadership. Ukrainian party boss Petr Shelest, for
example, was ousted from the political leadership in May 1972, in
part because of his opposition to Brezhnev's attempt to use détente
as a way of reorienting spending away from the military toward the
greater satisfaction of consumer needs.

Grechko and Détente

Shelest was not the only opponent of détente in the upper ranks
of the Soviet hierarchy. It is reported that Shelepin was ousted from
the Politburo in 1975 also because of his opposition to détente. For
his part, Grechko continued his stubborn opposition despite Brezhnev's introduction of a "peace offensive" at the Twenty-fourth Party

[84] Grechko, *The Armed Forces of the Soviet State*, p. 156.
[85] David Holloway, *The Soviet Union and the Arms Race*, 2d ed. (New Haven: Yale University Press, 1984), pp. 118–19.

Congress in 1971 and his increasingly laudatory comments on behalf of improved East-West relations. Kulikov shared his superior's skepticism.

Thus, despite the progress that was being made at the SALT I negotiations—in which Grechko most certainly was involved, given his position as defense minister—Grechko continually emphasized the threat presented by the West in his writings and speeches. In an article published in *Pravda* in February 1971 he accused the West of trying to crush socialism, of engaging in military provocations, and of accelerating the arms race.[86] He continued this hard line at the Twenty-fourth Party Congress in April, responding to Brezhnev's suggestion that an improvement in relations with the U.S. was possible by blasting Washington for using "political pressure, military threats, and provocation in order to dictate another country's policies" and claiming that the "increasing aggressiveness of imperialism, the sharpest of which is aimed at the Soviet Union, creates strains in international relations." Furthermore, he observed that "the preparations of the imperialists of the U.S. for aggression have not ceased and continue at an undiminished tempo."[87] Zakharov adopted a similar stance in an article he wrote shortly before stepping down as chief of the General Staff: "The imperialists continue the arms race, once again form a bloc, and threaten peace."[88] Likewise, Grechko argued that "the danger of a new war remains."[89] In an article published in 1971 in the authoritative party journal *Kommunist*, Grechko did appear to compromise somewhat in his dispute with Brezhnev and the political leadership over arms control. However, his support was lukewarm at best. For example, while ritualistically praising the recently concluded Non-Proliferation Agreement and the Seabed Treaty, he continued his attack on imperialism, which he called "malicious and perfidious," claiming that it "is ready to commit any crime for the sake of its mercenary interests." In addition, he warned that "the aggressive essence of imperialism has not changed" and claimed that imperialism was

---

[86] A. Grechko, "V boyakh rozhdennaia" ("Born in Battle"), *Izvestiia*, February 22, 1971.

[87] "The Speech of Comrade A. A. Grechko."

[88] M. Zakharov, "Uroki istorii" ("The Lessons of History"), *Izvestiia*, June 22, 1971.

[89] Grechko, "On Guard for Peace and the Building of Socialism," pp. 28–29.

employing the "most refined" methods against the USSR.[90] Several of Grechko's comments are noteworthy. First, his reference to the unchanging nature of imperialism was directed at Brezhnev, who had argued that it was possible to do business with those in the West who had a more realistic understanding of the danger of a nuclear war and recognized the utility of improved relations for both sides. Second, coming at a time when the USSR was engaged in delicate negotiations with the West on a strategic arms limitation agreement, Grechko's reference to "most refined" Western methods could be read as a warning to the political leadership not to be taken in, not to sacrifice the country's vital interests on the altar of improved East-West relations.

Grechko continued to express skepticism toward arms control in 1972, as the Soviet Union moved closer to agreement with the U.S. on the SALT and Anti-Ballistic Missile (ABM) treaties. He called the international situation "complex," criticized U.S. military spending and American policy in Vietnam, and claimed that the U.S. was breaking "the norms of international law."[91] Likewise, in a *Kommunist* article published at the same time, he spoke of "the increasing aggressiveness of imperialism" and accused the U.S. of "open aggression."[92]

Kulikov followed Grechko's lead in commenting on détente. In 1972, for example, he warned that imperialism was increasingly relying on "military force" to achieve its ends.[93] In addition, it seems from press reports that when called upon to endorse the SALT treaties, he carefully avoided making a positive statement. He noted the Soviet regime's interest in lessening the danger of a nuclear war and maintained that the treaties served the interest of the peoples of both countries.[94]

[90] A. Grechko, "KPSS i vooruzhennye sily" ("The CPSU and the Armed Forces"), *Kommunist*, no. 4 (March 1971): 42.

[91] A. Grechko, "Nadezhnyi strazh sotsializma" ("Reliably Guarding Socialism"), *Pravda*, February 23, 1972.

[92] Grechko, "The Armed Forces of the Union of Soviet Socialist Republics," p. 35.

[93] V. Kulikov, "Oveiannye boevoi slavoi" ("Covered with Combat Glory"), *Izvestiia*, February 23, 1972.

[94] V. Kulikov, "V interesakh ukrepleniia mira i mezhdunarodnoi bezopasnosti" ("In the Interests of Strengthening Peace and International Security"), *Pravda*, August 24, 1972.

Grechko's endorsement of the SALT treaties was more upbeat. The defense minister noted that while these treaties "did not eliminate the danger of nuclear war, they did lessen it."[95] Despite the avoidance of critical comments concerning U.S. policy in his statement on SALT, however, the tone of Grechko's comments was significantly more negative than Brezhnev's. Speaking at a Central Committee meeting in December, Brezhnev called the treaties "the first limitation in history of the most modern and most powerful types of weapons" and noted: "that which was agreed in Moscow should be strengthened and developed. One of the goals of the continuing talks on these questions is to find a way to make the temporary treaty permanent." Finally, Brezhnev observed that recent talks in Moscow between himself and President Nixon proceeded from the premise that "in a nuclear age there is no other basis for bilateral relations than peaceful coexistence."[96]

Undeterred, Grechko continued his assault on the U.S. in February 1973, charging that "reactionary circles" in the West were trying to return the West to the "time of the cold war."[97] He appeared to tone down his criticism of the U.S. slightly in his May *Kommunist* article when he stated: "the change from the cold war to détente is taking place in the world. But reaction and militarism still have not been neutralized."[98] Kulikov followed up with an even more frontal statement the next month. Writing in the Party's primary journal in the military he warned that: "Events of recent years clearly show that as before, the policy of imperialism remains reactionary, and aggressive, regardless of whether the power of militarism has decreased. Under those circumstances the aggressiveness of international reaction is aimed at the socialist states and above all against the Soviet Union."[99] Needless to say, such comments, par-

---

[95] A. Grechko, "Vazhnyi vklad v ukreplenie mira i bezopasnosti" ("An Important Contribution to Strengthening Peace and Security"), *Pravda*, September 30, 1972.

[96] L. Brezhnev, "O piatidesiatiletii Soiuza Sovetskikh Sotsialisticheskikh Respublik" ("Concerning the Fiftieth Anniversary of the Union of Soviet Socialist Republics"), in Brezhnev, *On a Leninist Course*, vol. 4, p. 79.

[97] A. Grechko, "Na strazhe rodiny" ("On Guard over the Motherland"), *Pravda*, February 23, 1973.

[98] Grechko, "On Guard over Peace and Socialism," p. 13.

[99] V. Kulikov, "Vysokaia boegotovnost'—vazhneishee uslovie nadezhnoi zaschity rodiny" ("A High Level of Combat Readiness Is The Most Important Condition for the Reliable Defense of the Motherland"), *Kommunist vooruzhennykh sil*, no. 6 (1973): 14.

ticularly the one by Kulikov, were not appreciated by Brezhnev and his supporters, who had begun to make arms control and improved East-West relations one of the main pillars of their foreign policy.

Meanwhile, an open debate had broken out in the press between representatives of the media and academia who favored détente and some in the military who echoed the line taken by Grechko and Kulikov. In *Izvestiia*, in July 1973, Aleksandr Bovin wrote that a nuclear war would be an irrational act, given the losses that would result from it. Georgii Arbatov, the Director of the USA Institute, maintained in *Pravda* that efforts to escalate the nuclear balance beyond its existing level would lead to less rather than more security. Rear Admiral Sheliag from the Lenin Military-Political Academy responded in *Red Star*, arguing that only imperialism would be destroyed in any war it started. Other military officers, primarily political officers, adopted similar stances.[100]

Not surprisingly, Brezhnev came out on the side of Bovin and Arbatov, in a speech in Poland in July 1974. After praising positive developments in U.S.-Soviet relations, including Nixon's recent visit to the USSR, Brezhnev turned to the question of nuclear war and observed: "For centuries humanity, in striving to ensure its security, has been guided by the formula: if you want peace, be ready for war. In our nuclear age this formula conceals a particular danger. Man dies only once. However, in recent years a quantity of weapons has already been amassed sufficient to destroy everything living on earth several times over."[101] In August Brezhnev spoke of "constructive relations" between capitalist and socialist states and called for efforts "to deepen the process of détente."[102]

At least one Western observer has suggested that one of Brezhnev's primary motives for elevating Grechko with Foreign Minister Gromyko and KGB Chief Andropov to full Politburo status in 1973 was to elicit support for his foreign policy.[103] Indeed, given Brezh-

---

[100] See Thomas N. Bjorkman and Thomas J. Zamostny, "Soviet Politics and Strategy Toward the West: Three Cases," *World Politics* 36, no. 2 (January 1984): 198–207.

[101] L. Brezhnev, "Sotsialisticheskoi Pol'she–tridtsat' let" ("For Socialist Poland—Thirty Years"), in Brezhnev, *On a Leninist Course*, vol. 5, p. 120.

[102] L. Brezhnev, "V splochennom stroiu sovetskikh respublik" ("In the Solid Structure of the Soviet Republics"), in Brezhnev, *On a Leninist Course*, vol. 4, p. 248.

[103] Raymond Garthoff, *Détente and Confrontation* (Washington, D.C.: Brookings Institution, 1985), p. 354.

nev's overall style of leadership with its emphasis on balancing support from all the key institutions, his inclusion of Grechko in the Politburo may have been aimed at least in part at gaining greater cooperation from his defense minister in key areas such as arms control. In the short run this move appears to have been successful—at least in Grechko's case. Writing on May 9, for example, Grechko noted that Soviet policy had made possible "positive progress on the world situation" and spoke of "a turning away from the Cold War to peaceful coexistence." This was to be Grechko's most positive statement on East-West relations.[104]

By October Grechko's position had begun to harden again. Writing about the battle for the Caucasus, he accused the "reactionary forces of imperialism" of "considering war as a means for achieving their aggressive goals" and argued that "despite some relaxation in international tensions, the threat of war has in no way diminished."[105] Then, in February 1974, he maintained that "imperialism is making serious military preparations against our country, against all countries of the Socialist Commonwealth."[106]

From an internal Soviet standpoint, Grechko's strongest attack on Brezhnev's détente policy came in June, only weeks before President Nixon's visit to the Soviet Union. Writing in *Red Star*, Grechko warned: "Imperialism is still carrying out material preparations for war, expanding its production of military equipment and weaponry, and insistently perfecting its gigantic military machine. . . . The danger of war remains a stern reality of our time."[107] A week after Nixon left the country, Grechko again emphasized the danger facing the Soviet Union when he noted: "despite a certain thaw in the international climate, there is still a real military threat from imperialism. It was and remains the main bearer of military danger."[108]

---

[104] A. Grechko, "Velikii podvig" ("The Great Feat"), *Pravda*, May 9, 1973.

[105] A. Grechko, "Bitva za Kavkaz" ("The Battle for the Caucases"), *Pravda*, October 8, 1973, and Grechko, "V. I. Lenin and the Armed Forces of the Soviet Government," p. 23.

[106] Grechko, "On Guard over Peace and Socialism."

[107] *Krasnaia zvezda*, June 5, 1974, cited in Timothy J. Colton, "Civil-Military Relations in Soviet Politics," *Current History* 67 (October 1974): 163.

[108] A. Grechko, "The Order of Lenin on the Standard of the Transbaikal Soldiers," *Krasnaia zvezda*, July 12, 1974, in *FBIS, The Soviet Union*, July 14, 1974, p. v2.

From all appearances, the Soviet military was not happy with the Vladivostok Accords signed in November 1974. As Garthoff put it: "The Soviet leaders made major concessions to reach agreement. . . . What needs to be stressed here is that the Soviet military leaders regarded as unjustified militarily the Soviet concessions in agreeing to equal levels of strategic forces without allowance for U.S. FBS [Forward-Based Systems]. While they accepted the decision to do so for broader political objectives, they were not happy with the decision." In fact, as Garthoff noted, the American response to the concessions the Soviets had made at Vladivostok "had been simply to pocket that gain and then to press for more."[109]

Thus, it is not surprising that in March 1975, only five months after the signing of the Vladivostok Agreement, Grechko was again pointing to the aggressive nature of Western imperialism, arguing that in spite of Soviet efforts "military preparations of the imperialist states have not only not slowed down, but in a certain sense they have accelerated."[110] Such statements were embarrassing to Brezhnev, and not only vis-à-vis the Americans. Taken together they conveyed the message that while Brezhnev might want to push a policy of détente with the Americans, Grechko wanted no part of it. In addition, the article also conveyed a not too subtle suggestion that Brezhnev might have been taken in by the American leader.

CONCLUDING OBSERVATIONS

Andrei Grechko dominated the Soviet military while he was defense minister. His hand is evident everywhere. Despite strong personalities, neither Zakharov nor Kulikov appear to have been particularly influential. Their subordinate roles appear to have been primarily a result of the presence of a strong, effective professional soldier in the top position. There was no need, for example, for Zakharov to voice his opposition to policies being followed by the political leadership as he had done under Khrushchev. In the first place, the military appeared to be getting what the high command wanted, and second, Grechko was a strong defender of the military's

---

[109] Raymond L. Garthoff, *Détente and Confrontation*, pp. 464, 468.
[110] A. Grechko, "Velikaia pobeda i ee istoricheskie uroki" ("The Great Victory and Its Historical Lessons"), *Problemy mira i sotsializma*, no. 3 (1975): 10.

interests. As a consequence, both men played supporting roles, backing up their defense minister when necessary.

The Diagnostic Period

When it came to scientific-technical issues, Grechko presided over rather than designed the major changes introduced into the Soviet armed forces while he was defense minister. He made clear that he expected the important changes of greater adaptation to the technological revolution but did not attempt to micro-manage the process. He may have not had a clear idea of what the Soviet military would look like in the year 2000, but it was clear that he felt an urgent need for action.

The same is true of warfighting strategy. Grechko let it be known that he supported both a more balanced force structure and greater reliance on conventional weapons. But in contrast to future Soviet military leaders such as Ogarkov, he did not attempt to break new ground in this area and, as will become evident in the next chapter, did not force the service chiefs to subordinate parochial interests to those of a combined-arms strategy. Rather, he provided the backdrop and suggested a direction (toward greater reliance on conventional weapons), but also permitted a broad and relatively open discussion by his subordinates on how to proceed. This is not to suggest that he was not concerned about the country's military capabilities; in fact, it can be argued that he presided over one of the biggest buildups in Soviet military force structure in history. However, he did not appear to have a clear idea of where the Soviet military was heading in terms of warfighting strategy. Such problems were not his major area of concern.

Part of the reason for Grechko's lesser concern over technology or warfighting strategy is that his attention was focused primarily on the political-military interface, in this case on the budget and arms control. Grechko never really accepted the idea of arms control; neither were cuts in the rate of military budgetary increases acceptable to him, whether as a way of satisfying consumer demands or of improving the country's military security. In short, what he wanted was a large military budget and no arms control. To him, the best means of ensuring Soviet security was a strong defense. Consequently, while he recognized the economic difficulties facing the country, he believed that any cuts in military spending would only undermine his efforts to build a balanced military force. The same is true of arms control. The concept of sacrificing military systems in order to constrain the other side's force structure was an idea he found hard to understand, for the West simply could not be trusted. Even when he was forced to go along with the ABM and SALT agreements, he did so reluctantly.

Determining Strategy

Insofar as can be determined, Grechko decided the military's strategy for achieving its long-term goals. This is particularly true of the socio-political sphere, which was his primary area of concern. When it came to the budget and arms control, Grechko's strategy was as straightforward as it was simple. He refused to be moved. Any attempts to cut the rate of growth of the military budget would be opposed, as would any further movement in East-West relations. He expressed his views in a way that left no doubt in the minds of other Soviets as to where he stood on the issues. Furthermore, while Grechko eventually came to the conclusion that party discipline left him no alternative but to support the SALT and ABM treaties, the language he employed made it clear that he remained opposed both to arms control and the entire détente process as well. And while he undoubtedly recognized that his strong support for greater reliance on modern technology in the Soviet military supported Brezhnev's push for détente and greater contact with the West, he apparently felt that in this instance he could have his cake and eat it too. Technology in the Soviet military was too important not to receive primary attention, and, if Brezhnev attempted to use it to his own ends, Grechko was convinced he could limit the damage—and he was right.

Mobilizing Assets

Perhaps because he adopted a "laid back" approach in dealing with problems in the military-technical area, preferring instead to oversee rather than to dictate changes in this area, Grechko made no effort to mobilize the military as an institution in order to improve its adaptation to the demands of modern technology. He made clear that problems existed and that work was needed to correct them, but at this point these were not as central an issue for him as they would be in later years.

In a recent study of the Soviet high command, Jeremy Azrael labeled the Grechko period the "golden age" of civil-military relations and noted that "the Soviet high command got almost everything it wanted in terms of resources, programs, status and freedom of action in developing Soviet strategic concepts."[111] While Azrael is correct insofar as the budget is concerned, the relationship was far from symbiotic.

It was clear during the first half of the 1970s that Grechko would not succeed in getting more money for the military. Therefore, he set out to ensure that the politicians would at least be unsuccessful in their attempts to cut his budget. From Brezhnev's standpoint, it came down to the dilemma of either ousting Grechko or putting up with his hard-line approach to the budget. And, in fact, it was only in 1976, a month prior to Grechko's death, when he was already quite sick, that Brezhnev was successful in pushing through a cut in the rate of growth of the military budget. When it came to arms control, however, Grechko was less successful.

We will probably never know the details of the Politburo debates over the SALT and ABM treaties, but it must have been clear to Grechko by the early 1970s that the likelihood of blocking the treaties was low. Brezhnev's commitment to arms control was strong enough and his position within the political leadership secure enough to enable him to override Grechko's objections. The ouster of individuals like Shelest and Shelepin from the upper ranks of the political leadership obviously served to strengthen Brezhnev's hand in pushing détente. Despite the failure to have his policy preferences implemented, however, Grechko had sufficient support within the upper ranks of the political-military leadership openly to defy his general secretary—as he did during Nixon's visit by questioning U.S. willingness to adhere to arms control agreements. The easiest and most logical reason for Grechko's ability to stand up to Brezhnev is that while Brezhnev was able to drum up enough support for arms control within the Politburo, his power was not sufficient to silence his defense minister. Grechko's death on April 26, 1976, had important implications for the future of the Soviet military. From a

---

[111] Jeremy R. Azrael, *The Soviet Civilian Leadership and the Military High Command, 1976–1986*, Rand Report, R-3521, June 1987, p. 2.

political standpoint, it removed one of Brezhnev's most determined opponents regarding the budget or arms control. Within a short time it would also lead to the removal of Grechko's supporter, the chief of staff, another plus for Brezhnev. On the military-technical front, however, Grechko's death did little to change the general course the Soviet military would follow in coming months and years. The emphasis he and Kulikov placed on modern technology, as well as their interest in a balanced military, would be shared by their successors, even if they saw a more pressing urgency in the need for movement in this area. Indeed, it could be argued that in withstanding pressures to cut the military budget, Grechko's greatest legacy to the Soviet military was the success he achieved in overseeing the Red Army's transition from a predominantly nuclear equipped and oriented force to one packing both a conventional and a nuclear punch—as he himself noted shortly before he died. Speaking of improvements that had been made in conventional forces, he stated that there had been "great improvement in fire, shock and maneuver capabilities of troops, which permits assigning them very decisive missions on the battlefield capable of being accomplished without resorting to nuclear weapons."[112] And as most Western analysts will attest, Grechko was not exaggerating.

[112] Grechko, *The Armed Forces of the Soviet State*, p. 153.

PART III

The Ogarkov Era, 1977–1984

CHAPTER 5

The New Team Takes Over, 1977–1980

Seen from Brezhnev's perspective, the political situation midway through the 1970s was mixed. On the one hand, Brezhnev had finally consolidated his position to the point where he was indisputably primus inter pares within the upper ranks of the Soviet political leadership. He had succeeded, for example, in having Shelepin dropped from the Politburo in April 1975. Then, at the Twenty-fifth Party Congress in 1976, he was able to blame Polianskii for the disastrous agricultural failure of 1975 (Polianskii was dropped from the Politburo) and to have three of his supporters promoted to full membership in the Politburo—Dmitrii Ustinov, Grigorii Romanov, and Geidar Aliev. In addition, in October of the following year Brezhnev supporters Konstantin Chernenko and Vasilii Kuznetsov were made candidate members of the Politburo. Finally, Kosygin, who was already beset by health problems, was neutralized, and Podgornyi, who had been a constant thorn in Brezhnev's side, was forced in May 1977 into retirement. Brezhnev had won the leadership struggle.

Commensurate with his increased standing in the Politburo, Brezhnev also began to be singled out for special attention—in effect, a new personality cult began to appear. He received the Lenin Peace Prize, his speeches were constantly cited in the media, and his photograph was evident everywhere. He was consistently praised as one of the most outstanding figures in the history of the Soviet Union; reading accounts of the Second World War written at that time, one has the impression that instead of a mere political officer, Brezhnev had been one of the key strategists behind the Soviet victory. On his seventieth birthday in 1976, Brezhnev was referred to several times as *Vozhd'* ("the leader"), a title that had hitherto been reserved for Stalin.

Despite his growing strength within the political leadership, Brezhnev was also beset with serious problems. To begin with, his health was beginning to fail. He would be around for another six years, but by 1976 it was becoming clear that he had neither the energy nor the ability to sustain the demanding schedule of a general secretary. Similarly, it was becoming increasingly obvious that the country's economy was suffering very serious problems. The "aging" economy—to use Gregory Grossman's phrase—was still attempting to recover from two devastating crop failures, defense expenditures continued to absorb a major part of the budget, and the outlook for overall economic growth for the next decade was not encouraging.[1]

Brezhnev's undisputed strength within the upper ranks of the Soviet national security apparatus offered a possible way out of the situation. To begin with, like the rest of Soviet society, the military was guilty of inefficiency and considerable redundancy. Instead of following a single unified strategy, some of the services (most notably the SRF, the Air Defense Forces (PVO), and the navy) often gave the impression of having their own approach to fighting a war. Greater discipline, a more rational approach to allocating resources, and an increased emphasis on a combined-arms approach to warfighting might make it possible to put tighter controls on military spending. In addition, further arms control agreements with the U.S. offered the prospect of greater access to Western trade and technology. They also held out the possibility of both greater predictability in the development of weapons programs and, if they were successful over the long run, cutbacks in military spending.

What was needed, however, was one officer, or several officers, to lead the Soviet military, men who would on the one hand be supportive of Brezhnev's policy, while on the other be able to force an often reluctant officer corps to implement it. When Grechko died in early 1976, Brezhnev was presented with an opportunity to make the changes he wanted. In this regard, the announcement in April that Brezhnev was chairman of the Defense Council, together with

---

[1] Gregory Grossman, "An Economy at Middle Age," *Problems of Communism*, 25 (March–April 1976): 18–33.

his "promotion" the following month to marshal of the Soviet Union, may have been aimed in part at making the point that in contrast to the Grechko period, Brezhnev was now in complete charge of the armed forces and would be behind any personnel and policy changes in the security area.

Enter Ustinov and Ogarkov

The appointment of Dmitrii Ustinov as defense minister in April shortly after the death of Marshal Grechko came as a surprise to most Western observers. While Ustinov had been on most succession lists, the appointment of a civilian to this top military post was unexpected. In fact, Ustinov represents the first "political general" to hold that post since Nikolai Bulganin gave up the defense minister's mantle in February 1955 to become prime minister.

If the announcement of Ustinov's appointment as defense minister was unexpected, Ogarkov's replacement of Kulikov as chief of the General Staff on January 8, 1977, was not only unanticipated, it was almost ignored in Western press reports. These reports highlighted Kulikov's new role as commander of the Warsaw Pact. As the headline in the *New York Times* put it, "General Kulikov, 55, is made Warsaw Pact Commander."[2] It was not until the fourth paragraph of the story that the reader learned that Ogarkov had replaced Kulikov. And yet, within a month, Ogarkov had moved ahead of Kulikov as the second-ranking officer in the Soviet military and, for all practical purposes, was in charge of the day-to-day operations of the Soviet armed forces.[3]

While at first glance Ustinov and Ogarkov may appear to have had little in common, it is my contention that the two appointments were in fact interrelated and constituted an integral part of Brezhnev's effort to exert greater control over the military on the two issues where Grechko's opposition had been most troublesome—arms control and the military budget.

First, let us consider Ustinov. To begin with, his appointment contrasts with that of Grechko. In 1967 the thirteen-day lapse between the death of Malinovskii and Grechko's appointment suggested some difference of opinion in the upper ranks of the Krem-

---

[2] *New York Times*, January 9, 1977.
[3] *Krasnaia zvezda*, February 23, 1977.

lin's national security apparatus. Ustinov's appointment, however, had been almost instantaneous, indicating that Brezhnev had had it in mind for some time. Indeed, Ustinov's promotion at the Twenty-fifth Party Congress in March 1976 to full membership in the Politburo a month before Grechko died suggests that Brezhnev was already planning to promote him to the position of defense minister.

Ustinov's writings and speeches indicate that he was a long-time supporter of Brezhnev's arms control policy. For example, in 1974, at a time when the party leader was feuding with Grechko, Ustinov came out strongly in support of Brezhnev's peace policy, noting that "international relations have essentially changed toward a weakening of tensions, confirming the principles of peaceful coexistence between states with different social systems, toward the development of mutually beneficial economic and technical cooperation between socialist and capitalist countries."[4] Furthermore, while it is not possible to locate specific statements by Ustinov calling for cutbacks in the military budget—a highly unlikely occurrence given his position in the military-industrial complex—he was a manager who knew the military-industrial complex inside out and certainly knew how to rationalize military expenditures if anyone did.

Finally, while Kulikov had not been as outspoken as Grechko during the early 1970s, he clearly supported him on both arms control and the military budget. While the idea of selecting someone other than Kulikov from within the upper ranks of the military to succeed Grechko was a possibility, it meant finding a four- or five-star general officer who would support Brezhnev in these key areas. Moving such an individual into the top job would not only create problems within the military hierarchy, it would also mean appointing an unknown individual to a key post at a delicate time—when important budgetary limitations were about to be imposed.

Having appointed Ustinov, Brezhnev had the option of letting Kulikov remain as chief of staff. However, the naming of a civilian as defense minister put Kulikov, as the top professional soldier, in an even more important position: it would now be up to him to maintain support among the professional officer corps for Brezhnev

---

[4] D. Ustinov, "Delo partii, delo naroda" ("A Matter for the Party, a Matter for the People"), in D. F. Ustinov, *Izbrannye rechi i statii* (Moscow: Politizdat, 1979), p. 239.

and his policies as to arms control and the budget. Kulikov was not likely to carry out this task with much enthusiasm, and his acerbic personality left open the possibility that he might end up creating dissension within the upper ranks of the armed forces. In addition, Brezhnev needed someone who had sufficient intellectual capacity to justify conceptually what he was doing while at the same time ensuring that the Soviet military was moving efficiently and effectively to make the best use of available resources. The most likely candidate was Ogarkov.

Perhaps because of his background as a technical officer and a delegate to SALT I, Ogarkov understood better than most of his colleagues how limitations on strategic systems could be made to serve Soviet interests. As Garthoff observes: "the assignment of Ustinov as Minister of Defense and the death of Grechko and elevation of Ogarkov placed in key positions men better able to consider such questions as strategic arms limitations in a broader context."[5] Furthermore, Ogarkov supported Brezhnev's reliance on arms control from the very beginning. In fact, he openly defied both Grechko and Kulikov—his military superiors—by offering support for Brezhnev at a time when they were questioning the value of his policies. For example, commenting on arms control in 1973 Ogarkov stated that "in recent years definite progress has been achieved." Furthermore, he added, "the improvement in the international climate which is currently taking place will undoubtedly contribute to a further advance along the road of limiting the arms race."[6] Ogar-

---

[5] Raymond L. Garthoff, *Détente and Confrontation* (Washington, D.C.: Brookings Institution, 1985), p. 557. Technical-services officers in the Soviet military are involved in work that is both highly complex and at the same time basic. Their work runs the gauntlet from building roads and fortifications to constructing missile and radar sites. Ogarkov himself was a fortifications engineer during World War II. But it is clear that while a technical-services background may predispose an officer toward a strong interest in high technology, it is no guarantee. As one former Soviet officer put it to this writer, "There are two kinds of technical officers, simple road-builders and very bright technically oriented individuals." Conversations with present and former Soviet military officers suggest that as early as the late 1950s Ogarkov had the reputation of being one of the latter. Furthermore, the fact that he played a key role in the SALT I talks, where he demonstrated a formidable grasp of the details of the various complex weapons systems and made a strong impression on his Western counterparts, suggests that his interest in and understanding of technology had a long history.

[6] "Otvety na voprosy redaktsii gazety 'Krasnaia zvezda' " ("Answers to Questions from the Editors of the Newspaper 'Red Star' "), *Krasnaia zvezda*, July 10, 1973.

kov continued his optimistic comments in 1974 when he noted that "a general shift has occurred in favor of a relaxation of international tensions, the positions of peace have been consolidated, and a move has been made in the direction of reducing the danger of the outbreak of a world thermonuclear war."[7] Ogarkov also criticized undefined "forces" in the West for opposing movement toward détente, but his characterization of the situation—i.e., that a general shift had occurred, the positions of peace had been consolidated—carry a greater tone of permanency than was the case with Grechko and Kulikov. Then, in 1975, Ogarkov observed: "In recent years the positions of peace have been strengthened, and a shift is relentlessly taking place toward a relaxation of tensions."[8] Finally, some eight months before he was promoted to chief of the General Staff, Ogarkov made an even stronger public statement in favor of arms control and détente when he wrote that "the trend toward easing tension and toward organizing comprehensive mutually beneficial cooperation among states with different social systems has begun *to dominate* international life."[9]

Ogarkov's willingness to disagree openly with his military superiors suggests that Brezhnev and perhaps Ustinov as well had supported him for some time. A review of statements on arms control made over the past twenty years by senior Soviet military officers at the four-star level and above suggests that on international issues they almost always repeat whatever their defense minister says. They may be creative on doctrinal questions, but this is almost never the case when it comes to foreign relations. In this light, Ogarkov's behavior seems, at a minimum, unusual.

More importantly, however, the appointment of Ogarkov as the most senior professional military officer marks an important watershed in the postwar development of the Soviet armed forces. Not only was he a technical services officer, but in contrast to Grechko and Kulikov, he had a sophisticated understanding of the interrela-

---

[7] N. V. Ogarkov, "The Fatherland's Reliable Shield," *Sovetskaia Litva*, February 23, 1974, *FBIS, The Soviet Union*, March 1, 1974, pp. v6–7.

[8] N. Ogarkov, "The Great Patriotic War," *Sovetskaia Rossiia*, May 8, 1975, *FBIS, The Soviet Union*, May 15, 1975, pp. R1–3.

[9] N. Ogarkov, "Immortal Feat," *Pravda vostoka*, *FBIS, The Soviet Union*, May 20, 1976, v1. Emphasis added.

tionship between the four variables covered in this study. For example, on the military-technical side, Ogarkov believed that with the increasing role of modern technology, more attention had to be paid to developing a Soviet-style meritocracy and to incorporating into the armed forces the latest developments in science and technology. Likewise, when it came to warfighting strategy, Ogarkov had a relatively clear idea of the direction in which he wanted Soviet strategy to go (e.g., toward a greater reliance on high-technology conventional weapons) and how he wanted the Soviet military to be structured (i.e., by emphasizing maneuverability, mobility, and sustainability).

Turning to the sociopolitical sector, Ogarkov contrasted sharply with Kulikov and Grechko. Where the latter had adamantly opposed both cuts in the military budget and progress on arms control, Ogarkov believed that the military could absorb cuts in its budget's rate of increase through a vigorous arms control policy and by streamlining the Soviet officer corps and force structure to remove inefficiencies and duplications. In this sense, Ogarkov's decision to adopt a positive approach toward integrating all four variables was one of the most important contributions he made to the evolution of the Soviet high command. The problem with Ogarkov's approach was that to be fully effective, all four variables had to work together. In the end, circumstances would undermine his efforts to implement this integrated approach.

The Key Players

It would be hard to find two individuals who differed more from each other as well as from the other six individuals included in this study than Ustinov and Ogarkov. Ustinov was not a career soldier; indeed, his only military service had occurred in the 1920s when he joined the Red Army for one year as an enlisted man. The rest of his career was spent in the Soviet military-industrial complex, where he had responsibility for the development and production of increasingly wider varieties of Soviet weapons systems. Eventually, he rose to the position of minister of the defense industry. Indeed, if there was a military-industrial complex in the Soviet Union, he was its chief.

Ogarkov, by contrast, was a career military officer. However, unlike all other professional military officers, who came from line branches of the Soviet military (e.g., armor, infantry), he was a technical services officer. Indeed, one senior Soviet officer told me that Ogarkov was unique in the annals of the Soviet General Staff. "Never has an officer from the technical services ever gone so high in the Soviet military; he is unusual."[10] Ogarkov had numerous command assignments, but in the beginning all were in engineering units. It was only after the war that he began to get the broader assignments necessary for higher rank in the Soviet military.

Ustinov and Ogarkov differ in another respect. Ustinov's background was in management. He made his reputation as an individual able to oversee and run a vast complex of industrial enterprises and to ensure not only that the Soviet military was supplied with a wide variety of weapons and weapons systems, but also that the research and development process was operating efficiently and at top capacity. While Ogarkov also has a background in management— he had been commander of a division and of a military district—he also was an outstanding military intellectual and theorist. Indeed, in many ways Ogarkov ranks as one of the finest minds in the history of the Soviet military, on a par with officers like Frunze, Shaposhnikov, and Tukhachevskii. What made him so important for the Soviet military—and this is the primary reason why he continues to have significant influence despite his retirement—was his outstanding ability to conceptualize problems in a way that gave Soviet military policy coherence and order. What made Ogarkov most unusual was not any novelty in his operational ideas—all had their antecedents under Grechko—but his ability to interrelate them.

This difference in backgrounds is of more than incidental interest. Indeed, it had important implications both for the military itself and for civil-military relations in the USSR during this period. Perhaps because Ustinov had so little background in military-technical matters, he had little to say about Soviet warfighting strategy. Indeed, a search of his writings from 1976 to 1984 reveals not a single original comment by Ustinov on what is considered the military-technical component of Soviet military doctrine. When he did speak on the topic, it was to support the positions taken by his chief

---

[10] Based on a private conversation between the author and a senior Soviet military officer.

of staff. As a consequence, during this period Ogarkov was for all practical purposes the most authoritative military spokesman on Moscow's warfighting strategy.

A veteran of party struggles under Stalin and in the post-Stalin era, Ustinov was a political animal, one who played the political game very carefully. He understood the need for caution in expressing his views and the importance of maintaining his ties with Brezhnev and the political leadership. As a result, Ustinov tended to side with the political leadership on disputed issues.

Perhaps because he was a technical officer, or maybe just because of his personality, Ogarkov was outspoken. He demonstrated repeatedly that while he understood the importance of political connections and politics, he was not prepared to sit by idly if he believed the interests of the armed forces were at stake. When he did not approve of the policy advocated by Brezhnev, he said so openly, even if this put him at odds with his defense minister. Indeed, the early 1980s saw something very unusual in Soviet civil-military relations—open polemics between the defense minister and his chief of staff over Brezhnev's policy on arms control and the United States.

Finally, Ustinov and Ogarkov were similar in one regard. They were deeply committed to technology: both believed that its development, its adoption by the Soviet military, and its mastery by Soviet personnel represented the future for the Soviet armed forces. Ogarkov's ideas are better conceived, and his concern about the need for greater efforts to incorporate technology more urgent, but both recognized its critical importance.

MILITARY-TECHNICAL ISSUES

Warfighting Strategy

Ogarkov's conceptual and operational efforts to build up the Soviet military can be divided into two parts. During his first four years as chief of staff his primary concern was with improving the Red Army's operational capabilities. Toward that end, his attention was focused on actions that would improve the Soviet military's ability to operate successfully in all environments. It was only with the publication of his pamphlet *Always in Readiness to Defend the Fatherland* in 1982 that he began to outline the reasons why he believed that conventional arms were the weapons of the future and that there was an increasing likelihood that a war—including even one in Europe—might remain conventional, even if the superpowers were involved.

The Nature of War.   While Ogarkov did not discuss the nature of war in great detail, he did touch on all three levels of conflict: local wars, theater conflict, and world war. Writing in the *Soviet Military Encyclopedia*, Ogarkov condemned local wars undertaken by "imperialists" and warned that they are dangerous because they could "escalate to a world war." Turning to theater conflicts, Ogarkov warned that the U.S. and NATO foresaw the possibility of "carrying out military operations with the use of *only* conventional weapons and with the limited use of nuclear weapons." As one would expect, Ogarkov's biggest concern was a world war. He argued that such a conflict would be unprecedented in terms of both its scope and the extent of its destruction. It would in fact be "a decisive clash between two opposing world socioeconomic systems—socialism and capitalism. It is assumed that such a war, simultaneously or subsequently, could involve the majority of states of the world. It will be unprecedented in its scope and violence, involve a global struggle of millions of allied armed forces, and will be conducted uncompromisingly with the most destructive political and strategic goals."[11] Clearly, for Ogarkov, a world war would be a catastrophic event.

Escalation.   When it came to escalation, Ogarkov argued that "Soviet military strategy admits that a world war may begin and for a definite time be conducted with the use of only conventional weapons. However, the expansion of military action *may* lead to its transformation into a world nuclear war where the main weapon will be nuclear weapons, above all, strategic weapons."[12] This statement has been seized by one Western scholar as part of an argument that Ogarkov was here maintaining that "such a war might begin with conventional weapons, but *would* develop into an all-out nuclear war in which nuclear weapons, particularly strategic nuclear weapons, would become the decisive factors."[13] In fact, a close reading of what

---

[11] N. V. Ogarkov, "Strategiia Voennaia" ("Military Strategy"), *Sovetskaia Voennaia Entsiklopediia* (Moscow: Voennoe izdatel'stvo, 1979), pp. 563, 564.

[12] Ibid. Emphasis added.

[13] Tsuyoshi Hasegawa, "Soviets on Nuclear-War-Fighting," *Problems of Communism* 35,

Ogarkov said indicates that he was breaking new ground. He did not say that a war *would* go nuclear, but that it *might* (*mozhet*). It might also *not* go nuclear. In this sense, Ogarkov was less pessimistic than Grechko concerning the issue of escalation. He was suggesting that a war—even a world war—might remain conventional. Indeed, for Ogarkov, the only thing inevitable about the introduction of nuclear weapons into a conflict would be the inevitability of retaliatory strikes.

In 1977 Brezhnev delivered his now famous Tula speech, in which he rejected the concept of military superiority:

> it is nonsense and completely baseless to argue that the Soviet Union is doing more than what is necessary for defense or that we are striving to gain military superiority, to acquire "a first-strike" capability. . . . The Soviet Union has been and will be a firm opponent of such an idea.
>
> Our military power is directed at avoiding not only a first strike but also a second strike, and at preventing a nuclear war itself. We can sum up our ideas on this problem in the following way. The defense potential of the Soviet Union must be sufficient so that no one should risk threatening our peaceful life. No aspect of our policy aims at superiority in armaments. Our policy aims at reducing military power and at lowering the possibility of military confrontation.[14]

It has been argued that Brezhnev's "rejection of superiority was bound to precipitate . . . a debate on victory in nuclear war, since achieving victory in nuclear war clearly implied possessing superior military power."[15] In fact, a number of analysts believe that Ogarkov led a battle against Brezhnev on this issue, that he argued that victory in a nuclear war would be possible—and, by implication, that nuclear war remained a means for gaining political ends. The relevant statement by Ogarkov comes from the same 1979 entry in the *Soviet Military Encyclopedia* in which he stated:

> It is believed that given existing means of destruction, a world nuclear war will be relatively short. However, taking into account the

---

no. 4 (July–August 1986): 5. Emphasis added. See also George G. Weickhardt, "Ustinov versus Ogarkov," *Problems of Communism* 34, no. 1 (January–February 1985): 81.

[14] L. I. Brezhnev, "Vydaiushchiisia podvig zashchitnikov Tuly" ("The Outstanding Feat of the Defenders of Tula"), *Pravda*, January 17, 1977.

[15] Hasegawa, "Soviets on Nuclear-War-Fighting," p. 4.

tremendous military and economic potential of the allied belliger-
ents, the possibility is not excluded that if the Soviet Union is forced
into a nuclear war, the Soviet people and its armed forces must be
ready for the most severe and lengthy tests. In such a situation, the
Soviet Union and the fraternal socialist states will possess definite superiority in comparison to the imperialist states, as a result of the
just goals of the war and the progressive character of their society and
governmental system. *This creates the objective possibility for achieving
victory.*[16]

With the appearance of this article, these analysts claim, "the lines
were clearly drawn between the military and the supporters of
Brezhnev."[17]

The situation was in fact more complex than this analysis suggests. To begin with, as Erickson has noted, the term "victory" in
Soviet military thought, when used in connection with nuclear
weapons, means "survival." What the Soviets really mean when they
use this term is that if a nuclear war were to be forced upon them,
they would have a warfighting strategy—including the use of nuclear weapons—and would be prepared to fight such a conflict and
survive it.[18] If anything, Ogarkov was supportive of the concept of
parity at the strategic nuclear level and, therefore, of Brezhnev's
Tula formulations. Furthermore, Soviet military officers increasingly rejected the idea of victory in a nuclear war. In the mid-1970s,
for example, students at the Voroshilov Academy were told that
while victory in a nuclear war was achievable, "the characteristics of
such a war leads us to conclude that in nuclear war there will be no
winner."[19] Soviet forces might achieve their military aims in such a
war, but the cost in terms of war damage would be prohibitive.

Nuclear Parity.   While Ogarkov's language on the existence of
strategic parity was not as unequivocal at this time as it would become after 1982, there are several indications that in the late 1970s
he was already moving in that direction. First, in his 1978 *Kommunist* article he conceptualized Soviet military policy by employing the

---

[16] Ogarkov, "Military Strategy," p. 564. Emphasis added.

[17] Hasegawa, "Soviets on Nuclear-War-Fighting," p. 6.

[18] John Erickson, "The Soviet View of Deterrence: A General Survey," *Survival* 24, no.
6 (November–December 1982): 242–51.

[19] Cited in Notra Trulock and Phillip Peterson, "Soviet Views and Policies Toward
Theater War in Europe," forthcoming in Bruce Parrott, ed., *The Dynamics of Soviet Defense
Policy*, p. 12.

Marxist idea of quantitative to qualitative transformation.[20] As he used it, this concept referred to the process by which the accumulation of weapons would reach the point at which the nature of conflict would change. He did not appear to attach any direct policy relevance to this idea at the time. Later, however, he would use it to argue for the existence of nuclear parity. It was almost as if the category had been resurrected for that specific purpose, as if Ogarkov had waited for the right moment to tie it directly to strategic parity.

Second, in a 1978 article in *Pravda*, Ogarkov observed that "the existence of strategic arms and their state of combat-readiness make it possible to give any aggressor an immediate and crushing answer. And the advocates of war can no longer fail to take this . . . into account."[21] He repeated this theme in his *Kommunist* article that same year, arguing that Soviet strategic forces were capable of "immediately delivering a powerful retaliatory strike on an aggressor in any area of the globe."[22] He made it again in his 1980 *Izvestiia* article, where he noted "the existing, approximate correlation of the sides' military forces" and commented on "existing approximate equality in medium-range nuclear means in Europe."[23] Finally, in his entry on "Military Strategy" in the *Soviet Military Encyclopedia* he observed that in the event the Soviet Union is attacked, the other side would "receive an annihilating retaliatory strike."[24] While his statements did not directly mention the term deterrence, they followed the same general pattern of statements by Soviet military theoreticians who argued that since it was impossible for either side to deliver a crushing first strike, a condition of nuclear parity existed at the strategic level.

Third, Ogarkov publicly endorsed Brezhnev's Tula speech, with its renunciation of military superiority, only a month after he made it.[25] He reiterated this point in 1979 in *Partiinaia zhizn'*, quoting

---

[20] N. Ogarkov, "Voennaia nauka i zashchita sotsialisticheskogo otechestva" ("Military Science and the Defense of the Socialist Fatherland"), *Kommunist*, no. 7 (1978): 110–21.

[21] N. Ogarkov, "Velikii podvig sovetskogo naroda" ("The Great Feat of the Soviet People"), *Izvestiia*, May 9, 1978.

[22] Ogarkov, "Military Science and the Defense of the Socialist Fatherland," p. 118.

[23] Ogarkov, "The Great Feat of the Soviet People," and N. Ogarkov, "V interesakh povysheniia boevoi gotovnosti" ("In the Interests of Raising Combat Readiness"), *Kommunist vooruzhennykh sil*, no. 14 (July 1980): 26.

[24] Ogarkov, "Military Strategy," p. 564.

[25] N. Ogarkov, "Strazh rodiny" ("Guarding the Motherland"), *Sovetskaia Rossiia*, February 23, 1977.

Brezhnev's *Time* magazine interview, "we are not seeking military superiority over the West, we do not need that. We need only reliable security."[26]

While none of these statements taken by itself, is proof that Ogarkov believed nuclear weapons were an undesirable tool for fighting a war, taken together they suggest that he was clearly moving in that direction. More importantly, from 1963 to 1981 there is not a single place in any of his articles or speeches where he advocated the use of nuclear weapons. As a professional military officer, he recognized the need for the military to be in a position to fight such a war if it came to that, but he never spoke of nuclear weapons as his preferred weapons. Given Ogarkov's tendency to be outspoken on issues he felt strongly about, it seems highly unlikely that he would have remained quiet on such a key issue if he had disagreed with his political or military colleagues on it.

Enforcing a Combined-Arms Approach.   Given the budgetary constraints facing the Soviet military when he took over, it was clear to Ogarkov that Soviet resources had to be carefully allocated, even more so than in the past. Likewise, it was becoming increasingly evident that if the Soviet military was to be successful on the battlefield, Ogarkov would need the complete cooperation of all of the military services. In essence, this meant a combined-arms strategy (i.e., the actions of all services would have to be subordinated to the control of a single frontal commander). Indeed, improving coordination among Soviet forces became one of the hallmarks of Ogarkov's tenure as chief of the General Staff. He was seized with the need to develop operational concepts that would improve the performance of Soviet forces in a future war, be it nuclear, conventional, or a combination of the two. "War," Ogarkov argued, "consists of a complex system of interrelated, powerful, simultaneous, and successive strategic operations."[27] He warned:

> Military operations in different areas (on the ground, in the air, and on the sea) are conducted through the joint efforts of all the branches of the armed forces in the interests of achieving a single objective—victory over a possible enemy. Neglecting this requirement of the dialectic could lead to one-sided judgments and conclusions and to the

---

[26] N. Ogarkov, "Guarding the Soviet Motherland's Interests," *Partiinaia zhizn'*, no. 4 (1979), *FBIS, The Soviet Union*, Annex, March 27, 1979, p. 6.

[27] Ogarkov, "Military Strategy," p. 564.

exaggeration of the role of one or another branch of the armed forces or form of strategic operations to the detriment of the others.[28]

In short, Ogarkov's task was to ensure that all Soviet military operations would come under the control of central military authorities, with no room for those who favored independent operations.

When he took over as chief of the General Staff, Ogarkov faced three seemingly formidable opponents, senior military officers who had long been strong, vocal advocates for their services—Marshal Tolubko of the SRF, Marshal Batitskiy of the PVO, and Admiral Gorshkov of the navy. One of his first tasks was to bring these three independent and assertive officers into line, so as to ensure that Soviet military strategy, not SRF, PVO, or naval strategy, would occupy first place in the operational plans of their services.

Under Grechko, the SRF had been considered special—the "heart" or "basis" of Soviet military power—despite the increasing importance of the other services. Ogarkov, however, decided that this had to change: the SRF had to lose its privileged position.

To begin with, in contrast to his predecessor, during the late 1970s Ogarkov stopped ranking the various military services. Instead, he utilized the term "strategic nuclear forces" to describe the Kremlin's strategic nuclear arsenal. As he put it in his 1978 *Kommunist* article, "Following the creation of *strategic nuclear forces*, for the first time in the entire history of war, the strategic command acquired at its disposal means which could immediately hit the aggressor with a powerful counterstrike anywhere in the world."[29] Thus, as early as 1978, Ogarkov clearly considered all three of the services having strategic nuclear weapons (the SRF, the navy, and the air force) to be playing important, if not equally important, roles in this area. That Ogarkov was not alone in his attitude toward the SRF is evident from an article by General Cherednichenko, who utilized the term "strategic nuclear forces" in his 1979 entry on strategic operations for the *Soviet Military Encyclopedia* (which was edited by Ogarkov).[30]

Marshal Tolubko's retreat from his independent stance was evident by the end of 1977. In February 1977, for example, just after

---

[28] Ogarkov, "Military Science and the Defense of the Socialist Fatherland," p. 116.

[29] Ibid., p. 118. Emphasis added.

[30] M. I. Cherednichenko, "Strategicheskaia operatsiia" ("Strategic Operations"), in Ogarkov, *Sovetskaia Voennaia Entsiklopediia*, vol. 7, p. 551.

Ogarkov took over as chief of staff, Tolubko observed that "the current *basis* for the combat might of the Soviet armed forces is the Strategic Rocket Forces."[31] By December, however, Tolubko had retreated to more "Ogarkovian" language, observing that "the rocket forces have been transformed into the reliable shield of the motherland." He made a similar observation in an article in *Kommunist vooruzhenykh sil*.[32] Thus, by the time his *Kommunist* article went to press, Ogarkov could take satisfaction that this assertive head of the SRF was publicly supporting the new line. Taken together, Ogarkov's 1978 *Kommunist* article, the Cherednichenko entry in the *Soviet Military Encyclopedia*, and Tolubko's retreat suggest that this important change in Soviet military thinking occurred almost as soon as Ogarkov took over and not in 1981 as some have maintained.[33]

Ogarkov's efforts to enforce closer cooperation among the various services continued when he took on Admiral Gorshkov, long considered one of the most independent of the Kremlin's military leaders. In 1976 the first edition of Gorshkov's *Seapower and the State* had prompted considerable debate in Soviet military circles, as Gorshkov appeared intentionally to underestimate the role of other Soviet forces. In the new edition of 1979, however, Gorshkov compromised and accepted both the importance of a unified military strategy and the need to subordinate and integrate the navy in this strategy. "It is therefore right, in our view, to examine under today's conditions not a great number of strategies, even within the framework of one unified strategy, but rather the strategic employment of the branches of the Armed Forces brought about by their specific features and the sphere of their employment within the framework of the unified military strategy." While conceding the need for a unified strategy, Gorshkov also called for recognition of the navy's role in the nuclear area: "the tendency . . . to concentrate strategic nuclear means in the navy's sphere of operations calls for the further

[31] Speech by Army Gen. Vladimir Fedorovich Tolubko, USSR deputy minister of defense on the 59th Anniversary of the Soviet Army and Navy, Moscow Domestic Service in Russian, February 22, 1977, *FBIS, The Soviet Union*, February 30, 1977. Emphasis added.

[32] V. Tolubko, "Moguchaia sila" ("A Mighty Force"), *Krasnaia zvezda*, December 29, 1977; V. Tolubko, "Vsegda na strazhe, vsegda nacheku" ("Always on Guard, Always Alert"), *Kommunist vooruzhennykh sil*, no. 23 (December 1977): 10–11.

[33] Michael J. Deane, Ilana Kass, and Andrew G. Porth, "The Soviet Command Structure in Transformation," *Strategic Review*, Spring 1984, p. 63.

growth of the Soviet navy in ocean theaters and directions in war."[34] Within four years the symbolic equality of the navy (and of the SRF and air force) would be formally enunciated by Ogarkov in a key article in *Izvestiia*. Shortly thereafter the primacy of Soviet military doctrine was emphasized with the discontinuation of the separate degree in naval science. In the future, Soviet naval officers would receive the same degree as officers from the other services. However, Gorshkov was not the type of person to capitulate completely in such situations, and during the early 1980s he would again lobby for greater freedom for the Soviet navy. But Ogarkov had apparently succeeded in making his point: Soviet naval strategy would be subordinate to overall Soviet military strategy.

The third major obstacle to Ogarkov's effort to develop a more efficient combined arms strategy was the PVO. Writing in the mid-1970s, spokesmen from the PVO, including Marshal Batitskii, argued vigorously for an expanded Ballistic Missile Defense system. Their major argument was that since the Soviet Union still faced the danger of a surprise attack, and since antiair defense forces could play a role in limiting damage, it was important "that the air defense system be continuously upgraded and able to destroy not only air-breathing weapons, but also ballistic missiles and satellites."[35] In essence, this was an argument for further expanding the role of the PVO.

It soon became evident, however, that the PVO's push for a greater role in Soviet military planning had failed. For example, by 1977 Marshal Batitskii had published a pamphlet accepting a narrower definition of the PVO's mission, and a year later he was removed from his position as head of the PVO.

In contrast to the SRF, the navy, and the PVO, the other two service chiefs, Marshal Kutakov (air force) and General Pavlovskii (ground forces) did not oppose Ogarkov's efforts to coordinate service activities more closely. In Kutakov's case, this was probably due

[34] S. G. Gorshkov, *Morskaia moshch' gosudarstva* (*Sea Power and the State*), 2d ed. (Moscow: Voenizdat, 1979), p. 317.

[35] Bruce Parrott, *The Soviet Union and Ballistic Missile Defense*, Johns Hopkins School of Advanced International Studies (SAIS) Papers in International Affairs, 1987, pp. 34–35. As far as this writer can determine, Parrott is the first to note the PVO's independent line in this area.

to the fact that the air force looked upon strategic nuclear operations as one of its less important roles. For example, in listing the air force's primary tasks at this time, Kutakov places such actions ("the destruction of the enemy's military-industrial capability") in third place behind the maintenance of air supremacy and the carrying out of frontal operations.[36] Thus the air force stood to be only minimally affected by Ogarkov's push for greater integration among the services.

Insofar as Pavlovskii was concerned, the ground forces had the most to gain in the short run from closer coordination of the various services. After all, since the vast majority of the key integrated commands would go to ground service officers, Ogarkov's modifications would further enhance their role within the military establishment. Thus it is not surprising that Pavlovskii was one of Ogarkov's strongest supporters.

Ogarkov's disciplining of the various services laid the groundwork for a more effective and integrated combined-arms strategy. All services would henceforth be expected to work closely together in resolving problems. According to one source, a new Strategic Nuclear Force (SNF) was created, one which "integrated the nuclear weapons of the services into a single command."[37] Whether or not such a command was actually created—this is the only reference in the literature to it—Ogarkov had placed the three key services on an equal footing. And this in effect broadened the parameters of the nuclear planning process. Service-specific strategies would no longer be acceptable. It was becoming increasingly necessary to think on a broader scale in such matters. As a consequence, the focus for such planning was increasingly centered in the General Staff.

Ogarkov's success in developing a joint approach in dealing with nuclear weapons, like his disciplining of the PVO, also had important implications for the Soviet military's attitudes toward arms control. The message was clear: arms control is important, and service interests will not be permitted to stand in its way. Furthermore, the service-wide approach taken by the General Staff in dealing with these matters made it easier to integrate force structure and arms

---

[36] P. Kutakov, "Voenno-vozdushnye sily" ("The Air Force"), *Voenno-istoricheskii zhurnal*, no. 10 (1977): 43.

[37] J. L. Sherer, *Soviet Biographical Service* 2, no. 1 (January 1986): 1.

control questions. Service parochialism would not disappear as a result of Ogarkov's actions, but the ability of a Soviet general or admiral to influence the process in favor of one service or another would become increasingly difficult.

Having won the initial battle with the SRF, navy, and PVO, Ogarkov still faced the problem of implementing the new approach insofar as it impacted on particular weapons systems and operational concepts. It was to this task that he next turned his attention.

Ensuring Coordination at the Theater Level.   For Ogarkov, the key to operations at the theater level was mobility, maneuverability, sustainability—and surprise. As early as 1963 he had stated that "overcoming the opponent by means of energetic surprise maneuvers—that is the direction in which the creative plans of the commander and the organizing work of the staff should be aimed."[38] Indeed, if there was anything Ogarkov felt strongly, it was the need to avoid the "blind ally" of positional warfare. Throughout his writings, Ogarkov stressed the importance of mobility, speed, and decisive action regardless of what type of weapons were being employed. Not only was he opposed to the idea of positional defense, but he also did not agree with the concept of a driving frontal assault. In short, for Ogarkov the ultimate disaster would be static operations whether they be offensive or defensive. Perhaps partially as a result of his own personality, the idea of sitting back and waiting to absorb a blow from the enemy or blindly striking at a deeply entrenched foe in traditional Soviet fashion did not appeal to him. He was much more attracted by the prospect of amassing forces at a carefully selected point and then exploiting the success thus achieved with the swift action of armor, infantry, and other forces. In short, Ogarkov wanted to be in a position to call the shots and in this sense bears a striking resemblance to military commanders like Patton and Rommel. One suspects that in the event of a war Ogarkov's forces would have specialized in the unexpected: in swift movements of forces over large distances that would hit the enemy where he least expected it.

Recognizing a problem is one thing, coming up with an ap-

---

[38] N. Ogarkov, "Vremia i eshche raz vremia" ("Time and Once Again Time"), *Krasnaia zvezda*, September 7, 1963.

proach for dealing with it is another. While much work had been done toward developing and implementing many of these concepts before Ogarkov had become chief of the General Staff, it was clear that additional efforts would be required before the Soviet military would be in a position to implement the strategic principles he outlined. As he stated in 1978, "our military cadre understand that there are a number of insufficiently studied problems, the resolution of which will demand their intensive work and creative efforts."[39] But most of all, such a resolution would require the creation of a structure that would ensure the close integration of all forces at the theater level. As he put it:

> an operation of a group of fronts came into being and was given broad theoretical justification and practical application. The joint efforts of the unified organizations and formations of all branches of the armed forces seized space up to 1,000 kilometers long and were characterized by the high rate of offense and resulted, as a rule, in the encirclement and defeat of large groupings of the enemy. This was a basically new phenomenon in Soviet military art.[40]

Fascinated with this problem, Ogarkov suggested in his 1979 *Soviet Military Encyclopedia* article on military strategy that the introduction of an intermediate structure between Theaters of Military Action—an old concept in the Soviet military—and the high command offered a way to increase coordination at the theater level. In essence, Ogarkov was faced with the problem of fighting a war involving great geographical expanses, with a wide variety of weapons systems in which instantaneous decisions could and would decide the course of the war. Operations at this (continental) level would, in Ogarkov's words, involve the "operations of the fronts, while in maritime areas it will include operations by the navy, the air force, airborne troops, and naval infantry, combined airborne and other operations including the use of nuclear armed missiles and air strikes." Such operations would be different because of their size, fluidity, and the tremendous mobility of forces: "Contemporary op-

---

[39] N. Ogarkov, "Sovetskaia Voennaia nauka" ("Soviet Military Science"), *Pravda*, February 19, 1978.

[40] N. Ogarkov, "An Immortal Feat," *Oktiabr'*, no. 5 (May 1980), Joint Publications Research Service, 76226, p. 65.

erations will be characterized by increased scope, a violent struggle for gaining and retaining strategic initiative, a high degree of maneuverability, the movement of groups of military forces in different directions in situations where the front is undefined, where one side has made deep penetrations, where there are quick and sharp changes in operational-strategic directions." The only way to ensure success at this level was to make certain that all relevant TVD operations were under the direct command of a single combined-arms commander. For his part, Ogarkov did not go into the details of the new structure at this time. In fact, it appears that they were still being worked out. However, his subsequent discussion of the issue makes it clear that he looked upon them as a key, indeed, as *the* key element in ensuring "close and uninterrupted mutual operations in war and strategic operations."[41]

Deep Operations.   When it came to a mode of operations, to a concept around which Ogarkov could tailor actions at the theater level, he seized on deep operations, an idea that had been present in the Soviet military for many years. In fact, Ogarkov had singled out this concept as early as 1963: "In the course of combat it is necessary simultaneously to influence the entire depth of the opponent's battle formation."[42] Another sign of the importance he assigned to deep operations is the fact that of the three articles Ogarkov authored for the eight-volume *Soviet Military Encyclopedia*, one was devoted to deep operations. In 1976, a year before he took over as chief of the General Staff, Ogarkov discussed the historical background of the concept and wrote that as originally defined, it meant

> the simultaneous suppression of the enemy's defense by means of destruction to its whole depth and breaking through its tactical zone on a selected axis with a subsequent swift development of tactical success into operational by committing to the battle an echelon for the development of this success (tanks, motorized infantry, cavalry) and the landing of airborne assaults for the most rapid achievement of the assigned mission. The theory of the deep operation showed a way out of the positional blind alley which was created in military art during World War I. It represented a fundamentally new theory

---

[41] Ogarkov, "Military Strategy," p. 564.
[42] Ogarkov, "Time and Once Again Time."

for the conduct of offensive operations by massive, technically equipped armies.

Using World War II as a backdrop, Ogarkov explained that his concept called for concentrating forces at one specific point with the goal of achieving a breakthrough, or, as he put it, "the need for massive application of forces and weapons on the decisive axes." Once the breakthrough was achieved, it had to be exploited. Toward that end, mobile groups were created. As Ogarkov put it: "To develop success, second echelons of strong mobile groups, as well as reserves of all branches of arms, were created in fronts and armies. Mobile groups were intended to develop offensive operations to a great depth and at a high tempo. They were created in fronts, where they consisted of one to two tank armies, and in armies, where they consisted of 1-2 tank or mechanized corps." The primary function of such groups was to encircle and cut off enemy troops, a task that he reports as having been successfully carried out during World War II: "In carrying out operations, great successes were achieved in the art of encircling major enemy groupings by the forces of one or several coordinating fronts. The art of eliminating encircled groupings by splitting them into parts early in the course of the encirclement and subsequently destroying them was further developed." Turning to the postwar period, Ogarkov noted that the basic principles underlying the theory had continued to be developed. However, he added, the term has fallen into disuse: "The term deep operation has not been used in official documents since the 1960s."[43] Presaging the importance he would later attach to it, Ogarkov observed that it remained an important concept in Soviet military planning. Indeed, he maintained, the appearance of nuclear weapons and the mechanization of Soviet forces had led to a "qualitative leap in the development of the armed forces" which had "increased the capability for simultaneously impacting on the entire depth of enemy formations, breaking through the enemy's defenses at high tempos and swiftly developing success." In practice, this meant that Soviet forces were in a position to advance quickly, to change directions as necessary, and thus to hit the enemy before he knew what was hap-

---

[43] N. Ogarkov, "Glubokaia operatsiia" ("Deep Operations"), in Ogarkov, *Sovetskaia Voennaia Entsiklopediia*, vol. 2, pp. 574, 578.

pening. In short, even before his appointment as chief of the General Staff, Ogarkov had seen deep operations as key to the future development of the Soviet armed forces at the theater level.

From the Soviet standpoint, deep operations also had important implications for the Kremlin's efforts to "wage the war with conventional weapons and win it quickly . . . in order to make escalation less likely."[44] In practice, deep operations presented the possibility of not only striking quickly and deeply and defeating Western forces before they could make a decision to escalate to nuclear weapons, they also provided an opportunity to overrun large segments of Western nuclear force arsenals, thereby seriously degrading Western nuclear assets—which in turn could also raise doubts in the minds of Western policy-makers over the advantages of resorting to nuclear weapons.

Operational Modifications. While most of the operational changes were to become visible to the West later, Ogarkov began to introduce a number of modifications aimed at increasing coordination while at the same time enhancing the striking power of Soviet forces, especially at the theater level. As one source put it with regard to the latter, "From the mid-1970s, the Soviet armed forces started to absorb large quantities of high-performance weapons systems which enhanced considerably the effectiveness of their combat operations."[45]

Aviation. To begin with, shortly after Marshal Batitskii's retirement as chief of the air defense forces in 1978, air defense assets, including fixed-wing aircraft, were subordinated to the army front commander. He would control these assets in the event of a war. As Peterson put it, "At the Military District (MD) level, the new command and control relationships are apparently reflected in 'air forces of the MD' and 'air defenses of the MD' which would better facilitate the conduct of air and defense operations in any given continental TMO [Theater of Military Operations]."[46] In essence, it would be

---

[44] C. N. Donnelly, "Operations in the Enemy Rear," *International Defense Review* 13, no. 1 (1980): 35.

[45] "Soviet Intelligence: New Generation Weapons and the Doctrine of Tactics," *Jane's Defense Weekly*, June 14, 1986, p. 1102.

[46] Phillip A. Peterson, "Reorganization Trends," in Paul J. Murphy, *The Soviet Air Forces* (London: McFarland and Co., 1984), p. 275.

the front commander who would determine how such assets would be utilized, thereby ensuring that they would be better able to provide fire support of ground force operations at that level. Likewise, the subordination of air defense forces would also contribute to his ability to deal with intruding Western aircraft, a matter of great concern to Soviet ground commanders.

In retrospect, the buildup in frontal aviation had been under way for some time. For example, from 1967 to 1977 frontal aviation aircraft had "increased by about 50 percent its inventory of tactical aircraft." Indeed, by 1977 "over 60 percent of the fighters in Frontal Aviation were those that had entered production after 1969." Finally, a potent assault helicopter force based primarily on the Mi-24 Hind and Mi-8 Hip helicopters was added, and the Soviets began to conduct training exercises designed "to weld tank, motorized rifle, and attack helicopter units into mutually-supporting combat teams."[47] Helicopters not only provided a way of inserting troops near the front but were also equipped with a wide variety of ordnance to support Soviet ground forces.

Artillery. In addition to the air assets that were placed at the disposal of the front commander, the Soviets also enhanced his artillery holdings. To begin with, the number of artillery pieces increased. One study suggests that in comparison with 1965, the number of artillery pieces grew from 122 to 202 in a motorized rifle division and from 68 to 112 in a tank division.[48] According to another source, beginning in 1978 the amount of self-propelled artillery in a tank division was increased to "include the addition of a . . . battalion to every . . . regiment."[49] In addition, the firepower of artillery holdings also grew as the Soviets concentrated on heavy artillery. Self-propelled and towed 152mm guns, the 203mm gun, the 240mm mortar, and the 220mm multiple rocket launcher that were added during the latter part of the 1970s were all capable of striking deeper and harder than their predecessors. In practice, this

[47] James H. Hansen, "The Development of Soviet Aviation Support," *International Defense Review* 13, no. 5 (1980): 683, 684.

[48] Charles Dick, "The Growing Soviet Artillery Threat," *Royal United Services Institute*, June 1979, p. 70.

[49] Phillip A. Peterson and John G. Hines, "The Conventional Offensive in Soviet Theater Strategy," *Orbis* 27, no. 3 (Fall 1983): 724.

meant that "targets within 30 kilometers of the forward line of troops can be engaged with these heavy artillery weapons or by Hind assault helicopters."[50] On the one hand, this decreased the vulnerability of such weapons to Western counterattacks, while on the other enhanced their ability to support deep operations. Taken together, the modifications in aviation and artillery meant that the front commander—who must make instantaneous decisions—would now be better able to concentrate fire and forces where he believed it would do the most good: he would not have to wait for a service chief in Moscow or the General Staff to give him permission to use these weapons.

Air Assault Operations. In order to provide the front commander with a vehicle for conducting operations against targets deep in the enemy rear, air assault brigades were created. These brigades, "appear to be capable of conducting parachute, heliborne, or air and land operations in enemy rear areas. These brigades, which would be controlled at the front level, probably are equipped with amphibious airborne infantry combat vehicles (BMDs) and organic artillery support." Such units could be used to "disrupt or destroy nuclear weapons, airfields, command, control and communications facilities, logistic facilities and key terrain."[51] Assuming they were successful, these units would not only facilitate the forward movement of Soviet forces, they would also significantly increase the chances of degrading Western nuclear assets.

Intensified Pact Integration. Intensified Pact integration also became a priority item under Ogarkov. For example, a special meeting of Pact military leaders devoted to integrating scientific activity was held in Warsaw in late 1977. According to a Polish source:

> A conference under the title "Current Problems and the Main Directions of the Development of Military Science of the Socialist Countries" took place at the Academy of the General Staff on December 14–15. Delegations from the Soviet Army, the Bulgarian People's Army, the National People's Army of the GDR, and the Hungarian People's Army took part and the meeting was presided over by Chief

---

[50] "Soviets Refurbish Artillery for Deeper Attack Missions," *Defense Week*, December 5, 1983.

[51] John G. Hines and Phillip A. Peterson, "The Soviet Conventional Offensive in Europe," *Military Review* (April 1984) 23.

of the General Staff, General of Arms F. Siwicki. The Conference has become an important factor in the further integration of scientific activities in the armies of the Socialist Commonwealth.[52]

More important from a military perspective, former Polish Colonel Kukliński has argued that the Soviets scored a major victory in their effort to enforce Pact integration in 1979, when they gained East European acceptance (with the exception of the Romanians) of a document entitled "Statute of the Joint Armed Forces and Their Organs in Wartime." Under the terms of this statute the East European military forces are for practical purposes almost completely subordinated to the control of the Soviet high command during wartime. In essence, according to Kukliński, the Soviets now had the capacity both to bypass national commands in a crisis situation and to exert control over individual East European forces. The statute is so secret, according to Kukliński, that "even the branch and military district commanders know only those provisions that affect them directly."[53]

Theaters of Military Action (TVDs). By the mid-1970s the Soviets were working out their thoughts on how to structure TVDs. Students at the Voroshilov General Staff Academy were being told "that Europe had been divided into three continental TSMAs (TVD)."[54] In a broader context, the Soviets played with the possibility of various geographical divisions, including Near Eastern, Middle Eastern, Northeastern, and Northern TVDs. The Soviets were clearly attempting to come to grips with the problem of how better to coordinate military actions between the national command authorities and those at the theater level.

The second half of the 1970s was an important period for the

[52] "Kronika" (Chronicle), *Wojskowy Przeglad Historyczny*, no. 2 (1978). Details concerning this conference, which was singled out by Gareyev for special attention (Frunze, "Voennyi teoretik," pp. 374–75), are contained in "O dalszej integracje działalności naukowej w armiach wspólnoty socjalistycznej" ("Concerning the Further Integration of Scientific Activities in the Armies of the Socialist Commonwealth"), *Żolnierz Wolności*, December 16, 1977. I am indebted to Ross Johnson for bringing these two articles to my attention.

[53] "Wojna z narodem widziana od srodka" ("At War with the Nation Seen from the Center"), *Kultura*, no. 4/475 (Paris 1987): 54–55.

[54] John G. Hines and Phillip A. Peterson, "Changing the Soviet System of Control," *International Defense Review* 19, no. 3 (1986): 283.

Soviet military. Ogarkov had provided the general outline for the future course of Soviet warfighting doctrine—an emphasis on combined arms, mobility, maneuverability, and, if possible, the avoidance of escalation to the use of nuclear weapons. In addition, he had disciplined three of his subordinate commanders whose independent attitude toward the operation of Soviet force might make implementation of a closely integrated combined-arms strategy difficult. All of the services—at least in public—were now dancing to the same tune.

In addition, while many of the details of the operational modifications that would be made during the first half of the 1980s were still not evident to Western observers, it was clear that major changes were under way, that Ogarkov and his colleagues were looking for and experimenting with alternate ways of fighting a future war, specifically one at the theater level. A strategic conflict remained a possibility, but for Ogarkov, at least, the existence of nuclear parity at that level lessened significantly the chances of such an occurrence. The task was to ensure that a theater conflict remained conventional. Furthermore, in contrast to Grechko, whose only solution to the problems facing the Soviet military was increased military budgets, Ogarkov believed that money could be saved by streamlining structures and procedures within the armed forces.

Management, Technology, and Leadership

Ogarkov's strong commitment to technology put him solidly in line with Brezhnev. Unlike Grechko, who had also understood the importance of technology within the Soviet military, Ogarkov saw no incompatibility between the need for a technological restructuring of the Soviet economy and a relaxation of tensions in East-West relations. Indeed, this relaxation would provide the necessary breathing space to enable the USSR to get its economic house in order.

Meanwhile, Ogarkov was seized with the need to force the Soviet military to begin to think creatively about the application of modern technology to military affairs. In this context it is worth noting that Ogarkov had been a long-time advocate of greater attention to modern technology in the Red Army. For example, before becoming chief of the General Staff Ogarkov had been even more outspoken than Grechko and Kulikov in calling for the Soviet military to do more in this area. Writing in 1971 in *Red Star*, for example, he had argued that "nuclear missile weapons and other new combat equipment have radically changed the methods and forms of conducting military actions, have created completely new connections and interdependencies between strategy, operational skill, and tactics, have led to substantial changes in the organizational structure of troops, and have made it necessary to reorganize the system of educating and training personnel." While much work had been done to adapt the Soviet military to changing circumstances, more was needed:

> one must not think that we have already accomplished and learned everything. More thorough research is needed, for example, into the problems of improving the quantitative and qualitative relationships between people and equipment, and of establishing the most expedient relations between the branches of the armed forces and within them, and also into the problems of improving organizational forms, decisionmaking methods, the communication of mission information to troops and equipment for controlling troops.

Furthermore, Ogarkov added, military officers "can no longer be content with knowledge of the tactical and technical data and equipment." Present and future problems cannot be resolved on the basis of past solutions: "It is impossible to approach the assessment of possible future battles simply by using the yardstick of past battles." Or, as he had stated elsewhere, "The military leader must look ahead." Then Ogarkov lashed out at those officers who do not keep abreast of the latest developments in technology:

> There is also, I believe, a more substantial reason for the *shortcomings* pointed out. It lies in the fact that *individual military leaders* do not keep pace with life and the development of scientific thought. Our higher colleges and military academies give the cadets and students good theoretical knowledge. But when officers come to the troops, some of them get bogged down in petty business, do not supplement their theoretical knowledge and even lose it. A decisive struggle must be waged against such an attitude.[55]

---

[55] N. V. Ogarkov, "Teoreticheskii arsenal voennogo rukovoditelia" ("The Theoretical Arsenal of the Military Leader"), *Krasnaia zvezda*, September 3, 1971, *FBIS, The Soviet Union*, September 10, 1971, p. m2. Emphasis added.

Ogarkov has generally been considered the Soviet military's leading advocate of the importance of modern technology in the last twenty years. Indeed, from his writings he appears to be almost a technical determinist. However, with two exceptions, Ogarkov's views on the significance of modern technology mirrored those of Grechko and Kulikov. The exceptions were the greater fervor with which he approached the problem and his heavy emphasis on the need for Soviet military officers to avoid focusing on fighting the last war and instead think creatively about how to deal with future military threats. This latter idea was inherent in Grechko's writings, but Ogarkov made it explicit, gave it greater importance, and injected a special sense of urgency into his discussion of it. It was probably a combination of his tendency to focus on the need "to think new," his high public profile (by Soviet military standards) on such issues, and his advocacy of high-technology conventional weapons that led many in the West to believe that this issue had originated with him.

To Ogarkov, the modern military world was a scene of dynamic change; only by adapting to change—indeed, only by being ahead of it—could the Soviet military hope to be competitive. Ogarkov's efforts to force a traditionally conservative, backward-looking officer corps to focus on the future were evident from the beginning. As he observed in February 1978, "past experience cannot be blindly copied and mechanically introduced into contemporary practice, cannot be approached with the standards of the past. Life urgently demands that we make certain corrections in the theory and practice of military affairs."[56] Or, as he put it two months later, "The views which have developed in one or another area of military knowledge are not eternal. They change with our knowledge and the development of military affairs and together with changes in objective circumstances."[57]

This concern with change—a key aspect of Ogarkov's thought process—was the basic theme of his 1978 *Kommunist* article. The three laws of the dialectic, which Ogarkov outlined in his article and subsequently utilized to lay a foundation for understanding

---

[56] Ogarkov, "Soviet Military Science."
[57] Ogarkov, "Military Science and the Defense of the Socialist Fatherland," p. 117.

changes in Soviet warfighting strategy, also served as a vehicle for sensitizing Soviet officers to the need to keep up with the changing nature of military affairs. For example, as Ogarkov utilized it, the unity of the struggle of opposites becomes an object lesson in why Soviet military officers should never consider the current situation permanent. Instead, they should look at the present as a guide to the future. According to Ogarkov, the classic example of the unity and struggle of opposites in the military sphere was the interaction between offense and defense:

> The history of war convincingly proves, for example, the existence of a permanent contradiction between means of attack and of defense. The appearance of new means of attack has always led to the creation of corresponding contradictions, but in the final analysis, this led to finding new means for waging battles and combat and for the conduct of operations. Thus, with the fast development of tanks, aviation, and submarines, antitank, antiaircraft, antisubmarine weapons and corresponding methods of defense were developed.[58]

The lesson for the Soviet military officer was that whatever exists is subject to change and that he should always be on the look-out for the next weapon or new type of strategy. This is also true of changes in military organization. As Ogarkov observed in 1979, "modern weapons are introducing substantial changes into the forms and methods of conducting hostilities and the organization of troops and naval forces."[59] This put a premium on intellectual curiosity and flexibility. The stereotyped conservative, unimaginative Soviet officer who relied on traditional methods for operating in the armed forces had no place in Ogarkov's military.

Furthermore, as one analyst has noted, Ogarkov was primarily concerned not with evolutionary but with revolutionary changes. He distinguished between "a slow accumulation of experience (exercises, field trials, even operational experience in local wars), and a rapid assimilation of new technologies and technologies based on modeling and simulation." Indeed, Ogarkov reportedly established

---

[58] Ibid.
[59] Ogarkov, "Guarding the Soviet Motherland's Interests," p. 9.

a think tank within the General Staff to help elaborate his concept of a high-technology future for the armed services.[60]

Like Grechko, Ogarkov continually stressed the importance of science in meeting the demands of contemporary warfare. His message was simple. Military affairs have become increasingly complex, more and more dependent on developments in science and technology; the Soviet military must make greater use of science if it hopes to remain competitive in the contemporary world. To quote Ogarkov, "Together with the resolution of current practical problems, the most important task at the present time is the further implementation of fundamental and basic research and analysis, the increasing of the comprehensiveness and validity of scientific prognosis, and the further development of military affairs in general."[61] Indeed, in an effort to emphasize the significance of developments in the area of science and technology, Ogarkov argued that "our military science entered a qualitatively new stage of development."[62] Obviously, if military science was in a new stage of development, then new approaches were needed to deal with it.

Ogarkov's response to the question of how the Soviet military should respond to the increasing importance of science paralleled that of Grechko. Two things had to occur. First, scientific research had to have military relevance: "The interests of the further development of Soviet military science requires the optimal combination of basic with applied research." Second, scientific research had to go beyond the narrow confines of military science. It had to incorporate all the latest developments from throughout Soviet society. This called for closer contacts with civilian institutions:

> New forms of advancement of scientific research in military training institutions and the scientific establishments of the USSR Ministry of Defense are developing. There is a strengthening cooperation with the USSR Academy of Sciences, scientific-research institutes, design bureaus, and other scientific centers not only in our country, but in the other socialist states. The comprehensive study of military-politi-

---

[60] Rose E. Gottemoeller, "Conflict and Consensus in the Soviet Armed Forces," forthcoming in Parrott, ed., *The Dynamics of Soviet Defense Policy*.

[61] Ogarkov, "Soviet Military Science."

[62] Ogarkov, "Military Science and the Defense of the Socialist Fatherland," p. 136.

cal, military-theoretical, military-technical, and military-historical problems is achieved through joint efforts.[63]

Such an approach has obvious implications for the civilian-military interface in the scientific sphere. To the degree that scientific institutions—ones not previously involved in such relationships—are drawn into close cooperation with military institutes, their independence and ability to conduct unclassified research will be limited.

Like Grechko before him, Ogarkov was concerned about improving the education and training of Soviet military personnel. Ogarkov, however, added a new twist: military officers were to be trained not only to operate increasingly complex equipment, but to educate as well. As Ogarkov saw it, the educational level of the young soldier or sailor entering the Soviet armed forces was increasing. If officers hoped to interact with them in a positive fashion not only did they need to be technical experts themselves, they also required pedagogical skills. They had to be able to educate as well as to lead: "Every military training establishment must display greater concern not only for military-technical training and the instilling of high personal ideological-political and moral qualities in students, but also for shaping in them the ability and skill of a future personnel educator, instilling a taste for conducting educational work in subunits and units and on ships."[64] The blind obedience common to the Russian military of the past was not Ogarkov's preferred approach for dealing with problems in the increasingly complex, high-technology armed forces.[65]

According to a former career Soviet military officer, Ogarkov was thought to be the moving force behind the 1971 decision to introduce "warrant officers—the *michmen* of the navy and the *praporshchiki* of the rest of the armed services—into the Soviet armed forces. The primary purpose of this new rank, according to this of-

[63] Ibid., pp. 142, 143.

[64] N. Ogarkov, "Povyshat' vospitatel'nuiu rol' sovetskikh vooruzhennykh sil" ("Raising the Educational Role of the Soviet Armed Forces"), *Krasnaia zvezda*, June 5, 1980.

[65] This increased emphasis on science, technology, and education was also manifested in the quantitative and qualitative increase in articles written by senior nonacademic officers in specialized journals such as *Voennyi vestnik* and *Morskoi sbornik*. Articles by senior officers holding important operational commands began to appear regularly in the latter part of the 1970s.

ficer, was to provide a cadre of technically competent individuals at the tactical level, who would serve extended periods in the military and function as the primary interface between officers and enlisted personnel. The result, it was hoped, would be a military better able to meet the demands of modern warfare.[66]

In addition to pushing Soviet military officers to play a greater educational role, Ogarkov called upon all segments of the military establishment, "military councils, commanders and staffs, political organs, the party, and Komsomol organizations," to assume greater responsibility for ensuring that Soviet soldiers and sailors would be both well-trained and politically motivated.[67]

The education and training effort within the military was of special concern to Ustinov; in fact, during the latter part of the 1970s he focused as much attention on it and mentioned it as frequently as did Ogarkov. Writing in 1978, for example, he observed that "a great deal of effort is required from all personnel to achieve highly coordinated actions and to gain complete mastery of modern weapons." Ustinov observed that "the quality of the educational process . . . is changing" and admonished his readers that "soldiers are not born but made: and the higher the quality of training and educational work and the closer to battle conditions in which land, sea and air exercises take place, the faster the process will be."[68] For both these men, education and training were integral to the future of the Soviet armed forces, and while they did not discuss it in as much detail as they would in the early 1980s, it was clearly a matter of concern to them. For them, the military was only as good as the technical capabilities of its personnel.

Command and control (*upravlenie*) was an area of special importance to Ogarkov. In fact, he mentioned it in almost every one of his major articles during the latter part of the 1970s. In his first major article as chief of staff he singled it out as one of the Soviet military's major concerns and called upon his colleagues "to search

---

[66] Conversation between the author and a former Soviet navy commander now residing in the West.

[67] Ogarkov, "In the Interests of Raising Combat Readiness," p. 27.

[68] D. F. Ustinov, "Shest'desiat let na strazhe zavoevanii Velikogo Oktiabria" ("Sixty Years on Guard Over the Gains of the Great October"), Moscow Domestic Service, February 22, 1978, *FBIS, The Soviet Union*, February 24, 1978, pp. v12, v13.

for better means of controlling troops in all elements [i.e., land, sea, and air] with the use of modern means of communication and automation."[69] Several months later, he again focused on command and control, arguing strongly that a new approach to the problem was needed. He stated that commanders' possibilities, "based on the old control methods, can no longer meet such requirements. In this respect, the automation of troop management through computers plays a great role. In turn, success in the use of automated control systems calls for raising the level of military-technical standards of commanders, the scientific organization of the work of staff, and efficient communications at all levels."[70] Of particular interest is Ogarkov's reference to the work of staffs. Military staffs have been around for a long time, but with greater attention now being focused on command and control, their importance within the Soviet military grew. It is not an accident that one of the three articles written by Ogarkov for the *Soviet Military Encyclopedia* dealt directly with staffs.

In this entry, Ogarkov argued that command-and-control forms the brain of the military, especially in a combat situation. Thousands of pieces of data are received at headquarters, and a tremendous amount of data must be processed and analyzed before it is useful to a commander. As modern warfare becomes more complex and the decision time available to a commander diminishes, the role of a staff increases. Ogarkov remarked with regard to a 1970s staff:

> In connection with the equipping of the armed forces with a series of types of nuclear weapons, missile technology, and new means of communication and electronics, the staff has become more multifaceted and responsible, but the conditions of its work have become even more difficult. In the most developed armies the staff masters automated systems of command and control, including computer technology, immediate and secure communications: in the practical work of the staffs, new methods of work are being introduced.

Without an efficient staff, Ogarkov argued, no commander could hope to perform his duties effectively. He observed in concluding his entry on the topic that there was a need for a further improve-

---

[69] Ogarkov, "Soviet Military Science."
[70] Ogarkov, "Military Science and the Defense of the Socialist Fatherland," p. 117.

ment in staffs, their equipment, and personnel: "Under new conditions, the work of the staff produces increased demands on the level of theoretical, operational-tactical, and technological preparation of staff officers, who should be distinguished by high qualifications and staff culture, by a deep and detailed knowledge of their subject."[71] In a certain sense, Ogarkov was returning to the point he had made earlier about personnel—well-trained officers and soldiers are the key to the future of the Soviet military, especially in an era dominated by advanced technology.

While Ustinov had less to say on the subject, it is noteworthy that he as well spoke out on the need for improvements in command and control:

> The state of combat readiness depends to a considerable extent on standards of management of troops and naval forces and primarily on the commanders' ability to lead subordinate subunits, units, and ships in a skillful way, on the farsightedness of their operational and tactical prognoses, on the realistic nature of their intentions and plans, and on their ability to maneuver forces and facilities in a flexible and mobile manner. . . .
>
> The task is to introduce into wider practice progressive methods of combat management and everything new that has been developed into this sphere by the scientific and technical revolution. It is necessary to try to ensure that the readiness of the management system is always in advance of the general combat readiness of the formation, unit, or ship and is higher and more mobile than it.[72]

However one looks at it, both Ogarkov and Ustinov considered improvements in military management to be imperative.

Adaptation to the demands of modern technology was a matter of high priority to both Ogarkov and Ustinov. The latter put it best in 1980 when he observed: "A subject of constant concern of the Party and its Central Committee is *the further development of military science and military art, the modernization of party political work, the systematic preparation of cadres, and the practical training and education*

---

[71] N. Ogarkov, "Shtab" ("Staff"), in Ogarkov, *Sovetskaia Voennaia Entsiklopediia*, vol. 8, p. 535.

[72] D. Ustinov, "Na strazhe revoliutsionnykh zavoevanii" ("On Guard over Revolutionary Achievements"), *Kommunist voorruzhennykh sil*, no. 21 (November 1977): 12.

of the personnel of the Soviet army and fleet."[73] Clearly, this was an issue that would continue to figure prominently in the writings and speeches of both men.

SOCIOPOLITICAL ISSUES

Economic Pressures

According to the CIA, in 1977, shortly after Grechko's death, the rate of growth in Soviet defense spending began to drop from about four to five percent per year to about two percent per year. While the CIA claims that all services "shared in the reduced growth in spending," some services were hit harder than others: "for example, total outlays for the Strategic Rocket Forces declined in absolute terms after 1977." The same was true of the air defense forces. The "main source of slower growth in defense spending was a stagnation in spending for military procurement after 1976"; the report argues that since the "stagnation in procurement" had lasted for seven years, it must be the result of a conscious decision: "This plateau arguably lasted too long to be the result exclusively of bottlenecks or technological problems."[74]

Like any senior military officer, Ogarkov would have preferred a larger rather than a smaller budget. However, he was prepared to work within the parameters laid down by the political leadership—the military would have to do more with less. This approach was based on a number of assumptions. First, by streamlining Soviet military operations and by enforcing a combined-arms strategy, Ogarkov believed that money could be saved at all levels. We have seen how Ogarkov was successful in forcing Tolubko, Batitskii and Gorshkov to accept a joint approach to problems of military strategy and how he pushed concepts like deep operations and rejuvenated TVDs as vehicles for ensuring greater integration among services in combined-arms operations. Second, the de-emphasizing of the SRF

---

[73] D. Ustinov, "Rukovodiashchaya rol' KPSS v stroitel'stve sovetskikh vooruzhennykh sil" ("The Leading Role of the CPSU in the Development of the Soviet Armed Forces"), in Ustinov, *Izbrannye rechi i stat'i*, p. 494. Emphasis in the original.

[74] "Allocation of Resources in the Soviet Union and China—1984 Hearings before the Subcommittee on International Trade, Finance, and Security Economics, 99th Congress, 2d sess., pt. 10, November 21, 1984, and January 15, 1985, pp. 53, 54.

and the PVO cited by the CIA fits in well with Ogarkov's preference for increased attention to conventional weapons with a concurrent downplaying of strategic nuclear systems. In similar fashion, the transfer of air defense assets to frontal commanders would diminish the need to spend as much money on this service. As many people in the West have argued, money can be saved by combining forces. And third, Ogarkov recognized more clearly than most of his contemporaries that the greatest danger facing the Soviet military was technological obsolescence. If the lagging Soviet economy was to produce the high-technology weapons that Ogarkov believed to represent the wave of the future, then the USSR would need a respite as the economy and the Soviet military was restructured to deal with the Western threat. The key to Ogarkov's respite was arms control.

As those who met him can testify, Ogarkov was a hard-nosed and brilliant negotiator. He was not a person to make unilateral concessions. If he came out in favor of arms control—in this case, SALT I—at a time when his military superiors opposed the idea, it was because he believed it served Soviet military interests. In essence, from Ogarkov's standpoint, SALT I and II offered not only predictability but also the prospect of an environment of diminished threat, one in which the Soviet military would be able to focus its resources on restructuring the economy so that it might compete in the area that really counted: high technology. From his writings, however, one can see that in 1979 and 1980 Ogarkov began increasingly to believe that the premises upon which he based his expectations were collapsing. The result was his increased alienation from the Brezhnev leadership, a situation that by 1981 had led to a major split between the Soviet military's chief of staff and its defense minister.

This increasing sense of dissatisfaction was most evident in Ogarkov's comments on the defense budget. Writing in May 1977, for example, some four months after he had become defense minister, Ogarkov noted that "our glorious army and navy now have the most modern combat equipment and possess everything necessary to fulfill the tasks facing them."[75] Ogarkov continued to use this

---

[75] N. Ogarkov, "The Great Feat of the People," *Izvestiia*, May 9, 1977, *FBIS, The Soviet Union*, May 12, 1977.

formulation or close variants of it through May 1978, when he noted that the Soviet army and navy "have everything necessary" to defend the Soviet Union.[76] From this point on, however, his approach began to change. In his 1979 *Partiinaia Zhizn'* article, Ogarkov warned that "the socialist countries cannot turn a blind eye to the fact that the Western powers are continuing to implement and accelerate military preparations in every sphere."[77] In May 1980 he observed that "our army and navy now have the most perfect weapons and military equipment and their might and combat readiness have risen to a qualitatively new level." He added a few months later in an article in *Kommunist vooruzhennykh sil* that the party was "taking the necessary steps to further strengthen the defense of the country."[78] The interesting aspect of these latter two citations is that they both conveyed the impression that more needed to be done. To be sure, the party was working on the matter, but Ogarkov avoided saying that the military had everything it needs.

Ustinov's comments are of particular interest during this period; in contrast to those of the early 1980s, these tend to parallel those of Ogarkov. In 1977 Ustinov like Ogarkov, began by arguing that the Soviet military was "provided with everything necessary for sustenance, combat training, and military service."[79] By 1979 Ustinov had adopted a more cautious line and noted only that "our armed forces are at a level sufficient to ensure that no one can encroach with impunity on our motherland's security and prevent the building of socialism and communism."[80] Similarly, in 1980 he observed that in view of the threat facing the USSR, Moscow "is maintaining its defenses, the military strength of the Armed Forces of the USSR, at a level that ensures peaceful conditions for the construction of communism."[81] Clearly from both Ustinov and Ogarkov's points of view

[76] N. Ogarkov, "Velikii podvig sovetskogo naroda" ("The Great Feat of the Soviet People"), *Izvestiia*, May 9, 1978.

[77] Ogarkov, "Guarding the Soviet Motherland's Interests."

[78] N. Ogarkov, "Exploit for the Sake of Peace," *Komsomol'skaia pravda*, May 9, 1980, *FBIS, The Soviet Union*, May 27, 1980; Ogarkov, "In the Interest of Raising Combat Readiness," p. 27.

[79] D. Ustinov, "Strazh mirnogo truda, oplot vseobshchego mira" ("Guarding Peaceful Labor, the Bulwark of Universal Peace"), *Kommunist*, no. 3 (1977): 16.

[80] D. Ustinov, "Vysokii rubezh istorii" ("A High Point in History"), *Pravda*, May 9, 1979.

[81] Ustinov, "The Leading Role of the CPSU in the Development of the Soviet Armed Forces," p. 501.

something had happened which raised questions about the sufficiency of the military budget after 1978.

Ogarkov's and Ustinov's concern over the military budget appears to have been the result of three factors. First, as Ogarkov
noted, NATO's decision to adopt the Long-Term Development Program in 1978, which eventually led to the deployment of the Pershing IIs and ground-launched cruise missiles, meant that the military threat facing the Soviet Union was increasing. Second, by
1979, even before the invasion of Afghanistan, Ogarkov had begun
to suggest that SALT II was in trouble. Third was the American
military buildup initiated by the Carter Administration. Regardless
of who won the upcoming American election, the military threat
facing the Soviet Union in the form of the MX, the Trident II, the
B-1, and other programs was likely to increase. The internal political problem for Ogarkov was that while the most rational approach
was to throw money at the problem by building up Soviet forces to
match the Americans', he was running into opposition from the Soviet political leadership.

Serious differences existed between the political leadership and
the military. On January 11, 1980, for example, an editorial in *Red
Star* argued that in view of the American military buildup, "the
CPSU and Soviet government are compelled to strengthen the defensive capability of our country, of its armed forces" and went on
to argue that while raising the standard of living of the mass of the
population was the most important goal, for the time being priority
should be given to industrial production. *Pravda*, meanwhile, reversed these priorities, arguing that improvements in the living
standard of the people should come first.[82] From Ogarkov's standpoint, the situation had worsened throughout 1979.

Chernenko, who was to be Brezhnev's successor once removed,
delivered a speech in February which argued that the SALT II treaty
would "make it possible to transfer a considerable share of the resources that are currently swallowed by the arms-race to constructive
purposes."[83] Then Brezhnev argued in his November 1979 Plenum
speech that there was no alternative to improving the lot of the gen-

---

[82] This discussion is taken from Parker, *The Kremlin in Transition.*

[83] *Sovetskaia Moldaviia*, February 27, 1979, as cited in Jeremy Azrael, *The Soviet Civilian Leadership and the Military High Command, 1976–1986*, Rand Report, R-3521-AF,
June 1987, p. 15.

eral populace.[84] All hope of increasing military spending at the expense of consumer allocations ended with the emergence of political instability in Poland, initially caused by a hike in food prices, and the recognition that food shortages in the Soviet Union could lead to domestic turmoil. As Parker observes: "As the Polish and domestic food crisis mounted, Brezhnev and his supporters used the new situation to argue that scarce marginal resources should be committed to consumer programs rather than industrial investments."[85] By 1980 Brezhnev was arguing that the Soviet military indeed had everything it needed: "Today, on the eve of the holiday of the Soviet Army and Navy, the Central Committee is able to assure the Soviet people that we have everything necessary to repulse any type of military provocation."[86]

This put Ustinov in a difficult position. As defense minister he was expected to articulate the concerns of the military high command. As a civilian, however, he had been appointed to this post in order to bring—and keep—the military budget under control. While his silence during the late 1970s on whether or not the military had everything it needed was probably a part of his own effort to maintain credibility within the high command, he indirectly supported the Brezhnev position, stating that only by improving the country's overall economic situation would it be possible to enhance its military capabilities. For example, he remarked in 1977 that

> the Tenth Five-Year Plan represents an important new stage in our country's development along the path toward communism. There will be an even bigger growth in its economic strength, and there will be further beneficial changes in the Soviet people's socioeconomic appearance as a result of the fulfillment of the tasks set by the Twenty-fifth Congress. *All this will contribute to the strengthening of the Soviet state's defense potential and the further development of its armed forces.*[87]

---

[84] L. I. Brezhnev, "Rech' na plenume Tsentral'nogo Komiteta KPSS" ("Speech at the Plenum of the Central Committee of the CPSU"), *Pravda*, November 28, 1979.

[85] Parker, *The Kremlin in Transition.*

[86] L. I. Brezhnev, "Nash kurs—mirnoe sozidanie" ("Our Course Is Peaceful Creation"), *Krasnaia zvezda*, February 23, 1980.

[87] Ustinov, "Guarding Peaceful Labor and the Bulwark of Universal Peace," p. 6. Emphasis added.

The main point here was that a reinvigorated economy would be the key to a strong defense. This was to be Ustinov's only comment of this nature during the latter part of the 1970s. It seems reasonable to assume that Ogarkov was not the only one within the upper ranks of the Soviet military who was concerned over budgetary problems and that Ustinov avoided the issue, by letting political leaders such as Chernenko and Brezhnev carry the load, in an effort not to lose whatever standing he may have had among senior military officers.

Faced with the impossibility of obtaining a faster increase in the defense budget, Ogarkov adopted what seemed to him to be the only logical course of action—closer integration of the military and civilian economies. Ogarkov began by arguing that a strong economy is key to the country's defense. In 1978, for example, he quoted Friedrich Engels as follows: "Nothing depends on economic conditions so much as a country's army and navy. Weapons, structure, organization, tactics, and strategy depend above all on the level of production and the means of communication which has been achieved at a given point in time." To illustrate his point, Ogarkov pointed to examples from World War II: After the war broke out, the Soviet economy was restructured to meet the demands of the wartime situation; new problems were encountered and new solutions found. All of the USSR's resources were put to work developing new types of weapons. As a result, Moscow "in a short time exceeded fascist Germany in the area of production."[88]

The situation had changed since the end of the war, however. Ogarkov went on to say that given the nature of modern warfare, it would not be possible to mobilize all the country's resources over a period of months in the event of a war. This must be done quickly. As Ogarkov was to remark in 1981, "Now, as never before, the coordination of the mobilized deployment of the armed forces and national economy in general is required, especially in the utilization of human resources, communications, energy, and the protection of the stability and vitality of the country's economic mechanism."[89] While he waited until the early 1980s to outline the details of what

[88] Ogarkov, "Military Science and the Defense of the Socialist Fatherland," p. 112.
[89] Nikolai Ogarkov, "Na strazhe mirnogo truda" ("On Guard over Peaceful Labor"), *Kommunist*, no. 10 (1981): 89.

he had in mind, Ogarkov was clearly laying the groundwork for stronger ties between the economy and the military. If the armed forces could not obtain significant amounts of additional funds, Ogarkov was prepared to argue that given the danger of a surprise attack (and its potentially devastating impact) and the enormity of the scope and depth of a future conflict, close ties between the two economies would be vital. In essence, this was a call for the subordination of the civilian economy to the high command. If Ogarkov could not get what he wanted by using a traditional approach, he was perfectly prepared to adopt an alternative, more creative one.

Arms Control

Ogarkov's attitude toward arms control negotiations closely paralleled the line he took on the budget. Up to the end of 1978 he was supportive, although he had begun openly expressing his concerns over events in East-West relations. After that point he began to move toward increasing opposition until by the end of 1980 he was openly opposing the line advocated by the political leadership. While also critical of the West, Ustinov was less vigorous in his expressions of concern and, indeed, supported a policy of détente throughout the period, with one exception. This was his use of alarmist language, beginning in 1980, concerning the threat of a new war; in fact, his language was almost as alarmist as Ogarkov's on this point. This may reflect his concern not to appear too forthcoming within the military in dealing with political authorities. Insofar as the political-military interface was concerned, however, the important factor is that Ustinov continued to push Brezhnev's "peace program" despite his growing concern over the climate of East-West relations.

Shortly after taking over as chief of the General Staff, Ogarkov published an article in *Sovetskaia Rossiia* that was almost euphoric in its praise of the arms control process: "In recent years the climate of international relations has warmed considerably, and there has been a move away from the cold war toward a relaxation of tension. Thanks to the vigorous activity of the Soviet Union, the socialist community countries, and all progressive forces, the danger of a new world war has receded. Peace has become more reliable and durable."[90] While supporting the arms control process, Ogarkov took a step hitherto unknown among senior Soviet military officers. He made public his own position on a key issue under discussion between the U.S. and the USSR in such a way that could be read as critical of the political leadership. Remarking on the results of Secretary of State Vance's visit to Moscow at the end of March, Ogarkov stated:

> The talks held at the end of March in Moscow . . . showed that the U.S. is trying to obtain one-sided military advantages and to encroach on the interests of the Soviet Union. This is borne out in particular by attempts to transfer artificially our medium-range bombers to the ranks of strategic arms and at the same time legalize the uncontrolled and unrestricted production of cruise missiles in the United States and thereby open up a dangerous new channel of the arms race. The desire to ensure one-sided military advantages was also manifested in the course of the talks by the fact that the proposals of the U.S. do not affect their forward-based nuclear weapons in Europe and Asia or their carrier-borne aircraft, do not take into account the possession of nuclear weapons by the NATO allies of the U.S., and so forth.[91]

What is unusual about this statement is not Ogarkov's expression of concern over the proposals Vance brought to Moscow: Brezhnev himself had complained that the trip had shown that the U.S. was moving away from "a constructive approach and for the present is putting forth a one-sided position."[92] What is unique here is that by going public with his specific concerns—something neither Kulikov nor Grechko ever did—Ogarkov was putting the political leadership on notice that he was strongly opposed to any agreement

---

[90] N. Ogarkov, "The Guardian of the Motherland," *Sovietskaia Rossiia*, February 23, 1977, in *FBIS, The Soviet Union*, March 4, 1977.

[91] Ogarkov, "The Great Feat of the People."

[92] L. I. Brezhnev, "Rech' na obede v Bol'shom Kremlevskom Dvortse v chest' Pervogo Sekretaria Tsentral'nogo Komiteta Kommunisticheskoi Partii Kuby, Predsedatelia Gosudarstvennogo Soveta i Soveta Ministrov Respubliki Kuby Tovarishcha Fidelia Kastro Rus" ("Speech at a Dinner in the Great Kremlin Palace in Honor of the First Secretary of the Central Committee of the Communist Party of Cuba, the Chairman of State Council and the Council of Ministers of the Republic of Cuba, Comrade Fidel Castro Rus"), *Pravda*, April 8, 1977.

that did not include compensation for these Western systems. Akhromeyev may have provided the logic behind Ogarkov's actions when he told a group of visiting U.S. senators that "when Secretary Vance proposed major changes in the Vladivostok formula without also being willing to put FBS back on the table . . . the Soviets saw the United States asking for new concessions on top of those already given."[93] Whatever motivated Ogarkov's action, he had introduced something new to Soviet military politics—direct public involvement by the high command in a politically sensitive issue. Where Grechko would have utilized an indirect approach to make his point, Ogarkov acted in a straightforword fashion.

Throughout the remainder of 1977 and well into 1978, Ogarkov repeated the now standard phraseology in praise of détente: socialist countries had "succeeded in achieving a turn from a cold war to a relaxation of tensions,"[94] and the "principles of peaceful coexistence of states with different social systems have been quite firmly strengthened."[95] Beginning in mid-1978, in the aftermath of the NATO Long-Term Development Program decision, a new tone of skepticism began to creep into Ogarkov's description of the international situation. In one *Kommunist* article, for example, he commented that "despite détente, . . . the imperialist states are continuing to strengthen aggressive military blocs and are modernizing their armed forces, spending huge amounts on armaments."[96] And in an article in *Izvestiia* he warned that "the threat of war has not been totally eliminated, and . . . forces exist in the world that are interested in the arms race and in whipping up an atmosphere of fear and hostility."[97] By 1979 Ogarkov was beginning to sound even more pessimistic. Writing in *Partiinaia Zhizn'*, Ogarkov raised the polemical level of his commentary a decibel when he warned that "under these conditions, the danger of war from imperialism cannot

[93] "Senate Delegation Report on SALT Discussions in the Soviet Union: A Report to the Committee on Foreign Relations, *United States Senate*, November 1979" (Washington, D.C.: Government Printing Office, 1979), p. 9.

[94] N. Ogarkov, "60 pobednykh let" ("60 Victorious Years"), *Voennyi vestnik* (October 1977): 4.

[95] N. Ogarkov, "Guarding the Conquests of Great October," *Agitator*, no. 1 (1978), *Joint Publication Research Service*, 70948, April 13, 1978, p. 2

[96] Ogarkov, "Military Science and the Defense of the Socialist Fatherland," p. 137.

[97] Ogarkov, "The Great Feat of the Socialist People."

be underestimated" and then attacked (unnamed) individuals in the Soviet political leadership "who are surprisingly ready to believe the false arguments of the NATO apologists who are trying to conceal the scale of NATO military preparations and their aggressive thrust." Ogarkov acknowledged that the completion of the SALT or of the MBFR (Mutual Balanced Force Reductions) talks "could play a major role" in "freeing mankind from the threat of a new war."[98] Despite this latter reference, however, Ogarkov's comments at this time have a decidedly more pessimistic cast. Throughout the remainder of 1979, Ogarkov continued to express concern over the course of East-West relations. He mentioned the danger of a new military conflict and argued that the forces in the West were intensifying their efforts to undermine SALT II.

Ogarkov's skeptical comments during 1979 appear to have had little if any impact on the political leadership. Brezhnev gave an interview on January 18, 1980, that set the tone for the official Soviet attitude toward the U.S. While acknowledging that the Carter Administration and NATO had taken actions that increased tensions, Brezhnev reiterated the Soviet commitment to détente. "Now in the 1980s, as earlier in the 1970s, we stand for the strengthening and not for the destruction of détente."[99]

Ustinov was more upbeat than Ogarkov on détente. In 1978, for example, Ustinov wrote of "positive changes in the world" and of the existence of a relaxation of tensions.[100] In 1979, just when Ogarkov was beginning to express skepticism concerning détente, Ustinov was arguing that "the relaxation of tension has now become an objective reality."[101] By 1980 Ustinov had become somewhat more cautious, warning that the forces of imperialism were "intensifying the arms race, fanning the flames of military conflicts in a number of regions of the world, provoking new conflicts."[102] As a

---

[98] Ogarkov, "Guarding the Soviet Motherland's Interests," pp. 6, 7.

[99] L. I. Brezhnev, "Otvety na voprosy amerikanskogo zhurnala 'Taim' " ("Answers to Questions from the American Magazine 'Time' "), *Pravda*, April 17, 1979.

[100] D. Ustinov, "Shest' geroicheskikh desiatiletii" ("Six Heroic Decades"), *Kommunist*, no. 2 (January 1978): 25.

[101] D. Ustinov, "Ustinov Moscow Speech," *Moskovskaia Pravda*, February 24, 1979, *FBIS, The Soviet Union*, March 1, 1979.

[102] D. Ustinov, "Na strazhe mira i truda" ("On Guard Over Peace and Labor"), *Pravda*, December 11, 1980.

result, he argued, the Soviet Union would combine its "peace policy" with increased attention to defense needs. Whatever he had in mind as to improvements in the country's defense national security, it is obvious that they would include a policy of détente.

Ogarkov continued throughout 1980 to express concern over East-West relations. In February, shortly after the invasion of Afghanistan, he charged Washington with making "material preparations for war" and seeking military superiority.[103] In a TASS report of a speech given by Ogarkov, he reportedly warned that "the winds of war are again blowing in international life."[104] At the same time two new themes began to appear in Ogarkov's public statements. First, he dug up an old Soviet propaganda line that he had avoided in the past: the U.S., the U.K., and other capitalist countries "pinned great hopes on Hitler's Germany as a shock force in the struggle against the land of the Soviets and gave it generous aid in restoring its military industrial potential and developing and technically reequipping its army of many millions." He further charged that the West had encouraged the Germans to move against the USSR in the hope that Berlin and Moscow would destroy each other. Second, Ogarkov began contrasting the 1970s—a period of a "relaxation of tensions"—with the more "complex" situation brought by the West "at the turn of the eighties."[105] As Ogarkov put it in a speech to military personnel on June 3, 1980: "the situation at the start of the 1980s has become noticeably more complicated and is presently characterized by extreme instability, unexpected turnabouts, and a distinct tendency toward intensification of the aggressive aspirations of the imperialist countries and China."[106] Thus, by the end of 1980 Ogarkov's public stance on détente had evolved from one of ardent support to one of skepticism and pessimism.

By the beginning of 1981 it was becoming increasingly clear

---

[103] N. Ogarkov, "Zavetam Lenina vernyi" ("Faithful to the Legacy of Lenin"), *Izvestiia*, February 24, 1980.

[104] N. Ogarkov, "Winds of Cold War," Moscow TASS in English, May 8, 1980, in *FBIS, The Soviet Union*, May 12, 1980.

[105] N. Ogarkov, "Exploit for the Sake of Peace," *Komsomol'skaia Pravda*, May 9, 1980, *FBIS, The Soviet Union*, May 27, 1980. See also, Ogarkov, "An Immortal Feat," p. 68; and Ogarkov, "In the Interests of Raising Combat Readiness," p. 25.

[106] Ogarkov, "Raising the Educational Role of the Soviet Armed Forces."

that Ogarkov was emerging as the dominant figure within the Soviet
military. He was the primary motivating factor behind the major
changes in Soviet warfighting doctrine. With Ustinov's support, he
was pushing the need for the Soviet military to adapt to the demands
of modern technology. He was leading the military's effort to increase the military budget and was increasingly downcast about the
prospects for East-West relations. If Ogarkov was assertive during
the latter 1970s, however, that was nothing compared to the position he would assume during the first half of the 1980s. While Ustinov had abdicated responsibility for warfighting doctrine to Ogarkov, Ustinov was still considered an important spokesman for
military interests. During the first half of the 1980s the situation
would develop to a point where Ustinov would be increasingly identified with the political leadership while Ogarkov would be recognized as the military's primary spokesman on issues of importance
to the armed forces.

CHAPTER 6

Ogarkov in Opposition, 1981–1984

*T*he world as Ogarkov saw it in 1981 was anything but hospitable. On the external front, he faced a revitalized NATO committed, at least on paper, to rebuilding its sagging defenses, while in Washington he was up against a new administration determined to strengthen American military capabilities across the board, from strategic to conventional. For all practical purposes the arms control process had collapsed. Events such as Afghanistan and Poland were being used in Washington to justify larger military budgets, and, from all appearances, the Reagan administration would probably get the funds it needed. The result would be a much more potent and broad-based military threat.

The internal situation was not much better. The last two years of the Brezhnev regime were marked by increasing stultification and stagnation. Indeed, as Brezhnev's health worsened, the country seemed to put itself on "automatic pilot." Decisions of any type were hard to come by, and the kind of long-range, dynamic leadership necessary to get the country moving again was out of the question. As Gorbachev noted, commenting on the late 1970s: "Everybody started noticing the stagnation among the leadership and the violation of the natural process of change there." To make matters worse, the economy—on which the modernization of the Soviet military depended—was a mess and by all appearances the future outlook was for further deterioration. Again to quote Gorbachev: "The country began to lose momentum. Economic failure became more frequent. Difficulties began to accumulate and deteriorate, and resolved problems to multiply. . . . a kind of 'breaking mechanism' affecting social and economic development formed."[1]

---

[1] Mikhail Gorbachev, *Perestroika* (New York: Harper and Row, 1987), p. 22, 18.

Faced with these seemingly intractable external and internal problems, Ogarkov adopted a dual strategy. First, he would continue his efforts to build up Soviet conventional and high-technology forces and to force the Soviet military to do more to adapt to the needs of the technological revolution. Regardless of what happened on the international scene, Ogarkov was convinced that his approach of moving away from primary reliance on nuclear weapons toward increased emphasis on high-technology conventional forces was the wave of the future. There was still much to be done to introduce needed modifications operational procedures, and the concepts underlying his preferred approach needed further amplification and development.

Second, on the political front, Ogarkov would oppose any efforts to improve East-West relations. It was not so much that he opposed arms control per se; indeed, he had long been a leading advocate of the arms control process. In light of events in Poland and the Soviet Union's own internal problems, however, he felt he could read the writing on the wall. The political leadership would seize on any progress in arms control to justify cutbacks in military programs. Such an approach would make sense under two circumstances. First, it would have to contribute to the containment of military threat from the West. Seen from the perspective of 1981, the situation was not encouraging. The U.S. had refused to ratify SALT II, was conducting a polemical campaign against Moscow, one unprecedented in recent years, and, most importantly, was engaged in a massive military buildup. The Americans seemed to be primarily interested in expanding their arsenal. As a result, the prospect for meaningful arms control in the immediate future was not good.

A second concern of Ogarkov's was the Soviet economy. Not only was he faced with the prospect of a political leadership prepared to use arms control to control the rate of increase in military spending—this might have been acceptable if the economy had been strong enough to enable the Soviet military to compete with the Americans in the one area that mattered, high technology. But the reality was that the Soviets were falling further behind, and the only hope Ogarkov saw was in the allocation of increasingly greater amounts of rubles to the military—in essence, throwing money at the military's technological problems. What was really needed from Ogarkov's perspective was a political leadership that would combine an arms control agenda with a vigorous approach to revitalizing the

Soviet economy. In the early 1980s such a leadership was lacking. As a consequence, on both the arms control and economic fronts, Ogarkov saw no alternative to adopting a strategy aimed at minimizing his losses.

As was the case during the latter half of the 1970s, Ustinov found himself in a difficult position. He was a senior member of the political leadership, yet he was also the defense minister. He was thus forced to straddle two functions: it was his task to attempt to make Ogarkov and the other top generals accept Brezhnev's agenda, but it was also his task to make certain that the Politburo, of which he was a full member, understood the generals' concerns. Failure to carry out the latter responsibility would undermine his standing within the military. He could command under such circumstances, but hardly lead. For his part, Ustinov appears to have decided to continue to be supportive of Ogarkov's efforts in the military-technical area. In discussing Soviet warfighting doctrine, Ustinov avoided going into the level of detail that Ogarkov did, but he did make several statements in support of the line the former was pushing. This was primarily Ogarkov's area of responsibility, but Ustinov wanted to be supportive of his chief of staff's efforts to improve the effectiveness of Soviet forces. Meanwhile, he was also fully behind Ogarkov's efforts to force traditionally minded Soviet officers to take greater cognizance of the demands of the scientific-technological revolution. Ustinov was himself close to being a technological determinist, and he could not have been more supportive of Ogarkov's efforts in this area. When it came to sociopolitical issues, however, Ustinov held the line against the generals. Issues such as arms control and the military budget were too sensitive from a political standpoint to permit Ogarkov and his colleagues to dictate policy. But if Ustinov was to maintain his credibility within the military establishment, he, the outsider, had to be careful how he handled himself in public. The result was what often appeared to be a series of contradictions in Ustinov's comments. For example, while warning that the world was moving closer to the brink of war, Ustinov also reaffirmed the importance and viability of improved East-West relations. The problem with Ustinov's attempt to combine these two apparently contradictory approaches derived from his chief of staff's outspokenness and defiance in presenting his views on the policies advocated by the political leadership in these two critical areas. Ustinov soon found himself in open opposition to Ogarkov. Indeed, Ogarkov's single-minded stubbornness in arguing for what he considered to be the military's (and the country's) best interests in these areas forced Ustinov to make a choice in 1981, one that he had managed to avoid during the latter part of the 1970s. Not surprisingly, when push came to shove, the life-long party apparatchik came out on the side of his general secretary. This in itself may help explain the reports that Ogarkov enjoyed wide popularity among the rank and file of the Soviet armed forces. Not only was he a highly regarded thinker—his 1982 monograph was required reading in military schools and academies—but he, unlike Ustinov, was in the soldiers' view prepared to stand up to the politicians and "tell it like it is." In this sense, Ogarkov was a very unusual Soviet military officer, one who would almost certainly succeed in alienating many, if not most, of his political colleagues.

One of the most interesting aspects of the early 1980s was the degree to which Ogarkov's ideas in the military-technical area seem to mirror those later espoused by Gorbachev. For example, by the end of his tenure as chief of staff, Ogarkov appeared to be moving toward acceptance of many of the ideas of what was later called a doctrine of sufficiency; he argued in favor of utilizing science and technology to modernize the Soviet Union and claimed that the only way the Soviet military could be effective would be by producing a new Soviet man, one instilled with a spirit of personal responsibility, initiative, creativity, and competence.

MILITARY TECHNICAL ISSUES

Warfighting Strategy

Throughout the first half of the 1980s Ogarkov continued to develop his ideas and make changes in the operational procedures of the Soviet military to make it better able to fight in a conventional, non-nuclear environment.

Ogarkov's view on the nature of a future war, especially one involving the use of nuclear weapons, remained unchanged throughout this period. As he noted in his 1981 *Kommunist* article, such a war would:

—be a decisive clash between two opposing social systems;
—cover all continents of the world;
—involve the use of the entire arsenal available to each side; and
—not be comparable with wars of the past in terms of ferocity or scale of potential destruction.

Indeed, Ogarkov concluded: "The very nature of modern weapons is such that if they are put into play, the future of all humankind would be at stake."[2] Or as Ogarkov stated in 1983: "if sixty-one states had been dragged into the maelstrom of World War II, with total losses at more than fifty million people, in the next war, if imperialism unleashes one, the consequences simply cannot be foreseen. It could mean the threat of disaster for the whole of civilization. And this is what the transatlantic strategists and their NATO allies could bring humanity to unless they are stopped in time."[3] Finally, in his 1985 monograph entitled *History Teaches Vigilance*, Ogarkov added an additional characteristic of a future war in noting that, "military activity will occur in many areas at the same time, be distinguished by unprecedented destructiveness, have a highly maneuverable, dynamic character, and last until the *total defeat of the enemy.*"[4]

In understanding Ogarkov's logic, it is important to emphasize that he was not advocating the use of nuclear weapons. Indeed, he assumed that the West would be the first to utilize such weapons. This point is important, as a number of Western writers have asserted that Ogarkov opposed the political leadership on the nuclear question and argued for nuclear aggression not only in the late 1970s, but throughout his tenure as chief of the General Staff as well. In 1981 Brezhnev observed in an interview in *Pravda* that "he who has decided to commit suicide can start a nuclear war in the hope of emerging victorious from it. Whatever strength the attacker may have and whatever means of starting a nuclear war he may

---

[2] N. Ogarkov, "Na strazhe mirnogo truda" ("On Guard Over Peaceful Labor"), *Kommunist*, no. 10 (July 1981): 85. See also N. Ogarkov, *Vsegda v gotovnosti k zashchite otechestva (Always in Readiness to Defend the Fatherland)* (Moscow: Voenizdat, 1982), pp. 46–47.

[3] N. Ogarkov, "Miru—nadezhnuiu zashchitu" ("Reliably Defend Peace"), *Krasnaia zvezda*, September 23, 1983.

[4] N. Ogarkov, *Istoria uchit bditel'nosti (History Teaches Vigilance)* (Moscow: Voenizdat, 1985), p. 77. Emphasis added.

choose, he will not achieve his aims. Retaliation is unavoidable."[5] The Strodes cite an observation in Ogarkov's 1982 book—"The fundamental principal of this preparation was and remains, learn to defeat a powerful, technically equipped opponent in any condition of modern war"—as evidence that Ogarkov refused to accept Brezhnev's argument as to the futility of employing nuclear weapons as a means for achieving policy goals.[6] Similarly, Hasegawa argues that "the major emphasis" in Ogarkov's 1982 book "was on the necessity to have a nuclear-war-fighting strategy. Nuclear weapons were not set apart from other weapons; both would have to be integrated into operational planning."[7] Both writers are correct in one respect: Ogarkov was ruling out "neither the need to fight a nuclear war nor the necessity for the Soviet military to be in a position to prevail in a world war; after all, he remarked as noted above that any such conflict would result in the total defeat of one side or the other. Furthermore, Ogarkov denied neither the importance of nuclear weapons nor that a conflict might not involve their use. In fact, his 1985 monograph observed that even a local war could lead to a world war in which nuclear weapons would be utilized: "Under those circumstances, it is not excluded that a war, having begun as a local conflict, might turn into a world war, as happened with the Second World War, or that a war in which conventional weapons are utilized might turn into a war in which nuclear weapons will be employed."[8] However, his attitude toward such weapons was more nuanced than is sometimes assumed in the West.

In essence, what Ogarkov was arguing is that if a world war occurred and the West decided to go nuclear, the consequences would be catastrophic. He never ceased to point out that the Soviet Union was prepared for such a contingency and, if such a war was forced on it, had sufficient nuclear and conventional capabilities to survive and even prevail. But that was not his preferred option. Indeed, one could speculate that Ogarkov may well have been one of

[5] L. Brezhnev, "Otvety na voprosy korrespondenta 'Pravdy' " ("Answers to Questions from a *Pravda* Correspondent"), *Pravda*, October 21, 1981.

[6] Dan L. Strode and Rebecca V. Strode, "Diplomacy and Defense in Soviet National Security Policy," *International Security* 8, no. 2 (Fall 1983): 92.

[7] Tsuyoshi Hasegawa, "Soviets on Nuclear-War-Fighting," *Problems of Communism* 35, no. 4 (July–August 1986): 73.

[8] Ogarkov, *History Teaches Vigilance*, p. 13.

the strongest supporters of Brezhnev's "no first use of nuclear weapons" policy. Anything that helped keep the conflict from going nuclear was in the Soviet military's interest. And if such a pledge would help undercut Western willingness to use nuclear weapons, all the better.

Nuclear Parity. Ogarkov's attitude toward nuclear weapons was best illustrated by his comments on nuclear parity during the early 1980s when he expanded on previous statements and became more explicit than he had been in the late 1970s. In his 1982 monograph, for example, Ogarkov spoke openly of the existence of "parity," said that the main purpose of the strategic nuclear forces was as a deterrent, and argued that the most important task for the Soviet armed forces in the event of a war was to be able to deliver a "devastating retaliatory blow" if the other side initiated hostilities.[9] In May 1983 Ogarkov went even further, arguing that while nuclear weapons may have played an important role in the 1950s, this was no longer the case. Relying on the second law of the dialectic, the shift from quantity to quality, which he had first introduced in his 1978 *Kommunist* article, Ogarkov maintained that an important change had taken place: "The arsenal of various kinds of nuclear warheads and means of delivery stockpiled in the world runs to many tens of thousands. These quantitative changes have led to qualitative changes: that which could have been achieved by nuclear weapons twenty to thirty years ago is impossible for an aggressor now. A crushing retaliatory nuclear strike awaits him!"[10] Ogarkov elaborated on this point the next year in his now famous *Red Star* interview, where he observed that "the quantitative accumulation of nuclear weapons . . . has led to radical qualitative changes in the conditions and potential for the use of these weapons."[11] Ogarkov argued that because of the immense size of the respective nuclear arsenals, it would no longer be possible for either side to believe it could deliver a devastating first strike. No matter what the attacker

[9] Ogarkov, *Always in Readiness to Defend the Fatherland*, pp. 40, 49, 58. See also N. Ogarkov, "Nadezhnyi oplot sotsializma i mira" ("The Reliable Bulwark of Socialism and Peace"), *Krasnaia zvezda*, February 23, 1983.

[10] N. Ogarkov, "Pobeda i sovremennost'" ("Victory and the Present"), *Izvestiia*, May 9, 1983.

[11] N. Ogarkov, "Zashchita sotsializma: opyt istorii i sovremennost'" ("The Defense of Socialism: The Experience of History and the Present"), *Krasnaia zvezda*, May 9, 1984.

did, the other side would have many nuclear weapons left over that any potential originator of such a conflict would have to assume that he would suffer a crushing retaliatory strike. The quantity of nuclear weapons thus led to a qualitative change in the role of such weapons. Indeed, the idea of a nuclear war as a rational means for achieving policy goals had become meaningless: "The grim reality of our day is that in contrast to the past, the very correlation of very important categories like 'war' and 'policy' have changed. Only when you have definitely lost your sense of reason can you try to find arguments or to define a goal that would justify unleashing a world nuclear war, thus confronting human civilization with the threat of destruction."[12] Up to this point, Ogarkov's attention had been focused on a world nuclear war in which, he believed, nuclear weapons would inevitably be utilized. But what about the limited use of nuclear weapons?

Limited Nuclear War.   Ogarkov has been unequivocal in his attitude toward limited nuclear war since he first addressed it in 1982. In his view, a limited nuclear war is not only unrealistic, it is impossible. He observed in his 1982 monograph that "confining nuclear war to some kind of limited framework is impossible."[13] Then, in his *Izvestiia* article published a few months later, he reiterated his position, noting that "to confine nuclear war within some kind of limited framework is a fantasy."[14] He made the point again for Western readers in a 1983 interview with *New York Times* reporter Leslie Gelb, where he commented that "the idea of a nuclear war has never been tested, But by logic, to keep such a war limited will not be possible. Inevitably, such a war will extend to all-out war."[15] Ogarkov returned to this issue in his 1984 *Red Star* interview:

> The calculation of the strategists across the ocean, based on the possibility of waging a so-called "limited" nuclear war, now has no foundation whatever. It is utopian: any so-called limited use of nu-

---

[12] N. Ogarkov, "Nemerknushchaia slava sovetskogo oruzhiia" ("The Unfading Glory of Soviet Arms"), *Kommunist vooruzhennykh sil*, no. 21 (November 1984): 14.

[13] Ogarkov, *History Teaches Vigilance*, p. 16.

[14] N. Ogarkov, "Vo imia mira i progressa" ("In the Name of Peace and Progress"), *Izvestiia*, May 9, 1982.

[15] Leslie H. Gelb, "Soviet Marshal Warns the U.S. on its Missiles," *New York Times*, March 17, 1983.

clear facilities will inevitably lead to the immediate use of the whole of the sides' nuclear arsenal. That is the terrible logic of war. Their arguments about the possibility of a so-called "limited nuclear strike without retaliation" against the enemy's main centers and control points are even more groundless. Such arguments are pure fantasy.[16]

Ogarkov repeated this argument a year later in an article in *Kommunist vooruzhennykh sil*; in his 1985 monograph he made the same point even more strongly: "however limited the use of nuclear weapons, it will inevitably lead to the immediate use of the entire nuclear arsenal of the sides."[17] In dealing with this issue, Ogarkov was unusually categorical in ruling out the possibility of limited war, suggesting as one writer put it that "the intended audience may not be only in the West but his own military establishment."[18]

Conventional Warfare. Ogarkov's greatest contribution to Soviet military doctrine stemmed from his belief that nuclear weapons were becoming increasingly less useful, that their use would spell disaster for the Soviet Union. He believed that the future belonged to high-technology conventional systems. In this regard, Ogarkov had spoken of the importance of weapons based on new physical principles beginning as far back as 1971. He returned to this idea throughout his writings over the years, but only in the mid-1980s did he begin to explain how he saw them in relationship to other weapons systems. A key article in *Izvestiia* in 1983, where he also argued that a major change was taking place in the utility of nuclear weapons, highlighted the increasing importance of high-technology conventional weapons:

> At the same time, existing strategic as well as operational and tactical means of waging the armed struggle are being energetically improved, and new ones are being created on the basis of the latest achievements of electronics and other technical sciences. Considerably improved automated systems for the control of troops and weapons and highly effective new conventional means of the armed strug-

[16] Ogarkov, "The Defense of Socialism: The Experience of History and the Present."

[17] Ogarkov, "The Unfading Glory of Soviet Weapons"; Ogarkov, *History Teaches Vigilance*, p. 39.

[18] Notra Trulock, "Soviet Perspectives on Limited Nuclear Warfare," in Fred Hoffman, Albert Wholstetter, and David Yost, eds., *Swords and Shields* (Lexington, Mass.: Lexington Books, 1986), p. 68.

CHIEFS OF THE GENERAL STAFF

Matvei Vasilevich Zakharov
April 1960–March 1963 and
November 1964–September 1971

Viktor Georgievich Kulikov
September 1971–January 1977

Nikolai Vasil'evich Ogarkov
January 1977–September 1984

Sergei Fedorovich Akhromeyev
September 1984–December 1988

DEFENSE MINISTERS

Andrei Antonovich Grechko
April 1967–April 1976

Dmitrii Fedorovich Ustinov
April 1976–December 1984

Dmitri Timofeyevich Yazov
May 1987–present

Sergei Leonidovich Sokolov
December 1984–May 1987

gle are being developed and introduced. The framework of the armed struggle is also being considerably extended. In the United States, for instance, space strike systems for military purposes and weapons complexes based on new physical principles are being created.[19]

Ogarkov went into even greater detail in his 1984 *Red Star* interview. According to Ogarkov, three major changes had occurred in recent years in military affairs. The first was the decreasing value of nuclear weapons as a result of their quantitative proliferation. The second was the increasing importance of conventional high-technology weapons systems. As he put it:

> rapid changes in the development of conventional means of destruction and the emergence in the developed countries of automated reconnaissance-and-strike complexes, long-range, highly accurate, terminally guided combat systems, unmanned flying machines, and qualitatively new electronic control systems make many types of weapons global and make it possible to increase sharply (by at least an order of magnitude) the destructive potential of conventional weapons, bringing them closer, so to speak, to weapons of mass destruction in terms of effectiveness. The sharply increased range of conventional weapons makes it possible immediately to extend active combat operations not just to the border regions, but to the whole country's territory, which was not possible in past wars. This qualitative leap in the development of conventional means of destruction will inevitably entail a change in the nature of the preparation and conduct of operations, which will in turn predetermine the possibility of conducting military operations using conventional systems in qualitatively new, incomparably more destructive forms than before.

For his third major change, Ogarkov argued that "the rapid development of science and technology in recent years creates real preconditions for the emergence in the very near future of even more destructive and previously unknown types of weapons based on new physical principles."[20] Work on such weapons, Ogarkov warned, is already under way; he went on to argue that it would be a serious mistake not to consider their implications "right now." In his 1985 monograph Ogarkov argued that "conventional weapons approach

---

[19] Ogarkov, "Victory and the Present."
[20] Ogarkov, "The Defense of Socialism: The Experience of History and the Present."

nuclear [weapons] in terms of their combat characteristics and effectiveness."[21]

The emergence of such weapons raised questions about the existing Soviet structure and, according to one analyst, led to a major debate within the Soviet armed force over the role of tanks.[22] For his part, as early as 1978 Ogarkov had expressed doubt over the utility of tanks, suggesting that they might not be able to withstand contemporary precision-guided missiles.

As far as the issue of high-technology weapons is concerned, Marshal Kulikov appears to have been on Ogarkov's side. He warned in February 1984 that NATO was equipping its troops with a new "generation of conventional weapons, and above all long-range precision weapons, modern means of air defense and radio-electronic combat, and projected command and control and communications systems."[23] In the convoluted world of Soviet military writings, warnings of the development of new systems by the other side are more often than not aimed at a domestic Soviet audience; in this case, Kulikov was affirming to other Soviets his belief in the importance of these weapons in their own arsenal. Numerous other articles appeared in the Soviet military press extolling the importance of such weapons. For example, General Vorob'ev published an article in *Red Star* just a week after Ogarkov was ousted praising the value of conventional weapons.[24]

Meanwhile, other officers, led by ground forces' chief Petrov, indirectly attacked Ogarkov's questioning of the role of tanks by arguing that despite the emergence of high-technology weapons, tanks continued to play a critical role on the contemporary battlefield. It is reported that Petrov himself threatened at one point to resign when Ogarkov attempted to have the ground forces disbanded as a separate service; Medvedev has suggested that Ogarkov's relations with his colleagues on this issue lacked "total mutual un-

---

[21] Ogarkov, *History Teaches Vigilance*, p. 25.

[22] Rose Gottemoeller, "Conflict and Consensus in the Soviet Armed Forces," forthcoming in Parrott, ed., *The Dynamics of Soviet Defense Policy*.

[23] V. Kulikov, "Guarding Peace and Labor," *Sovetskaia Rossiia*, February 23, 1984, FBIS, *The Soviet Union*, February 24, 1984.

[24] I. Vorob'ev, "Sovremennoe oruzhie i taktika" ("Modern Weapons and Tactics"), *Krasnaia zvezda*, September 15, 1984.

derstanding."[25] As long as Ogarkov was chief of staff, however, the focus would be on conventional weapons and, in particular, on those relying on high technology.

By the end of 1984 the outlines of Ogarkov's conceptual model for future war was becoming clear: nuclear weapons would be useful primarily to deter other nuclear weapons, and, unless forced to this by the other side, he would not advise their use. Indeed, he would agree with Ustinov's observation in 1982 that such weapons should be utilized only in "exceptional" circumstances.[26] Even the limited use of nuclear weapons represented a serious danger for the Soviet Union. Ogarkov wanted to keep all conflict conventional, especially one in Europe with its potentially serious implications for the Soviet heartland. The future of conventional war, however, lay in high technology. After all, as the Israelis had shown so recently, high-technology weapons in the hands of well trained and motivated soldiers could have a devastating impact. Indeed, the existence of reconnaissance strike complexes by the Israelis had enabled them to score their one-sided victory over the Syrians: the destruction of some eighty Syrian (and Soviet-made) aircraft without a single Israeli loss made clear that this development could not be ignored. The Soviets believed that these new weapons were already present in the West, and, with the normal Soviet military pessimism concerning their ability to compete with the West technologically, the situation was likely to get worse. A rethinking of Soviet strategy, tactics, and perhaps even force structure was in order.

To a large degree it was this belief, that the future lay with conventional arms and high technology, which motivated Ogarkov as he attempted to modify Soviet military operations to the point where they would be better able to operate in this new environment. This was not a sudden decision on his part; Ogarkov was not one given to quick changes. There is a clear direction to the development of thought in his writings. He may have avoided noting in the late 1970s that nuclear weapons were becoming less and less useful, but the logic of his entry on Soviet military doctrine in the *Soviet*

---

[25] As reported in John Parker, *The Kremlin in Transition*, forthcoming from Unwin and Hyman. For more complete description of Petrov's position, see Gottemoeller, "Conflict and Consensus in the Soviet Armed Forces."

[26] Ogarkov, *Always in Readiness to Defend the Fatherland*, p. 72.

Military Encyclopedia indicates that he was already moving in that direction. Other examples abound: Ogarkov's introduction of the dialectic in 1978; his acceptance of the concept of parity from the very beginning; the evolving nature of his ideas on the relationship between conventional and nuclear weapons; and his outright rejection of limited nuclear war in 1983—all, to varying degrees, made his primary point—that high-technology conventional weapons were the wave of the future. Furthermore, it could be argued that all the operational modifications he had pushed since taking over as chief of the General Staff were made in order to place the Soviet military in an increasingly better position to fight a conventional war and, if that option failed, to enable it to prevail in a nuclear conflict.

Finally, while it is impossible to establish a definite link between Ogarkov and the policy of "military sufficiency" introduced under Gorbachev, it is interesting to note that Ogarkov's last article utilized a formulation that could be construed as containing the basic principles, at least, of the Gorbachev line: "The Soviet people and their allies in the Warsaw Pact are not seeking military superiority over other countries, and our military doctrine has always been and is of a strictly defensive orientation. *But they have sufficient forces and potential to prevent others from gaining superiority over them.*"[27] It could be argued that in introducing the concept of military sufficiency in his 1985 Supreme Soviet speech, Gorbachev was repeating an idea that Ogarkov (and others) had hinted at earlier. Furthermore, Ogarkov's idea of preventing the other side from gaining superiority was soon to become party policy. It would thus be incorrect to suggest that the idea was solely Gorbachev's. He was certainly responsible for making it a political imperative and perhaps for ensuring military support for it, but Ogarkov had already suggested certain aspects of it one year earlier.

Operational Modifications

During the first half of the 1980s Ogarkov continued to introduce important changes in operational procedures and force struc-

---

[27] Ogarkov, "The Unfading Glory of Soviet Weapons," p. 24. Emphasis added.

ture, ones aimed at streamlining the Kremlin's military force structure.

Joint Operations. One of Ogarkov's key concerns throughout his tenure as chief of staff was to improve the ability of the various services and branches to operate jointly. This in his eyes was not only militarily sensible, it was also an economic necessity. Less money meant that the Soviet military had to be able to do more with less, and, as the budgetary squeeze tightened, pressure on the various services to subordinate their own special interests to those of military operations in general grew. This was particularly evident in the strategic nuclear area, where Ogarkov formalized the subordination of all three services having strategic nuclear weapons by symbolically giving them joint responsibility for the carrying out of strategic nuclear operations.

In his 1981 *Kommunist* article Ogarkov again utilized his phrase of 1978, "strategic nuclear forces." These, he claimed, formed the main element deterring an aggressor.[28] Then, in 1983, he revived a term which was to become the standard codeword for the subordination of all the services to the interests of the whole: he spoke of the "harmonious" (*garmonichnoe*) development of the Soviet armed forces. As he put it: "In view of the changes taking place in military matters and the aggressive preparations of the United States and its allies, a particularly well-conceived and harmonious development of the Soviet Armed Forces, categories of troops, and special troops is required.[29] Ustinov had made a similar observation in his 1982 monograph calling for the "rational and balanced development of all types of weapons."[30] Ogarkov continued to stress the importance of the "harmonious" development of all branches of the Soviet military and never deviated from his use of the term "strategic nuclear forces" throughout his tenure in office. In fact, he made it clear in a 1983 *Red Star* article that his use of the term was not accidental: "The main component of the combat might of the Soviet Armed Forces under present-day conditions, and the basic factor for deterring the aggressor, is our Strategic Nuclear Forces, which consist of groupings and formations of the Strategic Missile Forces, the Navy, and

[28] Ogarkov, "On Guard over Peaceful Labor," p. 87.
[29] Ogarkov, "Victory and the Present."
[30] Ogarkov, *Always in Readiness to Defend the Fatherland*, p. 71.

the Air Force.''[31] If there was any lingering doubt in the minds of those in the Soviet military over the symbolic equality of all three services possessing strategic nuclear weapons, Ogarkov had eliminated it.

On the theater level, however, much remained to be done. Greater awareness on the part of the officers and soldiers who would be involved in conflicts at the tactical level had to be achieved. Ogarkov's view on this became evident in several books published at this time. Here the most important factor characterizing war at the theater level, be it nuclear or conventional, was its increasing complexity. The solution was a greater emphasis on a combined-arms approach. General Reznichenko, for example, published a landmark book in 1984 with the title *Tactics*.[32] In this book Reznichenko outlined the basic premises for combat on both nuclear and non-nuclear battlefields. Reznichenko argued that tactics were changing constantly as a result of improved technology and made the point that without a combined-arms strategy it would not be possible to succeed on the battlefield—regardless of whether it would be conventional or nuclear. The successful outcome of the conflict would be dependent on successful combined-arms operations. Ustinov adopted a similar position when he noted that "in modernizing military readiness great importance is attached to the close cooperation of the various services of the Armed Forces, of branches and special types of troops."[33]

Theaters of Military Operations (TVDs).   Ogarkov stressed the importance of TVDs in his writings throughout the early 1980s. For example, his 1981 *Kommunist* article included a lengthy discussion of TVDs in which he reiterated his contention that the increased scale of operations necessitated the creation of a new structure:

> Now the situation is different. The army groups' command has at its disposal means of destruction (missiles, missile-carrying aircraft, and so forth) whose combat potential considerably transcends the bounds of army group operations. There has been a sharp increase in the maneuverability of troops, and the methods of resolution of many stra-

---

[31] Ogarkov, "Reliably Defending Peace."

[32] V. Reznichenko, *Taktika (Tactics)* (Moscow: Voenizdat, 1984).

[33] D. F. Ustinov, *Sluzhim rodine, delu kommunizma (We Serve the Fatherland, the Communist Cause)* (Moscow: Voenizdat, 1982), p. 87.

tegic and operational tasks by groupings and formations of branches of the Armed Forces have changed. As a result, earlier forms of the use of formations and groupings have largely ceased to correspond to the new conditions. In a possible future war not the army form, but a larger-scale form of military operations—theater strategic operations—will prevail.[34]

Ogarkov made the same points in his 1982 monograph, adding that "in the course of such an operation, each front (fleet) may be put into operation sequentially, with short pauses and even without them, on two or more frontal operations."[35] The clear implication of such a development was, as he noted in his 1985 monograph, that a more elaborate structure—a command between the TVDs and the high command—would be needed to ensure the smooth operation of these forces.

To date, the most authoritative Western study of TVDs holds that the Soviets have created "an intermediate level of strategic leadership between the national command authority and the Soviet/Warsaw Pact front."[36] This means that as Ogarkov suggested, one officer is given command over a vast geographical area comprising a number of TVDs. It is his task to coordinate, maneuver, and generally operate all of the forces under his command. The thought is that given the high degree of fluidity that is expected to characterize operations in a new war, one person must be in overall command. His presence will ensure that all Soviet military forces in the region react quickly and effectively, thereby greatly increasing their ability to cope with the unexpected.

At present, the Soviets appear to recognize five continental or strategic TVDs around the periphery of the USSR. These include: the Northwestern (Scandinavia), the Western (essentially Central and Western Europe), the South Western (the Balkans), the Southern (the Middle East), and the Far Eastern.[37] Within each of the strategic TVDs there are a number of what the Soviets call "operational directions," a term that in essence refers to a geographical

[34] Ogarkov, "On Guard over Peaceful Labor," p. 7.

[35] Ogarkov, *Always in Readiness to Defend the Fatherland*, p. 35.

[36] John G. Hines and Phillip A Peterson, "Changing the Soviet System of Control," *International Defense Review* 19, no. 3 (1986): 281.

[37] Ibid., p. 283.

focus of operations. It may involve several fronts. Furthermore, the commanders of these strategic TVDs enjoy a considerable amount of autonomy.

Deep Operations.   Even though he mentioned deep operations in his writings, Ogarkov's comments on this term are far less revealing than those he made on the changes the Kremlin had introduced into operational procedures. For example, Ogarkov mentioned the concept in his 1982 book and again in his 1984 interview, but only to note that it represented a major new development in military science in general, and in Soviet military science in particular.

Meanwhile, important changes were occurring in the Soviet military's ability to carry out deep operations. A Western specialist, relying primarily on Polish military journals, revealed in 1982 that the Soviets had developed a new operational concept—the Operational Maneuver Group (OMG). Based on the World War II idea of mobile groups, the OMGs were intended to help bring a war against NATO to a rapid close before the West could make a firm decision to utilize nuclear weapons. The OMG represented "an extra, highly mobile, operational force that is uncommitted when the defender has just committed his own reserves."[38] It would be made up of self-contained formations consisting of contributions from all services, although tanks would probably continue to play the major role, much as they did in the World War II mobile groups:

> At army level, an OMG would probably consist of at least one tank division or motorized rifle division, whereas at the front level it would be somewhat larger, possibly a tank or combined-arms corps of two or more divisions, or even an entire army. The most likely reinforcements to the OMG would include: 1) airborne or heliborne assault forces; 2) an aviation element (especially helicopters); 3) additional engineer elements (especially river-crossing and road-clearing support); 4) special logistic support including resupply by air; and 5) additional air defense support.[39]

---

[38] C. N. Donnelly, "The Soviet Operational Manoeuvre Group," *International Defense Review* 15, no. 9 (1982): 1177, 1181. Soviet military officers, however, have vigorously denied the existence of such units: "The facts are that these formations do not exist in the Soviet Armed Forces." See A. I. Gribkov, "Doktrina sokhraneniia mira" ("A Doctrine for Maintaining Peace"), *Krasnaia zvezda*, September 25, 1987.

[39] John G. Hines and Phillip A Peterson, "The Warsaw Pact Strategic Offensive," *International Defense Review* 16, no. 10 (1983): 1303.

Reflecting Ogarkov's commitment to develop a military that could operate under both conventional and—if necessary—nuclear conditions, the OMG would be equally suited for either environment.

In practice, the OMG would initially be held as a reserve some distance behind the front line. It would be subordinated to a first-echelon army. Once a breakthrough was achieved or a serious weakness detected on the other side, the TVD commander could release the OMG to exploit the situation, hopefully wreaking havoc behind enemy lines. It could have as its goal the capture of important targets (e.g., nuclear missile sites, key towns, or communication junctures) or be utilized to disrupt the West's ability to reinforce its front lines. The OMG concept has apparently passed beyond the theoretical stage. One source states that in the spring of 1981 "a motorized rifle division exercised . . . as part of the forces assigned to Warsaw Pact operations as the OMG of its parent army." In addition, in the winter of 1982 "a Soviet tank division exercised in the role of an OMG, this time by paying special attention to echeloning within the OMG itself."[40] OMGs, however, are only one part of Soviet frontal operations. Other elements also play important roles.

Improving Combined-Arms Operations. Everything Ogarkov tried to do as chief of the General Staff was aimed at improving the ability of the Soviet armed forces to operate together in a smooth fashion. This was evident both in his efforts at the theater and strategic levels.

Aviation. The Soviets continued to build on the progress they had made during the late 1970s in building up their aviation assets, both fixed-wing and helicopter. The focus of such operations was "the destruction of enemy air and air-defense assets, nuclear resources, and associated C3."[41] As a consequence, Moscow continued to improve its ability to carry out such missions; in the case of fixed-wing aircraft this meant building more fighter bombers. In 1985 one source estimated that out of a total 2800 aircraft, the Soviets would have some 1200 available for a first massed strike against

[40] Michael Ruehle, "The Soviet Operational Maneuver Group: Is the Threat Lost in a Terminological Quarrel?" *Armed Forces Journal* (August 1984): 55.

[41] Hines and Peterson, "The Warsaw Pact Strategic Offensive," p. 1392. "C3" refers to "Command, Control, and Communications."

Western targets.[42] The aircraft most suitable for performing this task in 1984 were the MIG-27, the Flogger, and the SU-24. The latter could hit the U.K. flying from the GDR, where it was deployed.

Meanwhile, the use of helicopters was expanded for both ground support and transporting troops and supplies. Beginning in 1981, for example, helicopters began to play a key role in Warsaw Pact exercises.[43] Their armor was improved, and they were integrated into Soviet ground units. As a result, not only was the firepower of Soviet units increased, their mobility was also enhanced. Soviet forces now had "air-assault units (a batallion per army and a brigade at the front level), specially designed for insertion among the enemy's forward formations, to help convert the ground forces' initial breakthroughs into operational level success." Recognizing the danger represented by helicopters, the Soviets also began to give increased attention to the importance of developing an antihelicopter weapon: "A new dedicated helicopter is understood to be in development and existing machines may be modified for the purpose."[44]

Armor.   Ogarkov presided over a further improvement in Soviet tank forces. The T-80, with its compound armor making it more survivable against Western antitank weapons, and the T-72, with its "rubber composition side plates designed to deflect antitank missiles, began to appear."[45] In addition, the Pact greatly expanded its holdings of antitank weapons to counter NATO's new generation of tanks.

Artillery.   Under Ogarkov's leadership the Soviets continued to upgrade their artillery holdings. For example, it was reported in 1983 that the Soviets were expanding the number of artillery pieces in a variety of units: "Army level independent artillery regiments which now normally consist of two battalions of 130mm field guns and one battalion of 152mm howitzers (in addition to their head-

[42] Phillip A. Petersen and John R. Clark, "Soviet Air and Antiair Operations," *Air University Review* (March–April) 1985): 46.

[43] C. N. Donnelly, "The Soviet Helicopter on the Battlefield," *International Defense Review* 17, no. 5 (1984): 562.

[44] C. J. Dick, "Soviet Operational Art, Part I: The Fruits of Experience," *International Defense Review* 21, no. 7 (1988): 757, 563.

[45] James H. Hansen, "Countering NATO's New Weapons," *International Defense Review* 77, no. 11 (1984): 1622.

quarters battery, target acquisition battery, and service troops), are now being converted to artillery brigades, equipped with two battalions each of field guns and howitzers."[46] In addition, some battalions had reportedly had their strength increased from eighteen to twenty-four guns, and the Soviets were making greater use of computers in their fire control system. Furthermore, BM-21 multiple-rocket launchers were now integrated into artillery regiments, and the T-64 replaced the obsolete PT-76. This expanded firepower became very important in helping to keep a conflict conventional. As has been pointed out several times, for Ogarkov and his colleagues it was absolutely crucial that Soviet forces—whether in the form of an OMG or regular front-line troops—be able to stage a breakthrough early on so as to achieve a quick and decisive victory before NATO might decide to escalate to the use of nuclear weapons. The greater mass of artillery would not only help them increase the chances of a breakthrough—it would also permit them to transfer a few of the tasks that would previously have been assigned to tactical nuclear weapons to conventional systems, thereby further decreasing the chances of escalation.

Logistics.   Throughout his writings Ogarkov spoke of the tremendous destructive power of modern weapons and of the major losses that would be a part of any war in the future. Consequently, it is not surprising that the Soviets made increased efforts to improve their logistic capabilities. For example, the creation of TVDs gave "the Soviets the ability to allocate resources from the center not just in wartime but during the crucial period before war breaks out."[47] This would better enable the field commander to move supplies and reserves from one area to another as the course of the battle shifted. In this regard it is worth noting that the Soviet decision to increase both stocks of fuel and ammunition in forward-staging areas and vehicle repair facilities enhanced the commanders' flexibility and made them less dependent on long supply lines subject to interdiction by the other side.

Short-Range Ballistic Missiles.   The decision on the part of the

[46] David Isby, "Soviets Refurbish Artillery for Deeper Attack Missions," *Defense Week*, December 5, 1983.

[47] C. N. Donnelly and M. J. Orr, "Soviet Logistics Flexibility," *International Defense Review* 19, no. 7 (1986): 948.

Soviets to develop dual-capable tactical missiles was almost certainly encouraged, if not instigated, by Ogarkov. These systems provide the Soviets with a critically important weapon, one that can hit a number of critical Western targets with a conventional warhead. Their accuracy means that in practice conventional warheads can destroy targets which previously had to be taken out by either aircraft or nuclear weapons.

Special Operations Forces.   While the West has probably exaggerated the overall significance of Moscow's special operations forces, they are an important component of the Kremlin's military strategy, especially in a potential war with NATO. Their primary task appears to be to destroy Western nuclear weapons before they can be employed. As one source noted, "These forces represent a flexible, diverse and unconventional attack capability against NATO. Dressed possibly in civilian clothing or in NATO uniforms, speaking German or English, they are to perform deep reconnaissance and sabotage missions, with particular emphasis on nuclear targets." The Soviet Union's seven airborne divisions represent another potent force. While lightly armed, they have the ability to operate independently and can "be tasked to neutralize critical rear-area targets such as nuclear units, headquarters and control points and airfields."[48]

Air Defense.   Of all the weapons possessed by the West, with the exception of nuclear weapons, the Soviets are most afraid of fixed-wing aircraft. Consequently, it is not surprising that under Ogarkov considerable efforts were devoted to strengthening Moscow's air defense forces. The number of tactical surface-to-air missiles and antiaircraft artillery was increased, and work was well under way on fourth generation fighters, including the MIG-29 and SU-27. Both planes reportedly have "look-down, shootdown radars," which "enable the Soviet fighters to engage enemy aircraft despite ground clutter."[49] After all, Ogarkov's conventional variant would have little chance of succeeding if all of the Pact's tanks and other equipment were to be destroyed by Western air power before they could be thrown into action.

---

[48] James H. Hansen, "Countering NATO's New Weapons," p. 1618.
[49] Ibid., p. 1619.

Airborne Warning and Control System.   When he spoke about reconnaissance strike complexes, Ogarkov had Western battle management systems in mind. These are complexes which coordinate aerial and ground-based systems in order to ensure that targets deep behind enemy lines are destroyed. The Israelis had shown how such a system could work when they inflicted such one-sided casualties on the Syrians. From Ogarkov's standpoint, the most effective counters to Western AWACS and related systems were fighter aircraft or perhaps a long-range antiradiation missile. Two new models, the AS-11 and AS-12, entered service in the early 1980s, but it is not yet known how effective they are. Meanwhile, Ogarkov had the Soviet military working on an AWACs aircraft of its own.

It is difficult to focus on any particular date as key to the evolution of Soviet warfighting doctrine under Ogarkov. In his 1982 book Ustinov writes of the need to modify Soviet operational art as a result of the demands of military technology, but he does not date when such changes should be made.[50] Based on the available evidence, it would appear that the changes or modifications that occurred in Soviet warfighting strategy were more evolutionary than revolutionary. Ogarkov's hand can be seen in almost all of the new developments, but even with his increased emphasis on high technology conventional weapons and the need for a revolutionary breakthrough in military technology, there is no indication that he reversed the overall orientation of Soviet strategy. Rather, he gave it direction and introduced a sense of urgency into its development.

Management, Technology, and Leadership

Despite his opposition to the foreign policy of the political leadership, Ogarkov, like Grechko before him, recognized the critical importance of advanced technology for the armed forces. In fact, of all the matters he felt most strongly, advanced technology must rank near the top. The future was in high technology, and unless the Soviet military met the demands of this revolution in military affairs, it would not be competitive. In this regard, it is interesting that Ogarkov's comments on the role of technology and the need for Soviet military officers to react in better ways to it bear a strong

[50] Ogarkov, *Always in Readiness to Defend the Fatherland*, p. 75.

resemblance to the policy of perestroika introduced by Gorbachev after he came to power in 1985.

As with Gorbachev, Ogarkov and Ustinov continued to single out science and technology—in this case, military science—as areas of vital concern. Writing in February 1981, for example, Ogarkov called military science the key to the future of the Soviet armed forces: "Under the conditions of sharp scientific-technical progress, it [Soviet military science] is becoming an even more effective means for increasing the quality of combat and operational preparations, of systems of training and educating troops."[51] Or, as Ustinov put it: "Now, in the epoch of the scientific-technical revolution, V. I. Lenin's warning that without science it is not possible to construct a contemporary army takes on special meaning. Today, to lead troops or train and educate them without scientific knowledge or contrary to science is inconceivable."[52] In his first major speech in 1985, Gorbachev called for an acceleration of social and economic progress "by making use of the achievements of the scientific-technological revolution."[53] Whether in the civilian or military world, all three men considered a greater reliance on science and technology to be critical.

As in the past, Ogarkov, joined by Ustinov, continued to harp on the need for Soviet military officers to concentrate on the future, not on the present or, even less so, on the past. (This is another of Gorbachev's basic concerns.) Given the dynamic nature of modern warfare and the fact that weapons systems are changing at a very fast pace, Ogarkov argued, the officer must look to the future: "Military art has no right to lag behind the combat potential of the means of armed struggle, particularly at the present stage, when on the basis of scientific and technical progress the main arms systems change practically every ten to twelve years."[54] Or, as he put it a year and a

[51] N. Ogarkov, "Na strazhe mirnogo truda" ("On Guard over Peaceful Labor"), *Sovetskaia Rossiia*, February 22, 1981.

[52] "Doklad Ministra oborony SSSR Marshala Sovetskogo Soiuza D. F. Ustinova" ("Report of Minister of Defense of the USSR Marshal of the Soviet Union D. F. Ustinov"), *Krasnaia zvezda*, May 12, 1983.

[53] M. Gorbachev, "O sozyve ocherednogo XXVII S"ezda KPSS i zadachakh, svyazannykh s ego podgotovkoi i provedeniem" ("Concerning the Convening of the 27th CPSU Congress and the Tasks Associated with its Preparation and Implementation"), *Pravda*, April 24, 1986.

[54] Ogarkov, "On Guard over Peaceful Labor," p. 6.

half later, "Stagnation in thought, and the stubborn, mechanical, unthinking clinging to old ways are dangerous under present-day conditions."[55] Indeed, Ogarkov added in his 1985 monograph that what is required is a "perestroika," a restructuring, of the scientific-technical thought process in the military.[56] Without it, he reiterated, the Soviet military could not hope to keep up with the demands of contemporary conflict: "A belated restructuring of views, obstinacy in working out and implementing new questions of military art and military construction, is fraught with serious consequences."[57] Ustinov was just as hard on Soviet military officers. In a speech before graduates of the senior military academies he observed that "military affairs do not remain in place."[58] Instead, he argued, as Ogarkov had many times, that given the speed with which developments in the areas of science and technology are forcing changes on the military, it is imperative that officers always update their education, always look to the future to find new solutions to new problems. For both these individuals, the key to winning future battles, especially in an age of high-technology weapons, lies in the individual's ability to think creatively and show initiative.

In the end, when it came to implementing a policy of technological modernization in the Soviet armed forces, Ogarkov and Ustinov argued as Gorbachev would several years later that the individual was key. If his or her educational level was not raised, there was little or no chance for success. For Ogarkov this meant not only academic and training institutions but training in the field as well. Presaging Dmitrii Yazov, the future defense minister, Ogarkov argued for a "hands-on approach." Officers must not only be competent themselves, they must also be prepared to train those under their command. And officers should never be satisfied with what they or their soldiers know. Instead, it was important that they look upon education as a life-long process. Graduation from an officer school or even a higher academy was not the conclusion of the

---

[55] Ogarkov, "Victory and the Present."

[56] As far as I can determine, this is the only time in his writings that Ogarkov used this term in this context.

[57] Ogarkov, *Always in Readiness to Defend the Fatherland*, p. 47.

[58] "Doklad Ministra oborony SSSR Marshala Sovetskogo Soiuza D. F. Ustinova" ("Report by Minister of Defense of the USSR, Marshal of the Soviet Union D. F. Ustinov"), *Pravda*, May 12, 1982.

educational process; it was just one stop on the way to becoming a competent, well-trained officer.

But there were problems. In one case, for example, Ogarkov complained that many young Soviet servicemen lacked a strong knowledge of the Russian language:

> In examining the question of the preparation of young people for military service, the importance of a good knowledge of the Russian language should be particularly mentioned. Unfortunately, a significant number of young men enter the army with a weak knowledge of the Russian language, which seriously hampers their military training. As is known, in the Armed Forces all regulations, instructions, educational supplies, directions for military technology, and weapons are written in the Russian language.[59]

The consequence, according to Ogarkov, is a lowering of combat readiness, as it is very difficult to train such people to master Soviet weapons systems.

Ustinov could not have been more supportive of his chief of staff in pushing Soviet military personnel to improve their technical qualifications. In fact, he commented on the problem throughout his 1982 monograph. And he laid full responsibility for improving the situation on the Soviet officer. Not only did officers have an obligation to be fully qualified in a technical sense, they also had to improve their pedagogical skills. In light of the ever increasing educational level of most people entering the armed forces as well as the fast pace of technological change, the "form and method" of training Soviet military personnel had to be constantly updated.[60]

With the structural changes that were being introduced into the Soviet armed forces (e.g., the TVDs), the role of command and control increased. For the Soviets, "it is . . . essential in certain areas to exercise control at the highest possible level to avoid frittering away resources on secondary objectives and to ensure coordination: Air and air defense operations and logistic management are exam-

---

[59] Ogarkov, *Always in Readiness to Defend the Fatherland*, p. 64. See also A. A. Yepshiv, *Sviashchenyi dolg, pochetnaia obiazannost'* (*Sacred Duty, Honorable Obligation*) (Moscow: DOSAAF, 1983), pp. 75–76.

[60] Ibid., p. 103.

ples."[61] Thus, it is not surprising that both Ogarkov and Ustinov were especially concerned with command and control. Ogarkov, in fact, devoted an entire article to the subject.

Speaking before a party conference of the General Staff in 1981, Ogarkov called for the "further modernization of the planning, style, and method of command and control, an increase in the efficiency, development, creativity and initiative of cadres."[62] In recent years, Ogarkov continued, the demands on the command-and-control system had increased, but while there had been some successes, there were also some "inadequacies." Ogarkov singled out in particular the "style" and "method" of leadership within the armed forces: too often leadership was a mechanical, formalistic process; given the need for instantaneous decisions, leaders had to become creative, to show initiative. Mechanical devices could be of assistance, but the key factor remained the individual officer. If he would not react quickly and creatively, there was little that machines could do:

> Under current circumstances, when a probable opponent has at his disposal such means of destruction that makes it possible to deliver surprise attacks, to carry out quick maneuvers, and regrouping of forces, only several weeks or even several fortnights will be given for a response. For that reason, under conditions of an increasing dynamism in combat operations and combat operations that will be untypical for the commander and staff, a high degree of flexibility and operational leadership is demanded as never before.[63]

While Ustinov in particular devoted a whole section of his monograph to the issue of command and control, both individuals give the strong impression that while the equipment is on hand, the major problem is the individual officer.

It would be tempting to suggest the existence of a personal tie between Ogarkov and Gorbachev, given the similarity of their views on a variety of issues, but there is no evidence that their relationship was anything but what would be expected between a chief of the General Staff and a high party official, one who—for at least part of

---

[61] Charles Dick, "The Soviet C3 Philosophy: The Challenge of Contemporary Warfare," *Signal* (December 1984): 49.

[62] N. Ogarkov, "Sovershenstvovat' upravlenie voiskami" ("Improving Control of Troops"), *Krasnaia zvezda*, January 7, 1981.

[63] Ogarkov, *Always in Readiness to Defend the Fatherland*, p. 36.

his tenure as chief of the General Staff—was the country's second-ranking political leader. Nevertheless, both could be considered technological determinists in that they believed that the application of the latest developments from science and technology could play a significant role in improving the Soviet Union whether on the domestic or the military front. Similarly, both men appeared to be convinced that the key to the future of the Soviet Union would be the individual. As Ogarkov put it in 1983: "Now more than ever officers are required to display competence, supreme discipline, an acute sense for what is new; [they must] see the long term, not rest on their laurels, [and must] work creatively, persistently implement practically verified forms and methods of action, and not be afraid to assume responsibility for resolving complex tasks."[64]

Personal responsibility, initiative, creativity, and competence were all characteristics both men agreed to be crucial if the USSR was to pull itself out of its current economic and social malaise. In this sense, Ogarkov's constant harping on the need for the Soviet military to do a better job in reacting to the demands of modern technology helped lay the groundwork for the implementation of Gorbachev's policy of perestroika in the armed forces.

SOCIOPOLITICAL ISSUES

The Economy

The battle over resources continued throughout the remainder of Ogarkov's tenure as chief of staff. From Ogarkov's standpoint the problem was simple. Not only did he have to come up with money to cover the costs of new exotic high-technology weapons—not an easy task given the technological backwardness of the Soviet economy—he also had to pay for continuing improvements in conventional forces and, as a result of Washington's buildup in strategic and space systems, in those arenas as well. Consequently, he felt he had no alternative but to go all-out in his effort to keep up with the West. Given the sad state of the Soviet economy and the increasing lack of political leadership, the only solution he felt to be available to him was to throw money at the problem. While he probably did

---

[64] N. Ogarkov, "Nadezhnyi oplot sotsializma i mira" ("The Reliable Bulwark of Socialism and Peace"), *Krasnaia zvezda*, February 23, 1983.

not deceive himself into thinking that even a significant increase in the military budget would solve all of his problems, he felt that any increase would help.

From the standpoint of the political leadership, however, the situation was more complicated. While defense needs were a matter of concern, the satisfaction of domestic demands were weighted even more heavily. The reality of unrest in Poland and reports of disturbances in the USSR over food shortages combined to convince Brezhnev and his colleagues that this area should receive priority. And the point of focus became the Eleventh Five-Year Plan.

From Brezhnev's standpoint, the focus of the upcoming five-year plan had to be the food problem. In addition, he argued in favor of expanding the production of consumer goods as well as improving their quality. As he put it at the Twenty-sixth Party Congress, "What we are talking about—foodstuffs, consumer goods, the services sphere—is a question of the daily life of millions of people. . . . It is according to how these questions are answered that people largely judge our work. They judge us strictly, exactly. And comrades, this must be borne in mind."[65] This was followed in November by an article by Chernenko in the authoritative party journal *Kommunist* in which he warned that neglecting consumer demands could lead to serious domestic problems.[66] In the end, the Eleventh Five-Year Plan, approved in May 1982, placed a premium on the growth of agriculture and light industry.[67] Increases in military expenditures would have to be deferred. This was not good news for Ogarkov and his colleagues. Writing several months before the adoption of the new five-year plan, Ustinov tried to reassure his readers that the approach proposed by Brezhnev was in the military's interest: "There is no doubt that implementation of the economic

[65] L. Brezhnev, "Otchetnyi doklad Tsentral'nogo Komiteta KPSS XXVI S'ezdu kommunisticheskoi partii Sovetskogo Soiuza i ocherednye zadachi partii v oblasti vnutrennei i vneshnei politiki" ("Report of the Central Committee of the CPSU to the 26th Congress of the Communist Party of the Soviet Union and the Current Tasks of the Party in the Area of Internal and External Policies"), *Pravda*, February 24, 1981.

[66] K. Chernenko, "Leninskaia strategiia rukovodstva" ("The Leninist Strategy of Leadership"), *Kommunist*, no. 13 (1981): 6–22.

[67] Daniel Bond and Herbert Levine, "The 11th Five-Year Plan, 1981–1985," in Seweryn Bialer and Thane Gustafson, eds., *Russia at the Crossroads* (London: Allen and Unwin, 1982), pp. 82, 87, 107.

plan adopted at the Twenty-sixth Congress of the CPSU will at the same time facilitate the technical outfitting of the Armed Forces."[68]

In fact, Ogarkov had long been waging a vigorous campaign against the general secretary's attempts to hold down military spending and foil Ustinov's efforts in the same direction. On May 9, 1981, he had argued that "the lessons of the past for present conditions in the world demand a constant raising of the level of combat readiness of the Soviet armed forces."[69] Ogarkov again called for an increase in the USSR's "defense capabilities" in his *Kommunist* article later that year.[70] Then on October 1, 1982, he hosted a conference of the General Staff at which he spoke on the continuing relevance of the famous Soviet General Staff officer, Marshal Boris Shaposhnikov. According to the report in *Red Star*, Ogarkov emphasized Shaposhnikov's observations on the interrelationship between "war and politics, war and economics."[71] By itself such a comment might seem harmless, but it was accompanied by an article by General Kozlov, the rector of the General Staff's Voroshilov Academy and formerly first deputy chief of the General Staff. In his article, Kozlov appeared to be arguing against certain unnamed individuals in the Soviet political-military leadership who, he implied, were not paying enough attention to conventional forces:

> There is no doubt that today it [a nuclear missile] is the basic means of attack in a nuclear war; it must not be underestimated. However, overrating such weaponry is also inadmissible, since it is fraught with reduced attention to conventional, traditional means of armed struggle, without whose proportional development it is impossible effectively to make use of the results of employing nuclear weapons, impossible to achieve the ultimate goals of war.[72]

While Khrushchev's name was never mentioned, this type of language was very similar to that utilized in the mid-1960s in the mil-

---

[68] Ustinov, *We Serve the Fatherland, the Cause of Communism*, p. 70.

[69] N. Ogarkov, "Uroki istorii" ("The Lessons of History"), *Krasnaia zvezda*, May 9, 1981.

[70] Ogarkov, "On Guard over Peaceful Labor," p. 91.

[71] N. Ogarkov, "Tvorcheskaia mysl' polkovodtsa" ("The Creative Thought of a Commander"), *Pravda*, October 2, 1982.

[72] M. Kozlov, "Vydaiushchiisia voennyi deiatel' i teoretik" ("A Distinguished Military Figure and Theoretician"), *Krasnaia zvezda*, October, 2, 1982.

itary's attempt to liberate itself from the grip of Khrushchev's single-variant strategy.[73] Everyone knew that conventional weapons, especially high-technology conventional weapons, were more expensive than nuclear weapons, and Ogarkov's mention of the close relationship between politics, economics, and war at a time when Brezhnev was putting his emphasis on satisfying consumer goods intended to get the point across: defense is important and costly.

Brezhnev clearly heard and understood the concern articulated by Ogarkov and Kozlov. In fact, he had been gradually giving ground in his rhetoric on the military budget. For example, Brezhnev had noted at the Twenty-sixth Party Congress that the Soviet military had "everything necessary in order to reliably defend the socialist achievements of the people."[74] He added, however, that the party would do everything necessary to ensure that this remained the case in the future.

By the end of 1981, however, Brezhnev was commenting in an interview with the West German journal *Der Spiegel* that if it turned out to be necessary (indicating that perhaps it might), the Soviet people were prepared to take additional steps to ensure their country's defense.[75] In his trade union speech in mid-1982, Brezhnev went even further, pointing out that in light of actions by the U.S. and NATO, it had been necessary for the Party to take additional steps to raise the country's defense capabilities.[76] Assuring his listeners that such steps were "an absolute necessity," Brezhnev emphasized that "not a single ruble more will be spent than is absolutely necessary." For his part, Ustinov again entered the debate on August 19 in Kuibyshev where he "repeatedly—three times stressed the adequacy of the Soviet defense effort."[77]

Finally, in October 1982, shortly before his death and only some three weeks after the Ogarkov-Kozlov articles had appeared, the

---

[73] See Parker, *The Kremlin in Transition*, for suggestions of such a connection.

[74] "The Report of the Central Committee of the CPSU to the 26th Congress."

[75] "Otvety L. I. Brezhneva na voprosy redaktsii zapadnogermanskogo zhurnala 'Shpigel' " ("L. I. Brezhnev Answers Questions from the Editors of the West German Journal 'Spiegel' "), *Krasnaia zvezda*, November 3, 1981.

[76] L. Brezhnev, "Zabota o liudiakh truda, zabota o proizvodstve—v tsentr vnimaniia profsoiuzov" ("Concern over Working People, Concern over Production—at the Center of Attention of the Trade Unions"), *Krasnaia zvezda*, March 17, 1982.

[77] Parker, *Kremlin in Transition*.

matter came to a head as Brezhnev addressed a major conference of senior Soviet military officers in the Kremlin. Brezhnev strongly defended his food program but gave the impression of a man under siege on the issue of military spending, assuring his listeners that

> everyone knows that the Soviet armed forces are a mighty factor for peace and security, a reliable means for repulsing aggression. And the people are not sparing any efforts to ensure that they are always equal to the task. We are equipping the armed forces with the most modern weapons and military technology. The CC [Central Committee] is taking measures to ensure that they have everything they need. And the Armed Forces should always be worthy of this concern.[78]

Brezhnev went on to argue that it was up to the military itself to raise its level of combat readiness. The message to Ogarkov (who was present at the meeting) and his colleagues was simple: the party is doing the necessary, make do with what you have—because it is all that you will get. Ogarkov's conspicuous absence from the photograph of military leaders published in *Pravda* and *Red Star* reports of the meeting was hardly accidental and suggests that at a minimum, he was being censured—at least in part—for his outspoken opposition to Brezhnev's economic policies. Chernenko emphasized the supremacy of consumer over military economic interests in even stronger terms two days later in Tbilisi, observing that "we are strong enough and we can wait."[79]

Faced with intransigence on the part of Brezhnev and the political leadership over the military budget, Ogarkov did the only thing available to him: he pushed his plan for a closer integration of civilian and military economies even harder. As in other instances, Ogarkov was outspoken in his willingness to take on Brezhnev and others. For example, at the same time Kozlov was publishing his article in *Red Star*, Ogarkov penned one in *Pravda*. In it he reminded the political leadership that "war, that former knightly joust, is nowadays not such a simple and delicate type of social relationship . . . . *We must prepare seriously, . . . fully mobilizing the efforts and resources of*

[78] "Soveshchanie voenachal'nikov v Kremle" ("A Meeting of Military Commanders in the Kremlin"), *Krasnaia zvezda*, October 28, 1982.
[79] K. Chernenko, *Zaria vostoka*, October 30, 1982, as cited in Parker, *Kremlin in Transition*.

the country."[80] It is probably not an exaggeration to suggest that such an assertion, coming as it did just before the October 27 meeting between Brezhnev and the generals, was not appreciated by the political leadership. Furthermore, Ogarkov's expression of concern in this area was bound to come across as more than a debating point.

The mobilization of Soviet forces in 1980–1981 as part of the Kremlin's effort to put pressure on the Poles had revealed serious operational problems, and Ogarkov emphasized the need to improve the USSR's capabilities in this area in his 1981 *Kommunist* article. He argued that in order to improve the effectiveness of Soviet defense efforts, actions in two areas would be necessary. First, there was a need for increased centralization of control during periods of tension. He noted the important role played in World War II by the State Defense Committee and the General Staff. In addition, he argued that it would be impossible to concentrate all leadership in the hands of the State Defense Committee. Instead, national security authorities would have to make greater use of lower level organs: "In future wars, if we are going to stop imperialism, it will be necessary to significantly enhance the role and importance of the relevant local party, Soviet, and economic organs in the resolution of defense tasks."[81] Ogarkov continued to harp on closer economic-military integration in his 1982 book, where he referred to the need for "a system of centralized control of the country and the armed forces"[82] and again mentioned the experience of World War II as to both the State Defense Committee as well as the use of local organs. Closely associated with Ogarkov's call for a more centralized leadership was his emphasis on the importance of military reserves. Reservists would play a vital role in the age of modern, high-technology weapons systems, and it would be important for former Soviet military and naval personnel to be both immediately available and properly trained in the event of a crisis. Given the needs of the Soviet economy, however, the release of even a limited number of reserves to the military would be bound to have an important impact on production.

Finally, Ogarkov mentioned the significance of rear action in a

---

[80] Ogarkov, "The Creative Thought of the Commander." Emphasis added.
[81] Ogarkov, "On Guard over Peaceful Labor," pp. 89, 90.
[82] Ogarkov, *Always in Readiness to Defend the Fatherland*, p. 60.

war. In a future war, he observed, "it will be difficult to determine where is the front and where is the rear."[83] He claimed in 1981 that the rear "takes on particular importance" under contemporary conditions. However, Ogarkov warned, the rear must "in a very short period of time replace the losses of massive amounts of military technology and weapons, without which it would be practically impossible to maintain the combat readiness of the armed forces at the necessary level."[84] In order to achieve such an end, the rear must be subordinate to the high command.

Given the stress on the importance of surprise throughout Ogarkov's writings, it seems logical to conclude that the kind of steps he outlined must be taken ahead of time. Indeed, his 1983 article in *Izvestiia* argued for the creation of a command that "would operate immediately at the start of a war." Improvements to coordination between central and local organs, the use of reserves, and the incorporation of the rear into the country's war economy must all be undertaken during peacetime. However such modifications of the military's role in the economy were to be implemented, they would have serious implications for the civilian-military interface. Ogarkov's 1983 comment that the Soviet party and government were "taking important steps to increase further the defense potential and mobilization readiness of industry, agriculture, transport, and other segments of the national economy" suggests that he may have achieved some success in having his ideas adopted, although empirical evidence that any specific structural modifications affecting the Soviet military-economic interface had been introduced is not available.[85] Obviously, as chief of staff in any scenario, Ogarkov would have played a key role in making and implementing decisions.

The second and, from an economic standpoint, even more important area where Ogarkov sought systematic growth was Soviet weapons systems. Dissatisfied with what he saw as a haphazard approach to military spending, Ogarkov argued in his 1981 *Kommunist* article in favor of "planned growth of our armed forces."[86] Needless

---

[83] Ogarkov, "Victory and the Present."
[84] Ogarkov, "On Guard over Peaceful Labor," p. 87. The same phrase is repeated in *Always in Readiness to Defend the Fatherland*, p. 40.
[85] Ogarkov, "Victory and the Present."
[86] Ogarkov, "On Guard over Peaceful Labor," p. 88.

to say, if Brezhnev had agreed to put money into the military budget in this "planned" fashion, it would have both undercut his flexibility in dealing with unexpected contingencies and made it impossible for him to shift funds to agricultural or consumer goods. In effect, the country's economic future would have been mortgaged to the military. Brezhnev, however, did not yield to Ogarkov's efforts in this area.

From Ogarkov's standpoint, the situation did not improve under Brezhnev's successors. In his report to the November 22, 1983, Plenum, for example, Andropov emphasized his commitment to Brezhnev's approach: "It is important to emphasize that the Party's line toward raising the people's standard of living is maintained. . . . It is planned to ensure the priority growth of group 'B' industries and an increase in the manufacture of consumer goods. Large material and financial resources are allocated for the further development of the agro-industrial complex. The people's real incomes will continue to grow." When it came to defense spending, Andropov remarked that "defense requirements, as usual, have been sufficiently taken into account." Andropov was to follow this line throughout his short fifteen months as general secretary.[87]

Chernenko was not much better from Ogarkov's standpoint. Shortly after taking over as general secretary in February 1984, for example, Chernenko argued that his prime concern was a "further increase in the well-being of the working people, the strengthening of the state's defense potential, and improvement in planning and economic management."[88] Military spending was important, but it was clearly to be subordinate to satisfying consumer demands. In March Chernenko again touched on this topic, noting that while defense needs were important, "we did not think of curtailing social programs."[89] Chernenko continued this line for the remainder of his time in office.

[87] "Zaiavlenie General'nogo Sekretaria TsK KPSS, Predsedatelia Prezidiuma Verkhovnogo Soveta SSSR Yu. V. Andropova" ("Statement of the General Secretary of the CC of the CPSU, Chairman of the Presidium of the Supreme Soviet of the USSR Yu. V. Andropov"), *Krasnaia zvezda*, November 25, 1983.

[88] K. Chernenko, "Po puti sovershenstvovaniia razvitogo sotsializma, po puti sozidaniia i mira" ("On the Road to Improving Developed Socialism, on the Road to Creation and Peace"), *Pravda* February 22, 1984.

[89] TASS, March 2, 1984, as cited in Parker, *The Kremlin in Transition*.

Ogarkov, in the meantime, maintained his defiant tone on military spending. In 1983, for example, he argued that the Second World War not only had shown the need for vigilance, but "also makes it crucial that they [the socialist countries] show tireless concern for the defense capability."[90] He returned to this theme in 1984, observing at a party meeting that "never before has the . . . economic struggle . . . acquired such an all-encompassing and menacing nature." Given the threatening situation facing the Soviets— the Americans were moving forward with their plans to station intermediate-range missiles in Europe—there was no alternative but to "develop and implement appropriate steps to strengthen the country's defense capability."[91] Finally, in his 1985 monograph published several months after his "transfer" from Moscow to the command of the Western TVD, Ogarkov lashed out at Chernenko and the political leadership in what was one of the strongest statements on the need to increase the military budget by any senior Soviet military officer to date: "The strengthening of the defensive capabilities of the USSR and the states allied with us, in the face of the increasing threat and military preparations on the side of the USA and NATO bloc, is an *objective, vital necessity*. And the more serious the threat, the greater should be our defensive capability, which is a mighty factor of peace."[92] While Ustinov had used this exact language some two years earlier, it took on a special significance in Ogarkov's writings primarily because Ustinov had used this language in arguing that the possibilities for improving the state of East-West relations had become considerably better. This was not the case with Ogarkov in his 1985 monograph.[93]

When he left Moscow in 1984 for his new assignment, Ogarkov must have carried with him a considerable sense of frustration as to the defense budget. From his perspective the situation was becoming desperate. He had not succeeded in convincing the political leadership of the need for an expanded defense budget, and, worse,

---

[90] Ogarkov, "Victory and the Present."

[91] N. Ogarkov, "S pozitsii vozrosshikh trebovanii" ("From a Position of Increased Demands"), *Krasnaia zvezda*, January 11, 1984.

[92] Ogarkov, *History Teaches Vigilance*, p. 80. Emphasis added.

[93] D. Ustinov, "Za vysokuiu boevuiu gotovnost' " ("For a High Level of Combat Readiness"), *Krasnaia zvezda*, November 12, 1983.

his attempts to increase the number of ties between the civilian and military economies had not compensated for the many demands on his limited budget. To make matters worse, he required additional money to develop and build the high-technology weapons he had talked about in 1983 and 1984. Finally, there was the Soviet economy itself. The situation had not only not improved during his eight years as chief of the General Staff, it had deteriorated still further. Unless something were done to address this latter problem in particular, the prognosis for the future would be bleak indeed.

Ustinov, meanwhile, had had his hands full in attempting to control his assertive chief of staff. Indeed, there are reports that Ustinov may have actively worked to have Ogarkov replaced. In any case, insofar as the military budget was concerned, Ustinov continued his efforts to straddle both sides of the fence. In 1983, for example, he had argued in front of a Soviet military audience that defense spending was under control and that the Party was working hard to satisfy consumer demands.[94] Then, in a 1984 speech published in *Pravda*, he remarked that

> expressing the Soviet people's will, the party and government stress that the USSR will not permit the disruption of the established military equilibrium, and that jointly with the other Warsaw Pact states we are adopting the necessary countermeasures to strengthen our security. At the extraordinary February (1984) Plenum of the CPSU Central Committee Comrade K. U. Chernenko, general secretary of the party Central Committee, said, "Let nobody have the least doubt: we will continue to take care to strengthen our country's defense capability so that we have sufficient resources with which to cool the hot heads of the bellicose adventurists." Soviet people may be sure that their peaceful labor is reliably secured by the full might of the Soviet state and its Armed Forces.[95]

This statement was a masterpiece of political maneuvering. Ustinov managed to address military concerns while at the same time affirming his support for Chernenko. The USSR was "adopting the necessary countermeasures," he assured his readers. Thus, in contrast to

---

[94] D. Ustinov, "Za ratnyi podvig i slavnyi trud" ("For Military Feat and Glorious Labor"), *Krasnaia zvezda*, September 10, 1983.

[95] D. Ustinov, "Nesokrushimaia i legendarnaia . . ." ("Invincible and Legendary . . ."), *Pravda*, February 24, 1984.

Ogarkov, Ustinov gave the impression that everything that needed to be done was being done. Furthermore, his reference to Chernenko's comment at the February Plenum not only invoked the general secretary, it also assured the reader that should additional steps be required, the party leadership would do what was necessary. While Ogarkov and Ustinov differed in their attitudes toward the Soviet military budget, the intensity of their differences of opinion in this regard was nothing compared with their public dispute over the USSR's policy toward East-West relations and arms control.

Arms Control

The public disagreement between Ogarkov and the Brezhnev leadership from the 1981 to 1984 centered around the utility of the arms control process as a vehicle for achieving Soviet foreign policy goals. Both sides were critical of the West in general and of the U.S. in particular. However, where Ogarkov argued that the arms control process was bankrupt and that the key to defending Soviet security interests was therefore a strengthened Soviet military, Brezhnev, Andropov, Chernenko, and Ustinov consistently maintained that however bad things might be for the moment, improved East-West relations remained a viable alternative. In short, for Ogarkov only a strong military would guarantee Soviet security, while the others maintained that arms control would also play an important part. Under the surface, however, the real problem from Ogarkov's standpoint was first that he feared an arms control agreement would be seized upon by the political leadership to justify an even further cutback in military spending, and second that given the Carter and Reagan administrations' buildup in the military programs of the U.S. and NATO, any limitations likely to be acceptable to the other side would seriously undermine Soviet security.

Brezhnev outlined his attitude toward the new Reagan administration in his address to the Twenty-sixth Party Congress in February 1981. He attacked Washington for increasing its military budget and for changes in its military doctrine, in particular its adherence to the idea that nuclear war could be limited.[96] He continued this line of attack in his *Spiegel* interview as well as in two

---

[96] "Report of the Central Committee of the CPSU to the 26th Congress."

speeches in 1982. His October 27 address to military officers accused the U.S. of "acerbating tensions, of aggravating the situation to the maximum extent."[97] Brezhnev also argued that the international situation was getting progressively worse. For example, in a speech in Kiev in May 1981, he maintained that peace was "seriously" threatened and, in his *Spiegel* interview, called the international situation "disquieting."[98] Finally, in a speech in March 1982, Brezhnev labeled Western policies "a course toward political catastrophe."[99]

Despite this criticism of the Reagan administration and these suggestions that the international situation had worsened, Brezhnev continued to voice support for détente and especially for improved U.S.-Soviet relations. In his address to the Twenty-sixth Party Congress, he stated his strong support for détente and expressed his hope that those who determine U.S. policy would adopt a more "realistic" approach in dealing with Moscow. Brezhnev went so far as to note that existing international problems could only be resolved by an "active dialogue at all levels." The Soviet Union, Brezhnev added, was "ready for dialogue." Furthermore, Brezhnev repeated his call for better ties a paragraph later, maintaining that "the USSR wants normal relations with the U.S."[100] Brezhnev reiterated his call for "normal relations" in his *Spiegel* interview later that year.[101] He also made the same point in his trade union and Komsomol speeches the following year and, in his October 1982 speech to senior military officers, went out of his way to emphasize that despite all the problems on the international scene, Soviet policy remained one of "détente and a strengthening of security."[102]

While he had previously questioned the Brezhnev leadership's

[97] "L. I. Brezhnev Answers Questions from the Editors of the West German Journal 'Spiegel' "; L. Brezhnev, "Zabota ob interesakh naroda—delo chesti komsomola" ("Concern for the Interests of the People—A Matter of Honor for the Komsomol"), *Krasnaia zvezda*, May 19, 1982; and "A Meeting of Military Commanders in the Kremlin."

[98] L. Brezhnev, "Bessmerten podvig, sovetskii narod!" ("Eternal Is the Feat, Soviet People!"), *Krasnaia zvezda*, May 10, 1981.

[99] L. Brezhnev, "Concern over Working People, Concern over Production—in the Center of Attention of the Trade Unions."

[100] "Report of the Central Committee of the CPSU to the 26th Congress."

[101] "Answers by L. I. Brezhnev to Questions from the Editors of the West German Magazine *Spiegel*."

[102] "A Meeting of Military Commanders in the Kremlin."

détente policy, Ogarkov's criticisms had been somewhat muted. By 1981, however, the debate over East-West relations broke into the open and became increasingly acrimonious.

In *Pravda* on May 9, 1981, Ustinov attacked those in NATO who seemed to believe that "the new weapons of mass destruction give them the possibility of threatening socialist and other countries." Despite this criticism, however, Ustinov avoided making any direct linkage between World War II and the present, except to note that "ruling circles" in the West had not learned from the defeat of Germany, but instead continued to rely upon militarism in their foreign policies: "They base themselves on military force, on a policy of military adventurism and aggression."[103] Equally noteworthy was Ustinov's somewhat hopeful prognosis for the future of détente. After listing efforts made by the USSR to improve the international situation and relations with the U.S., Ustinov noted that, "it is hoped that those who determine the policies of the leading capitalist countries will be able to think soberly, to look at things more realistically."[104] While this latter formulation was at least partially intended to influence the Western debate over Intermediate-range Nuclear Forces (INF) deployments, from an internal Soviet standpoint it carried the clear implication that such "realistic" people exist and that if successful, they could have a positive impact on a lessening of tensions.

Ogarkov, by contrast, published an article in *Red Star* that same day that was much more skeptical about relations with the West and the possibilities of a return to détente. He pointed out the suffering and costs of the Second World War and the hostility shown by imperialism toward the Soviet Union since its founding. Ogarkov stated that while it might have been hoped that the defeat of Germany and Japan would have led to a better world, this had not been the case because imperialism had remained hostile to the USSR: "These lessons are a powerful reminder of the *unchanging* aggressive nature of imperialism." To make the linkage between the past and the present even stronger, Ogarkov argued that there were "definite similarities between the present and the 1930s. Furthermore, Ogar-

---

[103] D. Ustinov, "Uroki velikoi pobedy" ("Lessons of the Great Victory"), *Pravda*, May 9, 1981.

[104] Ibid.

kov claimed that actions by "the class enemy against the socialist countries" were becoming even more "refined and perfidious" and added that the U.S. was "trying to destroy everything that has been done and is being done in the interests of détente and of international security, clearing the path in order to feed the appetite of military industrial magnates with the goal of making specific war preparations." In short, Ogarkov claimed that such actions were leading to an increasing "military danger."[105]

The contrast between Ustinov and Ogarkov at this point was striking. Where Ustinov reiterated continued Soviet commitment to détente, Ogarkov not only failed to support it, the logic of his argument suggested that it was dead as a policy option. After all, if the U.S. was following a course just like that of Nazi Germany, and if the warlike tiger had not changed his spots, the only rational course for the USSR would be to place increased reliance on its military forces—not on American "realists" or other "peaceloving forces" who may or may not be able to influence events.

Ustinov appeared to respond to Ogarkov's criticism of détente in a June 22 article in *Pravda*. Citing Brezhnev to the effect that the USSR's most important task was to strengthen peace, Ustinov took issue with Ogarkov's claim that the essence of imperialism had not changed. Admitting that the threat to peace and security, "as in the past, comes from imperialism," and that imperialism's aggressive nature was increasing, Ustinov nevertheless argued that it was possible to negotiate with imperialism. The correct course for the USSR, he maintained, was not only one of military strength, but of working with "peaceloving, realistic circles in the West" as well.[106] Ustinov thus concluded that although the threat came from imperialism, its essence could at least be modified to the point where developments within political circles in the West could have a positive impact on the international situation. Détente, in other words, was not dead.

Despite Ustinov's criticism of Ogarkov, the latter remained unrepentant. This was particularly clear in the debate that occurred between the two men in their 1982 monographs dedicated to the

---

[105] Ogarkov, "The Lessons of History." Emphasis added.
[106] D. Ustinov, "Otstoiat' mir" ("Defending Peace"), *Pravda*, June 22, 1981.

Twenty-sixth Party Congress. Ogarkov's 70-page monograph, en-titled *Always in Readiness to Defend the Fatherland*, was sent to press on December 17, 1981, and published on January 26, 1982, in 100,000 copies. Ustinov's 127-page monograph, entitled *We Serve the Fatherland, the Cause of Communism*, was sent to press on February 2, 1982, and published on February 15, 1982, also in 100,000 cop-ies.

Ogarkov used his book to reiterate and expand on the themes noted above. On the nature of imperialism, for example, Ogarkov not only repeated his previous comment that its "nature is un-changed," he also devoted a considerable amount of his work to dis-cussing its "aggressive" and "predatory nature." In the end he con-cluded that its aggressiveness had increased even more.[107]

Turning to the issue of détente, Ogarkov began his book by discussing the importance of the party's peace program adopted at the Twenty-sixth Party Congress and even appeared to give détente a backhanded endorsement, stating in the introduction that "the situation in the world demands new, additional efforts to preserve peace on our planet. Therefore, in the interest of further deepening détente, . . . Soviet communists adopted a Peace Program for the 1980s." He quickly qualified his support for détente, however, by noting only two paragraphs later that "in fighting for peace . . . it has been necessary to constantly keep the question of ensuring a reliable defense of our country, its allies, and its friends at the center of our attention." In fact, Ogarkov used the peace program through-out his monograph primarily to prove the "peaceful" nature of So-viet foreign policy, not to argue for a return to a policy of détente. The book does not once mention any forces of realism in the West or any value in arms control agreements. Instead, Ogarkov repeats the criticisms he made in his earlier writings. His solution to the international problems facing the USSR was to call again for in-creased reliance on the Soviet Union's military might. For example, in his conclusion he took on those who put faith in political rela-tionships by quoting Lenin, "Our efforts toward peace should be accompanied by intensifying our military preparedness, certainly not by the disarming of our army. Our army is the real guarantee

---

[107] Ogarkov, *Always in Readiness to Defend the Fatherland*, pp. 27, 5, 6, 17, 69.

that not the smallest effort nor the smallest encroachment by imperialist powers will be successful."[108] Once again, it was military
force and not détente that was the key to the USSR's security.

In his monograph, Ustinov repeated the Brezhnev line: there is
"no rational alternative to détente," and the USSR is in the forefront
of the battle for improved East-West relations. Furthermore, he reiterated his earlier arguments concerning the existence of positive
forces in the West, attacked the Reagan administration for attempting to undermine détente, and claimed that the latter was becoming
increasingly aggressive.[109]

While Ustinov did not directly attack Ogarkov, one of his criticisms of the Reagan administration could be perceived to be directed in part against Moscow's senior military officer: "The Washington administration attempts to cast doubt on everything positive
that was jointly achieved in the area of Soviet-American relations in
the 1970s."[110] Ustinov had repeatedly blasted the Reagan administration for undercutting détente, but this particular formulation,
with its emphasis on underestimating the positive achievements of
U.S.-Soviet relations, was unusual: it may have been aimed not only
at Washington, but also at Ogarkov, who had had nothing good to
say about U.S.-Soviet relations, past or present, beginning with his
May 1981 *Red Star* article.

Given the prominent role Ogarkov assigned to the Soviet armed
forces in ensuring Soviet security, it is noteworthy that Ustinov did
not mention that factor until twenty-three pages into the text, and
then only in the context of arguing for a strong economy to help
maintain the country's defenses. His main treatment of the Soviet
military did not appear until the second chapter, a third of the way
through the book and well after he made his pitch for détente. A
strong military was vital, Ustinov argued, since it would permit the
USSR to avoid American "blackmail."[111] Throughout his monograph, however, Ustinov made it clear that a strong military was
only one of the tools available for protecting the USSR.

---

[108] V. I. Lenin, quoted in ibid., pp. 4, 70.
[109] Ustinov, *We Serve the Fatherland, The Cause of Communism*, pp. 5, 7, 8, 22, 50, 53,
126.
[110] Ibid., p. 6.
[111] Ibid., p. 43.

With the Soviet walk-out from the Geneva INF negotiations in mid-1983, Ogarkov appeared to have been vindicated. It turned out that realistic forces in the West could do little to stop the deployment of American INF systems in Europe. In the long run, however, this walk-out was to be a major diplomatic blunder by the Kremlin—a mistake for which Ogarkov was at least partially responsible. For the present, however, Ogarkov's primary concern was to freeze East-West relations to the point where he would not be faced with a political leadership prepared to make concessions to the West, concessions that from his standpoint would make his own task much more difficult. The Soviets had announced a number of military steps in response to the deployment of American INF systems in Europe. Most of these appeared to be primarily symbolic: Soviet missile-carrying submarines were moved closer to American coasts, and new INF missiles were deployed in the GDR and Czechoslovakia. However, as noted above, there is no indication that significant increases were made in the military budget.

While the evidence is fragmentary, it appears that in articulating a hard line on arms control, Ogarkov was reflecting the views of many of his colleagues. Kulikov, for example, had compared Reagan with Hitler in June 1981, only a month after Ogarkov's *Red Star* article. A year later, in speaking to a military audience, Ustinov adopted a defensive posture toward arms control. In an apparent attempt to undermine those who believed that military power was the key to an effective foreign policy, Ustinov noted that "conditions in the world are not simple." Turning to the issue of arms control, he seemed to be pleading with his listeners to understand the importance of arms control, observing that "the peaceloving policy of the USSR . . . is not a sign of weakness."[112] He repeated this latter point a year later in an article in *Pravda*.[113] While such comments may have been in part intended for Western audiences, there is no question that his comments to senior military officers were aimed at calming their anxiety. And there is some evidence that objections from Ogarkov and some of his colleagues did impact

---

[112] "Report of the Minister of Defense of the USSR Marshal of the Soviet Union D. F. Ustinov," *Krasnaia zvezda*, May 12, 1982.

[113] D. Ustinov, "Moguchii faktor mira i bezopasnosti narodov" ("A Mighty Cause of Peace and the Security of Peoples"), *Pravda*, February 23, 1983.

directly on Soviet arms control policy, most notably Moscow's rejection of Paul Nitze's famous "Walk in the Woods" proposal, which was advanced in June–July 1982.[114]

From Ogarkov's standpoint, with the deployment of SS-20s in the latter part of the 1970s and early 1980s an approximate balance existed in Europe at the nuclear level. It is important to emphasize that Ogarkov counted British and French systems as well as those of the U.S. in calculating this balance. Indeed, as noted earlier, it was his concern over the presence of such systems that had caused him in 1977 to take the unprecedented step of commenting critically on the details of an ongoing negotiation with the U.S. Both Ogarkov and the political leadership were united in their efforts to stop the possible deployment of some 572 nuclear-armed Pershing IIs and ground-launched cruise missiles; they disagreed, however, on how to go about it. During the early part of the 1980s emphasis had been placed on a two-pronged course of attempting to use the peace movement in Western Europe to undermine Western support for the new missiles, while at the same time continuing negotiations for their eventual removal. One suggestion, the result of a private discussion between Soviet negotiator Yurii Kvitsinkii and Paul Nitze, was that the Soviets decrease the number of SS-20s in Europe to 75 in return for an agreement from the U.S. to limit the deployment of intermediate range missiles to 75 Tomahawk launchers (each carrying four missiles). In terms of warheads this meant 300 tomahawk warheads for the West to 225 SS-20 warheads for the Soviets. Bombers would have been limited to 150 each.[115] Soviet military leaders opposed this deal for the simple reason that it would have endorsed the presence of American warheads in Europe while at the same time failing to mention British and French systems. Not only would this have raised the nuclear threshold—the very opposite of what Ogarkov was seeking—it would have put additional Soviet targets at risk. This was, reportedly, one of the reasons why it was rejected by the Soviet side. It is perhaps noteworthy that the Soviet rejection of any such deal was the subject of a lengthy interview by Ustinov. On

---

[114] For a discussion of this proposal, see Strobe Talbott, *Deadly Gambits* (New York: Knopf, 1984).

[115] Ibid., pp. 124–25.

this question Ogarkov's concerns were apparently shared by a number of his colleagues.

Throughout the remainder of Ogarkov's time as chief of the General Staff the Soviets continued to insist on compensation for the British and French systems in INF discussions. During 1983, for example, in the so-called "Walk in the Park" proposal, the Soviets offered to limit SS-20 deployments to 120 if the U.S. would halt its plans to go ahead with the deployment of any Pershing IIs or Tomahawk cruise guided missiles. The issue of British and French systems would be deferred until later. In fact, the 120 SS-20s would have given the Soviets compensation for British and French systems. The proposal did not succeed and was eventually rejected by the Soviets themselves, lest anyone believe they were willing to live with British and French systems. As a consequence, the military status quo on the nuclear systems held by London and Paris was upheld.

Despite Ogarkov's success in getting the political leadership to remain firm on the arms control front, it was obvious that this was only a temporary lull. In essence, the leadership remained committed to arms control. Andropov expressed his commitment to détente on March 27, 1983, and invited the U.S. to join Moscow in working toward "preventing a nuclear catastrophe."[116] Several months later in a Plenum speech he resurrected the idea of "realistic" forces in the West with which the Soviet Union could work: "However, in today's capitalist world there are other tendencies, other policies, which more realistically take into account the situation in the international arena. [These people] understand that in the world an irreversible process has occurred, they understand the necessity for mutually acceptable, protracted peaceful coexistence between systems with different social systems. We for our part have said and repeat that we are ready for that.[117] In September, just before the arrival of U.S. missiles in Europe, Andropov reiterated his commit-

---

[116] "Otvety Yu. V. Andropova na voprosy korrespondenta 'Pravdy' " ("Answers by Yu. Andropov to Questions from a *Pravda* Correspondent"), *Krasnaia zvezda*, March 27, 1983.

[117] "Rech' General'nogo sekretaria Tsentral'nogo Komiteta KPSS tovarishcha Yu. V. Andropova na Plenume TsK KPSS 15 Iiunia 1983 goda" ("Speech of General Secretary of the Central Committee of the CPSU Comrade Yu. V. Andropov at the Plenum of the CC of the CPSU June 15, 1983"), *Krasnaia zvezda*, June 16, 1983.

ment to détente: "Our course, as before, is aimed at preserving and strengthening peace, at détente, at ending the arms race, at broadening and deepening cooperation between states."[118] And Chernenko was no better. In March 1984, for example, he called on all countries to work for peace and expressed the conviction that the world's problems could be resolved positively: "All that makes it possible that in the end the course of events will turn out well and again turn in the direction of strengthening peace, limiting the arms race, and leading to the growth of international cooperation."[119]

There was a certain irony in the position Ogarkov had achieved on arms control by September 1984. Having started out as the military's leading advocate of the process, he was now one of its strongest dissenters. Indeed, one of his most important successes during the last four years he spent as chief of the General Staff was a negative one: he had helped persuade the political leadership not to compromise the military's interests on the altar of improved East-West relations in Europe.

CONCLUDING OBSERVATIONS

There is no doubt that Ogarkov was the dominant figure within the Soviet military establishment during the period he served as Chief of the General Staff. Ustinov, as defense minister, certainly had a lot to say on general military issues, but he was not a professional soldier. The result was that he delegated a number of issues to Ogarkov, especially those in the military-technical area.

The Diagnostic Period

When it came to military-technical issues such as warfighting strategy, Ogarkov was the primary architect of Soviet policy. In fact, he helped to design a new conceptual approach, one that placed increasing importance on conventional and high-technology weapons. Ogarkov's work made it possible to justify intellectually,

[118] "Zaiavlenie General'nogo Sekretarya TsK KPSS Predsedatelia Prezidiuma Verkhovnogo Soveta SSSR Yu. V. Andropova" ("Statement of the General Secretary of the CC of the CPSU, Chairman of the Presidium of the Supreme Soviet of the USSR Yu. V. Andropov"), *Krasnaia zvezda*, September 29, 1983.

[119] "Rech' tovarishcha K. U. Chernenko" ("Speech by Comrade K. U. Chernenko"), *Krasnaia zvezda*, March 3, 1984.

within a Marxist-Leninist framework, the reasons for the decreasing importance of nuclear weapons. It is more difficult, then, to dismiss his work than if he had dealt with the issue in Grechko's piecemeal fashion. Ogarkov also oversaw—and may have designed—the implementation of a whole series of structural and organizational changes aimed at enabling the Soviet military to carry out more effectively the conventionally oriented strategy he favored. In contrast to Grechko, Ogarkov was not aloof from the doctrinal process—he dominated it. There were certainly those within the military establishment who did not agree with him on all issues, but by and large he appears to have gotten his way on almost all matters of substance. Ustinov, for his part, decided early on that issues of military management were for the professional military to work out— and Ogarkov, as the army's top professional soldier, appears to have been given a relatively free hand in diagnosing the military's problems in this area.

When it came to technology, Ogarkov again appears to have dominated the stage. He issued the loudest calls for greater reliance on science, for a better prepared, more forward-looking officer corps, and for intensified work on command and control. However, it would be wrong not to note that Ustinov also played an important role in this area. But his role was more that of a supporting actor. He agreed with Ogarkov on all of these issues and saw it as his duty to lend his chief of staff as much support as he needed.

While there may have been some disagreements within the high command on both the budget and arms control, there is no question that Ogarkov was the military's primary diagnostician on both counts. Whether he designed the military's positions or they resulted from close consultations with other senior military officers is not known. What is clear, however, is that he was not only the most visible advocate of what he saw to be military interests, he was also uncharacteristically (for a senior Soviet military officer) prepared to take on the political leadership as to both issues. Based on what we know of Ogarkov's dominating personality, I suspect that by and large his views and that of the high command were one and the same during his tenure as chief of the General Staff.

Ustinov's actions in the arms control and budgetary areas suggest that he tended to take his guidance from the political leadership. However sympathetic he might have been to Ogarkov's call for greater budgetary allocations to the military, or on the need to ensure compensation for British and French nuclear systems, when matters came to a head he advocated the policies put forth by his general secretary, as one might expect in the Soviet system. Indeed, it is Ogarkov, not Ustinov, who was unusual in his actions.

Determining Strategy

When it came to determining what strategy to adopt in furthering the military's interests, Ogarkov again appears to have been the dominant figure. While this is probably not surprising on military-technical issues, it is unusual for a senior party member of the Soviet political-military establishment to pursue a confrontational approach on politically sensitive issues. And Ogarkov not only pursued such a course, he seemed to relish it. Furthermore, given the dangers involved in this, one suspects that he decided on strategy and tactics himself: getting others involved would only have complicated matters.

While he took his marching orders from the Politburo, Ustinov appears to have shown considerable creativity in deciding how to deal with both his chief of staff and the issues themselves. From the public record it seems that he tried to avoid disagreements as much as possible: if the matter could be papered over, so much the better. If Ustinov could articulate the military's interests as was the case on INF, he did. When, however, he collided head-on with Ogarkov over a sensitive issue such as the budget or the role of arms control, he was perfectly prepared to deal with him in a (by Soviet standards) firm and direct manner.

Mobilizing Assets

Despite all of his public attention and creative efforts, Ogarkov was not completely successful in mobilizing assets to achieve what he believed to be the military's primary interests. He designed and oversaw the implementation of major changes in Soviet warfighting strategy, and it appears that he had some success in making the Soviet officer corps more aware of the demands of the technological revolution. On the political front, however, the most he was able to do on arms control was to prevent the things he opposed from happening. When it came to the economy, he was unable to convince the political leadership to increase the military budget, and it appears that he had only limited success in his efforts to achieve a better integration of the military and economic spheres. Ustinov's task, on the other hand, was primarily limited to two areas: keeping his chief of staff in line and, to the degree he was able, ensuring support from the military for policies favored by the political leadership when these diverged from those advocated by Ogarkov. Ustinov was operating from a position of strength, having as he did the entire party-governmental apparatus behind him.

PART IV

The Akhromeyev Era, 1984–1988

CHAPTER 7

New Approaches to Military Issues, 1984–1988

*T*he mid-1980s were a period of considerable change in the Soviet Union. The last five years had been characterized by a further decline in the economy, stagnation within the party and governmental apparatus, and a feeling throughout the country that the USSR had lost direction—that it was running, as it were, on automatic pilot. The succession of three old, sick, and in two instances increasingly lethargic general secretaries in a period of three years served further to intensify the image of the USSR as a system ready for the scrap heap of history. Now, however, a new, young (by Soviet standards), and vigorous man had appeared on the scene. This man spoke of the desperate condition of the country's economy, of the pervasiveness of corruption, inefficiency, incompetence, and irresponsibility within the party and state apparatus. What is more, he was talking about a need to bring about radical changes within the Soviet Union, arguing that the depth of the problems left the country no other choice: either it radically reformed itself, or it would fall hopelessly behind the West.

The military was also going through a period of significant change. In terms of personnel, major shifts were under way. Sergei Gorshkov had yielded command of the navy to his deputy, Vladimir Chernavin; the air force commander Pavel Kutakhov was succeeded by Aleksandr Yefimov; and Aleksei Lizichev became head of the Main Political Directorate, replacing the ailing Aleksei Yepishev. In addition, Vasilii Petrov moved up to become a first deputy minister of defense and was replaced as chief of the ground forces by Yevgenii Ivanovskii, and Vasilii Tolubko stepped down as head of the SRF in favor of Yurii Maksimov. With a few exceptions, there would be almost a complete turnover in top-level military officers by the end of 1988. And if there was any single factor that seemed to characterize the new top level military command, it was a commitment to combined-arms strategies and an understanding of the importance of technology in modern warfare.

The new general secretary's comments about the need to get the Soviet economy moving again found a resonance in the military. After all, the marshals recognized better than most the seriousness and depth of the economic problems facing the Soviet Union. Some of the steps the general secretary was taking irritated them—such as his public slights of the military and hints of cuts in the military budget and force structure—but these were things that they could live with if he could make the country competitive in the area of high technology. However, the jury was out and would stay out until he was able to prove not only that he meant what he said but also that he could successfully implement his policies. But we are ahead of ourselves. For the high command, the most immediate problem occurred in 1984, some six months before Gorbachev took over as General Secretary.

Exit Ogarkov

While Ogarkov's days as chief of the General Staff had long been assumed by most observers to be numbered, the TASS announcement on September 6, 1984, that he had been "transferred to other duties" and that Akhromeyev had been appointed chief of the General Staff came as a surprise. The suspense over Ogarkov's ouster was further heightened by the absence of any sign of praise in the announcement for the former chief of staff or any indication of what his new assignment involved. The implication was that Ogarkov had been demoted, an impression that seemed borne out as American diplomats in Moscow were told by a senior Soviet diplomat that Ogarkov had been replaced because he exhibited "unpartylike" tendencies.[1] A number of explanations have been advanced to explain Ogarkov's removal.

Budgetary Pressures?   The most commonly suggested reason for

---

[1] Bernard Gwertzman, "Soviet Dismissal Now Being Laid to a Policy Split," *New York Times*, September 13, 1984.

Ogarkov's ouster is that his demands for increases in the defense budget had reached the point where the political leadership had no alternative but to replace him in favor of a more pliant individual. There is no question that Ogarkov was on the hunt for more resources for the military budget. Indeed, one of the major implications of his May 9, 1984, *Red Star* interview, in which he had called for greater reliance on conventional, high-technology weapons, had been that more money was needed to keep pace with the U.S. and NATO in the crucial area of "emerging technologies."[2] Ogarkov quoted Chernenko to the effect that "the contemporary situation demands constant and manifold efforts to maintain the security of the country and a reliable defense," and went on seemingly to chide the general secretary when he noted that "this requirement must be fulfilled unconditionally." In essence, this put Ogarkov in the position of demanding that the general secretary allocate greater resources to the military. For his part, Chernenko had warned two months earlier that international pressures had "forced us to divert sizable resources to meet needs related to strengthening our country's security. *But even in these circumstances we have never even contemplated any cutting back of social programs.*"[3] Seen in this light, Ogarkov's May interview could hardly be interpreted as anything but a direct challenge to Chernenko and his budgetary priorities. And given Ogarkov's dynamic, aggressive personality, the chances that he would back down from such a deeply held belief were slim. The political leadership had little choice but to get rid of Ogarkov if it hoped to maintain its economic priorities.

Doctrinal Differences?   As noted above, there were some signs that Ogarkov's preference for high-technology conventional weapons had not been shared by all of his military colleagues. While the evidence is tenuous, there is no doubt that in pushing his policies within the Soviet military he had stepped on the toes of many of his colleagues. His argument in favor of arms control during the 1970s had certainly not been popular in all quarters of the high command.

---

[2] N. Ogarkov, "Zashchita sotsializma: opyt istorii i sovremennost' "("The Defense of Socialism: The Experience of History and the Present Day"), *Krasnaia zvezda*, May 9, 1984.

[3] K. Chernenko, "Rech' tovarishcha K. U. Chernenko" ("Speech of Comrade K. U. Chernenko"), *Pravda*, March 3, 1984. Emphasis added.

Likewise, those from more traditional services such as the ground forces had felt threatened by his continued emphasis on high technology at the expense of tanks, for example, just as those whose future was tied to strategic weapons had not welcomed his suggestion that the basic purpose of nuclear weapons was to deter the use of nuclear weapons.

High Profile?   In addition to his assertive nature, Ogarkov had also assumed an unusually high public profile while chief of staff. For example, he had been given the somewhat dubious honor of publicly explaining the Soviet action in downing a Korean airliner off the island of Sakhalin on August 31, 1983. While Leonid Zamiatin, chief of the International Information Department of the Central Committee, and Georgii Kornienko, a first deputy foreign minister, were also present at the press conference on September 9, it was dominated by Ogarkov. His skillful, even arrogant performance immediately began to raise questions in the minds of Western observers, since the tradition is for military officers to defer to civilian officials. Not this time, however. To a degree, Ogarkov's prominence could be attributed to an effort on the part of some within the political leadership to discredit him. After all, the military had bungled the job, and Ogarkov—the man who was always calling on his fellow officers to accept personal responsibility for their actions—would have to pay the price. Whatever the motivations behind Ogarkov's solo performance at the September 9 press conference, the fact remained that it gave him a public—and international—stature not enjoyed by a senior military officer for many years. When in early December the same three men gathered at a press conference to announce Moscow's response to the West's deployment of intermediate range missiles in Europe, the pique felt by the civilians seemed evident: Ogarkov's role here was limited to discussing military-technical issues.

Ogarkov's willingness to disagree openly with senior politicians, together with his performances at the September press conference, combined to give him a stature, particularly in the West, that may have been hard for many civilian party officials to accept. Indeed, if nothing else, the level of jealousy on the part of many of them must have been high.

A Power Struggle?   It is now clear that throughout the early 1980s a power struggle was going on behind the Kremlin walls.

There were, in fact, three death watches, as Brezhnev became increasingly incapacitated only to be succeeded by Andropov, who lasted a mere fifteen months, and Chernenko, who was already suffering from advanced emphysema when he took over as general secretary. Under these circumstances the chief of staff and defense minister took on considerable importance. In fact, there is some evidence that there had been other attempts to remove the assertive Ogarkov. For example, on March 25, 1983, TASS announced that four military officers had been promoted to marshal of the Soviet Union. Among these individuals was Ogarkov's deputy, Sergei Akhromeyev. What was so surprising about Akhromeyev's promotion is that it was the first time a first deputy chief of the General Staff had been promoted to marshal of the Soviet Union. Furthermore, three months later Akhromeyev was promoted from candidate to full membership in the Central Committee; he was clearly a man on the rise. But why the promotion? There are two—and as is so often the case in the Soviet Union, two contradictory—interpretations.

One explanation is that Akhromeyev was being prepared to take over from Ogarkov once the latter had been ousted. He now had the appropriate rank for the job. Alternatively, it is possible that Ogarkov was getting ready to take over Ustinov's position as defense minister.[4] Neither explanation is particularly convincing. To begin with, while there is no doubt that some in the political leadership would have liked to get rid of Ogarkov, he continued to enjoy a high degree of status up to the time of his ouster in September 1984. Indeed, on May 8, 1984, Ogarkov was singled out for special attention at an award ceremony in the Kremlin. It seems unlikely that he would have been the recipient of such an honor if a full-scale campaign were under way to have him removed. The idea that Ogarkov, with his tireless demands on the defense budget, might be chosen as defense minister seems equally unlikely. It would be like putting a fox in the chicken coop. Ogarkov's fortunes may have gone down in 1983 when Akhromeyev was promoted, but they apparently bounded back by early 1984. Why then was he ousted?

---

[4] For an in-depth discussion of this question, see John Parker, *The Kremlin in Transition*, forthcoming from Unwin Hyman, Inc.

In this writer's opinion the most immediate reason for Ogarkov's removal is that he fell victim to the succession struggle. By late 1984 the leadership struggle had become so intense that the thought of a person like Ogarkov in a policy-making position was unbearable. Chernenko was clearly living on borrowed time. It then became clear that Ustinov was terminally ill.[5] If Ustinov died in office and Ogarkov remained as chief of staff, the chances were that Ogarkov would probably become the new defense minister. Despite the similarities between Ogarkov and Gorbachev on many issues, at this point they clearly differed as to the military budget. Thus, given what we now know of Gorbachev's attitude toward the defense budget, and of Ogarkov's seemingly insatiable appetite for funds to finance high-technology programs, Ogarkov had to go. The way in which Ogarkov was treated after his transfer further supports the interpretation that Moscow's primary concern was not so much to discipline him as to ensure that he would no longer be involved in Kremlin politics. For example, former Politburo member Romanov told Western reporters in Helsinki that Ogarkov "was commanding the Soviet Union's largest Western forces."[6] By the time of the Twenty-seventh Party Congress, it was evident that Ogarkov did indeed have a very important position—commander of the Western TVD. Having revived and developed many of the ideas associated with a potential conventional war in Europe, he was now being given the chance to implement them. And given the preeminence enjoyed by the Western TVD, it was very likely that the changes Ogarkov made there would be emulated elsewhere. In addition, Ogarkov continued to publish. His November *Kommunist vooruzhennykh sil* article appeared two months after he was ousted, and his monograph entitled *History Teaches Vigilance* was published in April 1985. Ogarkov again appeared in print in October 1986 when an article purportedly written by him was published in the aftermath of the U.S.-Soviet summit at Reykjavik. The main message of this short piece was to warn the political leadership against making un-

---

[5] According to Ustinov's obituary, he died "after a prolonged illness," suggesting that he had been sick for some time. "Dmitrii Fedorovich Ustinov," *Krasnaia zvezda*, December 22, 1984.

[6] Reuters, Helsinki, October 14, 1984.

necessary arms control concessions to the West.[7] However, since all of the material in this article was taken verbatim from his 1985 monograph, it is not clear whether Ogarkov himself submitted the article for publication or if others were using his earlier writings to send their own messages. Meanwhile, despite a spate of rumors in 1986 that Ogarkov would soon become defense minister, he remained commander of the Western TVD until it was announced in October 1988 that he had in effect been retired by being transferred to the Main Inspectorate. (Soviet marshals by law never retire but are instead usually transferred to the Main Inspectorate when they finish their active duty.) He was again seen in public in November 1988 at the celebrations surrounding the October Revolution among members of the Main Inspectorate.

Ogarkov was a hard act for anyone to follow. In appointing Akhromeyev to succeed him the political leadership chose an individual who both agreed with most of Ogarkov's ideas concerning the future of Soviet warfighting doctrine and was more circumspect politically. Like Ogarkov, Akhromeyev would also participate in news conferences and make his views known on issues of concern to the high command, but he would adopt a lower and less confrontational public profile.

With Ustinov's death on December 20, 1984, the political leadership made the best choice possible for a succession period: they selected a man who had never shown any political ambitions, nor any special interest in matters such as strategy or arms control. In essence, Sokolov was a bureaucrat's bureaucrat. The political leadership had wanted an individual who would not make waves; in Sokolov they found the perfect man.

The tasks facing these men were not easy. The world seemed to be in flux. Not only was Soviet warfighting doctrine undergoing important changes, the economic outlook was uncertain. From the perspective of January 1985 it was not clear whether the political leadership would seriously attack the country's underlying economic

---

[7] N. Ogarkov, *Istoriia uchit bditel'nosti* (Moscow: Voennoe izdatel'stvo, 1985); N. Ogarkov, "Nemerknushchaia slava sovetskogo oruzhiia" ("The Unfading Glory of Soviet Arms"), *Kommunist vooruzhennykh sil*, no. 21 (November 1984); "Marshal Ogarkov: Military Technical Aspects of Soviet Military Doctrine," Moscow, *APN Military Bulletin* in English, no. 2 (October 1986): 5–6.

problems. Similarly, it was far from certain that it would provide the military with sufficient funds to sustain the needed force posture. Andropov had attempted to do something about the economy, but under Chernenko the situation had again stagnated. And even if he won out in the succession, Gorbachev was an unknown quantity. Then there was arms control. The political leadership appeared to be taking a greater interest in it, but with Chernenko on his deathbed it was unclear what would happen. This was an important issue for Soviet force structure. Would Sokolov and, more importantly, Akhromeyev be faced with demands for cuts in forces at a time when they faced additional budgetary problems? If so, could they hold the line as Ogarkov had? The high command faced an uncertain future. For the present, Akhromeyev in particular decided to adopt a "wait and see" attitude. He would see how far the new party leader was prepared to go—and how effective he would be—before deciding whether or not to throw his, and the General Staff's, support behind Gorbachev.

Enter Yazov

If Ogarkov's ouster was a surprise, the appointment of Dmitrii Yazov as defense minister on May 31, 1987—several days after the youthful West German Mathias Rust succeeded in flying a Cessna 172 through seven hundred kilometers of Soviet air space to land at the gates of the Kremlin—was totally unexpected. Only some four months previously Yazov had been moved to Moscow from the Far East to take over the position of deputy defense minister in charge of personnel. And he had not been on any Western lists for probable successors to Sokolov!

In retrospect it appears that the primary factor behind Yazov's appointment was his long-time support for the principles of Gorbachev's policy of perestroika. Indeed, a careful reading of the military press indicates that there were signs that Yazov had for some time been headed for bigger and better things under Gorbachev.

It has been rumored in the Western press that Gorbachev first met Yazov when the General Secretary visited the Far East in July 1986. Whether or not this was the case, Yazov had already been singled out for special attention in the military press. For example, on July 10, even before Gorbachev's visit, *Red Star* reported a meeting of party activists of the Far Eastern Military District at which

Yazov was the principal speaker. According to that account, Yazov was outspoken in his criticism of shortcomings in his own command. Many collectives, he stated, were passive and had failed to introduce new methods for dealing with problems; moreover, they had overrated their achievements and hidden their shortcomings. It is reported that he "sharply criticized" leadership styles, arguing that too much reliance was being placed on paperwork and a formalistic approach to dealing with subordinates.[8] Coming at a time when most other senior military officers were avoiding discussion of perestroika, Yazov's comments caused him to stand out.

Yazov's meeting with Gorbachev shortly after the publication of the article in *Red Star* certainly did nothing to hurt his standing in Moscow. In October he and the late Army General Valerii Belikov, commander of the Group of Soviet Forces in Germany, were singled out for their outstanding work with the Komsomol organization.[9]

However, the most important article praising Yazov's efforts on behalf of perestroika came in January 1987, only days before he was appointed chief of personnel. The article was written by a *Red Star* correspondent who had been sent to the Far East to evaluate changes introduced in that military district since Gorbachev's visit six months earlier. Yazov emerged from this article as the model commander, one who is willing to go to the field with his troops, who knows them and their problems and is bluntly objective in his evaluations. The article states that during his meeting with Gorbachev, Yazov told the general secretary that "discipline in the district had not improved recently and had even worsened in individual units and subunits. He presented accurate figures. Hundreds of officers and dozens of generals attended this talk. Now this talk is called in the district nothing other than a lesson in truth."[10] The article also observed that officers under Yazov's command who were caught concealing information were given severe party and military punishments. Finally, it noted the emergence of the first positive results of

[8] D. Yazov, "Povyshat' trebovatel'nost' " ("Increase Exactingness"), *Krasnaia zvezda*, July 10, 1986.

[9] D. Yazov, "Trebuetsia lichnost' " ("Personality is Required"), *Krasnaia zvezda*, October 31, 1986.

[10] D. Yazov, "Siloi pravdy" ("With the Force of Truth"), *Krasnaia zvezda*, January 16, 1987.

Yazov's efforts: officers spending more time with their troops, more accurate reporting of shortcomings, increased effectiveness of party organizations, a decline in disciplinary problems, and improved combat training. All sweet music to Gorbachev's ears, coming as it did at a time when the majority of those in the high command appeared to be opposing the implementation of perestroika.[11] Furthermore, the speed with which Yazov was appointed and the increasingly high profile he had begun to assume in the military press prior to May 30 suggest that Gorbachev had had his eye on Yazov for some time.

The Key Players

There was not only a generational split between Sokolov, on the one hand, and Akhromeyev and Yazov, on the other, there were also important differences in temperament and outlook. Sokolov had held a senior position of responsibility during the Second World War, while both Akhromeyev and Yazov had been junior officers. Likewise, Sokolov had spent the greater part of his career—and had made his reputation—as an administrator, with special expertise in logistics. He was an officer who could be relied upon to ensure that any organization with which he was associated would run smoothly. He was unlikely to come up with new approaches for dealing with the problems facing the Soviet military. Indeed, in reviewing all of his articles from 1969 to the present I have been unable to come up with a single idea that could be considered either new or profound. If the requirement was for an officer who would keep the military running without rocking the boat, Sokolov was the right person. It would have been hard to come up with an individual who was a greater contrast to Ogarkov.

Akhromeyev and Yazov, on the other hand, each in their own way, bore some resemblance to the former chief of staff. Despite his quiet demeanor and nonconfrontational approach when dealing with sensitive political issues, Akhromeyev shared some of Ogarkov's intellectual approach in dealing with the problems facing the military. From his writings it also appears that he shared the key tenets of Ogarkov's thinking on warfighting. His understanding of arms con-

---

[11] See Dale R. Herspring, "On Perestroika: Gorbachev, Yazov, and the Military," *Problems of Communism* 36 no. 4 (July–August 1987): 99–107.

trol had developed from superficial, when he became first deputy chief of the General Staff in 1979, to encyclopedic, by 1988. He reportedly did not use or even refer to his notes in arms control negotiations, but carried his facts with him in his head. Yazov, by contrast, appears to have had little interest in issues such as strategy, tactics, or arms control. Like Ogarkov, however, he was deeply interested in developing a new Soviet man, one who would be able to meet the demands of contemporary warfare. In fact, Yazov's view of what a Soviet soldier, and particularly a Soviet officer, should look like bore an uncanny resemblance to what Ogarkov called for: personal responsibility, initiative, and creativity in solving problems, a willingness to look to the future rather than to the present or past, concern for his troops, and personal competence. Indeed, in his writings over the past ten years Yazov treated the issue of creating a new socialist military officer with an almost religious fervor. This was his cause—one to which he was personally and deeply committed.

Thus while there are differences, and important ones, between Ogarkov and Akhromeyev and Yazov, the latter two advocated ideas very similar to those of their former chief of staff. As a result, as long as they were in the high command Ogarkov's influence would continue to be felt, not only because of the changes he was introducing as chief of the Western TVD, but through these influential leaders as well.

MILITARY-TECHNICAL ISSUES

The period after Ogarkov's ouster was one of considerable flux in Soviet military thinking about both warfighting strategy and personnel issues. This was particularly true of the period after mid-1986. Gorbachev's suggestion that the Soviet Union should move from an offensive strategy to one sufficient only for defense and his strong advocacy of perestroika (which had serious implications for how technology and personnel issues are to be handled in Soviet military) opened a new chapter in Soviet military affairs. Will the Soviet Union modify its strategy? If so, will this involve major changes in force structure? Will it produce a more formidable military force? What about perestroika in the armed forces? How will it impact on the officer corps? Will it bring about an upgrading in the quality of Soviet military officers? Will it produce a more efficient army and navy, better able to incorporate the latest developments from the world of high technology? Most important, will Gorbachev and Yazov succeed in gaining the acceptance of their policies not only in the military but also in the Soviet Union in general? From the perspective of 1989 these questions remain unanswered. Indeed, it may be another five or ten years before it will be possible to evaluate critically just how far things will go in the national security realm under Gorbachev. Nevertheless, given their potential significance, it is important to understand the important changes that occurred in military technical affairs while Akhromeyev was chief of the General Staff. It may help us better understand where the Soviets think they are going and the implications of this for both the USSR and the West.

Warfighting Strategy

During Akhromeyev's tenure as chief of the General Staff a major change occurred in the discussion of warfighting strategy. Where Ogarkov had concerned himself with many of the basic concepts underlying Soviet force structure and deployment, the two men who in one way or another succeeded him tended to speak in more general terms. Thus, where Ogarkov was concerned about subjects like deep operations and TVDs, Akhromeyev, who appears to have had primary responsibility for warfighting, avoided going into much detail on these issues. He mentioned the importance of fronts in the Second World War and made clear that such developments had implications for the present. For example, he used the experience of World War II to make a point about the importance of combined-arms operations: "The experience of the first period of the Great Patriotic War once again convincingly proves the accuracy of the most important conditions of the military art, in that victory in a battle with a strong opponent can be won only with the combined strength of all types of armed services and their *close integration*."[12] Akhromeyev goes on to point out the continuing importance of the

---

[12] S. Akhromeyev, "Prevoskhodstvo sovetskoi voennoi nauki i sovetskogo voennogo iskusstva—odin iz vazhneishikh faktorov pobedy v velikoi otechestvennoi voine" ("The Superiority of Soviet Military Science and Soviet Military Art—One of the Most Important Factors of Victory in the Great Patriotic War"), *Kommunist*, no. 3 (February 1985): 53. Emphasis added.

World War II experience for the present, thereby making the point that combined-arms operations remain the key to a victorious war. Although he discusses many of these factors, he does not develop his ideas on them in any detail. Akhromeyev's primary concern appears to have been with broader issues such as the role of nuclear weapons.

There are at least two possible explanations for this change in style. First, the nature of the future Soviet force structure was clearly a matter of discussion within the high command; until the details were worked out, it was an issue that the high command preferred not to talk about in detail. Second, given Ogarkov's transfer to the command of the Western TVD and his dominating personality, it is possible that he had been given primary responsibility for implementing these concepts within the Western TVD. This TVD would then presumably serve as a model for others. Whatever the reasons for the reluctance to discuss these issues in detail, it is clear that at least on the written and verbal level, major changes in how the Soviet military operates were under way.

The Nature of War. There was very little change in basic Soviet positions on most issues compared with those espoused by Ogarkov. The concept of strategic nuclear parity, for example, was an accepted fact in the writings of all three individuals. Sokolov reiterated what the politicians had been saying, namely, that a nuclear war "could not be won."[13] Akhromeyev discussed the issue several times in his writings and on every occasion came to the same conclusion: given the quantity of nuclear weapons available to both sides, and given the assurance that an attack by one side would be met by a swift and devastating retaliation from the other, nuclear war would be senseless: "Nuclear war can only lead to mankind's destruction," or, as he put it at the end of 1987, "Today it is impossible to achieve any political goals in a nuclear war."[14] Likewise, Yazov argued in 1987 that any kind of war would threaten humanity's very existence.[15]

The same is true of Ogarkov's skepticism concerning limited

[13] S. Sokolov, "Pobeda vo imia mira" ("Victory in the Name of Peace"), *Pravda*, May 9, 1987.

[14] S. Akhromeyev, "Velikaia pobeda" ("The Great Victory"), *Kraznaia zvezda*, May 9, 1987. See also "The Doctrine of Preventing War, Defending Peace and Socialism," *Problemy mira i sotsializma*, no. 12 (December 1987), *FBIS, The Soviet Union*, January 4, 1988, p. 3.

[15] D. T. Yazov, *Na strazhe sotsializma i mira (On Guard Over Socialism and Peace)* (Moscow: Voennoe izdatel'stvo, 1987), p. 31.

nuclear war. Yazov argued in 1987, for example, that the Western idea that a nuclear war could be limited to a single theater "is groundless."[16] And Akhromeyev argued against the use of any nuclear weapons, "since they cannot be used without catastrophic consequences for the whole of humanity."[17] The major concern of both writers was that any use of nuclear weapons could very well escalate to the point where central systems would inevitably become involved.

Conventional Weapons. The most important developments in the warfighting area over the past four years came in the area of conventional weapons. To begin with, all three Soviet military leaders accepted Ogarkov's primary thesis concerning the increasing importance of conventional weapons. Not surprisingly, this is particularly true of Akhromeyev, who as chief of the General Staff had primary responsibility for such matters. In February 1985 Akhromeyev accused the West of developing "new, highly accurate conventional weapons."[18] In a *Kommunist* article he argued that such weapons were more lethal, had a greater range, and were more accurate.[19] Two months later, in an article published in *Novyi Mir*, Akhromeyev picked up on a line Ogarkov had used, maintaining that such weapons were approaching nuclear weapons in terms of their "lethal nature, range, and accuracy."[20] Sokolov adopted a similar line, often accusing the West of "increasing the effectiveness of its conventional forces," and in his address to the Twenty-seventh Party Congress warned that the United States is "developing weapons based on new physical principles."[21]

Such weapons played an important role in Soviet discussions of the nature of a future conventional war. Writing in 1987, for example, Yazov argued that there were three types of wars: nuclear,

[16] Ibid., p. 30.

[17] Akhromeyev, "The Great Victory."

[18] S. Akhromeyev, "Na strazhe mira i sotsializma" ("On Guard over Peace and Socialism"), *Krasnaia zvezda*, February 22, 1985.

[19] Akhromeyev, "The Superiority of Soviet Military Science and Soviet Military Art—One of the Most Important Factors of Victory," p. 62.

[20] S. Akhromeyev, "Velikaia pobeda i uroki istorii" ("The Great Victory and the Lessons of History"), *Novyi mir*, no. 5 (1985): 19.

[21] S. Sokolov, "Velikaia pobeda" ("The Great Victory"), *Kommunist*, no. 6 (1985): 64; "Rech' tovarishcha Sokolova, S. L." ("Speech by S. L. Sokolov, USSR Defense Minister"), *Pravda*, March 2, 1986.

conventional, and local. The nuclear conflict, as noted above, was seen as a catastrophe for all of humankind. Yazov pointed out that some people thought that a conventional war would be like World War II. This was wrong for two reasons: first, there was a very real danger that such a conflict could escalate to the use of nuclear weapons, and second, in terms of their combat characteristics, some of the highly accurate weapons that would be utilized approached "small nuclear weapons" in terms of how lethal they were.[22] The clear implication was that if a war were to occur the casualties and destruction involved would approach that of a nuclear war, a point Gorbachev also made in *Perestroika*: "military technology has developed to such an extent that even a non-nuclear war would now be comparable with a nuclear war in its destructive effect."[23]

This tendency to equate nuclear and conventional weapons was particularly evident in an article Akhromeyev wrote in May 1987. In it Akhromeyev observed:

> The Soviet Union and its allies unreservedly reject war as a means of resolving political and economic disputes between states. They are convinced opponents of war in any form. The allied socialist states proceed from the premise that under present-day conditions neither nuclear nor conventional war must in any circumstances be allowed; it must not be unleashed. Nuclear war can only lead to humanity's destruction. A world war involving the use of conventional means will, if it is launched by an aggressor, also bring humanity incalculable and even unpredictable disasters and suffering.[24]

And a year later, during his visit to the United States, Akhromeyev came close to equating the two kinds of war when he noted in his address before the Council on Foreign Relations that "a world war (both nuclear and, we believe, conventional) under present conditions cannot be fought. It must not be unleashed. There will be no winners in any version of such a conflict."[25] Thus, the two kinds of war were perceived, by both Akhromeyev and Gorbachev, to be

---

[22] Yazov, *On Guard Over Socialism and Peace*, p. 31.

[23] Gorbachev, *Perestroika*, p. 141.

[24] Akhromeyev, "The Great Victory."

[25] Presentation of the Chief of the General Staff of the Armed Forces of the USSR Marshal of the Soviet Union S. F. Akhromeyev at the Council on Foreign Relations in NYC, July 11, 1988, p. 2. Typewritten manuscript.

much more closely related in terms of their destructive consequences than was the case, for example, in 1976.

Up to this point it could be argued that these men, particularly Akhromeyev, were doing little more than elaborating on ideas Ogarkov had already articulated. His preference for conventional weapons, his belief that the primary purpose of nuclear weapons was to deter nuclear weapons, his rejection of limited nuclear wars, and his concern over high-technology weapons were all taken over by his successors. Indeed, with the publication in early 1985 of a book by the Soviet theoretician and General Staff officer Colonel General Makhmut Gareyev, Ogarkov's ideas appeared to have achieved canonical status. In this book, entitled *M. V. Frunze—Military Theorist*, Gareyev referred to the key doctrinal work written some twenty years earlier by Marshal Sokolovskii and noted that "over the more than twenty years [since its publication] not all the provisions of this book have been confirmed." Gareyev went on to explain what he had in mind:

> In the 1960s and 1970s the authors of this and many other books proceeded primarily from the view that a war under any circumstances would be waged employing nuclear weapons, and military operations employing solely conventional weapons were viewed as a brief episode at the start of a war. However, the improvement and stockpiling of nuclear missile weapons have reached such limits where the massed employment of these weapons in a war can entail catastrophic consequences for both sides. At the same time, there has been a rapid process of modernizing conventional types of weapons in the armies of the NATO countries. The main emphasis has been put on the development of highly accurate, guided weapons which in terms of effectiveness are close to low-power nuclear weapons. Under these conditions, as is assumed in the West, there will be a greater opportunity for conducting a comparatively long war employing conventional weapons and primarily new types of high-precision weapons.[26]

As in the comments by Sokolov, Akhromeyev, and Yazov, all the main points made by Ogarkov were included: the diminished utility of nuclear weapons, the increased likelihood that conventional

[26] M. A. Gareyev, *M. V. Frunze—Voennyi Teoretik* (*M. V. Frunze—Military Theorist*) (Moscow: Voennoe izdatel'stvo, 1985), pp. 183–84.

weapons would be used, the importance of high-technology systems, and so on.

Despite this seeming confirmation of Ogarkov's major ideas, by late 1985 Gorbachev was articulating a new concept, that of military sufficiency, which, if it were implemented along the lines currently being discussed in the USSR, would have wide-ranging implications for the Soviet military.

Military Sufficiency.   Gorbachev's discussion of the concept of sufficiency can be traced to his address to the Supreme Soviet on November 27, 1985. In this speech he called on the U.S. and the USSR to "reach a common understanding of what level of weapons on each side could be considered relatively sufficient from the point of view of its reliable defense."[27] Gorbachev returned to this theme in his address to the Twenty-seventh Party Congress. As he put it, "Our country stands for . . . restricting military potentials within the bounds of reasonable sufficiency."[28] In making this argument, Gorbachev was maintaining that Soviet security depended on reducing nuclear weapons. In the past, while the desirability of reducing such weapons had always been acknowledged, indeed stressed, emphasis had been placed on the maintenance of strategic parity. For Gorbachev, however, what was important was a reduction in forces. Former Soviet Ambassador to the United States Anatoli Dobrynin picked up on Gorbachev's comment in an article published later that year in *Kommunist*. Dobrynin called for a reduction in conventional and nuclear forces to the point where "a rational sufficiency exists."[29] After some hesitation Akhromeyev adopted a similar stance the following February when he stated that Soviet military doctrine was "based on maintaining the country's defense capability at a strictly

---

[27] M. Gorbachev, "Ob itogakh sovetsko-amerikanskoi vstrechi na vysshem urovne v Zheneve i mezhdunarodnoi obstanovke" ("Concerning the Results of the Soviet American Summit in Geneva and the International Situation"), *Pravda*, November 28, 1985. Khrushchev had previously used this term in his 1960 Supreme Soviet Speech to justify his decision to reduce the forces by 1.2 million men, and Brezhnev had used the terms as early as 1966 in his March 29, speech to the Twenty-third Party Congress.

[28] M. Gorbachev, "Politicheskii doklad Tsentral'nogo Komiteta KPSS XXVI S'ezdu Kommunisticheskoi Partii Sovetskogo Soiuza" ("The Political Report of the Central Committee of the CPSU to the 26th Congress of the Communist Party of the Soviet Union"), *Pravda*, February 26, 1986.

[29] Anatoli Dobrynin, "Za bez'iadernyi mir, navstrechu XXI veku" ("For a Non-nuclear World, Toward the 21st Century"), *Kommunist*, no. 9 (1986): 27.

necessary level, precluding military strategic superiority on the part of imperialism."[30]

The campaign for military sufficiency was internationalized at the Budapest meeting of Warsaw Pact chiefs in 1987 when the communiqué issued at its conclusion called for "the reduction of armed forces and conventional armaments in Europe to a level where neither side, while making sure of its own defenses, would have the means for a surprise attack on the other side or for mounting offensive operations in general."[31] As a part of this communiqué, the Pact went on to propose the reduction of half a million troops by each side by the early 1990s.

The first high-level military response to the Budapest call was very positive. General Lushev, who is a first deputy defense minister, observed that the Soviet Union was interested in limiting forces to those "needed only for defense, but which are not capable of attacking."[32]

Talking in vague generalities about restructuring forces is one thing; actually deciding what that means, however, is another. And here there were some hints from Soviet sources during the Akhromeyev era on what they had in mind. First, Soviet writers suggested that forces should be restructured in order to discourage offensive operations. As retired General Mil'shtein put it, "if troops with offensive weapons are withdrawn—mobile units, strike aviation, tanks—. . . then, before organizing an offensive, it would be necessary to regroup, concentrate, and so forth."[33] Likewise, General Gareyev, in an article published in the West shortly before Akhr ⲏ-meyev's retirement, argued that "it would be expedient for the sides to withdraw their troops to a distance which would rule out surprise attacks on the territory of adjacent states without the necessary re-

[30] S. Akhromeyev, "The Glory and Pride of the Soviet People," *Sovetskaia Rossiia*, February 21, 1987, *FBIS, The Soviet Union*, February 27, 1987, p. 18

[31] "O voennoi doktrine Gosudarstv-uchastnikov Varshavskogo dogovora" ("Concerning the Doctrine of the States of the Warsaw Pact"), *Izvestiia*, May 31, 1987.

[32] P. Lushev, "Na strazhe zavoevanii revoliutsii" ("On Guard over the Gains of the Revolution"), *Mezhdunarodnaia zhizn'*, no. 8 (1987): 67.

[33] Statement by Vadim Makarevskii in an anonymous report of a roundtable discussion. "On Reasonable Sufficiency, Fragile Parity and International Security," *Novoe vremyia*, no. 27 (July 3, 1987): 20, as cited in James H. McConnell, *Reasonable Sufficiency in Soviet Conventional Arms-Control Strategy*, Working Paper, Center for Naval Analysis, CNA 87–1988, p. 3.

deployment of troops from in-depth areas." This would make it more difficult, he continued, for either side to carry out "offensive operations."[34] Restructuring Soviet forces, whether unilaterally or together with the West, would mean making some hard choices as to which types of forces would have to be cut. And while it was not clear exactly what the Kremlin had in mind during Akhromeyev's tenure as chief of the General Staff, it was evident that major changes were being contemplated. Akhromeyev himself argued that the implementation of a defensive policy would bring about changes in almost every area of activity, "in the nature and substance of military planning and military development, in the training of armed forces, and in the demands made on the development of our military art—strategy, operational art, and tactics."[35] And shortly before Akhromeyev stepped down, a relatively junior officer argued that the Soviet military would be well advised to move toward a smaller force posture, one that had more in common with the cadre/professional type army of the late 1920s and early 1930s than with the mass conscript armies of the present. The small size of such an army would make it easier to train and equip forces with the latest in modern high-technology weapons systems.[36] While this idea has been strongly opposed by the General Staff, it remains very much an issue in the USSR.[37]

---

[34] Makhmut Gareyev, "The Revised Soviet Military Doctrine," *Bulletin of the Atomic Scientists* 5, no. 10 (December 1988): 32. See also the same author's comments at a press conference in June 1987. "Doktrina predotvrashcheniia voini" ("A Doctrine for Preventing War"), *Krasnaia zvezda*, June 23, 1987.

[35] Akhromeyev, "The Doctrine of Preventing War, Defending Peace and Socialism," p. 3.

[36] Aleksandr Savinkin, "Kakaia armiia nam nuzhna" ("What Kind of an Army is Necessary for Us?"), *Moskovskie Novosti*, November 6, 1988. For public reactions to this article see, "Soldat—eto professiia" ("Being a Soldier Is a Profession"), *Moskovskie Novosti*, January 8, 1989, and "Nuzhna li reforma armii?" ("Does the Army Need Reforms?"), *Moskovskie Novosti*, January 22, 1989. For his part, Akhromeyev made it clear that he opposed such an approach: "Marshal of the Soviet Union Sergei Fedorovich Akhromeyev Answers Questions from *Sovetskaia Rossiia* Readers," *Sovetskaia Rossiia*, January 14, 1989, in *FBIS, The Soviet Union*, January 18, 1989.

[37] For a statement of the high command's attitude, see D. Yazov, "Armiia naroda" ("The Army of the People"), *Pravda*, February 23, 1989; M. Moiseyev, "S pozitsii obronitel'noi doktriny" ("From a Position of Defensive Doctrine"), *Krasnaia zvezda*, February 10, 1989; S. Akhromeyev, "The Army and Restructuring," *Sovetskaia Rossiia*, January 14, 1989, in *FBIS, The Soviet Union*, January 18, 1989 and A. Lizichev, "V tsentre perestroiki—chelovek" ("In the Center of Perestroika—the Individual"), *Krasnaia zvezda*, Feb-

The idea of a defensive orientation marked a radical departure in Soviet strategic thought. This was true even of Akhromeyev. Throughout his writings he discussed the role of the offensive in the Second World War and stressed its implications for the present. His 1982 comment in *Red Star* was typical: "The basic type of military action leading to the achievement of decisive military-political goals is the strategic offensive."[38] Similarly, as one Western analyst has noted, even the most recent edition of the *The Military Encyclopedic Dictionary* (published in 1986) blessed defense only "as an expedient when confronted with a superior opponent, or when it is necessary to economize on forces on secondary axes in order to accumulate a preponderance of forces for an offensive on the main axis."[39] It is thus not surprising that many in the West did not take Soviet talk of military sufficiency and a defensive doctrine very seriously. It was hard to believe that the Soviets could or would make such radical changes in their force structure or military thinking.

Management, Technology, and Leadership

While top-level military officers had called for improved management techniques, a greater emphasis on management, and a more viable personnel force, it was only after Gorbachev took over and introduced his policy of perestroika that the problems inherent in the military system began to be attacked vigorously. Akhromeyev, for example, wrote about the need to improve the methodological training of commanders and officer cadre in 1984.[40] Likewise, in February 1985 he repeated one of Ogarkov's favorite themes: namely, that it was critical for officers to focus not on past wars, but on the future. History, he stated, "offers many examples

---

ruary 3, 1989. The issue also reportedly played a role in the defeat of a leading Soviet general in the elections held in March 1989 for the Congress of People's Deputies. See Michael Dobbs, "Soviet General Faces Challenge," *Washington Post*, March 24, 1989.

[38] S. Akhromeyev, "Vtoraia mirovaia voina: itogi i uroki" ("The Second World War: Results and Lessons"), *Krasnaia zvezda*, December 18, 1982.

[39] McConnell, "Reasonable Sufficiency in Soviet Conventional Arms-Control Strategy," p. 6.

[40] S. Akhromeyev, "Rol' Sovetskogo Soiuza i ego Vooruzhennykh Sil v dostizhenii korennogo pereloma vo vtoroi mirovoi voine i ego mezhdunarodnoe znachenie" ("The Role of the Soviet Union and its Armed Forces in the Achievement of a Fundamental Breakthrough in the Second World War and its International Significance"), *Voenno-istoricheskii zhurnal*, no. 2 (1984): 24.

when the armies of some states prepared for future wars basing themselves only on the experience of the past without taking into account evolution in the military field." The same was true of technology. Leaders like Akhromeyev saw just as clearly as Ogarkov had the importance of science and technology: "A key place in the strengthening of the military might of the Armed Forces is occupied by *military science* as it plays the leading role in the theoretical elaboration of the armed means of achieving political ends."[41] Furthermore, Akhromeyev was just as aware of the need to improve the technical qualifications of officers and enlisted personnel. The difference between Akhromeyev prior to Gorbachev and Akhromeyev after Gorbachev had been in office for a year was that the former's comments tended to be ritualistic, while after the middle of 1986 the latter's statements revealed an increasing urgency and determination. Indications are that the initial reaction to perestroika in the military, including the high command, was cool.[42] It was one thing to recognize the need for change, another to deal with the confusion and instability that major modifications in bureaucratic procedure entail. Furthermore, there was no need to rush into a lot of probably unnecessary changes when it was uncertain how serious or effective the new general secretary would be.

Gorbachev outlined the key elements of his new policy of *uskorenie* (acceleration), as it was called at the time, in his speech to the Party Plenum in April 1985, shortly after becoming general secretary.[43] This address criticized the Soviet economic system, and especially the party political apparatus, for having failed to keep up with the demands of the times. He called for an acceleration of social and economic progress to be attained "by making use of the achievements of the scientific-technological revolution and by making the forms of socialist economic management fit contemporary conditions and demands." Gorbachev focused on the need for a more effective use of both human and material resources, a more creative

---

[41] Akhromeyev, "The Superiority of Soviet Military Science and Soviet Military Art," pp. 50, 62.

[42] See Herspring, "On Perestroika: Gorbachev, Yazov, and the Military."

[43] M. Gorbachev, "O Sozyve ocherednogo XXVII s'ezda KPSS i zadachakh, sviazannykh s ego podgotovkoi i provedeniem" ("On Convening the Regular 27th CPSU Congress and Tasks Connected with Preparing for and Holding It"), *Pravda*, April 24, 1985.

approach to management, the acceleration of the tempo of work, and the revitalization of the party apparatus. He asserted that ideological-political education should emphasize the "acceleration of the country's socioeconomic development." With regard to the human factor, Gorbachev spoke of the need to reinforce order and discipline, to hold workers responsible for their actions, and to develop a more creative leadership style: "It is now no longer sufficient merely to be able to take executive action . . . [T]he significance of such business-like qualities as competence, a sense of what is new, initiative, boldness, a readiness to take on responsibility for oneself, the ability to set a task and to see it through to the end, and the ability not to lose sight of the political meaning of management is growing greater and greater."[44] Implicit in this speech was the view that the existing Soviet system—with the help of science and technology, improved discipline and work habits, and other measures— was fully capable of putting the country's economy back on its feet.

The military press was ambivalent in its response to this speech and the new policy it expressed. On the one hand, the military tended to view economic acceleration as an issue for the civilian world in general and for the party in particular. On the other hand, the military agreed that it was necessary to improve the level of military preparedness and efficiency. In the words of *Red Star*: "In accordance with the decision of the April Plenum of the CPSU CC, Soviet soldiers have the responsibility to strive even more persistently to master combat skills, to raise vigilance and combat readiness, to strengthen discipline and regulatory order, to organize and, with a high degree of expertise, conclude the winter period of training."[45] With regard to military management, three specific areas were singled out for special attention in editorials in the military press: closeness to people (*bliznost' k liudiam*), "exactingness"—the quality of being exacting or demanding (*trebovatel'nost'*), and personal responsibility (*lichnaia otvetstvennost'*).

The first of these themes emphasized that officers who work closely with their subordinates and therefore know their strengths and weaknesses and who set high standards for themselves and their

---

[44] Ibid.
[45] "Navstrechu XXVII s"ezdu KPSS" ("Toward the 27th Congress of the CPSU"), *Krasnaia zvezda*, April 25, 1985.

troops can expect fewer disciplinary problems and a greater willingness on the part of the troops to carry out their missions. Exactingness was seen as a means of improving efficiency. As a June 6, 1986,
Red Star editorial put it, "It is a question of activating the human
factor, of the need to strive so that everyone works conscientiously
at his place with full efficiency, deeply conscious of the purpose of
the demands placed on him."[46] Persuading the leaders of an army
that had tended to rely on harsh discipline and unquestioning obedience of the efficacy and desirability of this approach would not be
easy.

In the past, in an effort to avoid responsibility for their actions—which had been the key to bureaucratic success in the Soviet
Union to date—many senior officers apparently had routinely failed
to provide their subordinates with clear, consistent instructions.
This practice led to confusion and loss of combat readiness. It is not
surprising, therefore, that the linchpin of management reform in the
military—as elsewhere in Soviet society—was personal responsibility.

Consistent with Gorbachev's April speech, the military assigned
primary responsibility for improved performance to the party apparatus. A May 1985 meeting of party activists called on party organizations to increase their efforts to raise the level of exactingness
and personal responsibility.[47] A month later, Admiral Aleksei Sorokin, first deputy chief of the Main Political Directorate of the Soviet army and navy, complained to a directorate gathering that the
political apparatus in the military had failed to meet the demands of
the April Plenum in a number of areas. In particular, he stated that
Communists, i.e., party members, were not doing enough to ensure
that plans for training exercises were carried out, nor were they setting good examples by improving personal qualifications or meeting
disciplinary standards. He concluded that in the future "the main
efforts are to be concentrated in ensuring the basic perestroika of the
work of individual communists towards supporting strict regulatory
order, in creating healthy conditions of morals and morale in the

[46] "Partiinaia trebovatel'nost' " ("Party Exactingness"), *Krasnaia zvezda*, June 6, 1985,
p. 27.

[47] "Povyshat' boegotovnost', krepit' distsiplinu" ("Increasing Combat Readiness,
Strengthening Discipline"), *Krasnaia zvezda*, May 25, 1985.

military collective."[48] A week later, addressing a meeting of officers of the Southern Group of Forces, Sorokin was again critical of the work of party organs, especially of their failure to eliminate "formalism" from political-educational work.[49]

It is clear from Sorokin's comments that Gorbachev was meeting resistance—or at least inertia—from the military regarding the proposed new forms of management. A review of articles published during this period by the country's three first deputy ministers (Akhromeyev, Kulikov, and Petrov) confirms one's sense of a general lack of interest in the subject.[50] Even Sokolov's expressions of concern appear perfunctory and show none of the urgency evident in Sorokin's comments.[51]

Gorbachev was not pleased with the military's low-key response. He met with senior military officers in Minsk in July and told the generals that "we now need energetic leaders who can command and communicate, people with initiative who are competent in their work." Despite this threat, the attitude of the military changed little in the months leading up to the Twenty-seventh Party Congress. Although there was an increase in the number of articles devoted to perestroika appearing in the military press, the issue was still primarily viewed as one for the attention of the party apparatus.[52] In fact, it is worth noting that Akhromeyev failed even to mention the term perestroika in his 1986 Armed Forces Day speech (published two days before the opening of the Twenty-seventh Party Congress) and that Sokolov, on the same occasion, limited himself to the following brief reference to the subject: "In line with the demands of restructuring, the following are of paramount importance: in-depth knowledge and precise execution of official duties by every serviceman, absolute truthfulness, the faculty of self-criticism in the as-

[48] A. Sorokin, "XXVII S"ezdu KPSS—dostoinuiu vstrechu" ("A Worthy Greeting for the 27th CPSU Congress"), *Krasnaia zvezda*, June 25, 1985.

[49] A. Sorokin, "Povyshat' deistvennost' politicheskikh zaniatii" ("Raising the Effectiveness of Political Work"), *Krasnaia zvezda*, July 2, 1985.

[50] V. Kulikov, "Nasha gordost', nasha slava" ("Our Pride, Our Glory"), *Izvestiia*, February 23, 1986; V. Petrov, "Urok surovy: pouchitel'nyi" ("Stern, Severe Lessons"), *Krasnaia zvezda*, September 1, 1985; S. Akhromeyev, "Na strazhe mira i sotsializma" ("On Guard Over Peace and Socialism"), *Krasnaia zvezda*, February 23, 1986.

[51] "Rech' Tovarishcha S. L. Sokolova" ("Speech by Comrade S. L. Sokolova"), *Krasnaia zvezda*, November 8, 1984.

[52] "Gorbachev: What Makes Him Run," *Newsweek*, November 18, 1985.

sessment of the state of affairs, and the ability to organize and unite subordinates in an uncompromising struggle against shortcomings and deficiencies."[53]

Although the main focus of the Twenty-seventh Party Congress was the economy, Gorbachev brought up the human aspect of perestroika once again, and with renewed vigor. The call at the April 1985 Plenum to improve economic performance by making use of reserves had not worked. Gorbachev now emphasized that progress depended on modifying behavioral patterns, on developing a new Soviet-style meritocracy in which party or family connections would play little or no role. As he put it, "the criteria for all advancements and transfers are the same—the political and professional qualities, abilities, and real achievements of a worker, and his attitude toward the people."[54]

In contrast to the April 1985 Plenum, the high command now appeared to take the general secretary somewhat more seriously. Increasing numbers of articles on restructuring were published in military journals and newspapers. *Red Star* inaugurated a special section devoted to problems of perestroika and published a number of letters to the editor on the topic as well. However, there was still considerable complacency. In a lengthy article published shortly after the Twenty-seventh Party Congress, the chief of the Main Personnel Directorate, Army General Ivan Shkadov, mentioned perestroika only once. His one comment, that "in recent years, a series of steps have been taken to modernize the system of training officer cadre, to improve the complex of military-training establishments for officers and cadre" suggested that he had the situation well in hand.[55] However, if one is to believe Lizichev, there were problems in the party organization within the military itself. At a November 1986 meeting he complained:

[53] S. Sokolov, "Reshaiushchii istochnik boevoi moshchi" ("A Decisive Source of Combat Might"), *Pravda*, February 23, 1986.

[54] M. Gorbachev, "Politicheskii doklad Tsentral'nogo Komiteta KPSS XXVII S"ezdu Kommunisticheskoi Partii Sovetskogo Soiuza" ("The Political Report of the Central Committee of the CPSU to the 27th Congress of the Communist Party of the Soviet Union"), in *XXVII S"ezd kommunisticheskoi partii Sovetskogo Soiuza: stenograficheskii otchet* ("The 27th Congress of the Communist Party of the Soviet Union: Stenographic Report"), vol. 1 (Moscow: Politizdat, 1966), pp. 24, 98.

[55] I. Shkadov, "Delo bol'shoi vazhnosti" ("A Matter of Great Importance"), *Krasnaia zvezda*, March 16, 1986.

Even the election-and-report meetings are far from taking a demanding look at perestroika, from [achieving] fully collective work in the search for new forms and methods in effectively resolving tasks. In some places, criticism carries a formal, superficial character. At many meetings, criteria characteristic of bygone days, an insufficiently fresh form of analysis, [and] a lack of sharp conclusions and self-criticism predominate.[56]

By the beginning of 1987 it was clear that if the military was not openly resisting perestroika, neither was it rushing to embrace it.

Gorbachev's comments at the January 1987 Plenum betrayed his irritation with the slow progress made in implementing perestroika. Acknowledging that "the cause of perestroika is more difficult and the problems that have accumulated in society more deeply rooted than we first thought," Gorbachev called for "truly revolutionary, comprehensive transformations in society." The key to his approach was cadre. "It . . . happens that certain executives find themselves in the wrong position and in no way up to the mark. . . . It seems essential to admit such errors, to rectify them, and without dramatizing them, to assign the person concerned to a job that corresponds to his abilities."[57]

Gorbachev's speech clearly sent a shock wave through the military. Top Soviet generals began to vocalize their support for perestroika. Numerous articles on the subject were written by the Soviet military leadership and appeared in the Soviet press early in 1987. Sokolov devoted an unusually large part of his Armed Forces Day article to restructuring, while Akhromeyev, who had tended to avoid the topic, singled it out for special attention. Lushev wrote several articles devoted to cadre and restructuring. Similarly, the chief of the SRF, Army General Yurii Maksimov; the head of the navy, Admiral Vladimir Chernavin; and the head of the air defense forces, Marshal Aleksandr Koldunov all published articles citing perestroika as a key factor in maintaining a high degree of combat readiness.[58]

---

[56] "Ostree otsenivat' reshitel'no deistvovat' " ("Evaluating More Critically, Acting Decisively"), *Krasnaia zvezda*, November 15, 1986.

[57] "O perestroike i kadrovoi politike partii" ("On Restructuring and the Party's Personnel Policy"), *Krasnaia zvezda*, January 28, 1987.

[58] S. Sokolov, "Na strazhe mira i bezopasnosti rodiny" ("On Guard Over the Peace and

The appointment of Yazov to be defense minister had important implications for the handling of perestroika in the Soviet military. In fact, Yazov appears to have been selected primarily because of his devotion to and expertise on personnel-related issues. Indeed, Yazov differs from many of his military colleagues because of his intense interest in personnel-related questions rather than in those of strategy or doctrine.

In 1978 Yazov authored an article in *Red Star* which outlined the most important characteristics of a commander. They included initiative, creativity, a spirit of innovation, competence, selflessness, good relations with the troops, a high standard of discipline, and a willingness "to assume responsibility for decisions."[59] The following year he wrote another article for *Red Star*—this one devoted to adapting military affairs to the scientific-technological revolution. In it he criticized officers who believed that training troops to deal with high technology was a problem only for specialists.[60] In 1981 he wrote of the need to develop innovative approaches to training[61] and in 1983 of the importance of the commander's moral example in maintaining a high degree of combat readiness.[62] In 1984, he called on officers to assume greater personal responsibility for discipline and in another piece that year criticized preconscrip-

---

Security of the Motherland"), *Pravda*, February 23, 1987; S. Akhromeyev, "The Glory and Pride of the Soviet People," *Sovetskaia Rossiia*, February 1, 1987, trans. in *FBIS, the Soviet Union*, February 27, 1987, pp. v1–4; P. Lushev, "Armiia Velikogo Oktiabria" ("The Army of the Great October"), *Krasnaia zvezda*, February 23, 1987; P. Lushev, "Vysokaia otvetstvennost' voennykh kadrov" ("The Lofty Responsibility of Military Cadres"), *Kommunist vooruzhennykh sil*, no. 5 (March 1987): 9–17; Yu. P. Maksimov, "Perestroika ekzamenuet kazhdogo" ("Restructuring Puts Everyone to the Test"), *Krasnaia zvezda*, February 5, 1987; V. Chernavin, "Avtoritet plavsostava" ("The Authority of Seagoing Personnel"), *Krasnayia zvezda*, March 21, 1987; and A. Koldunov, "Talk" Moscow Television Service, April 12, 1987, *FBIS, The Soviet Union*, April 12, 1987, pp. v2–4. Given the circumstances of his ouster a few months later in the aftermath of the Rust flight to Moscow, Koldunov's comment to the effect that "commanders, political organs, and staffs are acting with increasing responsibility and are raising and improving combat readiness, organization and discipline of personnel" has a certain ring of irony.

[59] D. Yazov, "Sluzhebnoe rvenie" ("Official Zeal"), *Krasnaia zvezda*, April 2, 1978.

[60] D. Yazov, "Na polnuiu moshch' " ("At Full Power"), *Krasnaia zvezda*, November 23, 1979.

[61] D. Yazov, "Chuvstvo novogo" ("A Sense of What's New"), *Krasnaia zvezda*, November 24, 1981.

[62] D. Yazov, "Nravstvennyi primer" ("A Moral Example"), *Krasnaia zvezda*, July 9, 1983.

tion training processes and called on responsible officials to "bravely draw conclusions and take timely measures."[63]

Two additional articles by Yazov appeared in 1985. The first stressed the need for close ties with the troops: "Closeness to people is not determined by the number of hours spent with them, but by actual influence on them and an ability to listen to the soldier and understand him."[64] In the second article Yazov focused on the need for commanders to take full responsibility for their units, something that would require a demanding attitude toward oneself and one's subordinates, no tolerance for shortcomings, a concern for people, initiative, and an irreproachable moral character.

In reviewing his writings one finds a striking congruence between his ideas and those of Gorbachev. Although Yazov did not use the term perestroika, his views clearly mirrored those of Gorbachev.

Yazov has made it clear that he is serious about perestroika. On July 27, 1987, *Red Star* reported a Yazov speech which blasted senior officers for failing to wipe out "negative tendencies" in the armed forces: "We must "look the truth in the eye: certain of us have lost our sense of duty and responsibility for the fulfillment of our duties and tasks."[65] Furthermore, Yazov's monograph published at the end of 1987 focused heavily on the issue of perestroika and its implications for the future of the Soviet military.

All indications are that in Yazov, Gorbachev found a military officer as committed to perestroika as the general secretary. As long as the Gorbachev/Yazov team is in place, management, technology, and personnel issues will have a high priority in the Soviet military.

SOCIOPOLITICAL ISSUES

The Economy

The attitude of the high command changed considerably once Gorbachev took over the reins of power. Where Ogarkov had been

[63] D. Yazov, "Rabotat' s Komsomolom" ("Working with Komsomol"), *Krasnaia zvezda*, June 12, 1984.

[64] D. Yazov, "Blizost' k liudiam" ("Closeness to People"), *Krasnaia zvezda*, October 17, 1985.

[65] D. Yazov, "Voennaia doktrina Varshavskogo Dogovora—doktrina zashchity mira i sotsializma" ("The Military Doctrine of the Warsaw Pact—A Doctrine of Peace and Socialism"), *Pravda*, July 27, 1987.

confrontational, Sokolov, Akhromeyev, and Yazov were much more accommodating on the military budget, at least in public. Furthermore, as Gorbachev's tenure as general secretary wore on, it became increasingly clear that one of his primary goals was to hold down if not cut back on military spending. That Gorbachev adopted such a policy is not surprising; what was unexpected was that in contrast to Ogarkov and his strong opposition to Gorbachev's predecessors, the country's top military officers gradually became more and more willing to support their general secretary.

Gorbachev made clear his intention to gain greater control over the military budget in a number of ways. Shortly after taking over as general secretary he met with a group of senior military officers in Minsk and told them they would have to do more with less.[66] Then, at the Twenty-seventh Party Congress, Gorbachev carefully avoided saying anything about the need for the party to help ensure a strong military as his predecessors had. Furthermore, the program adopted by the Congress contained an important change in language. Brezhnev had stated in 1982 that the party was "taking measures to ensure that they [the armed forces] have everything they need."[67] The new program, however, limited itself to saying that "the CPSU will make evey effort to ensure that the USSR's Armed Forces are at a level that excludes strategic superiority on the part of imperialism's forces."[68] Instead of guaranteeing the marshals that they would obtain everything they needed to maintain a strong defense, the new formulation made clear that the political leadership would limit itself to trying to supply the military with what it needed to ensure that the other side would not obtain military superiority over the USSR. Such a formulation carries with it the clear implication that the party leadership might *not* be able to provide

[66] It is rumored that at a meeting in Minsk in July 1965 Gorbachev told senior military officers that they would have to do more with less. M. D. Popkov mentioned this meeting in an article entitled "Partiia—um, chest' i sovest' nashei epokhi" ("The Party—the Mind, Honor, and Conscience of Our Epoch"), *Voennyi vestnik*, no. 2 (1986): 5. On the rumored substance of the meeting, see "Gorbachev: What Makes him Run."

[67] "Soveshchanie voennachal'nikov v Kremle" ("Meeting of Military Commanders in the Kremlin"), *Krasnaia zvezda*, October 28, 1982.

[68] "Programma Kommunisticheskoi Partii Sovetskogo Soiuza" ("The Program of the Communist Party of the Soviet Union"), in *Materialy XXVII S"ezda Kommunisticheskoi Partii Sovetskogo Soiuza* (Moscow: Izdatel'stvo politicheskoi literatury, 1986), p. 16.

the high command with everything it believed necessary: other approaches might have to be found to help guarantee the country's security. In time it was to become obvious that one of the factors Gorbachev had in mind was arms control and, eventually, unilateral force reductions.

Gorbachev also pushed the military to increase its contribution to the civilian economy. The Soviet armed forces have control over many segments of industry—those which produce goods primarily for the armed forces. In the past most of these enterprises also produced goods for the civilian economy. So the concept of the military contributing to the civilian economy was not new; what was new under Gorbachev was the public pressure directed at the military-industrial complex to increase the amount of work it was doing for the civilian sector. Prime Minister Nikolai Rizhkov, for example, noted on June 18, 1986, the leadership's intention to involve all machine-building industries, including the defense industries, in light industrial production.[69] Similarly, Lev Zaikov, a Politburo member and secretary of the Central Committee, stated in a speech in Irkutsk on July 29, 1986 that "it has been decided that the military sectors of industry will not only take an active part in the production of civilian production and nationally needed goods, but also combine it with the technical reequipping of light industries, food industries, public services, and trade."[70] And on August 28, 1986, a front-page editorial in *Red Star* called on military personnel to derive the "maximum benefit from a minimal outlay of time and resources." The message was clear. The military, like the rest of Soviet society, would be expected to contribute directly to the country's economic revitalization: this was not to be merely a problem for civilians.

Based on his comments only two days prior to the Twenty-seventh Party Congress, Akhromeyev appears to have been unaware of the major change in budgetary language about to be introduced. He was still using the older formulation, stating "the Communist Party

[69] N. I. Rizhkov, "O gosudarstvennom plane ekonomicheskogo i sotsial'nogo razvitiia SSSR na 1986–1990 gody" ("Concerning the State Plan for Economic and Social Growth of the USSR for the Years 1986–1990"), *Pravda*, November 19, 1986.

[70] L. Zaikov, "Nagrada rodiny—stimul dlia novykh svershenii" ("The Reward of the Motherland—the Stimulus for New Achievements"), *Pravda*, June 29, 1986.

is doing everything to ensure that the Soviet armed forces have at their disposal all of the necessary means to perform their constitutional duty of reliably defending the Socialist Fatherland."[71] This suggests that Akhromeyev was unaware of or opposed to the new formulation. Assuming that such a key document was circulated throughout the upper ranks of the Soviet government prior to its adoption by the Twenty-seventh Party Congress, as is the normal practice, Akhromeyev would have had to have known that this new formulation was at least being considered. His decision to go ahead with old terminology could signify opposition on his part, or it could be an indication that the language was still a matter of discussion within the top political-military leadership.

Sokolov appears to have been more supportive of the political leadership from the beginning of Gorbachev's tenure. For example, in his *Kommunist* article published just before Gorbachev's appointment as general secretary, Sokolov argued that fulfillment of the five-year plan "will further strengthen the economic basis of our military capabilities, of the combat power of the Soviet Army and Navy."[72] The important point is that rather than pushing for additional funds, Sokolov placed primary emphasis on fulfilling the five-year plan. Sokolov was in essence parroting the political argument put forth by Chernenko, Andropov, and Brezhnev: namely, that military power would come from the implementation of the basic economic plan, and would not be the consequence of a special emphasis on the military alone. Similarly, his speech at the November 7 parade clearly placed the satisfaction of consumer needs in first place. Referring to industrial growth, he observed, "These rates are dictated by life itself, by the need to enhance the welfare of Soviet people, to maintain the country's defense capability at a level that guarantees the security of our state and of its allies."[73] What is important in this statement is the fact that Sokolov clearly placed the satisfaction of military needs below meeting consumer demands. The following February, in his speech to the Twenty-seventh Party

[71] Akhromeyev, "On Guard Over Peace and Socialism."

[72] S. Sokolov, "Velikaia pobeda" ("The Great Victory"), *Kommunist*, no. 6 (1985): 67–68.

[73] S. Sokolov, "Rech' tovarishcha Sokolova, S. L." ("A Speech by Comrade S. L. Sokolov"), *Pravda*, November 8, 1985.

Congress, Sokolov reiterated the language adopted by the Congress and noted that "the CPSU will make every effort to ensure that the USSR Armed Forces are at a level which precludes the military superiority of imperialist forces."[74] And in case his listeners had not gotten the message, he observed a few days later that "Army and Navy personnel see it as their task to maintain the Armed Forces at the level of modern requirements by making the most rational use of everything with which the country provides them."[75] This idea of making the best use of available resources was to become a common theme within the armed forces.

For his part, Akhromeyev quickly adapted to the new line. In an *Izvestiia* article published on May 9, 1986, he commented that the "CPSU and the Soviet Government are paying unremitting attention to maintaining the country's defense potential at the appropriate level."[76] By the following year Akhromeyev was asserting that "our principle is to maintain the Armed Forces and our military potential in a state of rough military equilibrium and at a level sufficient to ensure reliable defense of the Soviet Union and the Warsaw Pact states."[77] This latter formulation, with its emphasis on "rough" equilibrium, represented a marriage of "military sufficiency" to the phrase utilized at the Twenty-seventh Party Congress. The combination of the ideas of rough equilibrium and sufficiency expressed the idea that there could be no absolute measure of military power and that as a consequence, the military would be provided with what was needed to keep the USSR more or less equal with the West: in some areas the USSR might be ahead, in others behind. By the time Yazov joined the high command, the concept of providing the military with what was needed to maintain overall parity was becoming standard, and Yazov showed no sign of wishing to change matters. In his monograph, for example, Yazov commented that "the USSR and its allies . . . take the necessary steps to maintain at the necessary level their military power."[78]

[74] S. Sokolov, "Rech' tovarishcha Sokolova, S. L., Minister Oborony SSR" ("Speech by S. L. Sokolov, USSR Defense Minister"), *Pravda*, March 2, 1986.

[75] S. Sokolov, "Decisive Source of Combat Might."

[76] A. Akhromeyev, "Uroki istorii" ("The Lessons of History"), *Izvestiia*, May 9, 1986.

[77] Akhromeyev, "The Great Victory."

[78] Yazov, *On Guard Over Socialism and Peace*, p. 20.

The bottom line in the comments by Sokolov, Yazov, and Akhromeyev—once Akhromeyev had accepted Gorbachev's policy—was one of confidence that the party was doing everything required to provide for the country's defense, that overall economic strength was the key to military power, and that the Soviet military had to take renewed steps to ensure that it would handle the resources available to it in the most rational and effective manner. This latter point was emphasized in a number of articles published in *Red Star*. Their message was simple: the people had entrusted the military with valuable resources at a time when the country was undergoing serious economic dislocations; it was up to the armed forces to show themselves worthy of this trust by making the best of what was available.

By 1988 the high command had come a long way from Ogarkov's blatant advocacy of more funds for the military. In fact, based on comments by Akhromeyev and Yazov, the military had come to grips with Gorbachev's belt-tightening. What had changed? One obvious explanation for Akhromeyev's change of heart is that he had sold out to the Gorbachev leadership. While such an action cannot be ruled out, and may have played a role, Akhromeyev adopted a less confrontational approach in dealing with the political leadership from the very beginning of his tenure as chief of the General Staff. For example, while he clearly understood the importance of mobilization and the need for the civilian economy to be heavily integrated with the military, he did not attempt as Ogarkov had done, to get around the budgetary question by trying to tie the economy to the military sector. For Akhromeyev it was a fact of life that the two were closely related: in the event of a war close connections would be necessary, but this was not something to make into an issue. By his nature, Akhromeyev attempted to avoid confrontations over disputed issues.

It is also possible that in Gorbachev Akhromeyev saw someone at long last attacking the country's underlying economic problems. No one knows better than the military the degree to which the country's military might is dependent on its economic efficiency. This was exactly Ogarkov's point: the defense of the Soviet Union depended on the economy, and, given the leaderless situation in Moscow, the only viable approach was to seek more rubles. The assertive position taken by Gorbachev at the Twenty-seventh Party Congress may have served to convince Akhromeyev that the country was now being led by an individual serious about introducing needed changes. Furthermore, there appears to have been an increased willingness on the part of the marshals and generals to admit that the military budget had been a burden on the Soviet economy. As General Chervov put it in mid-1986, "It is in the interests of the country's security and stability to have a lull in the arms race that will permit us to construct new and better cities and to give the people more consumer goods."[79]

In practical terms, this meant that the military was faced with the prospect of short-time sacrifices in return (it hoped) for long-term gains. Such a process would be painful, and numerous bureaucratic oxen would be gored. There would be screams and wails from those whose programs and weapons systems were to be cut back. Furthermore, it was not even clear that Gorbachev would succeed. Nevertheless, he offered the first real hope the military leadership had seen in almost ten years. At least he was attacking the country's problems.

In order to succeed, however, Gorbachev needed a breathing space, or *peredyshka*. This was equally true of the marshals. If they even hoped to see the reform of the economy, the infusion of the high technology they needed so badly, and the modernization of the armed forces, including its restructuring, they too could agree to the desirability of a pause, their own peredyshka. The obvious goal of such a policy would be an improvement in East-West relations followed by the signing of arms control treaties. These would provide the Soviet Union with both the predictability and the lessened threat it needed to direct economic resources from the military to the civilian sector. The outcome from the marshals' standpoint, assuming the process would work, would be a more proficient military machine. It might even be a smaller one. But its key was arms control. Akhromeyev 's prominence in the Soviet arms control process—which went beyond even the role played by Ogarkov—suggests that one of the reasons Akhromeyev decided to go along with Gorbachev was that he saw the possibility of attaining meaningful arms control agreements with the West, agreements that would en-

---

[79] La Republica, June 17, 1986, *FBIS, The Soviet Union*, June 20, 1986, p. AA5, as cited in John Parker, *The Kremlin in Transition*.

hance Soviet security and provide the time needed to improve Soviet military forces.

Arms Control

One of the most interesting aspects of the post-Ogarkov period was the extent to which Akhromeyev dominated the arms control field. He was an active participant in U.S.-Soviet summit meetings from Reykjavik on, and he regularly took part in important press conferences and meetings with Western delegations. When there was a need for an authoritative statement on an issue like the Strategic Defense Initiative (SDI), Akhromeyev was generally the one to write it. In essence, he was assigned primary responsibility within the armed forces for matters dealing with arms control. This is not to suggest that neither Yazov nor Sokolov before him were involved in the process; indeed, both made authoritative statements on a number of occasions. By and large, however, their comments just repeated statements previously made by other leading Soviet military officers. When the top ranks of the military expressed concern over problems of verification, for example, it was Akhromeyev who took the lead. And when Gorbachev met with the American President, it was Akhromeyev who was at his side.

Under Gorbachev Akhromeyev adopted an optimistic approach toward arms control. He did so by combining two interrelated themes. First, he played up the danger inherent in the current international situation: "Never before has the danger of nuclear war loomed so large as it does today." Or: "sinister plans for a new world war are being hatched in the United States."[80] The other half of the equation was his refusal to tie the current situation to the 1930s. Thus, in May 1985 he wrote in a *Kommunist* article that

> whereas the lack of unity among the forces of peace in the West at that time permitted Hitler to start the Second World War, the situation today is fundamentally different. Although the source of wars, i.e., imperialism, still exists, the CPSU believes that war can and must be prevented. Today humanity possesses far greater strength and possibilities for curbing new claimants to world domination than on the eve of the Second World War. These possibilities are repre-

---

[80] Akhromeyev, "The Lessons of History."

sented by the majority of peace-loving states and progressive public opinion in the world, all of which come out in a united front for international détente and disarmament and peace on the planet.[81]

This comment contrasted sharply with what Ogarkov had said throughout his time as chief of the General Staff. Where Ogarkov drew direct analogies between the 1930s and the present, Akhromeyev denied such a connection. Furthermore, where Ogarkov had claimed that the only way of protecting the USSR was through military power, Akhromeyev advocated a line very close to that followed by Brezhnev and Ustinov, that one could avoid a war by working with peaceful forces in the West.[82] He stated: "The main lesson of World War II—namely, that war must be combated before it has begun—therefore assumes special topicality today. Historical experience indicates that joint, concerted, and vigorous action by all peaceloving forces against the aggressive actions of imperialism is necessary in order to defend peace."[83] Indeed, Akhromeyev argued in early 1986 that only through the "collective efforts of all countries and peoples" would it be possible to avoid a war. In comparison with the 1940s, he continued, the situation had *"fundamentally changed."*[84]

By mid-1987 Akhromeyev like Gorbachev was arguing that military power by itself would not guarantee the USSR's security: "Nowadays it is impossible to ensure security merely by improving one's sword and shield." Arms control would be vital: "The security of each state is directly dependent on the security of all. It can only be achieved by limiting and reducing armaments and by strengthening confidence-building measures and international cooperation among countries."[85]

[81] Akhromeyev, "The Superiority of Soviet Military Science and Soviet Military Art," p. 60.

[82] See also Sokolov, "The Great Victory," pp. 65–66; Sokolov, "Speech by S. L. Sokolov, USSR Defense Minister," November 8, 1985; S. Sokolov, "Pobeda, obrashchennaia v nastoiashchee i budushchee" ("A Victory Oriented Toward the Present and the Future"), *Pravda*, May 9, 1986; "I Serve the Soviet Union," Moscow Domestic Service, August 2, 1986, *FBIS, The Soviet Union*, August 15, 1986, p. v2; S. Sokolov, "Pobeda vo imia mira," ("Victory in the Name of Peace"), *Pravda*, May 9, 1987.

[83] Akhromeyev, "The Lessons of History."

[84] Akhromeyev, "On Guard Over Peace and Socialism." Emphasis added.

[85] Akhromeyev, "The Great Victory."

Despite this optimistic approach, Akhromeyev openly voiced concerns in two areas. First, he complained about unilateral concessions on the part of the USSR. At a press conference in August 1986 Akhromeyev reacted to Gorbachev's decision to extend the Soviet moratorium on nuclear testing a second time (until January 1, 1987) by suggesting that the moratorium had damaged Soviet security and given the United States a military advantage: "If we were to take a purely military point of view, conducting nuclear explosions—specifically, eighteen in one year—has given the United States certain purely military advantages. We have to face this squarely. We had to allow a certain amount of damage to ourselves, . . . but we took into account that this damage was within tolerable bounds. Furthermore, Gorbachev reportedly told President Reagan at the Geneva summit that getting the nuclear test moratorium had been difficult, and there are reports that Soviet military officials complained to Western diplomats that they opposed the second extension announced in May 1986.[86]

Several days later Akhromeyev made a major speech before the Conference on Disarmament in Europe (CDE) that betrayed further Soviet military concern about Gorbachev's arms control initiatives, this time in the area of confidence-building measures. Akhromeyev's comments centered on two concerns. First, he stated that while the Soviet Union had accepted the idea of reducing the level for giving notification of its land-force maneuvers, the postponement of a notification requirement for independent air and naval exercises till the second stage of the CDE "was very difficult for us." Akhromeyev also appeared piqued by the Soviet government's decision to agree to exclude U.S. territory from confidence-building measures. As he put it, "If maneuvers of troops near the Volga river and the Urals are subject to notification and verification, legitimate thoughts come to people's minds as to why these same activities are not verified near the Missouri River and Cleveland."[87] The sensitivity of

[86] Gary Lee, "Soviets Successfully Use Nuclear Test Ban for International Campaign," *Washington Post*, August 31, 1986.

[87] Statement by Marshal Sergei F. Akhromeyev, Chief of the General Staff of the Armed Forces of the USSR, First Deputy Minister of Defense of the USSR, Stockholm, August 29, 1986. This statement was handed out by the Soviet Delegation to the Conference on Disarmament in Europe.

these issues within military circles became evident when the *Red Star* summary of Akhromeyev's speech, published the next day, failed to mention them. This summary gave a more positive tone to Akhromeyev's speech, limiting his critical comments to an expression of concern on "the outside limit to garrison activity of troops proposed by NATO."[88] The second area of concern to Akhromeyev was verification. At a press conference on January 18, 1986, he argued that MBFR monitoring "must not turn into intelligence activity."[89] He repeated this warning on several subsequent occasions.

Given Ogarkov's long-standing opposition to the elimination of INF systems from Europe, Akhromeyev's support for the treaty may at first glance appear surprising. However, there are a number of reasons why Akhromeyev in particular supported the agreement, both privately and publicly. First, there was the fact that in contrast to the stagnation of the early 1980s, Gorbachev appeared to have the country moving again, even if it remained unclear whether he would succeed in revitalizing its economy in the long run. For the present, he was the only hope the high command had for rebuilding the economic and technological substructure on which the country's military power was based. Second, while the Soviet military was probably forced to accept more intrusive verification than some would have liked, this phenomenon was becoming more widespread in the USSR. Visits of Congresspeople to the radar station at Krasnoiarsk and of other U.S. officials to the chemical weapons plant at Gomel, the presence of Western teams on Soviet territory to verify the size of Soviet nuclear tests, the challenge inspections carried out under the Stockholm agreement, and the presence of American inspection teams, at Votinsk and other places, to verify compliance with the INF Treaty all suggest that a basic decision had been taken to open up the security sector of the Soviet Union—even if far more remained hidden than was being exposed. Third, the agreement made good sense from the military standpoint. The Soviet military had long been concerned about the presence in Europe of ground-launched cruise missiles and the Pershing II. This latter missile had

---

[88] S. Akhromeyev, "Na Stokgol'mskoi Konferentsii" ("At the Stockholm Conference"), *Krasnaia zvezda*, August 30, 1986.

[89] S. Akhromeyev, "Osvobodit' mir ot iadernogo oruzhiia" ("Freeing the World from Nuclear Weapons"), *Pravda*, January 19, 1986.

been a matter of particular worry to the generals, who viewed it as a highly accurate weapon with the ability to decapitate Soviet command-and-control facilities in the Western regions of the USSR. The INF agreement eliminated this missile from Western Europe. As should be obvious by now, the Soviet high command was also interested in any agreement that would lessen the danger of escalation to nuclear weapons in Europe in the event of a war. While approximately four thousand nuclear warheads would still remain in Europe after the weapons covered by the INF agreement had been withdrawn, this agreement diminished the possibility of any automatic escalation to the use of nuclear weapons in a conflict. Nuclear weapons could still be utilized, but a nuclear-armed aircraft can be recalled, and it also takes longer to launch it.

There was also some question of how useful, for warfighting purposes, systems like the SS-20 would be. The primary military use of the SS-20 appears to be to deter similar Western systems in Europe. Its use would not only guarantee escalation up the nuclear ladder, it would also mean that even if the Soviet military succeeded in a war with NATO, it would inherit a nuclear wasteland—something of dubious military, industrial, and economic utility.

INF also set the stage for a START agreement, something that was of considerable interest to the high command. If the Kremlin could obtain an agreement that cut Western strategic forces by fifty per cent, this could have the effect of constraining Western efforts in this area. Since the high command believed that the only thing that nuclear weapons deter was other nuclear weapons, the money saved from further research and development on strategic or theater nuclear weapons was—or could be—available for work on high-technology conventional systems. In addition, agreements such as INF and START helped make the Western arsenal more predictable. Given the scarcity of resources available to the Soviets and the increasing technological gap separating them from the West, a greater degree of predictability was welcome.

Finally, the Soviet military realized that it could not compete with the West in a technological arms race. And people like Akhromeyev understood that national security was composed of more than weapons and weapons systems. Diplomacy was also important, as Gareyev recognized when he observed that, "the significance of the diplomatic struggle is even more evident. Skillful diplomacy not only creates favorable conditions for the conduct of military actions, it can [also] lead to the creation of an entirely new military-political situation for the conduct of the armed struggle."[90] In fact, it was much more difficult for the West to sustain a military buildup during a period of détente than when tensions were high. Consequently, if a period of détente would serve to undermine—or at least lessen—Western willingness to support a buildup in high-technology conventional weapons at a time when the USSR was struggling to restructure its economy, then arms control agreements would serve the country's security interests.

This is not to suggest that the high command did not make some sacrifices to get the INF agreement. The principle of asymmetrical reductions and intrusive verification were accepted for the first time. In addition, the Soviets agreed to eliminate the SS-23. The high command had long opposed movement in these areas. In the case of the SS-23, there were rumors that the system was plagued with troubles. However, even if it was beset with problems (assuming such deficiencies could be corrected), removal of the missile would eliminate the Kremlin's most reliable system for attacking targets deep in NATO's rear, such as ports needed to sustain the American reinforcement of Europe. Such targets could obviously be covered by a multitude of other nuclear-capable aircraft, but the degree of certainty that they would reach their target on a regular basis was not as high as it would be with a missile.

The Soviets also made concessions at the INF talks. From the high command's standpoint, the Soviet Union agreed to leave French and British systems unrestrained, postponed the question of mid-range aviation, and expressed "its readiness to eliminate all its intermediate-range and operational tactical missiles not only in Europe but also in the Asian part of the country."[91] Some in the military were probably upset over certain aspects of the agreement. The important element, however, was that the key military officer—in this case, Akhromeyev—supported it. And if Akhromeyev supported the agreement, there were reasons for this; he was not the

---

[90] Gareyev, *M. V. Frunze—Military Theorist*, p. 381. I am indebted to Ted Neely for pointing out this citation.

[91] Akhromeyev, "The Doctrine of Preventing War, Defending Peace and Socialism."

kind of individual to make unnecessary concessions or to sacrifice his country's national interests.

Several participants in arms control negotiations with Akhromeyev commented not only on his command of the material and nonpolemical style, but on his authority to make important decisions as well. None of the other seven men focused on in this book enjoyed such power in this area. On some occasions an individual exerted a negative influence (Grechko is the prime example), but in the case of Akhromeyev one had the impression that he was granted considerable leeway in actually *making* important decisions. One explanation for Akhromeyev's unprecedented role in the arms control arena is that because he recognized the extent of the country's economic problems and the need to restructure Soviet forces so that the USSR might be able to compete with the West technologically, and also supported perestroika and military sufficiency, he was given a relatively free hand to negotiate the best deal he could with the West. He understood that an arms control agreement was necessary, that without it the Soviet Union would never gain the peredyshka it so desperately needed in order to restructure its economy and begin to build the technological base to support a modern military and civilian economy. Gorbachev had publicly—and, one assumes, privately as well—made clear that he wanted progress in this area. There is no doubt that he and the Politburo provided Akhromeyev with guidance on the broad principles underlying any agreement. When it came to details, however, one has the impression that this was a matter over which Akhromeyev had considerable authority. In essence, it was to a large degree up to him to craft an agreement in such a way that it did the least amount of damage to the Soviet side while at the same time undermining Western military capabilities to the maximum degree possible.

CONCLUDING OBSERVATIONS

One key way in which the Akhromeyev period differed from the periods under Ogarkov or Grechko was the degree to which the general secretary appeared to dominate almost all segments of military policy. Gorbachev forced through changes that, while generally supported by the top military leadership, probably would have never been implemented had he not been on the scene. In a sense, Gorbachev was the lever forcing through changes, some of which had long been sought by Ogarkov and others. It is probably no exaggeration to suggest that without Gorbachev many of the major changes that took place within the Soviet military would probably not have occurred. However, Gorbachev was not Khrushchev. Khrushchev had attempted to dictate the details of military policy—most of which were strongly opposed by the high command—even in the military-technical sphere. Gorbachev, on the other hand, while he made it clear that changes were needed, left it to the marshals to design a suitable strategy and decide how to allocate funds. Furthermore, in contrast to the early 1960s, Soviet warfighting strategy—even if it were eventually to undergo significant modifications—was building on existing Soviet military thought. This, together with the other factors noted above, may help to account for the better relationship Gorbachev had with his high command.

The Diagnostic Period

Soviet warfighting strategy provided a perfect example of the importance of Gorbachev's role. Many top Soviet military officers recognized that something needed to be done to update the armed forces, to permit them to fight the kind of a war that Ogarkov spoke of in the early 1980s. Nevertheless, given the complexity of the Soviet military machine and the likelihood of major resistance within the military to far-reaching changes, it is unlikely that any single military officer could have brought about the needed reforms. Ogarkov presided over the introduction of a variety of very important modifications in Soviet force structure, but even he was not fully successful in his efforts to get the armed forces to make all the changes he believed to be necessary.

The same is true of management and personnel. Beginning in the early 1970s Ogarkov spoke constantly of the need for major changes in this area. In fact, reading some of his articles and speeches, he occasionally sounds like early vintage Gorbachev. And while he did much to improve the operation of the Soviet military in this area, it was Gorbachev's policy of perestroika that forced the armed forces—even if reluctantly, in some cases—to make the needed changes.

As to the military budget, the situation changed fundamentally once Gorbachev took over. While the military, in the persons of

Akhromeyev and Yazov, was presented with an opportunity to make its views known and present its case, all available evidence suggests that it was Gorbachev and the Politburo that made the key decisions. Furthermore, while it could be argued that this was the way it had always been, the Grechko period suggests that the military could have and has had a direct impact on the formation of the military budget.

Turning to arms control, the contrast with the Ogarkov period is striking. Again the main impetus was the new political leadership. Gorbachev made it known that he was interested in arms control and expected progress in this area. And senior military officers like Akhromeyev understood that arms control treaties could benefit Soviet security.

In all four areas, the problem was not a failure to diagnose the problem: the high command had long understood the need for changes. But now, for the first time in many years, they had a political leadership that was forcing them to make these changes. Not all military officers approved of or even benefited from them. But as long as Gorbachev was in power and officers like Yazov and Akhromeyev occupied the top positions in the military, they had no alternative but to implement them.

Determining Strategy

Gorbachev's approach to the many bureaucracies in the USSR had been to place in leadership positions individuals who supported his policies and, having given them general guidance, to leave it to them to implement these policies. This appears to be what he did with the high command. In Akhromeyev and Yazov Gorbachev had officers with whom he was comfortable. The high command was told that military sufficiency would be the country's military doctrine, but it was largely left to individuals like the former chief of the General Staff to oversee the details of how it was to be achieved. The situation was similar when it came to personnel and management questions. The military gradually, if reluctantly, understood that perestroika would be necessary. In Yazov Gorbachev had someone determined to implement it. As long as Yazov did not slacken in his devotion to perestroika, and as long as his perestroika followed the general guidelines being applied in the rest of Soviet society, it would be up to him to determine how reforms would be applied in these areas.

The budget issue was closely related to both warfighting and arms control. From comments made by Gorbachev and others it soon became evident that the military would be allocated less money in the future. The key point, however, was that it would be up to the chief of the General Staff and his subordinates to decide how best to spend it. For example, with cuts in force structure there would be questions on whether or not additional money should be put into the research and development of high-technology weapons or devoted to additional procurement to attempt to offset any cuts. Likewise, it was asked, what should be done with any money that is saved? Should all of it be put into military-related programs? Or should it be allocated to the civilian sector in an effort to provide the incentives necessary to improve the economy? No doubt there would be differences of opinion between the high command and some civilians in the upper ranks of the political leadership. It remained to be seen how successful senior military officers would be in this area.

Finally, Akhromeyev's unprecedented influence—for a professional military officer—in the arms control arena followed the same line that Gorbachev adopted in other areas: Find an individual who will support your general approach, get him to agree to work within specified guidelines, and then leave it up to him to work out the details.

Mobilizing Assets

Gorbachev's impact was also evident when it came to mobilizing assets. Both top military officers spoke in his name and with his authority when it came to mobilizing the armed forces for perestroika and military sufficiency. The same was true for arms control and the need to live within defined budgetary limits. The ambiguity that had existed under Ogarkov was gone. All concerned knew what was demanded of them, and all understood that Gorbachev expected compliance.

As long as Gorbachev was able to dominate the Soviet political scene as he did during the Akhromeyev period no senior military officer was likely to have problems mobilizing assets within the military. In effect, the military was instituting changes that were part of broader systemic modifications. But it paid a price for this "outside" assistance: Gorbachev set the parameters within which the generals had to work. By the end of 1988 the idea of a minister like Grechko, one who would openly advocate policies opposed by the political leadership, seemed very unlikely. To survive, senior military officers had to be team players. Furthermore, their authority— even within the military—remained to a large degree derivative. If Gorbachev were to have lost out in the political struggle in Moscow, their own ability to enforce their will in areas such as personnel and management would have suffered. They would have been forced into a situation analogous to that which prevailed under Ogarkov, where their ability to effect changes in the military had been dependent on their own standing within the armed forces. And if the case of Ogarkov is an example, they would more often than not have been frustrated.

PART V

Looking to the Future

CHAPTER 8

Gorbachev and the Soviet High Command

Gorbachev's *December 7, 1988,* speech to the United Nations announcing a unilateral reduction in conventional forces coincided with Akhromeyev's retirement "for reasons of health." Both came as a complete surprise to Western observers. Most analysts had believed what Soviet military and political leaders had said: namely, that there would be no unilateral cuts on the Soviet side, that any reductions in Soviet forces would have to be accompanied by similar, even if asymmetrical, decreases in the size of Western forces. Likewise, while there had been rumors for some time that Akhromeyev would retire and become an advisor to Gorbachev, his retirement was seen as a protest against the unilateral nature of the reductions.

Exit Akhromeyev

The cuts Gorbachev announced in Soviet forces are substantial. He stated that Soviet forces would be reduced by some 500,000 worldwide over the next two years. The USSR would withdraw from Eastern Europe and disband some six tank divisions (totaling 5,000 tanks and 50,000 troops). In addition, Soviet forces in the European part of the Soviet Union would be cut by 5,000 tanks, and total Soviet forces from the Atlantic to the Urals would be reduced by 8,500 artillery systems and 800 combat aircraft. Furthermore, as Gorbachev announced on January 18, 1989, of the 500,000 troops to be reduced, 240,000 would come from the European part of the country, 200,000 from the eastern sector, and 60,000 from the southern.[1]

---

[1] "Soviet Split on Military Cuts," *New York Times*, December 8, 1988; "Gorbachev Says Military Budget Faces Cutbacks," *Washington Post*, January 19, 1988.

The USSR's allies subsequently also announced cutbacks in force structure. Taken together, Soviet and East European force reductions in Europe will amount to a total of "296,300 troops, 12,000 tanks, 9,130 artillery systems, 930 warplanes and other armaments." Furthermore, with Western criticisms of the offensive orientation of Soviet forces deployed against NATO very much in mind, the Soviets decided to withdraw units which are primarily aimed at ensuring the success of offensive operations. Thus, General Yazov noted in a press conference at the end of April that Soviet withdrawals would include, "assault-landing and assault-crossing formations and units with their armaments and equipment. . . . This means the 'potential for a surprise attack' . . . is being removed."[2]

These cuts in forces will be carried out over a two-year period (December 1988–December 1990). During the first part of each year, the focus will be on changes in force structure aimed at giving the Soviet forces that remain "a more defensive thrust." This includes "converting combined-arms formations to a new organizational structure." In this regard, Yazov explained that in these countries tank regiments will be removed from motorized infantry divisions thereby decreasing the total number of tanks by forty per cent. In addition, the number of tanks in tank divisions will fall by more than twenty per cent, as a result of the elimination of one tank regiment. The number of antitank and antiaircraft weapons will increase, as will the unit's capability for laying mines. As far as the rest of the affected regions are concerned, Yazov stated that a number of motorized infantry divisions will be turned into machine-gun and artillery formations, "which, as is known, are earmarked only for defense."

During the second half of each year the units to be disbanded will be withdrawn to the Soviet Union. This means that during 1989 three tank units (two from the GDR and one from Hungary) will be withdrawn. In addition, "24 tactical missile launchers and about 2,700 tanks will be withdrawn."

Despite official Soviet protestations that Akhromeyev's retire-

---

[2] "V interesakh bezopasnosti" ("In the Interests of Security"), *Izvestiia*, February 28, 1989. The following details on the Soviet reduction plan are derived from this interview with Yazov.

ment was in no way tied to Gorbachev's first announcement of these reductions, many in the West thought otherwise. The immediate reaction to Akhromeyev's retirement was typified by a comment in the *New York Times*: "Gorbachev's decision to make substantial reductions in the Soviet armed forces may have caused a highly unusual rift between the Soviet leader and the chief of the General Staff, Marshal Sergei F. Akhromeyev, according to American officials."[3] Because of the timing of his retirement and the fact that both Akhromeyev and Yazov had publicly argued against unilateral cuts, it was assumed that they must have opposed Gorbachev's reduction plan.

We will probably never know the details surrounding the Kremlin's decision to go ahead with these cuts, i.e., who opposed them, who supported them, and the intensity of the debate. However, based on both circumstantial evidence and the findings of this study, this writer would argue that rather than opposing the cut, Akhromeyev probably played a key role in designing it. This is not to suggest that the idea of unilateral cuts was welcomed by Akhromeyev, or that he might not have disagreed with Gorbachev and others over details (e.g., how many troops or tanks to include). But in principle he probably supported it. At least this is the position he took in early January in an interview with the paper *Sovetskaia Rossiia* when he noted, "I would like to emphasize: the decision to reduce our armed forces by 500,000 men . . . is perfectly correct and justified from both the political and military viewpoints. *It was thoroughly considered from the military point of view* prior to the December 7 speech."[4]

Despite disclaimers by Akhromeyev, Yazov, and others—including Gorbachev—about the possibility of unilateral cuts, by the beginning of December it was becoming increasingly clear that major if not radical changes were being considered in Soviet force structure. Furthermore, it would have been stranger if Akhromeyev ac-

---

[3] "Marshal of the Soviet Union Sergei Fedorovich Akhromeyev Answers Questions from *Sovetskaia Rossiia* Readers," *Sovetskaia Rossiia*, January 14, 1989, *FBIS, The Soviet Union*, January 18, 1989. See also "Gorbachev Says Military Budget Faces Cutbacks," "Soviet Military Fought Cuts," *Washington Post*, December 9, 1988, and the interview with Aleksandr Yakovlev, "Yakovlev: Both Nations Weary of Accusations," *Washington Times*, December 9, 1988.

[4] "Gorbachev Says Military Budget Faces Cutbacks." Emphasis added.

tually *had* supported unilateral cuts in public and in meetings with Western officials. To have suggested that the concept was acceptable would have diminished the public-relations impact of the Gorbachev speech. Furthermore, since the exact nature of the cuts was apparently a matter of discussion in the highest ranks of the Soviet political-military leadership up until the day Gorbachev announced them, premature disclosure of any acceptance of the principle of unilateral cuts would have led to endless speculation, both in the West and in Moscow, over their size. This could have complicated the Soviet decision-making process as supporters and detractors attempted to seek public support for their positions.

Most important, the actions taken by Gorbachev fully accord with the general direction in which Soviet military thinking has been moving ever since Ogarkov became chief of the General Staff. The cuts were also advantageous from the point of view of the General Staff. A cut in the size of the Soviet military provides the high command with an opportunity to concentrate its limited resources on fewer high-cost items. Like Ogarkov, Soviet writers today increasingly recognize the importance of qualitative factors in modern warfare. Moiseyev, for example, noted that "the future of the armed forces must be conditioned by qualitative parameters, not quantitative ones," while General Lizichev commented that "the efficiency of Soviet military organizational development must be determined primarily by qualitative parameters with regard both to technology and military science, and to the composition of the Armed Forces."[5]

This increased emphasis on quality has a number of ramifications. For example, it is leading to new thinking in the military-technical sphere on a broad range of issues. In the past, with the exception of such outspoken individuals as Marshal Ogarkov, many Soviet writers tended to sidestep the issue of how to relate quantity and quality in calculating the military balance. Recently, however, more serious attention has been focused on this issue. For example, Colonel Strebkov, writing in *Kommunist vooruzhennykh sil*, argued that while determining the relative importance of qualitative and quantitative factors in the conventional sphere is very difficult (due

---

[5] "S positsii oboronitel'noi doktriny" ("From a Position of Defensive Doctrine"), *Krasnaia zvezda*, February 10, 1989; A. D. Lizichev, "V tsentre perestroiki—chelovek" ("At the Center of Perestroika—the Individual"), *Krasnaia Zvezda*, February 3, 1989.

to the "relatively large number of scenarios under which they could be utilized"), the situation is much simpler when it comes to nuclear weapons. In fact, he argued, a primary focus on quantitative factors distorts the situation. He then notes that while most observers agree that the ability to deliver a retaliatory strike is crucial, a determination of one's ability to deliver such a strike can no longer be made solely on the basis of the numbers of nuclear weapons. Moreover, he adds, the total number of nuclear weapons held by both sides is far in excess of what is needed to maintain parity.[6]

What is important about this article is not that it breaks new theoretical ground or provides a definitive answer to the question of how much is enough. The appearance of this article in a journal published by the Main Political Directorate, one aimed at a broad readership in the military and especially at political officers, who will draw on it in developing their own lectures, makes clear that the issue is open to debate and that the old answers are no longer acceptable.

Among the factors driving the Soviets' concern about the West, few are more important than its technological prowess. The Soviets themselves recognize that they are significantly behind in this area. As Colonel Strebkov put it, "We do not have parity with the imperialists in the economic and scientific spheres. In the middle of the seventies we began to fall behind the U.S. in the degree of increase of gross national product, and in recent years in the rate of growth of productive labor. According to the evaluations of our economists, the standard of living of the populace of the Soviet Union falls in the middle of states occupying fortieth to fiftieth place in the world."[7] By cutting back on the size of their military, the Soviets will be able to focus on developing a qualitatively better armed forces. This is particularly true for the officer corps.

Officer efficiency reports are normally prepared once every four years. During 1989, however, every officer in the entire armed forces

---

[6] V. Strebkov, "Kriterii voenno-strategicheskogo pariteta" ("The Criteria of Military-Strategic Parity"), *Kommunist vooruzhennykh sil*, no. 4 (February, 1989): 18–24. The same author expressed similar thoughts in an article in *Krasnaia zvezda*, "Voennyi paritet vchera i sevodnia" ("Military Parity Yesterday and Today"), January 3, 1989.

[7] Ibid. See also Robbin F. Laird and Dale R. Herspring, *The Soviet Union and Strategic Arms* (Boulder, Colo.: Westview, 1984).

will be evaluated. According to General Sukhorukov, who is in charge of cadres in the Ministry of Defense, each officer will be evaluated on "qualitative parameters" such as his technical competence, his knowledge of military science, and how he relates to enlisted personnel.[8] Those who do not pass this examination will be placed in the reserves.

Meanwhile, a number of military schools will be closed. Most cadets will be given the opportunity to continue their education at other facilities, while those who do not meet the appropriate standards will be transferred to the reserve or finish out their two-year obligation in regular units.[9] As with officers, the message to cadets is clear—if you want to be one of those retained in the military, with all of its advantages, it is up to you to prove yourself.

The high command is also seizing on these cuts to raise the quality of military educational institutions. In October 1988 a campaign to improve the quality of educational institutions was initiated with the appointment of General Vostrov as chief of the Main Directorate of the Military Educational Establishment. The work of these institutions has been singled out for special criticism. According to General Lobov:

> The problem of improving the methodological expertise of commanders may thus be said to be the most acute problem that we face at the present time. The source of the problem is to be found in military educational institutions, where future officers undertake only minimal study of even the most elementary methodological procedures. It is in the military educational institutions that the improvement of work with cadres must begin, because it is here that the foundations are laid down for the future of the Army and Navy.[10]

Some modifications are already being introduced into the educational system. For example, considerable effort is being devoted

---

[8] "O rabote s kadrami" ("On Work with Cadre"), *Krasnaia zvezda*, February 12, 1989.

[9] "Out of Uniform," *Sovetskaia Rossiia*, March 8, 1989, in *FBIS, The Soviet Union*, March 10, 1989.

[10] V. Lobov, "Vysokoe kachestov—glavnyi kriterii boevoi podgotovki" ("High Quality is the Main Criterion in Combat Training"), *Kommunist vooruzhennykh sil*, no. 1 (January 1989): 14. See also "Sluzhim Sovetskomu Soiuzu, po strogomu schetu" ("We Serve the Soviet Union—By a Strict Accounting"), *Pravda*, January 22, 1989, in which Yazov is cited as lamenting the state of training in the army.

to streamlining training procedures through the introduction of computers and computer-simulated training devices. In addition, greater emphasis is being placed in raising the psychological, pedagogical, and leadership skills of officers. Most important—and presumably most difficult—has been the effort to teach military educators to think in a more creative fashion.[11] Military academics in the Soviet Union enjoy a comfortable standard of living—access to housing, good schools, career and geographical stability—and if they hope to remain in their positions they will have to meet new standards. Failure to do so will lead to their replacement.

The high command has also seized on the changes currently underway in the personnel area to attack one of the most serious problems in the military; the harassment of junior, first-year enlisted personnel by second-year soldiers—the so-called *dedovshchina* problem. After years of refusing to discuss it, civilian criticism has forced the issue into the open. For example, a letter to the editor of *Literaturnaia gazeta* told of cases where individuals committed suicide as a result of the hazing they endured in the army. This article went on to call for the creation "of independent committees in each republic, *krai*, and *oblast'* for the social control of the Army."[12]

Cognizant of the impact such control structures would have on the military's ability to run its own affairs, the high command responded swiftly and firmly. Yazov condemned hazing as "an unlawful phenomenon," and General Lizichev went even further in a *Kommunist* article that not only recognized its existence but placed responsibility for its elimination solely on military officers themselves: "We and only we—commanders and political workers—are responsible for hazing, responsible before the people and our own conscience." Furthermore, he warned, "When commanders and political workers do not take decisive measures to curtail such ugly and shameful phenomena and use neither the educational possibilities nor the full force of the authority granted to them for this purpose,

[11] See, for example, the interview with General Konchits, commander of the Frunze Military Academy. "Kuznitsa voennykh kadrov" ("The Forge of Military Cadre"), *Voennyi vestnik*, no. 12 (1988): 6–12.

[12] "Pora pereiti k dely" ("Time to Get to Work"), *Literaturnaia gazeta*, no. 9 (March 1, 1989). See also Aleksandr Terekhov, "Bez sekretov" ("Without Secrets"), *Nedelia*, no. 46 (1988), and Stuart Dalrymple, *Radio Liberty Report*, RL 185/88, "Bullying in the Soviet Army," April 29, 1988.

we will make them strictly accountable. We will expel them from the party and the Komsomol."[13] Whether these steps will be enough to eradicate the problem remains to be seen. But there is no doubt that the high command is aware of the problem and is placing responsibility for it where it belongs—on the shoulders of the officers themselves.

Those military officers who think that this talk about creating a Soviet-style meritocracy in the military is merely empty rhetoric need only take a look at developments within the high command itself since Gorbachev came to power. The change overall has been significant in favor of younger, better-qualified officers. As reflected in Table 1, there have been many changes at the highest level. Changes in lower-level commands have been even more extensive. Admiral Chernavin, for example, noted that "besides me, all my deputies and all the fleet commanders have been appointed in the past three years."[14] Furthermore, while factors other than age may have influenced these changes, it is clear that seniority no longer ensures an officer's longevity. Indeed, conversations with Soveit officers suggest that even more extensive changes in favor of younger individuals are in store. Furthermore, looking at the changes that have occurred over the past ten years reveals a decided prejudice against officers such as Admiral Gorshkov, or Marshals Tolubko and Batitskii, with their strong service orientation.

The reduction in personnel and force structure under way in the USSR will be especially welcomed by Moscow's East European allies, who not only lag several generations behind the Soviets in equipment holdings, but who also have had a difficult time in keeping even, let alone significantly modernizing their forces. In fact, one factor driving the Soviets toward a revision of their strategy for fighting a war in Europe may be the sad state of their East European allies, who make up almost half of Pact troop strength on the Central Front.[15]

---

[13] D. T. Yazov, "Armiia naroda" ("The Army of the People"), February 23, 1989; A. D. Lizichev, "Armiia: razgovor o nasushchnom" ("The Army: A Discussion of Essentials"), *Kommunist*, no. 3 (February 1989), p. 21.

[14] "Ne mech—a shchit" ("Not the Sword—But the Shield"), *Izvestiya*, February 23, 1989.

[15] See, for example, Dale R. Herspring, "The Soviets, the Warsaw Pact and the East European Militaries," in William Griffith, ed., *Central and Eastern Europe and the West in the 1980s* (Boulder, Colo.: Westview, 1989).

While much depends on the way in which they are to be implemented, when taken together with the INF agreement the reductions announced by Gorbachev will lessen the probability, although not the possibility, of any kind of a war in Europe—nuclear or conventional. The lessening of the military threat will have important

TABLE 1.
MILITARY LEADERSHIP—AVERAGE AGE

Name	Year of Birth	Position
	1985	
Sokol'ov, S. L.	1911	Minister of Defense
Akhromeyev, S. F.	1923	Chief, General Staff
Kulikov, V. G.	1921	Chief, Warsaw Pact
Petrov, V. I.	1917	First Deputy Chief, Ministry of Defense
Altunin, A. T.	1921	Chief, Civil Defense
Gorshkov, S. G.	1910	Chief, Navy
Govorov, V. L.	1924	Chief, Main Inspectorate
Ivanovskii, Y. F.	1918	Chief, Ground Forces
Koldunov, A. I.	1923	Chief, Air Defense Forces
Kurkotin, S. K.	1917	Chief, Rear Services
Lizichev, A. D.	1928	Chief, Main Political Directorate
Maksimov, Y. P.	1924	Chief, Strategic Rocket Forces
Shabanov, V. M.	1923	Chief, Armaments
Shkadov, I. N.	1913	Chief, Personnel
Yefimov, A. N.	1923	Chief, Air Forces

Average Age—65.2 years

	1989	
Yazov, D. T.	1923	Minister of Defense
Moiseyev, M. A.	1939	Chief, General Staff
Lushev, P. G.	1923	Chief, Warsaw Pact
Kochetev, K. A.	1933	First Deputy Minister, Ministry of Defense
Govorov, V. L.	1924	Chief, Civil Defense
Chernavin, V. N.	1928	Chief, Navy
Sorokin, M. I.	1922	Chief, Main Inspectorate
Varennikov, V. I.	1923	Chief, Ground Forces
Tret'iak, I. M.	1923	Chief, Air Defense Forces
Arkhipov, V. M.	1933	Chief, Rear Services
Lizichev, A. D.	1928	Chief, Main Political Directorate
Maksimov, Y. P.	1924	Chief, Rocket Forces
Shabanov, V. M.	1923	Chief, Armaments
Sukhorukov, D. S.	1922	Chief, Personnel
Yefimov, A. N.	1923	Chief, Air Force
Yashin, Y. A.	1930	Chief, Radio-Electronic Combat

Average Age—63.3 years

SOURCE: Author's files.

implications for Western attitudes toward military spending and, in the minds of most observers, will lead to a diminished willingness to support a Western military buildup. This interrelationship between military security and public diplomacy is a concept that Ogarkov and Akhromeyev understood very well. Undercutting Western support for advances in high-technology conventional weapons is very much in the Soviet Union's security interest. And while it is still too early to tell what kind of an impact Gorbachev's announcement will have in this area, it is clear that he has succeeded in getting the attention of Western Europe.

Ogarkov stressed throughout his writings the tremendous losses that would accompany a future war. Given such a situation, cutting back on Soviet forces would at first glance appear to weaken Soviet ability to prosecute such a conflict. However, in addition to his emphasis on high-technology weapons, Ogarkov articulated the key elements of modern warfare as speed, sustainability, and maneuverability. Such a war could probably be better fought by smaller, highly mobile units—brigades or regiments, perhaps, rather than divisions. There is considerable talk at present about a major restructuring in Soviet force posture toward such smaller units. This would be Ogarkov's kind of war. Furthermore, while Gorbachev's decision to cut 10,000 tanks marks a major change in Soviet thinking, it accords with Ogarkov's skepticism about the utility of tanks and his belief that the future would belong to qualitatively new types of weapons systems.

Despite the apparent compatibility of the basic tenets of Ogarkov's thinking with the reforms occurring in the USSR, the new approach will not only mark a major change in the way Soviet officers think but also undo many of the operational modifications that Ogarkov introduced into the Soviet armed forces. For example, using the World War II battle of Kursk as a focal point, A. Kokoshin and V. Larionov recently argued that the emphasis on defense "assumes definite changes in the way military professionals think." It also necessitates

"rethinking" historical experience, specifically the Battle of Kursk fought in the summer of 1943, when Moscow deliberately chose to assume a defensive posture—of its own free will, and not out of necessity. "This was the first case in the history of war and the military art, where the stronger side assumed the defensive. As is known, the classical formula for the military art ran as follows: defense is the stronger type of military action; therefore the weaker side resorts to it." But the USSR was not the weaker part on this occasion; the Red Army "had no fewer than the Wehrmacht," and in a number of indicators was superior to it.[16]

A debate over the future of Soviet force structure has been raging in the Soviet Union for some time. Not only have civilian analysts been involved (mostly on the side of those who want smaller, less tank-heavy forces), but senior military officers have also debated the issue. Indeed, it is clear that there are a number of individuals who strongly disagree with the path advocated by Gorbachev, Akhromeyev, and Yazov. Too many bureaucratic fiefdoms are being affected not to expect considerable differences of opinion. General Tret'iak, for example, argued strongly against unilateral cuts in Soviet forces: "Any changes in the Army have to be weighed up a thousand times. For instance at the end of the 1950's the Soviet Union unilaterally reduced the Army by 1.2 million men. Economists have calculated that this enables us to increase old-age pensions two-fold, to create 100 house-building combines. But that step was hasty, it dealt a colossal blow at our defense potential."[17] Similarly, in an article ostensibly devoted to the World War II battle at Stalingrad, General Ivanovskii carefully qualified his support for a new defensive doctrine, arguing that while a defensive strategy had helped to wear the Germans down, it was only the counteroffensive that had made victory possible.[18] Finally, Marshal Kulikov, long considered to be one of the strongest "hard-liners" in the Soviet military leadership, wrote a book in which he attempted to restrict severely the flexibility of the political leadership when it came to national security affairs.[19]

---

[16] A. Kokoshin and V. Larionov, "The Battle of Kursk in Light of Today's Defensive Doctrine," *Mirovaia ekonomika i mezhdunarodnye otnosheniia*, no. 8 (August 1987): 32–33, 36, cited in McConnell, "Reasonable Sufficiency in Soviet Conventional Arms-Control Strategy," p. 7.

[17] TASS, February 17, 1988.

[18] E. F. Ivanovskii, "Vydaiushchaiasia pobeda Sovestkoi Armii" ("The Outstanding Victory of the Soviet Army"), *Voenno-istoricheskii zhurnal*, no. 11 (1987): 44–53.

[19] V. G. Kulikov, *Doktrina zashchity mira i sotsializma* (*The Doctrine of the Defense of Peace and Socialism*) (Moscow, Voennoe izdatel'stvo, 1988), pp. 82–83.

One suspects that as Colton has suggested on a number of occasions, the battle over the future of the Soviet armed forces will not be fought exclusively along bureaucratic lines. This is particularly true now that Gorbachev has announced that in addition to the unilateral cuts he announced in New York, the Soviet military budget will be cut by 14.2 per cent and the production of arms and military technology by 19.5 per cent.[20] Instead, there will be cross-cutting alliances between various military and civilian players; some will favor the major changes advocated by Gorbachev, others will push for only slight modifications, while still others will try to avoid any changes at all.

Enter Moiseyev

On December 15, 1988, the Kremlin announced the appointment of Colonel General Mikhail Alekseyevich Moiseyev to replace Akhromeyev as chief of the General Staff. This young, relatively junior three-star general, described by one source in Moscow as a "rising star," was selected over many more senior military officers.[21]

Compared with what is available on the eight other senior military officers discussed in this book, biographical data on Moiseyev is very limited. The forty-nine-year-old officer was born in 1939 in Khabarovsk to a working-class family. He joined the army in 1958 and graduated from an officer's school in 1961, and from the Frunze Military Academy in 1972. He then commanded a regiment and a motorized-rifle division. Subsequently, he graduated from the Voroshilov Military Academy in 1982 with the coveted Gold Star for academic excellence. As the top student in his class he was selected to give the commencement address. Moiseyev's rise since graduating from the Voroshilov Military Academy has been nothing short of meteoric. A major general when he graduated, by 1985 he had been promoted to lieutenant general. He was assigned to the Far Eastern Military District, where he commanded an army for a brief period of time before being promoted to Yazov's chief of staff. When Yazov was transferred to Moscow to take charge of personnel in the Ministry of Defense, Moiseyev was made commander of the Far Eastern Military District and promoted to colonel general.

---

[20] "Gorbachev Says Military Budget Faces Cutbacks."
[21] "Moscow Appoints Top Army Officer," *New York Times*, December 16, 1988.

As the first officer with no Second World War experience to occupy that post, and as one who does not appear to have had much experience on the General Staff (which is often, but not always, the path to the top in the Soviety military), Moiseyev's appointment marks a break with the recent past. He is also about fifteen years younger than most of the rest of the Soviet military leadership. Looking at the three articles Moiseyev authored prior to becoming chief of the General Staff, his primary interest has been personnel-related matters. He has expressed particular concern about science and technology, arguing in his 1985 article that "it is . . . disturbing that the technical horizons of some [Soviet officers] are not only failing to expand, they are actually diminishing."[22] Indeed, in this sense he is cut from the same mold as Yazov. He apparently has little background in matters such as arms control or doctrine and strategy. This has led some to speculate that with Akhromeyev's departure and Moiseyev's appointment, the Soviet military will have less impact on arms control policy in general.[23]

Moiseyev's appointment appears to be primarily aimed at providing support for Yazov in the personnel area at a time when the Soviet military is faced with the need to make both major cuts in personnel and potentially significant modifications in force structure. It does not necessarily follow, however, that Akhromeyev's retirement indicates a loss in influence for the uniformed professional military officer in areas such as arms control. To begin with, Akhromeyev, in retirement, has been appointed a special advisor to Gorbachev and the Defense Council. Assuming his health permits, Akhromeyev may well continue to play a major role in this area through his new position. And through him the military will have an important spokesman at the highest level when political-military issues are being discussed. Second, while the military appears to be in the process of losing its monopoly over national security information, and while there is clearly less emphasis on the military com-

---

[22] "Polkam nuzhny mastera" ("Regiments Need Experts"), *Krasnaia zvezda*, June 1, 1985. For other articles by Moiseyev see, "Splochenie voinskikh kollektivov—otvetstvennaia zadacha komandirov i politrabotnikov" ("The Unity of Military Collectives—the Responsible Task of Commanders and Political Workers"), *Voenno-istoricheskii zhurnal*, no. 12 (1987), and "Ukreplenie distsipliny—zabota kazhdogo dnia" ("Strengthening Discipline, the Task of Each Day"), *Kommunist vooruzhennykh sil*, no. 9 (1988).

[23] *New York Times*, December 16, 1988.

ponent of Soviet foreign policy, the number of military officers currently assigned to civilian institutions such as the Ministry of Foreign Affairs or Central Committee is at an all-time high. Indeed, the nature of national security decision making in the USSR appears to be changing. Instead of a bifurcated military-political decision-making process, Gorbachev appears to have decided in favor of greater interaction on the part of all participants. This means that while military officers will have to live with greater civilian involvement in their affairs, they are also beginning to play a greater role in a number of key foreign policy areas. Indeed, it would not be surprising to see increasing evidence of interaction between senior military officers from the General Staff and civilian officers in the planning of Soviet national security policy.

THE MARSHALS/GENERALS AND THE PROCESS

During the course of this study I have argued that there is a more symbiotic relationship at the top of the national security pyramid than is generally recognized in the West and that the Western tendency to see Soviet military politics as a zero-sum game distorts and oversimplifies the nature of the relationship. This has been particularly true of the period since 1977, when Ogarkov was appointed chief of the General Staff. In this writer's opinion, Ogarkov's appointment was one of the most important developments in postwar Soviet civil-military relations: Ogarkov, in contrast to Grechko, believed that closer interaction with political authorities could help advance the military's interests. Ogarkov's most important legacy is that he taught the high command how to take a multifaceted look at national security affairs. He himself was not successful in integrating the four variables analyzed in this study, but he laid the groundwork for much of what is occurring at present. The current Soviet military leadership—at least those on the General Staff—understand that provided they have a responsive political leadership, there is more to be gained from taking a broad view of national security affairs and working closely with politicians in a positive manner than by adopting the negative, self-isolating approach as did Grechko.

With the emergence of Gorbachev as general secretary, Akhromeyev at first adopted a wait-and-see attitude. Once convinced that

Gorbachev was serious about major modifications in the country's economy and that he seemed to have the ability to bring about some of these changes, he joined the Gorbachev team. The new defense minister, Dmitrii Yazov, is also clearly a member of this team, and there is no reason to believe that General Moiseyev will not be supportive of Gorbachev's policies as well. The result has been a more symbiotic relationship than was the case in the first half of the 1980s.

This does not mean that there are no important areas of disagreement among the top political-military leaders. Akhromeyev, Yazov, and Moiseyev certainly have misgivings about the direction in which a policy of military sufficiency might take them, and they cannot be happy about the loss in prestige the military has suffered since Gorbachev took over. But given the enormity of the problems facing the Soviet Union, they have decided that their best alternative is to support Gorbachev. He may not be the best possible general secretary, but he is certainly better than anything they have had in the last twenty years. Besides, Gorbachev has avoided Khrushchev's tendency to interfere in internal military affairs. It is up to the marshals to figure out how to revise Soviet force structure in accordance with a policy of military sufficiency—whatever that means.

To a degree, the fact that the new approach appears to be working is due to the personalities of the individuals concerned: Akhromeyev, Yazov, and presumably Moiseyev as well. All believe that it is the proper approach and that in Gorbachev they have a general secretary who shares their views. The longer this arrangement lasts, the more likely it is to become institutionalized in the sense that those who rise to the top of the General Staff will be accustomed to such behavior. Just as those who are not comfortable with a combined-arms strategy have found themselves moved out of key command positions, those who are unable to work with the politicians or think in broad political-military terms are unlikely to rise to the top of the military hierarchy. Likewise, the longer these procedures remain in force, the more likely they are to become routinized behavioral patterns on both sides. Senior political figures will regularly consult with their military colleagues on issues such as arms control, while the latter will attempt to explain the interrelationship between force structure and arms control. The old separation of military-technical and political affairs that Grechko felt comfortable with appears to be dead.

This study suggests that the immediate future for Soviet civil-military relations will be one of continued interaction between marshals and senior politicians on issues of mutual importance. In some cases there will be differences of opinion, in others agreement. In all cases, however, there will be an increased willingness, especially on the part of marshals and the generals, to take a broader view of the country's problems and to look for more creative solutions to them.

THE KEY PLAYERS

This study has argued that individual military officers can have an important impact both within the armed forces and in relations with the civilian political leadership. It has also suggested that the three-phased division of the leadership process suggested by Tucker offers a useful vehicle for analyzing the role played by these individuals in both areas. It is now time to take a closer look at these eight individuals and to place their actions in the broader perspective of Tucker's approach.

The Diagnostic Period

Based on the actions of the eight individuals included in this study, the question of who determines the military's interests depends on both the individual and the issue for its answer. In some cases the chief of staff is dominant, while in others it is the defense minister. One conclusion suggested by this analysis is that a civilian defense minister has less impact on the determination of military interests than does a professional military officer. In essence, a civilian appears to function as a mediator between the chief of staff and the political leadership.

Military-Technical Issues.   Turning to the question of management and personnel, primary responsibility seems to have shifted. Grechko himself assumed overall responsibility for this issue when he was defense minister, although Zakharov was assigned particular responsibility in the area of cadre. Likewise, Kulikov also spent considerable time on this subject. During the Ogarkov-Ustinov period, by contrast, responsibility for such issues was lodged primarily with Ogarkov, although Ustinov played an important supporting role.

Ogarkov was most outspoken on this topic and appears to have tried to do the most to upgrade the management/personnel system. With Sokolov's appointment as defense minister, the management/personnel issue tended to recede into the background. This is somewhat surprising, given Sokolov's long-time experience with logistical and personnel issues, but from his writings and speeches one can conclude that he was not particularly interested in this issue. For his part, Akhromeyev never indicated a special interest in personnel or management. Yazov, on the other hand, has clearly assumed primary responsibility for improving Soviet performance in this area; indeed, it is my contention that this was the primary reason why he was selected to be defense minister. The same is true for the Akhromeyev's newly appointed successor, Moiseyev.

When it comes to warfighting strategy, Grechko was the most authoritative voice during his time in power—which is not surprising, as he was defense minister. But as has been noted above, he was very careful not to prejudice the issue. His attention was focused primarily on making sure the military obtained everything it needed to develop a balanced force structure. Grechko's successor, Dmitrii Ustinov, delegated responsibility for warfighting strategy to Ogarkov, and it was he who dominated this area while he was chief of staff. Other officers occasionally questioned some of his premises— for example, on the use of limited nuclear weapons—but it was he who guided and determined the main points that underlie current Soviet warfighting strategy. With the appointment of Sokolov, responsibility for warfighting strategy was once again delegated to the chief of staff—in this case, Akhromeyev. Sokolov had never shown any interest in this area throughout his entire military career, and so it came as no surprise that he delegated it to Akhromeyev when he took over as defense minister. Based on the available evidence, the same pattern is being followed under Yazov.

If it is possible to generalize in the scientific-technical area, one may claim that with one exception, responsibility for warfighting strategy was delegated to the chief of staff. After all, it is the General Staff that has the greatest expertise in this area. In order for the defense minister to dominate the evolution of warfighting strategy, he would have to oversee closely the activities of his chief of staff. Although this is certainly within the realm of possibility, it is difficult, given the defense minister's many other responsibilities. It would be even more difficult for a civilian defense minister, who in most cases does not possess the prerequisite technical knowledge, to do so. He would indeed be in a position to issue general guidelines, but in most cases it would still fall to the chief of the General Staff and his subordinates, who constitute the primary repository of information and expertise, to implement modifications in war plans.

The picture is more mixed when it comes to personnel and management issues. While very much involved, Grechko was not nearly as dominant as Ogarkov. This is even more the case with Yazov. The latter appears to be consumed with the implementation of perestroika in the military. As a consequence, we have a situation in which the defense minister was dominant in two periods, the chief of staff in another.

Sociopolitical Issues.   With the exception of Grechko, the chief of staff appears to have had the major responsibility for determining the military's interests in the sociopolitical area. In the budgetary and arms control areas, for example, Grechko was clearly the military's main spokesman. He was the one who took the lead in opposing Brezhnev's attempts to cut back in the early 1970s. Under the Ogarkov-Ustinov leadership, it was Ogarkov who was most outspoken. This does not mean that Ustinov did not argue the armed forces case when Brezhnev's or Chernenko's proposed budgets were discussed. However, Ogarkov's outspoken opposition on the budgetary issue after 1981 made clear that the most authoritative voices within the professional military did not accept the Ustinov line. Based on the information currently available, the situation with Akhromeyev was somewhat different. In this instance, the chief of staff was deeply involved in arms control and force structure modifications. As a result, he was probably the key officer in determining the military's stance on budgetary issues. Yazov is also clearly involved, but his main attention is focused elsewhere. It is too early to tell what impact Akhromeyev's retirement will have on this relationship. But as pointed out above, it would be a mistake to assume that the military has lost influence in the process just because of Moiseyev's appointment as chief of the General Staff.

The situation is similar when it comes to arms control. During the 1960s and early 1970s Grechko determined the high command's attitude toward this issue. He was the military's spokesman in opposing Brezhnev's efforts to improve East-West relations, and he was the one who decided that arms control was not in the military's interest. Ogarkov, by contrast, began as an advocate of arms control but soon came to the conclusion that given the international and domestic situation in the early 1980s, progress in this area was not in the military's interest. In fact, recent revelations concerning the Soviet decision to invade Afghanistan suggest that both Ogarkov and Akhromeyev, who was on the General Staff at the time, advised against this action. Based on comments by Marshal Kulikov, the military was presented with a *fait accompli*: "I remember the situation well because I was a Deputy Minister of Defense. About midnight Ustinov arrived and declared. 'We will cross the border tonight.' And that was all! Who made the decision? I know only one [possibility]—the leadership. And we all know who was in charge at that time."[24] In this instance, the high command had no difficulty in diagnosing their military interests; the problem was that their advice went unheeded. And here Ustinov played the role of an emissary from Brezhnev to the high command.

After Ogarkov's ouster, Akhromeyev was crucial in determining the military's interests in arms control. From all appearances he was the military's major broker when it came to negotiating with the political leadership over the structure of a future agreement, and he continues to be influential in this area, despite his retirement.

Determining Strategy

Military-Technical Issues. Not surprisingly, there is a striking similarity between the individuals who played the key roles in determining the military's primary interests in this area and those who were most influential in determining strategy. Grechko's more relaxed approach to personnel/management and warfighting issues was reflected in the lack of a well-conceived strategy in either area. This situation differed markedly from that under Ogarkov. Here we have a situation in which, on the personnel/management front, the chief of staff with the assistance of his defense minister gave strong expression to the need for improving training, management, and use of technology in the armed forces. He repeatedly led the charge to

---

[24] "Afghanistan: Podvodia itogi" ("Afghanistan: Summing Up Results"), *Ogonek*, no. 12 (March 1989): 6; "Veterany i perestroika" ("Veterans and Perestroika"), *Krasnaia zvezda*, March 4, 1989.

get rid of incompetent officers and called for greater efficiency in running the military establishment. His strategy was to lead a public campaign within the armed forces in an attempt to force change on the institution.

Ogarkov adopted a similar stance when it came to warfighting. He went public with his call for major changes in the way Soviet military officers thought about warfare. As with personnel/management issues, he believed that the most effective approach was to guide a discussion of the issues. And if one assumes that the public discussion he led was accompanied by an even more open discussion behind the scenes within the ranks of the military, it becomes clear that Ogarkov believed the best way to deal with the issue was to keep it alive. If nothing else, this created a situation that helped to prepare his colleagues for the changes he was introducing in force structure, but, perhaps even more important, to make other officers and civilians accept the idea that military strategy is an evolving process, that one must expect constant change. Indeed, one of his main themes throughout his writings is that change is inherent in military affairs. Akhromeyev's approach to warfighting was quieter than Ogarkov's. While he presumably made his concerns known behind the scenes, he basically accepted the main principles laid down by Ogarkov. He saw military sufficiency to be compatible with these principles, and while Akhromeyev may not have believed that all aspects of sufficiency are fully in the armed forces' interest, he appears to have made a decision that it was in their interest—and, no doubt, his own—to support it. Consequently, he has been a strong advocate of the policy in his public statements.

Sociopolitical Issues.   The strategies adopted by the key players on these issues have differed considerably. Grechko's approach to both arms control and the budget was a simple one of outright opposition. He appears to have made very little attempt to work with Brezhnev in coming up with an agreement that would minimize damage to the military. Instead, he believed that outright opposition was the best approach. Ogarkov, on the other hand, began his tenure as chief of the General Staff believing that he could work with the political leadership on arms control and the budget. As a result of a number of factors, however, he soon became disillusioned and retreated into a two-pronged policy of working to diminish the chance that the political leadership would accede to an agreement before major changes had occurred in the country's scientific, technical, and economic structure, while also making an effort to obtain more funds for the armed forces. This latter strategy was, in turn, also made up of two parts: first, the open advocacy of more money for the military, and second, an effort to tie the civilian economy even more closely to the military sector under the rubric of greater military preparedness. Akhromeyev's strategy as to the military budget was closely tied to his approach to warfighting strategy and arms control. He saw them as closely intertwined and believed that it would be possible to work with the political leadership, in this case Gorbachev, to make meaningful progress in overcoming the country's many problems. As a consequence, Akhromeyev was very circumspect in his comments on the budget. He was careful to support Gorbachev's call for a more rational and efficient use of resources and warned that the military would be expected to do more with less. When it came to arms control, he had apparently decided that the best strategy was to become a major participant in the process. If nothing else, his presence at Gorbachev's elbow enabled him to shape an agreement that would minimize the damage any treaty might do to Soviet military preparedness.

Mobilizing Resources

Conceptually, a senior military leader needs to mobilize resources to prepare for two different scenarios. On the one hand, he may wish to oppose changes being forced upon him; on the other, he may advocate changes of his own. Each type of action requires a different approach. It is much easier, for example, to veto something than it is to initiate an action, especially in the conservative Soviet military. Assuming the presence of a strong individual, all that needs to be done to negate a policy is to ensure sufficient influence at the top to convince the decision maker that too much risk would be involved in initiating a new policy. On the other hand, when it comes to advocating a new approach, especially one that marks a radical departure from existing practice, the military officer must obtain strong political backing for his actions. A myriad of entrenched bureaucratic forces whose fiefdoms will be affected can be expected to oppose any change in the status quo. A major infusion of outside support is needed. Obtaining outside support, however, puts the senior military officer in a difficult position. If he accepts it, he runs the risk of having political authorities become directly involved in the process. Perestroika is acting as a strong impetus in the area of personnel and management, but it is dictating the general direction in which changes in the military must go.

Military-Technical Issues. Grechko's major concern was not with the introduction of new changes, but with holding the line on the budgetary and arms control fronts. As a consequence, he made no attempt to solicit outside support for changes in strategy or personnel/management. Indeed, as has been argued above, it is not clear that he knew exactly where he wanted to go, especially as to personnel/management.

Ogarkov began his tenure believing that he had Brezhnev's ear and that he would be able to obtain the political support necessary for implementing wide-ranging changes in the strategy and management areas. The reality, however, was quite different. The Brezhnev regime appeared to be too decrepit to mobilize itself for anything. How could one make a successful argument in favor of what amounted to a systemic change when faced with a political leader who was becoming less and less effective? Consequently, Ogarkov did what he could: he harped on the need for better management and greater use of technology and attempted to force Soviet officers to become more effective leaders. But the fact remains that his immediate impact was modest.

The situation was similar with regard to warfighting strategy. It is going too far to suggest that if Ogarkov had had his way, he would have introduced a policy of military sufficiency, however implemented, but it is indeed clear that the principles he laid down for the conduct of a future war are compatible with such a strategy—even if the force structure is not. In any case, one suspects that if he had had his way, he would have moved strategy in that general direction. But in light of the economic and technical problems facing the USSR, there was little hope of getting the necessary support. The situation did not improve under Andropov or Chernenko. So Ogarkov did the best he could: he modernized Soviet force structure and set the conceptual guidelines for the future development of Soviet warfighting strategy.

Yazov's success—if any—on the personnel/management front will be largely a result of the very strong support he is receiving from Gorbachev. Based on letters to the editor and other comments in the Soviet military press, the rank-and-file officers and NCOs are less than enthusiastic about perestroika. They all realize, however, that as long as Gorbachev remains in a strong position they have no alternative but to go along with the process. In the end, if Yazov and Moiseyev succeed, they will produce a military which is more formidable and effective, one closer to what Ogarkov was calling for.

While it is difficult to know where the impetus for military sufficiency originates, all of the indications are that it was not put forth by the high command, even if its main principles are compatible with those advocated by Ogarkov. Since Gorbachev is the main driving force behind it, Yazov and Moiseyev can rely on his support to gain acceptance within the military; when they turn to their colleagues they can argue that they are merely following orders. They do not have to mobilize the military in favor of military sufficiency; Gorbachev is doing this for them. Those in the military hierarchy who choose not to support such a policy will be shunted aside. And Yazov and Moiseyev can count on Gorbachev to back them up.

Sociopolitical Issues. When it came to mobilizing support for his preferred approach to the budget and arms control, Grechko's approach was to try to mobilize the high command to prevent Brezhnev from making the modifications he sought. While he had considerable success in this regard, Ogarkov's defection provided Brezhnev and Ustinov with the opening they needed. In Ogarkov they believed they had found the needed support within the high command and as a consequence he was appointed chief of the General Staff.

In the beginning, Ogarkov did attempt to mobilize the military behind Brezhnev's arms control and budgetary policies, but he soon grew disenchanted and began to work to mobilize the high command—together with other segments of the national security leadership—to oppose any movement on arms control while pushing hard for a larger military budget.

Akhromeyev and Yazov, after an initial period of hesitation, have worked to mobilize support within the military establishment for Gorbachev's policies. This does not mean, as noted above, that the Kremlin's top military officers support Gorbachev on all aspects of his budgetary and arms control policies. Nor does it mean that their support will continue for the indefinite future. However, they appear to have decided for the present that since he is attempting to attack the country's underlying problems, it is in the armed forces interest to support him and, accordingly, they are attempting to mobilize the support of the country's military behind him.

PREDICTING INFLUENCE

Predicting how much influence an individual will exercise either within the military or vis-à-vis political authorities is very difficult, if not impossible. Nevertheless, based on this admittedly small sample, a number of observations emerge.

To begin with, there are three types of personalities that have been most prominent over the past twenty years. First, there is the aggressive, confrontational individual, like Grechko or Ogarkov, who is not afraid to take on the political leadership directly. This approach works only when the political leadership is weak. The idea of a Grechko successfully opposing Gorbachev appears far-fetched at best. One of them would have to go. Second, there is the type who avoids confrontations and instead works with the political leadership. This is the road both Akhromeyev and Yazov have taken, with the result of increased influence for the military in the area of arms control. But this approach is dependent on the presence of a strong political leader; otherwise, the top generals have no one with whom they might work. Ogarkov was prepared to cooperate with Brezhnev on a variety of issues, but Brezhnev and his successors were too weak and beset with too many problems to be meaningful allies. Finally, there is the more passive, less assertive type of individual such as Sokolov, who was selected to be defense minister primarily because high officials believed he would not become a political force during a period of succession.

It is clear that the influence exerted by an individual is also a result of factors that go beyond personality. For example, Grechko's influence on the budgetary issue during the 1960s and the 1970s was not only a product of his hard-line approach, but also resulted from support he received from others—at first from the entire political leadership, and later certain segments of it. He made a difference, but it is doubtful that he could have held the line on any issue on his own. As it was, he lost on arms control and, in the waning days of his time as defense minister, must have known that he would lose on the budgetary issue as well.

A third indicator of possible influence is an individual's writing. This can provide clues both to his areas of interest and to the likelihood he will be assertive once he attains a high position. Grechko wrote on every topic imaginable, and his interests were catholic. When he focused on an issue of concern to him, it was clear that he expected compliance with his wishes. Ogarkov also had a broad range of interests, but was particularly concerned with strategy and force structure. When he focused on an issue important to him, his writings carried the cadence of command, as in his 1971 *Red Star* article on military training. Ustinov avoided most fields covered in this study, with the one exception of personnel/management, and when he did address one of the issues he avoided the categorical statements common to Ogarkov. Sokolov's writings indicated that he was neither interested in any of these issues nor felt strongly about them. Instead, he comes across as a man reading a speech or publishing an article prepared for him by someone else. Akhromeyev, by contrast, showed special interest in arms control and strategy. Personnel and management issues have never been his field of interest. Furthermore, he carefully avoided the confrontational language common to Ogarkov; indeed, he was careful not to antagonize others even when he made some of the same points as Ogarkov while working under him—an indication that he would be a person likely to work with rather than confront the political leadership. Finally, a reading of Yazov's writings over the years shows that his primary interest has long been personnel and management. It is therefore no surprise that he decided to make this his issue when he became defense minister. Furthermore, his strong language in pushing perestroika was evident in his writings long before he was selected to be defense minister.

Fourth, while training for the post of senior military officer is generally relativly homogenous (all must graduate from an officer school, a military academy, and the General Staff Academy), it is clear that those who are selected for the top positions tend increasingly to be well-educated and articulate. Ogarkov is generally recognized as one of the brightest officers in the Soviet armed forces to date, and Akhromeyev has impressed those who have met him as a man fully in command of his material, one able to carry on complicated arms negotiations without reference to notes. The same is true of Moiseyev, who Defense Secretary Carlucci called a "comer" after meeting him during his 1988 visit to the Soviet Union.[25]

Fifth, personal ties play a crucial role. Grechko had close ties to Brezhnev and probably owed his appointment to him. It is not clear who Kulikov's primary ally was in the high command, although one suspects that as commander of the Group of Soviet Forces in Germany, he must have come to Grechko's attention; after all, the latter took a special interest in this command, having himself formally been its commander. The reasons for Ogarkov's appointment to the General Staff are unclear, but his elevation to the post of chief of the General Staff appears to have been engineered by Brezhnev and Ustinov who perceived him to be a man who understood and was willing to support the arms control process. Sokolov's appointment appears to have been a marriage of convenience. He was an uninfluential first deputy minister of defense who could be expected to serve as defense minister without making waves. Akhromeyev had served under Ogarkov; indeed, from his writings he could be considered an Ogarkov protegée. In Akhromeyev the political leadership had an Ogarkov without his pugilistic personality traits. Yazov's connection with Gorbachev is obvious; the latter personally selected him for the position of defense minister. Finally, Moiseyev's ties with Yazov have been very close, and Yazov appears primarily responsible for Moiseyev's rise to power. While focusing on personal ties can be very difficult and often misleading, it can provide a guide in attempting to discover who will support whom in a crisis.

While it would be tempting to draw up a model of the average chief of staff or defense minister based on the eight individuals covered in this study, such a model would be misleading. There are only eight individuals involved, and much depends on circumstances. Who is general secretary? How much power does he possess? What is the personality of the chief of staff or defense minister (i.e., are they compatible with each other, and is either or both compatible with the general secretary)? What is the individual's area of expertise, and how does it fit the needs of the military establishment at the time? In short, the most that can be said about the

---

[25] "Young Obscure Officer is Named Leader of Soviet Armed Forces," *Washington Post*, December 16, 1988.

average chief of staff or defense minister—assuming he is a professional soldier—is that he will be well-educated, will have held a number of command- and particularly staff-positions, and will probably have served at some time on the General Staff.

EVALUATING THE INDIVIDUALS

Grechko. When it comes to the military budget, Grechko emerges as the most influential individual covered by this study. None of the others had anywhere near the influence he had on this issue. His power was admittedly negative—i.e., holding the line against cuts in the rate of increase of the military budget—but it was something none of the others was able to accomplish. Grechko also presided over a major buildup in Soviet conventional and nuclear forces. Indeed, the military force the West now faces is to a large degree a result of Grechko's efforts in holding the line on military spending. Grechko's limitations were most evident in his inability to interrelate the four issues dealt with in this study. For example, in looking at arms control, he was driven by fears that politicians would seize on any arms control agreements as pretexts for cutting weapons production. Consequently, his response was negative. Perhaps this officer who once commanded cavalry units can be excused if he did not understand the nuances of strategic arms control, but his attitude created tension between the high command and the political leadership.

Zakharov. In his relations with Khrushchev, Zakharov showed that he was prepared to take a stand and openly oppose the political leadership when it attacked military interests. Under Grechko's leadership, however, Zakharov seemed to concentrate his interests more on personnel-related issues. In fact, there was no need for Zakharov to speak out against the political leadership. The military was obtaining what it wanted, and Defense Minister Grechko appeared to have a special relationship with the country's political leader. Furthermore, Grechko's dominant position within the Ministry of Defense meant that it would have been difficult for anyone to have upstaged the defense minister.

Kulikov. Given his strong personality, it is surprising that Kulikov did not play a more important role as chief of the General Staff. To a large degree he was in the shadow of a powerful defense minister, a professional military officer with personal ties to Brezhnev. If anything, Kulikov was the model subordinate, carefully supporting whatever his defense minister said or did. This was the primary reason for his ouster as chief of staff so soon after Grechko died: he was so closely identified with the former defense minister that he had to go if the political leadership were to bring in the new kind of thinking that Ogarkov represented.

Ogarkov.   When it comes to warfighting strategy, Ogarkov was the most influential voice in the Soviet military in the past twenty-five years. His prestige derives not only from what he wrote and said, but also from the wide-ranging changes he introduced in Soviet force structure. Few of his ideas were original, and most of his force structure modifications had been around in one form or another for some time. But Ogarkov gave these ideas intellectual respectability and focused Soviet thinking in a direction that continues to be relevant. Ogarkov has also had lasting influence on the managerial and leadership front. The major improvements in command and control introduced at his behest, his greater emphasis on efficiency and personal responsibility, all fit the main tenets of Gorbachev's perestroika.

Ogarkov was also a leader in the field of arms control. A technical services officer and a key participant at the SALT I talks, Ogarkov understood better than most if not all of his contemporaries how to use arms control to improve Soviet security. One suspects that he would have been more than willing to work closely with Brezhnev and Ustinov in designing additional arms control arrangements, but the danger he perceived from the American buildup, not to mention the further decay he saw in the Soviet economy under Brezhnev's increasingly inept leadership, convinced him that until steps were taken to get the country moving again, arms control would only hurt Soviet security.

Ogarkov was so outspoken on the need for more money for the military that it is hard to imagine him supporting the kind of cutbacks that Akhromeyev and Yazov have faced. Yet his cries for additional funds were those of a military officer frustrated by an economy that offered no prospect of improvement at any point in the near future. What alternative was there but to throw money at the military's problems?

One cannot help but wonder what the situation would have been like if Ogarkov had been ten years younger and had appeared on the scene at the same time as Gorbachev. Assuming that he could have controlled his abrasive personality, he would have been faced with a general secretary who was everything he had been seeking in the late 1970s—a man prepared to go to great lengths to shake up and overhaul the Soviet economy; a man who believed strongly in the importance of technology; a man devoted to the idea that the individual would be the key to the future of the Soviet Union and prepared to turn the country upside down if necessary to get it moving again; and a man who understood how to use arms control agreements to improve Soviet security. One suspects that Grechko never would have adapted to the world offered by Gorbachev. His horizons were too limited. This was not the case with Ogarkov, who understood the political-military-economic basis of Soviet military power. Ogarkov and Gorbachev might have disagreed on some issues—for example, Ogarkov might have found it difficult to accept unilateral cuts or intrusive verification, and he might have balked at calls for a smaller force structure. Still, he had been prepared to work with the political leadership to enhance Soviet security and prestige. Unfortunately—or, for the West, perhaps, fortunately—he was faced with a different type of political leadership.

Ustinov.   Dmitrii Ustinov played a very important role during his time as defense minister. He acted as a conduit between the high command and the political leadership and provided Ogarkov with needed support in the latter's attempt to change managerial procedures in the Soviet military. However, it is difficult to detect any area where he had a long-term impact. He said almost nothing about warfighting strategy, and when it came to management and leadership he played only a supporting role. On arms control he attempted to argue the case for Brezhnev's approach within the military and in the process was drawn into a polemical debate with Ogarkov. And as the decision to invade Afghanistan illustrates, he sometimes acted as Brezhnev's "enforcer," forcing the military to comply with policy decisions they opposed. On the budgetary front he attempted to argue the military's case within the Politburo but as a civilian, his ability to advocate a position different from Brezhnev's was limited. In short, Ustinov was important primarily because as defense minister he opened the door for someone like Ogarkov to have such a pronounced impact within the Soviet military.

Sokolov.   A careful reading of Sokolov's writings and speeches over the past twenty years suggests that he is one of the most uninspiring of all senior Soviet military officers. Indeed, it was largely because of his bland personality and lack of ambition that he was selected to be an interim defense minister. He left almost no impact on any of the four areas covered in this book.

Akhromeyev.   On the question of arms control Akhromeyev emerged as the most important voice within the Soviet high command of the past twenty years. Ogarkov was influential in the early 1970s, but not even he had had the influence that Akhromeyev exercised as chief of the General Staff. Akhromeyev's power appeared to go beyond arms control. He played a key role in determining the nature of Soviet forces under a policy of military sufficiency and, as a consequence, undoubtedly had a major input into budgetary discussions. It was up to him, for example, to argue which weapons would be constructed and in what numbers, so as to compensate for force cutbacks and arms control limitations.

Yazov.   While it is still too early to know what the future holds for perestroika, based on his actions to date Yazov has the potential to have a major, even lasting impact on the Soviet personnel and management system. Assuming that perestroika as it has been outlined by Yazov is implemented, the Soviet military of tomorrow will be far more potent and effective than it is today. Indeed, if Yazov is successful in rooting out even half of inefficiencies that plague the Soviet military system, it will be possible for the Red Army to get along with fewer troops and weapons and still be in a position to deliver the same—or even greater—punch.

FUTURE RESEARCH

This study, like others of its type, raises as many questions as it answers. Indeed, we have just begun to scratch the surface when it comes to understanding the role Soviet officers can have within the military and in interfacing with the political leadership.

For example, just because the military's top military officers advocate a certain set of policies it does not follow that the officers beneath them share their views. For example, what about the deputy defense ministers? Do they agree with Akhromeyev when it comes to military sufficiency? Indeed, as this book goes to press there are signs that some of the service chiefs are becoming increasingly concerned over the implications any cutbacks will have for their services. Likewise, what about a possible START treaty? What happens if Gorbachev is removed from office and Akhromeyev and Yazov fall? In other words, just how deep into the Soviet officer corps does the support we see for Akhromeyev, Yazov, and Moiseyev go? What will happen if they themselves decide that Gorbachev is pushing the military too far?

Learning the extent of support for the country's top military officers within the military is also important from a methodological standpoint. It is possible that most officers at the level of colonel look upon themselves as executants of party directives, as Odom's model would suggest. It is also possible that they instinctively perceive their relationships to politicians to be more adversarial than their relationship to the high command. In short, it is possible that people like Akhromeyev, Yazov, and Moiseyev are the exceptions.

Finally, we need to know more about the types of individuals who rise to the top in the Soviet armed forces. What are their common characteristics? Are certain background command positions a prerequisite? If we could narrow the range of likely appointees, it would enable us to make an in-depth study of them *before* they are appointed, thereby improving our ability to predict future Soviet policy.

All of these questions are answerable. Biographical information is available on Soviet military officers, and almost all of them—down to the level of deputy defense minister—have written articles for the Soviet military press. This makes possible an in-depth study of them, their writings, and their personal connections. Such a study would contribute considerably to our understanding of the dynamics of politics both within the high command and in its relations to the political leadership.

We also need to know more about the interface between civilian and military officers on issues such as arms control and military strategy. When a military leader relies on civilians to push through needed changes, what kind of a price does he pay in terms of lost autonomy? Akhromeyev appears to have compensated for greater civilian involvement in the determination of force structure with his enhanced role in the arms control process. But is this always the case? If not, why not? Furthermore, when is the high command's influence the greatest: during a period like that which occurred under Grechko, when civilian-military relations were strained, or during a period like the present one, when the relationship between the political leadership and the high command appears to be more symbiotic?

Finally, it is important to recognize that this book has certain biases. It assumes that all major ideas or policy preferences favored by the eight individuals covered in this book can be observed in their writings. As a result, Sokolov appears to be the least influential. But, as one specialist has observed, perhaps Sokolov did not like to put his ideas on paper. After all, he appears to have played a major role in issues of Soviet military presence in the Third World and Afghanistan. While there is no doubt that Sokolov played an important role in the Defense Ministry, where he occupied a key position for many years, he does not appear to have had a major impact on the issues analyzed in this study.

This brings us to the last point: namely, that this study omits discussion of a number of issues of considerable importance to the armed forces, for example, those of Poland and Afghanistan. The omission of such key topics is regrettable, but for methodological reasons the focus of this study was limited to four areas. Other studies must now expand the issues covered here to deal with a multitude of other topics, including Soviet military involvement in the Third World, in Europe, and on other parts of the Soviet Union's periphery.

As this book goes to press, Soviet military affairs appear to be in considerable flux. There is talk of military sufficiency, radical arms control reductions, a major restructuring of the Soviet armed forces, budgetary cutbacks. While none of these ideas may ever be fully implemented, the long-term implications of even their partial enactment will be important not only for the Soviet Union, but the West as well. Greater attention to the role played by the high command can improve our understanding both of where the Soviets are going in critical policy areas as well as the nature of power relationships within the Soviet national security decision-making apparatus. Of course, a focus on the top military decision makers is no shortcut to an understanding of Soviet political-military affairs. But it does add another dimension.

APPENDIX:

Biographies of the Key Personalities

SERGEI AKHROMEYEV

1972–1974, first deputy commander, chief of staff of the Far Eastern Military District; 1974–1979, chief of a Main Directorate, deputy chief of the General Staff; 1979–1984, first deputy chief of the General Staff; 1984–1988, first deputy minister of defense, chief of the General Staff; 1988–present, senior advisor to the general secretary.

Sergei Fedorovich Akhromeyev was born in 1923 to a peasant family.[1] He entered the Soviet military in 1940, reportedly as a cadet at the naval academy in Leningrad. When the Second World War began, Akhromeyev was transferred to the Naval Infantry where he fought on the Leningrad Front. Two years later he reportedly transferred to the armored forces. Akhromeyev is listed as having commanded a platoon, held the position of senior adjunct in a battalion, and commanded a battalion during the war.

During the postwar period, Akhromeyev held a number of positions, including chief of staff and commanding officer of a regiment, commanding officer of an armored regiment, deputy chief of staff and commander of a division, chief of staff, first deputy commander and commander of a Unified Command (*ob"edinenie*).[2] As to educational background, Akhro-

---

[1] Biographical data on Akhromeyev is taken from "Akhromeyev, Sergei Fedorovich," in Akhromeyev, *Voennyi Entsiklopedicheskii Slovar'*, p. 56.

[2] There is a certain amount of ambiguity in this term. The *Soviet Military Encyclopedic Dictionary* defines it as "a military formation, including several 'soedinennyi' or 'ob"edinennyi' smaller staffs, as well as units (*chastie*) and formations (*uchrezhdenii*)." The problem is that it is not clear just how large a formation a *soedinenie* is. Some analysts have suggested that it may be as large as an army or a corps; others believe it to be somewhat smaller. Based on the definition included in the *Military Encyclopedic Dictionary*, and conversations with former Soviet military officers, its size depends on the task at hand. It is

meyev completed the Academy of Armored Troops in 1952 and the General Staff Academy in 1967. He clearly excelled in the latter—he was one of the few awarded a gold medal upon graduation.[3] Among those who attended the General Staff Academy in 1965, 1966 and 1967 were Generals Maksimov, Gerasimov, Zaitsev, Lushev, Varennikov, and, perhaps most importantly, Yazov. It is not known to what degree Akhromeyev knew these individuals; if he did, it might help explain the success that several of them have enjoyed once Akhromeyev became chief of the General Staff. It also suggests the existence of an Akhromeyev-Yazov grouping in the high command. Akhromeyev became a member of the Communist party in 1943, a candidate member of the Central Committee in 1981, and a full member in 1983.

In 1974 Akhromeyev became chief of the Main Operations Directorate and deputy chief of the General Staff; he held the latter position until 1979, when he moved up to become first deputy chief of the General Staff.

A number of interesting points emerge from Akhromeyev's career profile. First, his primary area of expertise appears to be in areas such as planning and operations. Second, he has not followed the traditional ladder to the top: he never held a major command such as one of the key military districts or Group of Soviet Forces in Germany. It is not clear why Akhromeyev was asked to join the General Staff in 1974. This occurred at a time when Ogarkov was first deputy chief of the General Staff and a deputy minister of defense. While solid evidence is lacking, it is possible that Ogarkov played a role in moving Akhromeyev into this key position. Given his later ascendancy within the military hierarchy, Ogarkov could probably have blocked Akhromeyev, if not at the time of his appointment to the General Staff, then in subsequent years. In any case, the areas of Akhromeyev's interest and apparent expertise closely parallel those of Ogarkov, thus ensuring that Ogarkov not only came in close contact with him, but probably took a personal interest in his career.

Akhromeyev has made a strong and positive impression on Westerners who have met him. He comes across as a highly competent, technically sophisticated military officer, one fully conversant with issues as divergent

---

interesting to note in this regard that a recent study by the Rand Corporation of major commands in the Soviet military lists Akhromeyev's last major field position before joining the General Staff as first deputy commander and chief of staff of the Far Eastern Military District. This suggests that Akhromeyev spent most of his military carrier in staff positions. Edward L. Warner III, Josephine J. Bonan, and Erma F. Packman, *Key Personnel and Organizations of the Soviet Military High Command*, Rand Note, N-2567-AF, April 1987, p. 32.

[3] V. G. Kulikov, *Akademiia General'nogo Shtaba* (*General Staff Academy*) (Moscow: Voennoe Izdatel'stvo, 1979), p. 262.

as arms control and the Third World. He eschews polemics and does not appear to be arrogant, preferring instead to present his case in a matter-of-fact fashion, thereby letting the facts speak for themselves. It is, of course, impossible to know how much of Akhromeyev's public behavior carries over into his private meetings within the Soviet political-military, but assuming there is a similarity, one suspects that he may be more effective than Ogarkov in interacting with the senior political leadership.

ANDREI GRECHKO

1960–1967, first deputy minister of defense and commander, Joint Armed Forces, the Warsaw Pact forces; 1967–1976, minister of defense. Died 1976.

Andrei Antonovich Grechko was born in the Ukranian village of Golodaevka in Rostov-on-Don Province in 1903.[4] His parents were peasants. His father had been a sergeant-major in the tsarist army and had taught Grechko to ride and use a saber. Grechko was a high school student when the Russian Civil War reached his village. Impressed by what he had seen of the Soviet forces, he left school at the age of sixteen and joined the Eleventh cavalry division of the First Horse army as an ammunition carrier. He fought in the battles of Taganrog and Rostov during the South Ukrainian Campaign. He became a member of the Komsomol in 1920.

Grechko graduated from the Taganrog Cavalry School in 1926, reportedly in the top ten per cent of his class. He was assigned to Moscow where he commanded a platoon and later a cavalry squadron in the First Detached Cavalry Brigade. In 1933 Grechko was selected to attend the Frunze Command and Staff Academy, at that time the most prestigious military school in the USSR. He graduated in 1936. He was named chief of staff of an independent cavalry division in the Special White Russian military district in 1938. He was involved in "freeing the Western regions from White Russia in 1939,"[5] i.e., he participated in the Soviet-German partition of Poland. Grechko, by then a colonel, also reportedly com-

---

[4] Primary sources for biographical material on Grechko are Alfred L. Monks, "The Rise of Marshal Grechko," in David R. Jones, *Soviet Armed Forces Review Annual*, vol. 3 (Gulf Breeze, Fla.: Academic International Press, 1979), 204–224; Seweryn Bialer, "Andrei Antonovich Grechko," in George Simmonds, ed., *Soviet Leaders* (New York: Crowell, 1967) and "Grechko, Andrei Antonovich," in N. V. Ogarkov, ed., *Sovetskaia Voennaia Entsiklopediia*, vol. 3 (Moscow: Voennoe izdatel'stvo, 1977), p. 49, and S. P. Ivanov, "Polkovodets sovetskoi shkoli" ("A Commander from the Soviet School"), *Voenno-istoricheskii zhurnal*, no. 10 (1983): 55–60.

[5] Ibid.

manded an infantry regiment during the Russo-Finnish War of 1939–1940. Purges in the Red Army during the latter part of the 1930s did little to hurt his career. After the conclusion of the Russo-Finnish War, Grechko was detailed to the prestigious Voroshilov General Staff Academy, from which he graduated in 1941 some three days before Hitler attacked the USSR. Despite his request for service at the front, Grechko was initially assigned to the General Staff. However, within twelve days he got his wish and was assigned commander of the Thirty-fourth Cavalry Division of the Fifth Cavalry Corps, located in the Southwestern Ukraine.

Grechko's first combat command was not a successful one. His division, made up primarily of reservists, was badly mauled by the Germans, and by December 1941 it was withdrawn from the front. Grechko must have impressed his superiors despite the losses suffered by his division, however, because a month later he was promoted to general major and made commander of the Fifth Cavalry Corps on the Southwestern Front. Grechko and the units under him played an important role in operations in the Kharkov area and in April 1942 he was appointed commander of the Twelfth Army of the Southern Front. Despite his best efforts to stem the tide of the German advance, Grechko's forces were again forced to yield to the military superiority of the Germans. However, he apparently again impressed his superiors despite his losing record because in September 1942 he was appointed commander of the Forty-seventh Army, which at that time was defending the city of Novorossiisk. On October 19, 1942, Grechko continued his rise, having been named to command the Eighteenth Army. This unit had a particularly difficult task, that of defending the city of Novorossiisk against a massive German onslaught. If this city had fallen, the gates to the Caspian sea and the oil fields would have been open to the Germans. He succeeded. As a Western source noted, "By the end of 1942 the 18th Army was pinning down fourteen German divisions. Soviet writers credit this with setting the stage for a massive counter-attack. The Red Army had blunted the enemy's drive to capture the Caucasus, a development which had an important bearing on the subsequent course of the war."[6] Grechko had played a key role in this. It is also worth noting that his main political commissar in this undertaking was none other than Leonid Brezhnev.

By January 1943, as the tide turned against the Germans, Grechko, now a lieutenant general, was given command of the Fifty-sixth Army. His task was to take the city of Krasnodar, which he did. By the end of October 1943 Grechko's forces had chased the Germans out of the Cauca-

---

[6] Monks, "The Rise of Marshal Grechko," p. 209.

sus. Now known as an officer who got things done—in fact, as one who appeared to relish difficult tasks—Grechko was promoted to the rank of colonel general and became deputy commander of the First Ukrainian Front. In another fortuitous encounter, Grechko met Nikita Khrushchev, the Front's political officer. Grechko subsequently played a major role in the retaking of Kiev and, having been promoted to the rank of army general, took command of the First Guards' Army, which subsequently liberated Czechoslovakia from the Germans.

During the postwar period, Grechko's importance within the Soviet military establishment gradually increased. He was appointed commander of the Kiev Military District early on and remained there until 1953. One Western observer has suggested that whereas Kiev was indeed an important military command, the fact that he served there for eight years "showed that he ranked only among the second echelon of the Soviet high command."[7] The one major advantage of this post was that until 1949 the Ukraine was under the control of Khrushchev, which enabled Grechko to solidify his personal ties with the future party leader. In 1953 he took command of the Group of Soviet Forces in Germany, was promoted to marshal in 1955, and in 1957 was given the post of commander of Soviet ground forces. By 1960 he was a first deputy minister of defense and commander of the Warsaw Pact. He became a full member of the Central Committee in 1961. In April 1967 he became minister of defense.

A number of observations emerge from Grechko's background. First, he was clearly intelligent. Soviet military academies are demanding institutions, and he reportedly did extremely well. According to one author, while serving as commander in chief of the Soviet ground forces, Grechko gained recognition as a "talented military thinker. . . . Grechko was responsible for developing tactical doctrine for the infantry and new weapons and equipment."[8] Second, his loyalty to the system was never in doubt. He joined the Red Army at an early age, and there is no sign that he was ever anything but loyal to his political superiors. Third, Grechko was politically well-connected. Fourth, Grechko, an infantry and cavalry officer, understood the intricacies of combined operations. He was certain to be skeptical—if not openly opposed—to simplistic solutions, especially ones that attempted to provide single-variable answers to the problems facing the Soviet Army. Yet in the key area of warfighting strategy, that was exactly what the Soviet military faced: Khrushchev had declared that nuclear weapons were a panacea to the country's military problems and had

---

[7] Bialer, "Andrei Antonovich Grechko," p. 119.
[8] Monks, "The Rise of Marshal Grechko," p. 214.

used them to justify his plans for major cutbacks in non-nuclear forces. Finally, the "can-do" attitude Grechko exhibited during the war suggests a man who is a leader, one who influences events rather than being influenced by them.

VIKTOR KULIKOV

1967–1969, commander of the Kiev Military District; 1969–1971, commander of the Group of Soviet Forces in Germany; 1971–1977, first deputy minister of defense and chief of the General Staff; 1977–1989, first deputy minister of defense and commander, Joint Armed Forces, the Warsaw Pact; 1989–present, member of the Main Inspectorate.

Viktor Georgievich Kulikov was born on May 7, 1921, in Verkhniaia Liubovsha, now called Novodereven'kovskogo, which is located in the Orel Oblast'. Kulikov entered the army in 1939, graduated from the Grodnenskoe Military School in 1941 as an infantry officer, and was assigned as a platoon commander to the Kiev military district. In the first part of the war Kulikov fought on the Southwestern, the Kalininskii, First Baltic and Second White Russian Fronts. During this period he held a number of positions including commander of a motorcycle regiment and chief of staff of an armored battalion. From 1943 to 1945 Kulikov was chief of staff of the 143d independent tank brigade. In this latter post he was in charge of planning the brigade's operations in the Smolensk, Belorussian, Rizhskii, and Eastern Prussian operations. In the course of these operations the brigade "carried out assignments directed at breaking the opponents strongly reinforced defensive lines, operated as part of a mobile group of forces, carried out defensive actions against counterattacks by enemy armored units, and participated in liberating Nevelia, Politska, Mitavy, Tukumsa, Danzig, Stettin, and other cities." Insofar as his own performance is concerned, his official Soviet biography notes that "in the course of organizing combat operations and directing the brigade, Kulikov acted in an expedient manner, thereby making it possible for the brigade to carry out its tasks successfully."[9] He was reportedly wounded six times during the war and was involved in negotiating arms deliveries from the Americans in Murmansk.

In the immediate postwar period, Kulikov was chief of staff and dep-

[9] Information on Kulikov is taken from, N. V. Ogarkov, ed., *Sovetskaia Voennaia Entsiklopediia*, vol. 4 (Moscow: Voennoe izdatel'stvo, 1977), p. 517.

uty commander of a brigade and commander of a regiment. From 1954 to 1957 he was chief of staff and commander of a division and in 1959 was appointed first deputy commander of an army. From 1964 to 1967 he was commander of an army in the Murmansk region. He was promoted to the rank of lieutenant general in 1965. "In commanding divisions [*soedineniia*] and operational armies [*ob"edineniia*], Kulikov demonstrated qualities such as a thorough military-theoretical preparation and the knowledge of how to translate into practice the rich experience of the Great Patriotic War." In May 1967 Kulikov was named commander of the Kiev Military District, and in October 1969 he became commander of the Group of Soviet Forces in Germany—a highly prestigious and sought-after position. In September 1971 he was named chief of the General Staff and first deputy minister of defense. In the latter post he took considerable interest in "further refining the development, technical equipping, [and] operational and combat readiness of branches of the armed forces and in raising their [level of] combat readiness."[10]

Kulikov joined the party in 1942, attended the Malinovskii Higher Armored Academy from 1945 to 1947, and graduated from the Frunze Military Academy in 1953 and the Academy of the General Staff in 1959. He became a full member of the Central Committee in April 1971, while still commander of the Group of Soviet Forces in Germany.

Like his superior, Grechko, Kulikov has seen the reality of combat and was probably equally opposed to simplistic solutions to the problems facing the armed forces. His many years in staff positions as well as his experience as a commander of increasingly larger formations also means that he probably understood the need for close cooperation, if not integration, between the civilian and military sectors. His lack of technical background, while it did not hinder his ability to understand the need for the Soviet armed forces to adapt to the technological revolution, may help account for his lack of enthusiasm concerning arms control. For a tank officer, entrusting Soviet security to esoteric arms control arrangements that may or may not improve the country's security situation is not a meaningful way to approach the country's problems. The only way to do so is to rely on its military might. Concepts like strategic parity and asymmetries in strategic force posture may be useful in understanding the correlation of military forces, but they are certainly not terms upon which the country's security should depend. For a man like Kulikov, combat is real, and anything that detracts from the state's ability to engage in it is to be opposed.

[10] Ibid., p. 518.

NIKOLAI OGARKOV

1965–1968, commander of the Volga Military District; 1968–1974, first deputy chief of the General Staff; 1974–1977, deputy minister of defense; 1977–1984, first deputy minister of defense and chief of the General Staff; 1984–1988, commander of the Western TVD; 1988–present, member of the Main Inspectorate.

Born in 1917 in what is now the Kalinin District, Nikolai Vasilevich Ogarkov completed the Worker's Power Engineering School in 1937.[11] He joined the Red Army in 1938 and was sent to the Kuibyshev Military-Engineering Academy from which he graduated in 1941.

Ogarkov's wartime service was spent as an engineering officer in the Technical Services. From September 1941 to February 1942 he was a fortifications engineer on the Karelian front. He then became a regimental engineer with the 289th Infantry Division and later a brigade engineer with the Sixty-first Naval Infantry Brigade. It is possible that Ogarkov met Akhromeyev at this time, as the latter began his wartime career fighting in the Naval Infantry on the Karelian front. In December 1942 Ogarkov was named deputy chief of staff for operations on the staff of engineering troops attached to an unspecified front. This was followed in December by a promotion to chief of staff of engineering troops on an unknown front and the following May he became the division engineer for the 122nd Infantry Division which fought on the Karelian and Ukranian fronts. Ogarkov is credited by Soviet sources with having played a major role in organizing engineering operations in the Zapoliap, Baltic, and Hungarian operations. Soviet sources characterize his wartime service as marked by "deep military and engineering knowledge, personal courage, and bravery."[12] Ogarkov joined the party in 1945.

It has been rumored that Ogarkov met and established working relationships with Andropov and the future Marshal Sokolov during his time on the Karelian front. Andropov was in charge of Komsomol work and the assumption is that since Ogarkov had responsibility for engineering/technical work, he would have worked closely with Andropov, who was also involved in supporting Soviet partisans. Similarly, it has been rumored that Ogarkov got to know Sokolov who served in the region at this time.

[11] Biographical data on Ogarkov is primarily drawn from "Ogarkov, Nikolai Vasil'-evich," in N. V. Ogarkov, ed., *Sovetskaia Voennaia Entsiklopediia*, vol. 6 (Moscow: Voennoe izdatel'stvo, 1978) p. 7 and "Ogarkov, Nikolai Vasil'evich," in Akhromeyev, *Voennyi Entsiklopedicheskii Slovar'*, p. 506.
[12] Ogarkov, *Sovetskaia Voennaia Entsiklopediia*, vol. 6, p. 7.

While such relationships cannot be ruled out, this writer has not been able to locate any evidence to confirm their existence.

Ogarkov's quick advancement during the war suggests two things: first, while many of his comrades were being killed, thereby opening up room for advancement, he must have done an outstanding job. Second, his experience as an engineer almost certainly convinced him of the value of utilizing technology to the maximum degree possible in combat operations.

Ogarkov's first postwar assignments were in the Carpathian and Maritime Military Districts, the latter of which is located in the Far East. Ogarkov was appointed head of a department in the Operations Directorate of the Eastern Theater of the Far East in 1948. In 1953 he became deputy chief and then chief of the Operations Directorate and, subsequently, deputy chief of staff of the Far Eastern Military District. His commanding officer at this time, first as commander in chief of Soviet Forces in the Far East (1947–1953) and then as commander of the Far Eastern Military District (1953–1956), was Marshal Rodion Malinovskii. While it is impossible to prove that a close relationship existed between the two, it is highly unlikely that Ogarkov would have been either accepted under Malinovskii's command into a responsible position or, more importantly, promoted to the position of deputy chief of staff, without Malinovskii's support. In March 1956 Malinovskii left the Far East to become a first deputy defense minister and commander of Soviet Ground Forces. Three years later Ogarkov followed him to Moscow, where he attended the prestigious Voroshilov General Staff Academy, an institution generally considered to be a stepping-stone to leadership positions in the Soviet military.

After completing the General Staff Academy, Ogarkov commanded a motorized infantry division in East Germany and in December 1961 became chief of staff (first deputy commander after 1963) of the Belorussian Military District. By December 1965 he was commander of the Volga Military District where he remained until 1968. According to the *Soviet Military Encyclopedia*, "Creatively applying the deep theoretical knowledge and rich practical experience that he had obtained during both peace and war, he skillfully organized combat operational training of troops under conditions of their being massively outfitted with new weapons."[13] Ogarkov was made a candidate member of the Central Committee of the CPSU in 1966.

Based on his performance as chief of the Volga Military District, Ogar-

---

[13] Ibid., p. 8.

kov was asked to join the General Staff as a first deputy chief in April 1968, probably by Marshal Zakharov, with whom he is rumored to have served in the past. Zakharov at that time was chief of the General Staff. While Soviet sources are silent on Ogarkov's exact duties at that time, his presence on the Soviet SALT I delegation as the senior military representative from 1969 to 1971 suggests that he had special responsibility for strategic weapons policy. Ogarkov became a full member of the Central Committee in 1971, a clear sign that he was destined for higher-level positions in the political-military hierarchy.

In March 1974 Ogarkov became a Deputy Minister of defense. According to one Western specialist, he had responsibility for "systems analysis, assessment of weapons systems effectiveness, and resource allocation. He also demonstrated a keen interest in the research, development and deployment of ADP systems within the Soviet Armed Forces, with particular relevance to command and control at all levels."[14]

Those who have met Ogarkov have found him a man of imposing intellect, possessing a brilliant analytical mind and an exhaustive knowledge of weapons and weapons systems. Gerard Smith, the chief U.S. delegate at the SALT I talks, characterized him as "a forceful individual." Smith also cites a Soviet diplomat who said Ogarkov was bright and intellectually strong and "by no means a run-of-the-mill army officer."[15]

SERGEI SOKOLOV

1964–1965, first deputy commander of the Leningrad Military District; 1965–1967, commander of the Leningrad Military District; 1967–1984, first deputy minister of defense; 1984–1987, minister of defense; 1987, relieved of duties.

Sergei Leonidovich Sokolov, a Russian by nationality, was born on July 1, 1911, in Evpatoriia in the Crimea.[16] His father was a clerk. He went to

[14] Richard Woff, "Marshal N. V. Ogarkov Moves On?" Rapid Report No. 22, October 1984, p. 4. Papers presented in Research with Defense Studies, University of Edinburgh, and the Center of Strategic Technology, Texas A and M University.

[15] Gerard Smith, *Doubletalk: The Story of the First Strategic Arms Limitation Talks* (New York: Doubleday, 1980), p. 46.

[16] Biographical data on Sokolov is taken from "Sokolov, Sergei Leonidovich," N. V. Ogarkov, ed., *Sovetskaia Voennaia Entsiklopediia*, vol. 7 (Moscow: Voennoe izdatel'stvo, 1979), p. 435; "Sokolov, Sergei Leonidovich," S. F. Akhromeyev, *Voennyi Entsiklopedicheskii Slovar'* (Moscow: Voennoe izdatel'stvo, 1986), 689–90; Harriet Fast Scott, "Soviet Defense Minister Sokolov," *International Defense Review*, 18, no. 12 (December 1985): p. 1902; and O. Losik, "Marshal Sovetskogo Soiuza S. L. Sokolov" ("Marshal of the Soviet Union S. L. Sokolov"), *Voenno-istoricheskii zhurnal*, no. 7 (1981): 64–66.

work in 1927 at an unspecified factory in the city of Kotel'nich in the Kirov region. From 1930 to 1932 Sokolov was engaged in full-time party work as secretary of the Komsomol organization at the Kotel'nich industrial enterprise and was a member of the regional Komsomol bureau.

Sokolov entered the army in 1932 as a student at the Gorki Armored Tank School, from which he graduated in 1934. Immediately after graduation, Sokolov was assigned to the Far East in tank units where he commanded a platoon, a company, and a section of a battalion. He took part in the battle of Hasan Lake in 1938 and by the time the Second World War broke out was chief of staff of a tank regiment on what was to become the Karelian Front. In October 1941 Sokolov was appointed deputy chief and in April 1942 chief of a section in the armored forces directorate. From January 1943 to March 1944 he was chief of staff of the command of armored and mechanized infantry forces on the Karelian Front. From March to September 1944, Sokolov was commander of armored and mechanized infantry forces of the Thirty-second Army. According to the *Soviet Military Encyclopedia* Sokolov "took part in the defense and liberation of Zapoliar'ia where he demonstrated personal courage and a high degree of organizational competency in commanding armored forces."[17] By the end of the war Colonel Sokolov was commander of armored and mechanized troops of the Fourteenth Army.

After the end of the war, Sokolov was sent to the Military Academy of Armored and Mechanized Infantry Forces from which he graduated in 1947. He was then assigned to be commander of a tank regiment and from 1948 to 1949 served as chief of staff of a tank division. Now a one-star general, Sokolov attended the General Staff Academy from which he graduated in 1951. In January 1952 he became commander of a mechanized division. The *Soviet Military Encyclopedia* notes that after he left that post Sokolov "served in command and staff positions."[18] From 1960 to 1964 he was chief of staff and first deputy commander of the Moscow Military District. The assignment presumably brought him into contact with Khrushchev, Brezhnev, Ustinov, and other top Soviet political figures. In June 1964 he became first deputy commander and, in October 1965, commander of the Leningrad Military District. Sokolov joined the party in 1937, became a candidate member of the Central Committee in 1966, and was elevated to full membership in 1968.

In 1967 Sokolov became one of the first deputy ministers of defense. It is generally believed in the West that during his tenure in this position

---

[17] Ogarkov, *Sovetskaia Voennaia Entsiklopediia*, vol. 7, p. 435.
[18] Ibid.

Sokolov had primary responsibility for logistics and rear services matters. He reportedly played an important role in planning the Soviet invasion of Afghanistan. He was promoted to army general in 1969.

Given his strong background in management affairs as well as his service in a variety of command and staff positions, Sokolov was a good choice from the political leadership's standpoint to succeed Ustinov in 1984. As he was a professional military officer, none of his colleagues could complain that the military as an institution was being slighted by the appointment of another civilian as defense minister, and his primary focus on managerial issues meant that he would be likely to avoid attempting to play a major role in matters such as arms control.

DMITRII USTINOV

1965–1976, secretary of the Central Committee; 1976–1984, minister of defense. Died 1984.

Dimitri Fedorovich Ustinov was born in Kuibyshev on October 17, 1908. Little is known about him prior to 1922 when, at the age of fourteen, he joined the Red Army.[19] After he was demobilized in 1923 he attended a technical school in Makar'ev, from which he graduated in 1927. At that time he joined the CPSU. In 1927 he began working as a metal worker in two different factories. In 1934 he graduated from the Mechanized Military Institute in Leningrad. From 1934 to 1941 he served as an engineer at the Artillery Scientific-Research Naval Institute, a bureau chief, a deputy chief designer, and director of the factory "Bolshevik." From 1941 to 1946 he was People's Commissar for Armaments. Soviet sources note that as People's Commissar for Armaments during the war, Ustinov "made a significant contribution to the development of the production of artillery and small arms [and] in resolving complex scientific-technical problems associated with creation of new types of weapons."[20] Ustinov was thus a major force in the production of weapons systems for Soviet forces during the war. In November 1944 he became a colonel general of the engineering artillery service.[21]

---

[19] Biographical data on Ustinov is drawn from "Ustinov, Dmitrii Fedorovich," in Nikolai Ogarkov, ed., *Sovetskaia Voennaia Entsiklopediia*, vol. 8 (Moscow: Voennoe izdatel'stvo, 1980), p. 227–28, and "Ustinov, Dmitrii Fedorovich," in Sergei Akhromeyev, ed., *Voennyi: Entsiklopedicheskii Slovar'* (Moscow: Voennoe izdatel'stvo, 1986), p. 769.

[20] Ogarkov, *Sovetskaia Voennaia Entsiklopediia*, vol. 8, p. 227.

[21] Harriet Fast Scott and William F. Scott, *The Armed Forces of the USSR* (Boulder, Colo.: Westview, 1979), p. 120.

From 1946 to 1953 Ustinov was minister of armaments and from 1953 to 1957 minister of the defense industry. During this period, Ustinov was in essence chief of the Soviet weapons industry. Indeed, if there is a military-industrial complex in the Soviet Union, he was clearly at its head during those years. In recognition of his increasingly important role in the Soviet military-industrial arena, Ustinov became a member of the Central Committee in 1952. In 1957 he became a deputy chairman and in 1963 first deputy chairman of the Council of Ministers, and was subsequently elevated to chairman of the Supreme Economic Council. In 1965 he was made a candidate member of the Politburo and appointed to be Central Committee secretary in charge of the defense industry where, according to the *Soviet Military Encyclopedia*, he

> coordinated and directed the work of scientific enterprises, construction bureaus, [and] industrial enterprises with the purpose of carrying out in a more complete fashion the party and government task of further strengthening the economic and defensive strength of the homeland, taking part in organizing work in the area of developing technology utilized for investigating and mastering the expanses of space.[22]

In short, over the years Ustinov played a major role "in changing the Soviet Armed Forces from horse-drawn artillery, which it possessed in vast quantities at the end of World War II, to a military force armed with the most modern and sophisticated weaponry of the twentieth century."[23] Ustinov was the USSR's top weapons expert not only in terms of design and development but in terms of production as well. If anyone in the Soviet Union understood the details of the Soviet military budget and weapons production process, it was Ustinov. Finally, in April 1976, after Grechko's death, Ustinov was appointed defense minister, an army general, and a month later a full member of the Politburo. In July of that year he was promoted to marshal of the Soviet Union.

DMITRII YAZOV

1974–1976, Main Personnel Directorate of the Ministry of Defense; 1976–1979, first deputy commander of the Far Eastern Military District; 1979–1980, commander, Central Group of Forces; 1980–1984, commander, Central Asian Military District; 1984–1987, commander, Far Eastern Military Dis-

---

[22] Ogarkov, *Sovetskaia Voennaia Entsiklopediia*, vol. 8, p. 227.
[23] Scott and Scott, *The Armed Forces of the USSR*, p. 121.

trict; Jan–May 1987, deputy minister of defense, Chief Main Personnel director-ate; May 1987–present, minister of defense.

Dimitri Timofeevich Yazov was born into a peasant family on November 8, 1923, in the small village of Yazovo in Omsk province.[24] He was one of four children (two boys and two girls); his father died in 1934. Yazov joined the army in 1941 and was sent to an accelerated course for infantry officers in Moscow. In 1942, at the age of nineteen, Yazov was commissioned and saw service on the Volkhov and Leningrad fronts. He was wounded during the war but returned to combat after a short period of convalescence. After the war, he served in a variety of positions and in 1956 graduated from the Frunze Military Academy. At various times during this period he commanded a company, then a battalion, and was in charge of training for a military district. In 1959 he was promoted to lieutenant colonel and in 1961 took command of a regiment in the Leningrad Military District. By 1965 he was a full colonel.

After graduating from the Voroshilov General Staff Academy in 1967, Yazov was given command of a division in the Transbaikal Military District. By 1970 he was a major general. From 1972 to 1974 he commanded a unit in the Transcaucasus and was then transferred to the Main Personnel Directorate of the Defense Ministry. In 1976 he became first deputy commander of the Far East Military District and in 1979 commander of the Central Group of Forces (in Czechoslovakia). In 1980 he was appointed chief of the Central Asian Military District and the next year gained candidate membership on the Central Committee. Yazov reportedly served with Army General Ivan Tret'iak and graduated from the General Staff Academy the same year as Akhromeyev.

As Yazov was commander of the Central Asian Military District at the time of the Soviet invasion of Afghanistan, it is possible that he played a role in that undertaking, if only in ensuring logistical support. However, there is no solid evidence directly linking him to it. Yazov is credited by one source as having introduced, during a tour as district chief, new techniques for combined-arms operations and new training techniques for upgrading the skills of Soviet soldiers.[25] In February 1984 Yazov was promoted to army general and placed in charge of one of the Soviet military's premier commands—the Far Eastern Military District. He remained there

---

[24] Biographical data on Yazov is drawn from "Yazov, Dmitrii Timofeevich," in Akhromeyev, *Voennyi Entsiklopedicheskii Slovar'*, p. 844; "Rodom iz Yazova" ("A Native of Yazovo"), *Krasnaia zvezda*, April 13, 1985, and Alexander Yanov, "Why Yazov?" RFE-RL, *Radio Liberty Research*, RL 212/7, June 1, 1987.

[25] Yossef Bodansky in *Jane's Defense Weekly*, March 31, 1984, as cited in Ibid.

until January 1987, when he was recalled to Moscow to become deputy minister of defense in charge of personnel.

Like Sokolov before him, Yazov has good credentials for a defense minister. He held most of the types of positions one would expect from a defense minister, and, while his selection was a surprise to Western observers, his extensive background in personnel issues—the focus of all of his articles prior to becoming defense minister—made him the perfect choice for defense minister under Gorbachev.

MATVEI ZAKHAROV

1960–1963, first deputy minister of defense and chief of the General Staff; 1963–1964, commander of the Voroshilov General Staff Academy; 1964– 1971, first deputy minister of defense and chief of the General Staff. Died 1972.

Matvei Vasilevich Zakharov, the son of a worker, was born on August 17, 1898, in the village of Voilov, now Staritskii, in the Kalinin Oblast'.[26] At the age of seventeen he became a mechanic. He joined the Bolsheviks shortly after the creation of the Russian Republic in February 1917, became a member of the Red Guards, and participated in the storming of the Winter Palace on November 8, 1917.

Zakharov joined the Red Army in 1918 and completed a course at an artillery officer's school that same year. During the civil war he commanded an artillery battery and an artillery division in the Tenth Army on the Southern Front, where he took part in the defense of Tsaritsyn. He was subsequently made commander of an artillery supply division and chief of staff of a brigade for operational affairs in the Thirty-fourth Infantry Division. The latter division fought against Denikin's forces on the Southeastern and Southern Fronts.

After the civil war Zakharov decided to stay in the army. He was assigned to the staff of a division and later to the staff of the White Russian Military District where he worked on mobilization and supply affairs. In 1925 he entered the Frunze Military Academy from which he graduated in 1928 with a specialization in supply. He returned to the Frunze in 1931 and graduated again in 1933, this time from the operations faculty. In

---

[26] Information on Zakharov is taken from, N. V. Ogarkov, ed., *Sovetskaia Voennaia Entsiklopediia*, vol. 3 (Moscow: Voennoe izdatel'stvo, 1977), p. 418; S. Rudenko, "Marshal Sovetskogo Soiuza N. V. Zakharov," *Voenno-istoricheskii zhurnal*, no. 8 (1988): 557–60; and Seweryn Bialer, "Matvei Vasilevich Zakharov," in George Simmonds, ed., *Soviet Leaders* (New York: Crowell, 1967).

1936 he became commander of a regiment and in the summer of the same year was sent to the newly established Voroshilov General Staff Academy. In June 1937 he became chief of staff of the Leningrad Military District. In May 1938 Zakharov was assigned to the General Staff and in June 1940 became chief of the staff of the Twelfth Army and then chief of staff of the Odessa Military District. He was now a major general.

As he had during the prewar years, Zakharov spent most of the Second World War in staff positions. He was chief of staff on a number of fronts, including the Northwest, Kalinin, Rezervno/Stepno, Second Ukrainian and Transbaikal Fronts. According to his official biography, he

> made a significant contribution to the planning, preparation, and carrying out of the Belgorodogo-Khar'kovskii, Kirobogradskii, Korsun'-Shevchen-kovskii, Umansko-Botoshanskii, Yassko-Kishinev, Debrecen, Budapest, Vienna, Prague, and Khingano-Mukdenskoi offensive operations.[27]

In short, Zakharov emerged from the war with a reputation of being an outstanding staff officer. He was now an army general.

Zakharov's first assignment after the war was as commandant of the Voroshilov General Staff Academy, where he remained until 1949. He was then transferred to the General Staff, where he stayed until 1952. The fact that he was then sent to the operationally insignificant Main Inspectorate suggests that he had run afoul of Stalin. This suspicion is strengthened by his appointment in May 1953—the month Stalin died—to the post of commander of the Leningrad Military District. He continued to move up the promotion ladder in 1957, when he was given the much coveted post of commander of the Group of Soviet Forces in Germany. In April 1960 he became chief of the General Staff and remained in that position until he ran into problems with Khrushchev, and was ousted in 1963. Zakharov then returned to the General Staff Academy where he remained as commandant until he was recalled in 1964 to become chief of the General Staff once more. He remained in this post until September 1971. He died in the following year.

Given his willingness to stand up to Khrushchev and, presumably, to some degree to Stalin, it is perhaps surprising that Zakharov was not more outspoken or dominant during his time as Grechko's chief of staff. In fact, as his biography makes clear, he was a professional staff officer and, while reportedly bright, not the type of officer to seize the limelight. His task was that of an implementer. If political authorities had launched an attack

---

[27] Ogarkov, *Sovetskaia Voennaia Entsiklopediia*, vol. 3, p. 418.

on what he considered to be the prerogative of the professional military, he might perhaps have responded, but in that regard Grechko appeared to have matters well in hand. Consequently, during the period covered by this study he appears to have focused his attention on military-technical and on personnel issues in particular.

Index